TOWARD
NEW
TOWNS
FOR
AMERICA

TOWARD
NEW
TOWNS
FOR
AMERICA
BY
CLARENCE S.
STEIN

With an
introduction
by
LEWIS
MUMFORD

THE M.I.T. PRESS
Massachusetts Institute of Technology
Cambridge, Massachusetts, and London, England

Fifth Printing, November 1973
Sixth printing, April 1978
SBN 262 69009 8 (paperback)
Copyright 1957 by Clarence S. Stein
Printed in the United States of America
Library of Congress Catalog Card Number: 57-6538

CONTENTS

TO ALINE

FOREWORD

The purpose of re-exploring this series of experiences in community building was to find guidance for all of us in making the next step toward building New Towns. I had in mind that both in America and in Europe the time is ripe for complete change in the form of urban environment. I believe that the best and easiest way to start that change is to build New Towns on new sites, as Sir Ebenezer Howard suggested. The opportunity to do this may come sooner than we had reason to expect. The creation of towns for industry and for living, of moderate size, widely separated from each other, may be imminent as a defense measure. This could be the beginning of a new era of nation-wide decentralization. For fortunately here the best policy for peace and for defense are the same: orderly, related dispersal of workers and working places in limited-sized communities, surrounded by open country.

On the other hand, as a result of the Redevelopment powers under the Housing Act of 1949 the way is now open for large-scale rebuilding of decaying sections of old cities. It is equally important that both the building of New Towns and the redevelopment of old ones shall be part and parcel of the future.

In the case of the redevelopment projects it seems clear to me that they will fail in their purpose and be merely patches on the past and passing framework of the old cities unless they are all conceived, planned, and carried out as large-scale units of new cities — new cities even though they are on the old sites. In finding the form of these future cities the preliminary experiments of which this book tells will, I hope, be of help to both planners and administrators.

Although this book deals with American experience it has strong ties with Great Britain. Much of the philosophy and experience in housing and city building from which Henry Wright and I and the rest of us started had its roots in English experience and thinking. To a great extent we carried on the work begun by Ebenezer Howard and Raymond Unwin. By a happy chance, much of this book was written during 1949 in Wyldes, the former home of Sir Raymond Unwin. The articles were prepared for a British publication, *The Town Planning Review,* edited by Gordon Stephenson of the Department of Civic Design at the University of Liverpool. It was he who suggested that I tell the story of some of my experiences in connection with the creation of new communities in America.

FOREWORD

I was at the time preparing a book on the three Greenbelt Towns. I put this aside to start on a series of articles because I had come to the conclusion that the Greenbelt Towns were only three links in the chain of experiences that led from Sunnyside and Radburn through Baldwin Hills Village toward the future New Towns of America. This fortunately resulted in its splendid presentation by the Liverpool University Press and to my association with Gordon Stephenson. To his thoughtful understanding and editorial guidance this book owes much of its form and beauty. So here I offer my affectionate thanks to Gordon Stephenson—and may I add to his American wife, who edited this in the American language in such a way that my British and European friends could understand it.

Of the many other friends and associates to whom I owe gratitude for their help in research or in reading the manuscript I can mention only a few. For research I thank Louise Blackham, Elizabeth Coit, Kate Edelman, and Helena Newman.

For suggestions and correction of manuscript I have had the assistance of those who promoted, planned or managed the various developments, including: Alexander M. Bing, Ralph Eberlin, and Herbert Emmerich on *Sunnyside* and *Radburn;* Ernest Schofield on *Phipps Garden Apartments;* Nathan Straus and Frank Jordan on *Hillside Homes;* Charles T. McDonald, James Gobbel, Samuel Ashelman, Jr., Win McCamy, and Mary Jane Kinzer on *Greenbelt;* Walter Kroening and Elbert Peets on *Greendale;* Lawrence Tucker and Roland A. Wank on *Greenhills;* and Lewis Wilson, Ray Knisely, Robert E. Alexander, and Edwin Merrill on *Baldwin Hills Village.*

For the living pictures of Radburn and Greenbelt, most of which were taken in the summer of 1949, we owe deep appreciation to Gretchen van Tassel. For assistance in the bibliography my thanks are due to Katherine McNamara, Librarian, Departments of Landscape Architecture and Regional Planning, Harvard University.

Finally, for inspiration and general assistance, my heartfelt gratitude to Benton MacKaye, Hugh Pomroy, Albert Mayer, and Lewis Mumford.

New York
November 1950

FOREWORD TO THE REVISED EDITION

Six years have passed since this book was published: six years of unprecedented production of mass housing, redevelopment, even New Towns. The ideas and forms that it describes have become widely accepted—even if not so widely practiced.

This book was called *TOWARD New Towns for America* because, although it described communities that were thoroughly contemporary, none of them was comprehensive enough in scale or functions to fully deserve the title of New Town.

Since then, that has changed. At least one such municipality has been planned and is being built in America, though not in the United States. Kitimat in British Columbia is the direct descendant of the communities that are the subject of this book. It has the same basic physical elements. The procedure by which the plan was developed grew out of the experience that is described here.

The influence of the Radburn Idea has travelled far. I am finding that even if the seeds of ideas are slow in propagating close by, they often are carried to distant points, there to bloom more fully. This is true of Vallingby, a veritable New Town for 60,000 people, built as an addition to Stockholm, which was started about when this book was written and is now practically complete—and fully inhabited.

The Radburn Idea is a basic element of the plan of Vallingby, conceived by the brilliant community architect Sven Markelius. It is carried out with much originality, imagination, and variety, to fit the special requirements of the site and of the people of Stockholm. The plan further develops the related Radburn elements of superblocks with central open greens forming a continuous chain of parks toward which buildings face, and specialized types of paths and roads completely separated from one another.

The same principles, modified to meet quite different local customs, in large part set the pattern for Chandigarh, the new capital of East Punjab, India, both as first laid out by Mayer and Whittlesey and as now being built according to the plans of Le Corbusier.

Thus three of the outstanding New Towns or cities of this decade demonstrate on a city-wide scale the principles and practices which were the basis of the pioneer communities with which this book deals. In Sweden, India, and British Columbia the New Towns toward which we in the United States have been moving these last thirty years have actually come into existence.

New York
November 1956

FOREWORD TO 1966 EDITION

This third edition of *Toward New Towns for America* follows the text of the 1956 edition without revision.

I have, however, added a short supplementary bibliography containing a few outstanding and particularly pertinent references with some description of their contents.

New York
November 1965

INTRODUCTION

BY

LEWIS

MUMFORD

Except for colonial times, hardly a beginning has been made, up to now, on the history of American city development and urban design. Not the least merit of Clarence Stein's account of the housing and planning experiments that began with Sunnyside Gardens in the nineteen-twenties is the fact that it is a valuable document toward this unwritten history. But it is happily far more than that: it is an account of certain new ideas in planning the urban environment; and it is a critical appraisal —often a strict self-appraisal—of the results. No book in this field could be more pertinent to our present task, or more salutary; for both the housing and the city planning movement have reached a point where, to justify their existence, they must depart from their familiar stereotypes and strike off boldly along the lines indicated by the planning work of Clarence Stein and Henry Wright, correcting the weaknesses time has disclosed and carrying further their many valuable contributions.

Seen in perspective, the positive phase of city planning began in America with the work of Frederick Law Olmsted, first in Olmsted and Vaux's plan for Central Park; while the positive phase of housing began, after the Civil War, with the building of the series of White model tenements in Brooklyn, dwellings whose good qualities never received adequate analysis or awakened emulation. Though Olmsted's was a reflective mind, his own work failed in some degree to produce the impression it might and should have had on a later generation. Perhaps one of the reasons for this was the fact that he did not write such a detailed account of his own achievement as Mr. Stein wisely has here attempted, with the providential and patient encouragement of Mr. Gordon Stephenson. Even the two-volume biography of Olmsted, published

in our generation, centers almost exclusively on one aspect of his work, park planning, and does not do justice to his many pioneering contributions, not merely to urban design but to regional culture.

Since the work of such strong individuals has been so easily forgotten—despite Olmsted's immense influence on his contemporaries—it is not perhaps singular that the excellent early planning of mill villages, like Lawrence and Lowell in Massachusetts and Manchester in New Hampshire, was passed over without even comment, till Mr. John Coolidge published his recent *Mill and Mansion*. Even more significant American initiatives in urban layout and site planning were forgotten: I refer not merely to the planning in long parallel rows in Jefferson's University of Virginia (triumphantly invented a century later by German planners) but to the creation of the super-block, with entrant cul-de-sacs. This admirable device for lowering road costs, increasing the amount of green space, and creating tranquil domestic quarters free from through traffic long antedated the motor car; in fact, it was widely employed in Cambridge and Longwood (both near Boston, Mass.) before the middle of the nineteenth century. Curiously it never attracted any later attention, not even from nearby planners like Olmsted and John Nolen, though the latter had his office in Cambridge and must have repeatedly visited these very super-blocks on friendly, if not on professional, errands.

The transition to modern planning and housing in America did not take place on any scale until the First World War. So far from building on American traditions, the planners turned mainly to England for their models: reverting to an old colonial habit. In 1915 Charles Harris Whitaker, the redoubtable editor of the Journal of the American

INTRODUCTION

Institute of Architects, then to enter on its most brilliant decade, began to publish reports of the new war housing communities built in England under Raymond Unwin. Mr. Frederick L. Ackerman made a special visit to England to gather materials for one of these articles; and the discussions that followed laid the foundations for the new housing policy courageously instituted by the Federal Government under Woodrow Wilson. The current shortage of housing in industrial towns, even before the United States entered the war in 1917, made it imperative for the government to plan and construct housing estates for munitions workers and shipbuilding workers: indeed, Washington created two independent authorities to plan and build adequate quarters in these respective fields.

Working in a realm where they had little preparation and less formal training, the accomplishment of American architects and planners was remarkably high; and the new housing communities, like the Black Rock development at Bridgeport and the Yorkship Village near Camden, gave an immense stimulus to socially minded architects throughout the country. Two such architects, F. L. Ackerman and Henry Wright, had worked on the United States Shipping Board's War Housing, under Mr. Robert D. Kohn, he who was to become first head of Public Works Administration housing under President Roosevelt in 1933; and sometime after the war Mr. Kohn, already associated professionally with Mr. Stein, brought Wright and Stein together. That meeting began their close association, a partnership in every sense but the legal one, which lasted for a decade. The results of that synergy are visible in this book.

In the post-war period, Mr. Whitaker performed one further service to the planning movement, when he moved his offices from Washington to New York: he brought together in friendly intercourse the group that was to become, in 1923, the Regional Planning Association of America; and he opened the pages of his Journal to reports and discussions on community planning, in a special department edited by Mr. Stein. To understand the scope of Stein's and Wright's contributions to planning, one must do more than appraise their individual work: one must also examine the close group in which they played such a dynamic part. But first a word about their own personalities.

As is usually the case in a good partnership, Clarence Stein and Henry Wright each possessed special abilities that complemented those of the other. Henry Wright was both an able technician and a dreamer: a man with a quick mind, fertile in suggestions, never rigidly committed even to his own best ideas, but ready to go off on a new trail at the first gleam of an opening. Trained as a landscape architect, he had settled down in St. Louis and raised a family of four, a large family for his generation. Wright's experiences with the difficulties and opportunities of a middle class household made him a most sympathetic interpreter of the needs of his new clients in low income housing: here he counter-balanced Stein, who had long been a bachelor, accustomed to the apartment house life of Paris or New York. Wright even lived with his family in Sunnyside, during its early days, and learned at first hand its advantages and drawbacks. He recognized the necessity of both lowering the cost of housing and doing a better job of it; and his analysis led him to emphasize the way in which control over the over-all pattern could contribute to both ends.

Henry Wright was a great lover of chess; and he used to say that his skill in chess made a better planner of him, ready with alternative solutions, able to think many moves ahead, trained to coordinate many variables; certainly planning itself had for him all the excitement of that noble game; and as with chess, he never thought he could exhaust all its possibilities. Both as a human being and as a thinker, he retained a youthful eagerness that matched his capacity for growth. This readiness to learn helped to make him an excellent teacher; and his openness to new ideas in architecture put him into sympathetic relations with the younger architects and planners, whom he gathered round him in a small summer school on his New Jersey farm. Some of the best of the younger generation, people like Robert Mitchell and Chloethiel Woodard Smith, were Wright's students. Wright had the independence and freedom of the unfettered intellectual, who has never been bribed into submission by the fleshpots; but his very independence and his occasional hot temper needed a moderating influence; and this, among many other things, his associate, Stein, provided.

Clarence Stein is a rare combination of artist and organizer; a man of fine taste, delicate discrimination, and a background of adequate means that gave him wide opportunities, not only for the exercise of these qualities but for travel as well. He had been chief designer for Bertram Gosvenor Goodhue and had been in charge of the planning of a model mining town at Tyrone, New Mexico. But during the years of his greatest activity, the organizer in Stein was perhaps uppermost: it was he who not merely kept the office running, but organized the Regional Planning Commission, and deployed the little squad of thinkers and technicians who surrounded him with such skill that their opponents treated them as respectfully as if they were a regiment. If Wright was the zealous bird-dog who was always picking up a new scent, Stein was the hunter who never forgot that he had to bring home the game. Stein combined an extremely conciliatory manner with a will of steel; and he had a happy faculty of being all things to all men: he was capable of smoking a long black cigar with Governor Smith or admiring a Renoir that Alexander Bing had recently purchased; of chewing over contractors' estimates with his engineer and man-of-all-work, Frank Vitolo, or of reacting intelligently to the latest idea MacKaye or Wright had evolved overnight.

Stein was an excellent appraiser of both men and ideas; and best of all, for the purpose in hand, he never permitted himself to lose sight of the broader social goals through overemphasis on any single set of details. Stein's persistence often kept Wright on the main track when the latter's curiosity or his love of intellectual adventure might have led him off along ultimately less rewarding paths; this very persistence was partly responsible for the final appearance of that early landmark in regional planning thought, the Plan for the State of New York: a task from which at one moment Wright was inclined to withdraw—only to come forward finally with the most brilliant historical summation, and a radically new concept of decentralization.

So close was the relation of the two men during the decade of their active association that it is hardly possible to assign credit to one or the other

for any particular part of the work; and it was of the essence of their relation to disregard such matters; for a good partnership, like marriage, disdains any close accountancy of personal disbursements and receipts. By training, however, Wright was the planner, with a specially fine eye for site planning and grouping; while Stein was predominantly the architect. When their association terminated, however, Stein devoted himself increasingly to planning. If the architecture always remained more traditional than the planning in the work they did together, this was at least partly because salesmen, contractors, and financiers, making principles out of prejudices, all fancied themselves as having more competence in the architectural department. So preposterous was the prevailing conservatism here in the twenties that it was only after a serious struggle that the planners of Sunnyside were permitted to paint the interior doors, instead of giving them the conventional hideous mahogany stain, or to use common brick throughout, instead of using special face-brick on the street side.

But, to sum up, what Wright and Stein had in common was even more important than what they held separately: they were united in personal modesty and generous public aims, in an absence of competitive self-display, in a keen sense of the essential values in art and life, in a desire to make the good things of our civilization available to all its members: above all, they shared a warm, abiding humanity. But for Wright's early death in 1936, it is conceivable that the two men might have come together again professionally; indeed each, independently, had a part in the development of Greenbelt.

In the case of Clarence Stein one further element must be added: his keen sense of public issues. Until his influence began to be felt, the housing movement in New York had confined itself, under Mr. Lawrence Veiller's leadership, almost exclusively to restrictive legislation. Even the model tenements built in New York by philanthropic groups were only a few shades better than those allowed by law; while the notion of having the State supply the capital and even take the initiative in publicly condemning land for housing purposes and subsidizing, further, the lowest income groups would

INTRODUCTION

have been regarded by the original housing reformers with more horror than the slums themselves.
More than any other single person, Clarence Stein
changed all this. As the dynamic chairman of the
Commission for Housing and Regional Planning,
he not merely established the widespread need for
new housing for the lower income groups, ill-
served by private enterprise: he also showed the
need of large scale enterprise, both private and
public, to do the job effectively; and pointed out
that money at low interest rates would be far more
effective in reducing costs than any conceivable
economy in construction. Stein also pointed to the
need, now only beginning to be recognized, to build
on open land, in order to eliminate wasteful street
patterns, provide open spaces, reduce density, and
drain off sufficient population from the central
areas to lower the grossly inflated land value based
on anti-social standards. Early and late, Stein advocated a public policy working for decentralization, industrial dispersal, new towns, and regional
reconstruction.

Without Clarence Stein's initiative, New York
State's constructive leadership in publicly aided
State housing in the late nineteen-twenties would
not have come about; and without this leadership,
the Roosevelt administration would not, in all probability, have been able to evolve the comprehensive
national housing policy that it actually embarked
on with such readiness. Finally, had it not been for
the ideas that the Regional Planning Association of
America, under Stein's presidency, had put into circulation during the twenties, the Greenbelt Towns
undertaken by the Resettlement Administration in
1934 would have been inconceivable, and the germs
of an American New Towns policy—still unfortunately aborted—would not have been implanted in
Washington.

The important thing to realize, then, is that the
work Clarence Stein took part in as architect and
planner, though largely of a private nature, up to
Greenbelt, went on against this background of
wider public education and effort; and it had as its
ultimate aim the use of the power and wealth of the
State to co-ordinate all the forces that create communities and to make them serve public, rather
than private and selfish ends, even though the enterprise itself was privately financed. Stein treated

these experiments in housing as Ebenezer Howard
treated the Garden City: as a proving ground for
methods that would later be used, if successful, on a
far wider scale. First private initiative to test the
validity of the new planning; then public enterprise, to extend it and co-ordinate it, when private
enterprise lagged or retreated or proved impotent.
Stein's purposes found a sympathetic echo in Alexander M. Bing, a public spirited citizen, who fortunately was also a shrewd and experienced real estate
operator, accustomed to handling large enterprises.
At the height of his business success, Mr. Bing put
his abilities at the service of housing improvement,
with the ultimate purpose of building a garden city;
and without such valiant practical co-operation
Stein would probably never have gone so far in
community design. As it was, Stein became something more than an architect and planner: he was
the foremost exponent in his generation of urban
statesmanship.

Having sketched in this political background, I
must complete it by outlining the intellectual foundations of Stein's and Wright's work: the vivid in-
terchange of ideas that took place within the Regional Planning Association, where the civic ideas of
Geddes and Howard, the economic analyses of
Thorstein Veblen, the sociology of Charles Horton
Cooley, and the educational philosophy of John
Dewey, to say nothing of the new ideas in conserva-
tion, ecology, and geotechnics, all had a part in
transforming the cut-and-dried procedures of the
earlier planners. The Regional Planning Association of America—not to be confused with the
Regional Plan Association of New York, a later
organization created to carry on the work of the
Russell Sage Foundation plan—is perhaps worth
more than a mere mention here, for its composition
and nature should be well understood by those who
erroneously believe that important movements can
be carried out only by mass organizations, supported by a heavy budget. The charter members of
this group, which first met in 1923, were the following: F.L. Ackerman, Frederick Bigger, A.M. Bing,
John Bright, Stuart Chase, R. D. Kohn, Benton
MacKaye, Lewis Mumford, C. S. Stein, C. H.Whi-
taker, and Henry Wright. In time, a handful of
others joined the association, including Edith Elmer
Wood, Tracy Augur, and Catherine Bauer; but at

no time were there as many as twenty members.

This group made up in intensity what it lacked in extension. A core of members met at least two or three times a week, sometimes more, for lunch or dinner; and from time to time somewhat more formal meetings were held over a weekend, at the Hudson Guild Farm in Netcong, New Jersey, for strenuous systematic discussions. (The members came with their wives and incidentally were among the first urban groups to revive the square dances and the Appalachian folk-ballads, under the guidance of MacKaye: the great geotect who conceived the Appalachian Trail, as a means of both using and conserving that primeval area.) Patrick Geddes was present at the first weekend meeting in May 1923; and at one of the last weekends, before Radburn was launched, Clarence Perry took an active part. But essentially this little group was a society of friends: people so close in aim, so freely co-operative in act, that the principle of unanimity, of laboring with each other till they had clearly focussed their agreements, spontaneously operated. On such a basis neither factionalism nor desire for priority or publicity marred the work in hand. This group's active years spanned the decade between 1923 and 1933; and its last public effort was to conduct a week's meeting on Regionalism for the Institute of Public Affairs at the University of Virginia. On that occasion, the principal address was delivered by Franklin D. Roosevelt, then Governor of the State of New York, soon to bring before the American people the ripest fruit of two generations of regional thinking, from Marsh and Olmsted onward—the Tennessee Valley Authority act.

After 1933, the members of the Regional Planning Association scattered, many of them to work actively on the projects for which the group had, with no thought of such early realization, laid the theoretic foundations and outlined the practical tasks. Both the public and the private work carried on by the members of this association was affected by the constant cross-fertilization of ideas that took place between its members; for their prime object was to re-educate themselves, rather than to diffuse the existing stereotypes. They could shift from one task to another without narrowing their objectives or losing sight of their goals: the building of balanced communities, cut to the human scale, in balanced regions, which would be part of an ever widening national, continental, and global whole, also in balance. They could dream, with Walt Whitman, of 'the place where the great city stands,' the city of the most faithful friends, because they had wrought that ideal into their own lives. Ultimately, it was out of this group as a whole, rather than simply out of those directly responsible, that some of its best products came forth: the Regional Planning Number of the Survey Graphic (May 1925), the Final Report of the New York State Commission for Housing and Regional Planning, (1926), and the Radburn plan itself.

Playing over Stein and Wright, then, as thinkers and planners, was the constant stimulus of this wider group, sympathetic yet critical, idealistic but shrewd, not committed to immediate success but working patiently and effectively toward ultimately practical goals. Because of the general misdirection of effort in housing and planning during the nineteen-twenties, with its sprawling cities, its extravagant subdivisions, its areas of standardized blight, hastily sold off (under the aegis of the Own Your Own Home movement) to people already sufficiently insecure without this extra burden—because of this Stein and Wright were the only living links, along with Ackerman, between the admirable community planning of the war communities in 1918 and the efforts in housing and urban re-development undertaken, all too ignorantly of past efforts, in the early days of the Roosevelt administration.

Without this link, that work could hardly have gotten off to such an early start. Yet here, perhaps, is the place to make an observation entirely outside Mr. Stein's province as historian: namely, that the inadequate employment of Henry Wright and the all but total neglect of Mr. Stein in the housing and planning work of the thirties was, to speak in the mildest terms possible, one of the great oversights of the Roosevelt administration. And the country has paid for that neglect in dull stereotyped plans, in poverty of amenities and social facilities, in the notable lack of the human touch, which characterizes so much of the public housing and planning in the United States during the last 15 years. That work has been unexpectedly large in quantity, compared with the modest hopes entertained in the

INTRODUCTION

twenties; but it has been unnecessarily low in quality, compared with Sunnyside, Radburn, Greenbelt.

If the significance of the work of Stein and
Wright had been fully understood, the reckless
overcrowding of the land that has now become
standard practice in urban re-development—pi-
ously concealed under the 'low-coverage' which its
density makes almost meaningless—could never
have taken place. Projects like the Metropolitan
Life Insurance Company's Parkchester and Stuy-
vesant Town, and the New York City Housing
Authority's many slum clearances of equal density,
should have been unthinkable, in view of these
better precedents, had not wilful indifference to the
side-reaction from this overdensity, upon both the
occupants and the city, become almost a qualifica-
tion to posing as an allegedly practical expert on
these matters. The invisible costs of such projects—
the increased burden on non-existent parks, playgrounds, schools, the excessive costs of traffic congestion and avenue widening in cities developed
now for five or six times their original density—
heavily outweighs all the visible economies. Stein
and Wright had demonstrated on the basis of a
careful cost analysis, which included long term as
well as immediate costs, that the prejudice in favor
of high buildings and high densities simply could
not stand up under rigorous appraisal. In short,
they had verified for themselves Sir Raymond
Unwin's dictum: Nothing gained by overcrowding.
In community development it is not the first costs
but the final costs that count.

If in housing Stein and Wright's work carried on
the wartime traditions in group housing and row
(terrace) housing that were otherwise being abandoned or forgotten, on the side of community
planning they were conscious disciples of Barry
Parker and Raymond Unwin, and unconscious
disciples of their own great precursor, Olmsted.
Olmsted's complete separation of pedestrian walks
from vehicular and horseback traffic, by means of
overpasses and underpasses, in Central Park, was
certainly the major forerunner of the Radburn
plan. Unfortunately, Olmsted himself never apparently grasped the general significance of this
separation for modern planning, particularly on
land whose contours offer different levels. But one
can hardly doubt that Stein's daily walks through

Central Park during this formative period encouraged him to hold to it tenaciously, once Radburn
was built: more so than Henry Wright, who, when
he came to plan Greenbrook in 1935—it was never
built—went back to a more traditional layout. In
Hampstead Garden Suburb, on the other hand,
Parker and Unwin had explored the possibilities
of the superblock even in the early units, and had
used it in the same fashion as the earlier subdividers around Boston. But these English planners never
erected the super-block into a universal principle
of laying out a modern residential quarter: hence
they never carried it through as systematically as
the planners of Radburn did. Similarly, Parker
and Unwin had, in Hampstead, created on a limited scale the continuous inner park; but they did
not follow this to its logical conclusion by inter-
weaving this continuous green throughout the
whole development. But it was the systematic
application of these two planning elements that
created a radically new urban layout, the Radburn
plan, in which the avenue itself was pushed to its
logical conclusion to function solely as a means of
circulation, not as a promenade for shops and
offices. This is not indeed the only possible solution
for the problem of traffic in a motorized age; but
it is one that had many excellent features never
before utilized.

Like Olmsted, Stein and Wright dared put beauty
as one of the imperative needs of a planned environment: the beauty of ordered buildings, measured to the human scale, of trees and flowering
plants, and of open greens surrounded by buildings
of low density, so that children may scamper over
them, to add to both their use and their aesthetic
loveliness: a freedom not possible, incidentally, on
land occupied at a density over a hundred persons
to the acre, where the green exists only to be
looked at, not used. These planners insisted on
including open spaces and generous plantings as
part of the essential first costs of housing. In the
effort to achieve utmost economy, at a time when
building costs were still prohibitively high, they
doubtless sometimes allowed the inner quarters of
the house to become a little cramped. Their excessive economy here was re-enforced, probably,
by their memory of the fate of Forest Hills, the
garden suburb built on Long Island before the First

World War by the Russell Sage Foundation: meant to serve as a working-class community, but destined by the very generosity of its housing to become an entirely middle class, indeed upper middle class, community. When they came to Radburn their parsimony—say rather their prudence—somewhat relaxed, though never so much as a long term view would have justified; but even in the earliest work they provided generous open spaces and play areas, in a fashion hitherto unknown in New York since the middle of the nineteenth century. The results of their open designs speak for themselves; and they will continue to speak for many years; for their communities—and later ones patterned after them, like Baldwin Hills Village in Los Angeles and Fresh Meadows in New York—will sturdily resist that endemic disease of urbanism, blight: a disease that fatally overtakes places people quickly cease to love, once the first glow of possession is over, because they were never in fact lovable.

Comeliness and neighborliness are the qualities that Clarence Stein and Henry Wright wrought into their designs. Before Clarence Perry wrote his able treatise on the Neighborhood Unit, Stein and Wright had, in Sunnyside, carried out many of his theoretic suggestions in concrete detail. Their growing attention to the promotion of social life, through the timely provision of schools, shopping centers, community meeting rooms, informal outdoor meeting places, and even, in Radburn, swimming pools, distinguishes the work here presented from the more rigorous but somewhat less genial schemes that were current in Europe, particularly in Germany, during the same period, a moment when the tenants' 'minimum of existence' seemed to represent the modern architects' maximum of desire. These American planners had indeed something to learn, in clean modern form, from the best of their colleagues in Zurich, Berlin, and Frankfurt-am-Main; and Wright spent the better part of a year in Germany and Switzerland, zealously familiarizing himself with the fresh work there, which reached such a high level in Zehlendorf, Roemerstadt, and Neubuehl. But in turn these Americans had something to teach their European colleagues; and in current healthy reaction against a one-sidedly mechanistic mode of planning, in which the main human objec-

tives are forgotten, Stein and Wright still have something to teach to the younger generation. Stein's direct influence on Greenbelt, Md., and Baldwin Hills Village, and his indirect influence on Fresh Meadows, have contributed in no small measure to their excellence.

No one knows better than Clarence Stein that the work he has here described is but a beginning. What he and Wright demonstrated are not forms to be copied, but a spirit to be assimilated and carried further, a method of integration to be perfected, a body of tradition to be modified and transmitted—and in time transmuted into new forms that will reflect the needs and desires and hopes of another age. But the educated man is he who can best make use of the wisdom of the past, economizing his own time by not blindly and ignorantly repeating experiments that have failed, or by following blind trails that lead to bankrupt enterprises. Those who would go beyond the work Mr. Stein has spread before the reader in the following pages must at least catch up with it; and some of those who fancy themselves most in advance of it are actually lagging far behind: witness such a Fourierist antique as the new skyscraper village in Marseilles.

Sunnyside Gardens and Radburn and the Greenbelt towns were but finger exercises, preparing for symphonies that are yet to come: preliminary studies for the new towns that a bolder and more humane generation, less victimized by the false gods of finance, will eventually build. These planners dreamed generously; and their dreams will survive the weaknesses and imperfections of their execution. They achieved an outstanding degree of success, even when the economic tide was running against them, and when the more favorable political currents, represented in America by the New Deal and the more constructive elements in the labor movement, were not yet in motion. Their relative success and increasing influence is a pledge of what may be attained in the future under happier conditions.

Let the planners of the coming generation ponder this testament.

LEWIS MUMFORD
AMENIA, NEW YORK
1951

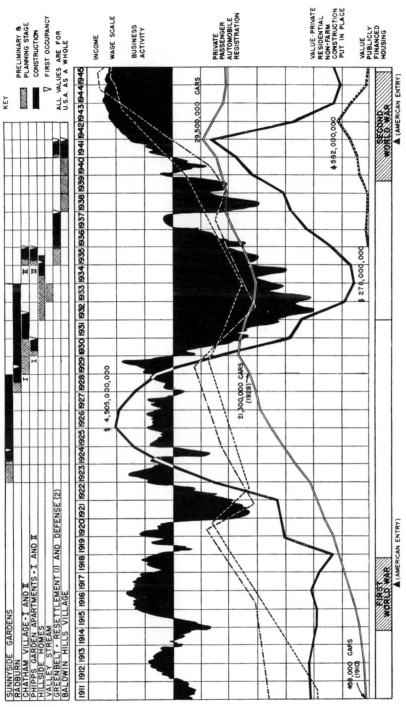

Fig. 1—Chart showing the years in which the various projects described were planned and constructed, and the time relation to the general economic climate. Sources included: U. S. Dept. of Labor; Poliak Foundation for Economic Research; Twentieth Century Foundation.

TOWARD NEW TOWNS FOR AMERICA

After the First World War there was a strong surge of enthusiasm for a better world. A group of us, including Lewis Mumford, Stuart Chase, Benton MacKaye, Charles Whitaker and Henry Wright, formed the Regional Planning Association of America, to discuss regional development, geotechnics and New Communities. New York's great democratic governor, Al Smith, planned to replace the slums in which he had grown up. As a result, there was created the Commission of Housing and Regional Planning. He made me Chairman. Up to that time in America our attack on housing had been regulatory—legal don'ts. I went abroad in search of more constructive action. In England 'New Towns' and 'New Towns after the War' were attempting to chart a new way; the second Garden City, Welwyn, was being built. I returned to America a disciple of Ebenezer Howard and Raymond Unwin.

Soon after, I walked uptown with Alexander M. Bing, the successful developer of massive apartments and skyscrapers. His war work had been connected with labor problems. He was trying to

decide whether he would be more useful in the field of labor or housing. I suggested the building of a Garden City.

That is how it started. We intended to create a Garden City in America. But time and place and the so-called economic cycle mold the ultimate reality of our dreams. So we first built Sunnyside, a community within the rigid framework of New York's gridiron. Then Radburn, realistically planned for the Motor Age, but not a Garden City as Howard saw it.

Before either of these we planned a Garden Community for a population of 25,000 on a square mile, at the undeveloped edge of New York City.[1] Here, in association with Henry Wright, the brilliant city planner and analyst, we developed the theoretical basis of land and community planning that was afterwards applied at Radburn, Chatham Village, the Greenbelt towns, and Baldwin Hills.

But the Garden Community was never realized: the purchase of the property could not be financed quickly enough to prevent the land being subdivided and thrown into the speculative market.

Fig. 2—Preliminary study of a proposed garden community in the New York region, 1923. In the normal subdivision plan, lower right, a street area of 190 acres, or 32.8 per cent of the whole, was required. In the proposed plan, upper right, 135 acres of streets, or 23.5 per cent, make ample provision for all needs, and park areas and space for other community needs are gained. The diagram below shows the use areas for apartments, row houses, communal space, parks, allotment gardens, light industry and store groups in the various centers.

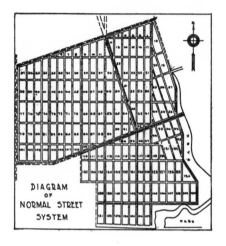

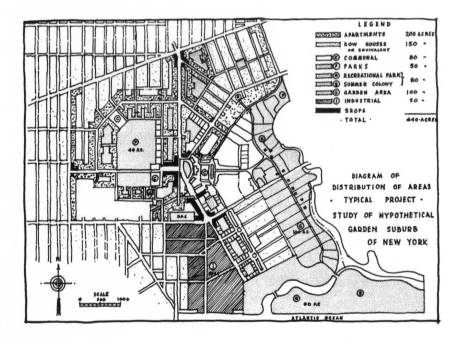

1

SUNNYSIDE
GARDENS

Clarence S. Stein and Henry Wright,

Town Planners

Clarence S. Stein, Chief Architect

Frederick L. Ackerman,

Architect of Blocks of Houses

The first development of the City Housing Corporation, the limited dividend company which Mr. Bing organized in 1924 for the ultimate purpose of building an American Garden City, was less spectacular than our proposed Garden Community. During the early years the Corporation required practice in large-scale planning, building, and community organization. Cautious, safe investment seemed a wise first step. Therefore we started in the Borough of Queens, on a large undeveloped site close to Manhattan's business center.

Construction of moderate-cost housing was once more slowly getting under way. It had been arrested during and after the First World War. This was in spite of the tremendous need, the crowding of our slums, and the doubling up of families. Building costs had almost doubled between 1914 and 1924.

Speculators feared the competition of lower future building costs. Ultimately, as the result of the tax exemption[2] offered by the city in 1920, a housing boom started in the practically undeveloped area across the East River. Land values were low, but street or utility improvements and recreational space were practically non-existent. Endless rows of cramped shoddy wooden houses and garages covered the land and destroyed natural green spaces (Fig. 7). The Metropolitan Life Insurance Company, as a result of tax-exemption, built, in Queens Borough, large-scale apartment groups to rent at $9 a room.

Near the largest of these the City Housing Corporation, in early 1924, purchased an undeveloped area which had been held by the Long Island Railroad for use as a railroad yard. With additional purchases, there were about 77 acres, 55.82 of which were used to create the Sunnyside Community of 1,202 family units. These were built during 1924-1928 as a continuous large-scale operation.

THE SITE was convenient for workers in the office centers of Manhattan. The rapid transit station at the corner of the property was 15 minutes travel time from the 42nd Street center. Land was cheap, averaging 50¢ per square foot, not including streets. It offered little difficulty, through rock or soil, for large-scale methods of excavating. Main utilities came to the edge of the property. We found it more economical to install sewers, and to build streets under City specification, than to have this done by the municipality. Our work was programmed so that each unit of building was completed without leaving vacant lots, and utilities were installed only as needed. This saved greatly on carrying charges as compared with the typical spotty methods of development.

1924-1928 were good years financially and for employment. Sunnyside houses were sold and apartments rented as soon as they were completed.

The City Housing Corporation had profited when in the autumn of 1928 it had finished its building of Sunnyside. This was not only because of good management, low-cost land close to rapid transit, economical planning, and orderly large-scale building in the brief period of 1924-1928. It was also a result of fortuitous circumstances. Among these were (1) the colossal post-war de-

SUNNYSIDE GARDENS

mand for homes, which filled houses as soon as they were finished; (2) and as a result of (1) the rapid rise of land costs. The 671 thousand square feet of land purchased by the corporation, but not used, increased in value from 50¢ a square foot (plus 15¢ carrying and improvement cost) to $1.62 a square foot.[3]

Objectives

PURPOSE.—The ultimate aim of the City Housing Corporation was to build a garden city. Knowledge and experience gained at Sunnyside was intended to serve that objective. The immediate purposes, as stated by Mr. Bing in 1926, were 'to produce good homes at as low a price as possible: to make the company's investment safe; . . . to use the work of building and selling houses as a laboratory in which to work out better house and block plans and better methods of construction and financing.'

These objectives guided us in planning Sunnyside.

1. It was a laboratory, an experiment, a voyage of discovery, and an adventure.

2. Economy in planning and building was essential. Most earlier well-intentioned American attempts at community housing for low-income workers had been tempted, by planners' delight in spacious elaboration, into becoming middle-class suburbs. Wright and I were determined to simplify and even squeeze our house plans so as to make them available at as low a price as possible. Economical spaciousness we hoped for as a result of judicious group planning.

LAND COST.—One of the principal reasons given for unhealthy, inhuman congestion is generally the high cost of urban land.

What we demonstrated for America, by our site and group planning at Sunnyside, and even more at Radburn, was the possibility of preserving open spaces for natural green, for recreation, for light, for healthful living, and for more spacious and beautiful living without additional cost, in fact at less than the normal price.

The basic theories by which we worked were not new. In England, Raymond Unwin, at the beginning of the century, in his revolutionary pamphlet 'Nothing Gained by Overcrowding,' had adequately proved that large open spaces could be preserved in block centers at practically no additional cost per lot, and with far less investment of capital or labor. Henry Wright brilliantly applied these principles to American conditions.

The division of land costs at both Sunnyside and Radburn illustrate the discrepancy between raw and improved land. The land at Sunnyside had been out of farm use for thirty to thirty-five years. During that period of 'ripening' the cost of the land rose from 3.3 cents per square foot in 1892 to the 48.5 cents that the City Housing Corporation paid the railroad for property it had held out of use for 18 years. There was no profit in this difference of 45 cents.

The increased value was mainly in carrying charges, taxes and interest. Up to the time of the City Housing Corporation's purchase in 1924, the railroad in 18 years had built up 38.3 cents production cost, of which less than one cent was for public improvements. The City Housing Corporation, through speedy use, minimized the carrying charges on the land. Of the production costs of 33⅓ cents between purchase and use for construction, 24 cents per square foot went for public improvements and interest on these, as compared with 8⅔ cents for taxes and interest on investment.[4]

Planning Sunnyside

THE GENERAL PLAN (Fig. 3).—There never was time to study the plan of Sunnyside as a whole. As soon as the tract of land owned by the Pennsylvania Railroad was purchased in February, 1924, planning for the first unit was started. Building actually commenced on April 1st, two months later.

Our previous studies, in 1923, of a garden community had proved the unnecessary costliness of developments based on the typical gridiron layout.[5] But the Sunnyside area was already laid out in city blocks 190 to 200 feet wide and about 600 to 900 feet long (Fig. 3). In spite of the evidence of economy and better living conditions shown in the various studies made by Wright, for the elimination of certain thoroughfares that became dead-ends by the railroad, the Borough Engineer's Office would have nothing of it. The streets were on the map

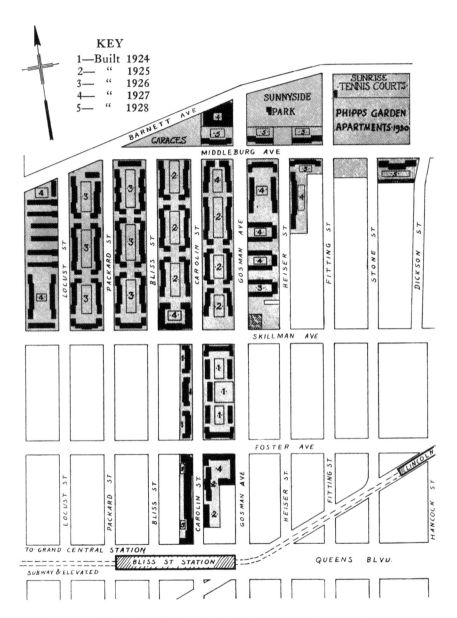

Fig. 3—General plan of Sunnyside Gardens showing the relation of the development to the city block system of layout, the position of the rapid transit station, and the site of Phipps Garden Apartments. The years in which the various stages of construction were completed are indicated. These streets have had their names changed. Locust, Packard, Bliss, and Carolin are now 44th, 45th, 46th, and 47th Streets, respectively. Middleburg Ave. is now 39th Ave., Foster Ave. is now 43rd Ave.

24

SUNNYSIDE GARDENS

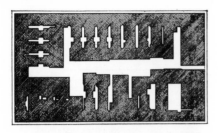

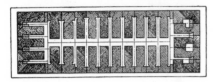

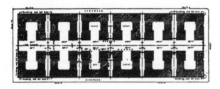

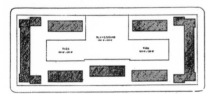

Fig. 4—Comparison of four ways of developing blocks in New York City. In the first three examples the subdivision into lots is the controlling factor in design. In the third, by the Metropolitan Life Insurance Company, the inner green space is greatly increased, but the persistence of lot subdivision causes bad side-lighting. In the fourth example, lot subdivision no longer controls design.

and there they must remain. A variation would be a dangerous precedent! Ultimately, only a few short ends of streets near the railroads were closed. These were advantageously used for garage groups, the Park, and in the end for the Phipps Garden Apartments. Elsewhere we were forced to fit our buildings to the blocks rather than the blocks to the living conditions, as we afterwards did at Radburn.

GROUP PLANS.—The first unit, built in 1924, was designed as a separate community (Fig. 5). By surrounding the perimeter of the block with narrow buildings, leaving no projecting wings, a great part of the block could be held for common use, even after allowing for private gardens connected with the single and two-family houses (Fig. 6). Playground and common garden space was dedicated as a private park for the use of surrounding residents, under the control of block trustees (Fig. 8). Experience showed that the single tennis court was an impractically small unit for operation. The playground activities were found annoying and noisy by those who dwelt around them (Fig. 5).

During the second and third years the use of the common block centers was continued, but in a somewhat different form. The long 900-foot blocks were divided into smaller quadrangles, almost completely enclosed and in scale with humans and their two-story houses. These interior garden courts were the equivalent of a park, some three-quarters of a mile in length and totalling six acres in area. Their appearance contrasted sharply with the typical speculators' developments nearby on similar blocks, crowded with garages and access roads, a mass of gray cement and roofs, barren of trees and grass. The characteristic Sunnyside block interior was some 120 feet wide between the rear of buildings. Each house had its private garden space, about 30 feet deep. The central areas, some 60 feet wide, though legally the property of the various owners, were used in common by all those in the surrounding houses under a 40-year easement agreement (Fig. 12). These common greens were intended for restful gatherings or for quiet play. They were not to be used as playground for any but the very young (Fig. 13). Adequate space was left between the rear of the end buildings to open up a vista through the length of the block. Between the three-family buildings, paths cross from street to street

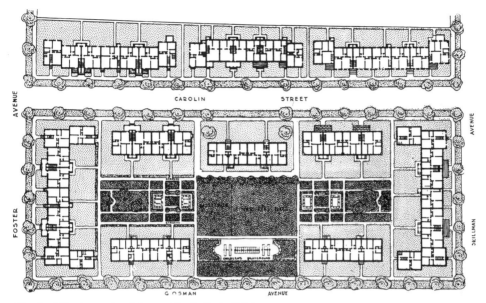

Fig. 5—*The first unit of Sunnyside, built in 1924.*

Fig. 6—*The interior of a block in the first development, showing the landscaping soon after completion in 1924. Apartment buildings and two-story single and two-family houses are on the perimeter. The central space is for common use and there are private gardens. From foreground to background may be seen decorative gardens, infants' play space with pergola, young children's recreation space, and then tennis courts. In the distance is the rapid transit line to midtown New York. Photo taken in 1924.*

SUNNYSIDE GARDENS

Fig. 7—The character of miles of boom development in Long Island City at the time when the Sunnyside Gardens project was conceived.

Fig. 8—Children's playground in court of the first unit, built in 1924. Photo taken in August 1949.

and give access to the center of the blocks. These cross-walks were staggered so as to create interesting vistas with terminal facades (Fig.9).

The carrying of coal, ice and food to the rear of row houses meant in the early work two areaways allowing passageway through the cellar. Later, on the basis of our observation in the English Garden Cities, Henry Wright and I decided to try passageways through the ground floor of some houses. These were not successful; they complicated the plans, and were difficult to maintain and police.

GARAGE COMPOUNDS.—The preservation of the Sunnyside block interiors required some other location of garages. They were grouped at the other side of Middleburg Avenue near the railroad. This was a daring thing to do, especially as the nearest house in the first unit was fully a thousand feet away, and there was nothing but barren waste between. However, this did not prevent the quick sale of houses. The parklike courts more than compensated for the lengthy walk to the garages.

The garages, which were grouped behind a brick wall, were factory-made metal units. They served well the first decade or so; they are now rather obsolete. Our large automobiles are cramped both in the garages and in the roads. The metal exteriors are rusted and worn. We have found masonry garages, in the later developments, more lasting. A little additional cost in construction, and above all in spaciousness, to prepare for possible change is generally a good investment.

At a later date, a large two-story concrete garage was erected nearby by the corporation. It was heated, and service was expensive. Therefore it was necessary to charge more rent, much more than most Sunnyside residents could afford. The large garage never paid. It has been my experience that in communities of this kind the simple type of low structure is the most successful and most satisfactory. Expensive, large structures require too much in overhead costs.

COURTS AND GARDENS.—In the last years at Sunnyside, at the edges of the property, we built courts opening off the streets. Our purpose was to front as few houses as possible toward the outside builders' monotonous rows. The continuous rows of buildings on three sides of a common green have

a pleasant sense of enclosure. Architecturally I find them more satisfactory than the broken line of free-standing houses on typical Radburn culs-de-sac (Fig. 11).

These courts worked very well at Sunnyside in spite of being fitted into the gridiron street pattern. There is a great deal of privacy on the garden sides, augmented by the height above Gosman Avenue of the three eastern groups (Fig. 14). The varied landscape design is rich with twenty years' growth, and has a restful beauty. The livingrooms and most of the bedrooms face toward gardens instead of streets. Services come directly to the kitchen or cellar entrance by private paved service lanes which connect two public streets.

Lewis Mumford, who lived in Sunnyside for 11 years, most of this time on one of these courts, has this to say:[6] 'It has been framed to the human scale and its gardens and courts kept that friendly air as, year by year, the newcomers improved in the art of gardening and the plane trees and poplars continued to grow . . .

'So, though our means were modest, we contrived to live in an environment where space, sunlight, order, color—these essential ingredients for either life or art—were constantly present, silently molding all of us.'

PLANNING ECONOMIES.—These courts opening off the street suggested methods of replacing some through streets with parks, as was afterwards done at Radburn. Let us compare their cost with a group of the same number of similar houses around the typical earlier inner courts. About the same amount of main street front is required on two streets for the two arrangements of two three-family houses, two two-family houses and 12 single-family dwellings. However if we had been permitted to close every second street without installation of main line utilities and street paving, wiring, etc., we would have had a goodly saving. This would have more than paid for adequate turn-arounds at private lane ends, or even for narrow U-shaped roads around each second dead-end group. It would also have covered the costs of replacing half the streets with well-planted parks, sixty feet wide.

GROUPING.—We mixed the different house types in the same rows throughout the development:

SUNNYSIDE GARDENS

single-family-home-owners next to landlord and tenant in flats. In spite of the speculative operators' fear of such indiscriminate grouping, and the zoners' preoccupation in keeping dwellings of similar types together, we found this did not cause sales resistance. I have heard of no social difficulty resulting from it. The tenants on the second floor were members of the Sunnyside Association as well as the house owners, and so were those of the apartment houses, both in the co-operatives and those operated by the Corporation as landlord.

In the block which was developed during the first year we grouped three-floor apartment buildings with the two-story rows of mixed single and two-family houses. The varied heights give far more interest than could any amount of pattern, horizontal or vertical massing of windows, or lines of brick ornament. Such a combination would not have been permitted if Sunnyside had been classified within the zoning laws as *residential*. Luckily, as a proposed site of a railroad yard, Sunnyside was mainly classified as *industrial*. Therefore we were free to design for community and aesthetic objectives.

We continued to experiment in this manner by locating an apartment building around a court which opened on the central green of the block. This gave the apartment tenants a view for 800 feet over trees and lawns and gardens and pergolas.

UNIT PLANS.—We aimed to simplify construction, heating and plumbing; to make every internal inch serve, to eliminate waste movement, to minimize frontage and thus utility costs. We studied every detail so as to save money and thus serve as low an income group as possible. We counted on the spaciousness of our gardens to compensate for any undue tightness inside houses.

The types of houses at Sunnyside were limited in number (Fig. 10). We did our best to standardize so as to keep down costs and resulting selling price. All residences were two stories high above a basement. They had maximum cross-ventilation as none was more than two rooms deep. The depth of 28-ft. 4-in. which was used through all five years, and for all single and two-family houses as well as for the earlier apartments, was based on stock framing lengths.

After a careful cost analysis was made by Henry Wright in 1925, we made some minor changes. The operation of all mechanics was carefully followed and timed, so as to find ways of improving plans and construction without increasing costs. What we learnt was very useful in developing broader types of economical houses at Chatham Village.

The *two-family* house had identical plans on both floors. The typical apartment, 25-ft. wide, had two bedrooms besides kitchen and livingroom. The end houses, 28-ft. wide, had in addition a diningroom that could be used as an additional bedroom. These were very economical houses. The first year we used identical plans for our first apartment building which was three stories high, for the purpose of comparing construction costs.

The *three-family* house was planned primarily as the end enclosure of our garden courts. It also filled the needs of larger families in the first floor apartments, and the two upper apartments, each with a single bedroom, livingroom and kitchen, served well for the newly-wed families.

These houses had windows on all four sides and were almost free-standing, having very little attachment to the row. They had more than the usual garden space. In fact, the family on the ground floor, in a number of cases I have noted of late, not only grows flowers, but even vegetables.

Both two- and three-family houses were purchased by single owners at Sunnyside, on the basis of the upper-floor tenants helping to pay operation charges and maintenance. As a result, all disputes between owner and tenant eventually came to the management office of the City Housing Corporation. When hard times came and rents could not be paid or tenants moved out, the owners of these multiple-family houses were in much worse straits than the individual house owners.

The predominant type of *apartment dwelling*, the four-room unit (which was similar to that of the two-family house), had one outstanding defect. One bedroom opened into the livingroom and not into the passageway leading to the bathroom. Another less important objection was that access to all rooms except kitchen was through the end of the livingroom. In spite of this the houses and apartments were popular. Therefore I continued to use these two types, because of their great economy and

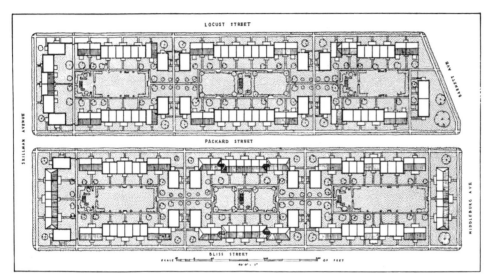

Fig. 9—Plan of two blocks with inner courts, built in 1926.

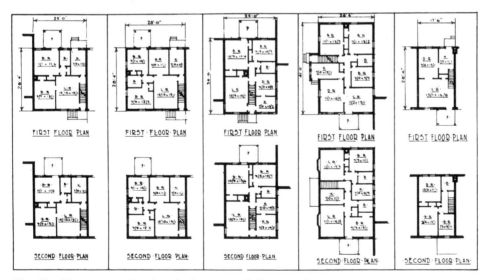

Fig. 10—House types, showing single, two- and three-family houses.

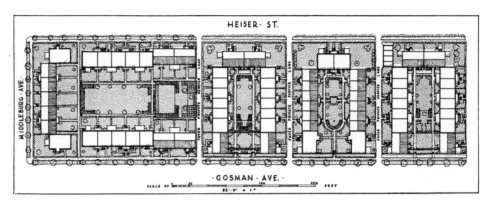

Fig. 11—Plan of part of a block with an inner court and three courts opening off the street, built in 1927.

Fig. 12—An inner court built in 1926. Photo taken in August, 1949.

minimum corridors for walk-up apartments, for years, gradually increasing the depth from 28 feet to 34. We must have built thousands of them at Sunnyside and Phipps. Then I finally developed a plan with all bedrooms leading to the corridor for Hillside, and used it again for the second unit of Phipps Homes (Fig. 97).

The Corporation looked upon Sunnyside as a social and economic, as well as an architectural, experiment. Therefore they tried co-operative ownership of the first apartment buildings. Only a few experiments in co-operative ownership of low-priced apartments had been tried in New York. These were mostly by groups of the same ancestry, from countries such as Finland where there had been practical experience in co-operation. The Sunnyside purchasers were of varied racial, religious and social background, and perhaps because of this the co-operatives were not successful. In later co-operative schemes success has been achieved. Perhaps we were too early with the Sunnyside experiment.

BASEMENT.—There is much to be said for and against cellars in single or two-family dwellings. Most governmental houses have been built without them, but they never have enough storage space. I am for cellars, ground conditions and water level permitting. A house should be lifted up a few steps as protection against rain and snow. In the north, footings have to go down below the frost level. Slightly more depth will suffice for a cellar. If ground is not rocky, a bulldozer will clear the whole space under the house as easily as cutting for footings and foundations only. It gives the cheapest possible space for heating and storage. If the ground slopes a little, as at Chatham Village, a large window can be put in at one end for a workroom or children's play space.

Brick Exteriors

USE OF BRICK, we found, had certain difficulties, such as leaking. This was not due to the use of comparatively cheap local (Hudson River) bricks, instead of the more extravagant face bricks. The leaks, experts told us, were through the joints—too much lime in our mortar. Keppler, the great master-builder of Amsterdam, said when I discussed our difficulties with him: 'In Holland we have built our walls almost exclusively of bricks for a thousand years. We should be experts, but they still leak.'

There is an architectural harmony at Sunnyside because of the common use of brick, as well as the repetition of simple details and the continuous roof lines. After twenty years or so, I am still strongly impressed by the advantage of brick over wood as an exterior material, whether it is used for bearing walls, as in Sunnyside's first year, or merely as a facing, as it was later used there and at Radburn. I am thinking of its effective appearance in a setting of natural green. That is the dominant feature at Sunnyside. The street trees that were so thin and scraggly when Marjorie Cautley, the Landscape Architect, planted them two decades ago now almost arch over the streets. The varied Hudson River brick, our common brick in New York City, forms a beautiful and contrasting background for the trees. And then there are the inner courts! In midsummer they seem almost too rich and luxuriant. But the dwellers in the surrounding houses are probably thankful for the protection from the sometimes torrid summer sun and in part from rain, as well as for the everchanging play of light and shadows on the opposite buildings. The courts seem well enough cared for after all these difficult years of depression and war. The planting of the little private gardens in many cases shows care and affection for natural beauty. There are even some home-owners who are growing vegetables, mainly in the larger lots around the three-family houses.

The brick exteriors remain more harmonious than wood because they are not painted. Therefore, there is no danger of assertive souls expressing their individuality, to the dismay of their neighbors, by coloring their dwelling with an inharmonious pigment. The natural quality of the brick eliminates the need of one expensive item of upkeep.

Life in Sunnyside

Although the orderly community character of Sunnyside drew to it teachers, artists, and writers, the intellectuals never were a dominant portion of the Sunnyside population. A census of house-owners in 1928 showed that non-professional workers—116 mechanics, 79 office-workers, 55

Fig. 13—An inner court built in 1926. Photo taken in August 1949.

*Fig. 14—A court opening off the street, built in 1927.
Photo taken in 1949.*

small tradesmen, 5 chauffeurs, 49 salesmen, etc.—were about four times as numerous as actors, artists, musicians, teachers, architects, engineers, doctors, and other professionals.

The Sunnyside population was a cross-section of those of moderate means (in 1926 the median income was $3,000). They were not the very poor who were afterwards to be housed by the Housing Authority with the aid of a governmental subsidy.

It was the pupose of the City Housing Corporation to create a setting in which a democratic community might grow. The Corporation supplied the place and equipment for community gathering and activity. In the beginning it also employed playground directors and encouraged the organization of a community association. Tenants and house owners had equal voice in community undertakings. The Corporation enthusiastically cooperated in the rapid development of social activity.

In the beginning there was no time to prepare a general community or physical plan. The two grew together. The neighborhood unit idea was still to be developed in America. Sunnyside was a pioneer in the community field as well as in housing.

As construction was gradually completed, court or block groupings served as centers for social activity and block organizations sponsored the program. Ultimately a recreation park served as a social center for the whole community.

In 1926 the City Housing Corporation set aside a park of three and a half acres and fully equipped it for the recreational use of children of all ages, as well as adults. A house already on the site was adapted to serve as a Community Building. The park was deeded to the Community Trust to be held in trust for the use of the 1202 families of Sunnyside.

With the establishment of this physical center for activity came the organization of a single Sunnyside Community Association. This was more effective than the several separate 'block' organizations. However, for the protection of property interests of the house owners and the maintenance of the block centers, the property owners' associations which had been organized for each block were continued.

Later, at Radburn, because of the Sunnyside experience, a single association was formed in the beginning with much broader functions than the Sunnyside Community Association.

The economic depression affected the people of Sunnyside as it did the great many who lived in the thousands of houses which sprang up in the Borough of Queens during the building boom period of the twenties. There was unemployment, savings were spent, and people were unable to pay the interest and amortization on their mortgages. In the end, many lost the homes they had thought were theirs.

There was one important difference between the people of Sunnyside and the others. Sunnyside was a community of people accustomed to meeting and doing things together—a real neighborhood community. The others were lone individuals with no organized social or other relations with the people who lived next door. At Sunnyside a home-owners' group was quickly formed; it comprised a majority of the community. The home-owners, as a community group, were soon ready to ask, and if necessary to fight, for a postponement of or a decrease in mortgage payments. In the end, they went on strike and, as a group, refused to make payments. Their attack was aimed at the City Housing Corporation. In this they were wrong, no matter how just might be their resentment.

The City Housing Corporation, in regard to the collection of charges on mortgages, was only the agent of the lending institutions that held the principal mortgages. The financial organizations had no personal contact with the home-owners of Sunnyside, or with any others who were being dispossessed. They insisted that the legal terms of the mortgages be fully carried out; basic economic conditions or sentiment were not within their province. The City Housing Corporation, though powerless, took the full brunt of the attack from the organized people of Sunnyside. The irony of the situation was that it had stimulated and helped community organization, and those living in Sunnyside had thus become accustomed to forming their own organizations.

The disunion growing out of the conflicts in the community, at that time, ended the most constructive development of community life, and Sunnyside has never regained its sense of unity as a neighborhood. However, the green commons, and their continued care by the block groups, have served as a basis of local unity; and, most important perhaps, the beauty of the garden-community, within the framework of the busy city, has been preserved. This pointed the way toward the 'Radburn Idea.'

Conclusions

I. GREEN COMMONS in block centers can be developed, even within the limitations of the characteristic American gridiron street pattern. They make a peaceful and beautiful setting for the surrounding homes.

Private deed restrictions can preserve such common green areas which are likely to disappear if protected solely by zoning.

II. THE GROUPING OF BUILDINGS of different heights and bulk, if well organized, increases the architectural interest and distributes the advantages of open spaces.

A combination in rows or groups of single-family, two-family and apartment houses, inhabited partially by tenants and partially by home-owners, need not cause social difficulties or sales resistance.

III. THE SIMPLE RECTANGULAR FORM of apartment unit gives maximum livability at minimum cost.

IV. SUCCESSFUL INVESTMENT HOUSING DEVELOPMENT for those of limited incomes requires:

1. *Low cost land,* adequate in size and easy of development.
2. *Transportation* to take people easily to working places in relatively short time.
3. *Continuous large scale building* of complete sections with installations of utilities and streets paralleling construction of buildings, the building to be followed immediately by marketing and use.
4. *Rapid development* so as to minimize carrying charges.
5. *Simple standardized units.*
6. *Grouping* for unity and variety of appearance as well as to add to the feeling of spaciousness given by the open areas.
7. *Limited interest rate* on capital invested.

All these elements existed in the development of Sunnyside. As a result it was a financial success until it was blighted by the depression. The disastrous results, both to the inhabitants and the City Housing Corporation, that followed were accentuated by the system of mortgage financing that functions to the advantage of owner or tenant only in the limited periods between economic deflation.

These periods, as shown (in Fig. 1), have been shorter, in the past, than the time required to pay off most residential mortgages. As the 'home-owner' has only a minority holding on his house, when inevitable depression comes, he discovers that 'home-ownership' for those with low incomes is a myth.

V. RESEARCH AND ANALYSIS should form an essential part of all community development. Every job should be a laboratory. Customary plans, forms or construction methods should be constantly questioned and analyzed. Fresh exploration and investigation is required to keep both architecture and community organization alive and contemporary.

Fig. 15—Houses and landscape are united in a spacious composition.

2

RADBURN

**Clarence S. Stein and Henry Wright,
Town Planners
Clarence S. Stein, Chief Architect
Frederick L. Ackerman, Architect of Blocks
of Houses and Radburn Building
Andrew J. Thomas,
Architect of Apartment Buildings
James Renwick Thomson,
Associate Architect for House Groups**

Economic Background

Early in 1928, after four years of success at Sunnyside, the City Housing Corporation was prepared to carry out its original objective, the building of a complete Garden City.

It had an experienced organization of technicians practised in economical planning, large-scale building, real-estate management, and community organization. It had confidence based on increasing success. By the end of the year Sunnyside would be completed; 1200 units would be sold or rented; 8 million dollars would be invested in Sunnyside, and after paying operating and carrying expenses and full annual 6 per cent stock dividend, a good surplus would remain to invest in the new venture. Mr. Bing was convinced of the security of the investment. He said[7] 'The larger the company becomes, the safer its operations will be, the greater the economy . . . of the company's work.' Land prices had risen so that ultimately the 20¾ acres at Sunnyside not used in the development were sold at a profit of over $646,000 — almost three times its cost. In short the Corporation was riding high on the waves of prosperity and booming real estate.[8]

The economic atmosphere in which Radburn was born was very different. The first home-owners moved into Radburn in May, 1929; that autumn the Wall Street market collapsed. Building went on around New York for a while, and for some years the City Housing Corporation continued to buy land and build at Radburn, though at a diminishing rate (twelve houses were built in 1933). Mean-

while the home owners of Radburn lost their jobs and incomes, and many of them their homes. The depression gave them the time and leisure to use the community opportunities provided by the physical and social plan. But it left a deep scar on their lives and little hope for the successful completion of Radburn. The City Housing Corporation was ruined. It lost most of the land outside the two developed superblocks. But in these there was enough to demonstrate a new form of town and community building: the Radburn Idea.

Conception of the Radburn Idea

Sunnyside was a dress rehearsal, but on a stage so limited that the authors' style was cramped. During the final year's performance, a search was started for an adequate theater in which to produce an American Garden City.

In our minds' eye we still had the theme that Ebenezer Howard had created so vividly in his book 'Garden Cities of Tomorrow.' We believed thoroughly in green belts, and towns of a limited size planned for work as well as living. We did not fully recognize that our main interest after our Sunnyside experience had been transferred to a more pressing need, that of a town in which people could live peacefully with the automobile—or rather in spite of it. The limitations which we found in the gridiron street pattern at Sunnyside, as a setting for safe motor-age living, made clear to all the staff what we planners had long seen and had planned to eliminate. So it was not surprising that at a staff discussion of the next project, the

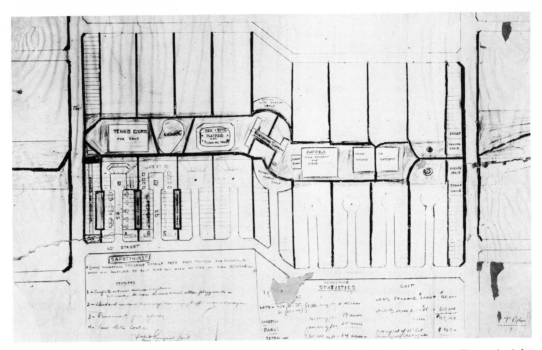

Fig. 16—Sketch plan made by Herbert Emmerich on December 3, 1927. The principles developed by the architects of Sunnyside are here set down by an administrator, who had joined in many discussions and was thoroughly conversant with the experience of Sunnyside. He called his superblock "Safetyhurst: a (highly) theoretical residence district free from traffic and congestion—which will doubtless be built someday when we tire of auto risks!"

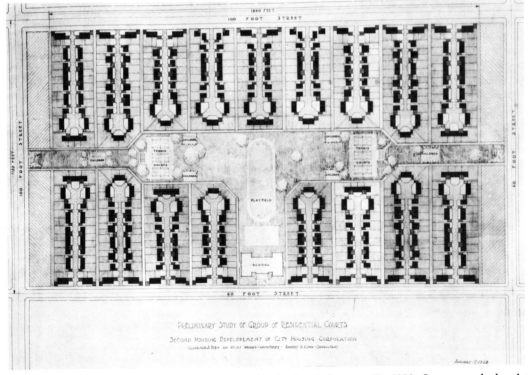

Fig. 17—Theoretical study of a superblock, dated January 17, 1928. It was made by the architects at the time when the idea was being discussed by all concerned, including Mr. Emmerich. It was soon to be the basis of the Radburn Plan.

young general manager, who was later to become head of the Federal Public Housing Authority, Herbert Emmerich, appeared with a crude, but complete, diagram of a superblock, which formed a neighborhood (Fig. 16).

The preliminary theoretical diagram of a rectangular superblock that the architects drew on January 17, 1928, included all the elements of the Radburn Idea (Fig. 17). The superblocks built at Radburn, although less geometric as a result of the topography—and therefore more interesting—were basically the same.

The Site

After examining some 50 possible sites, a large tract of undeveloped fertile farm land in the Borough of Fairlawn, New Jersey, only sixteen miles from New York, was chosen.

The speculative builders, who were already ruthlessly destroying the appearance of the land toward the proposed George Washington Bridge, had found this property too expensive. The good farmers, descendants of the Dutch, who had worked the land since Colonial days, were content and not anxious to sell. Careful maneuvering by real estate agents was required to prevent land prices from soaring beyond the possibilities of moderate cost housing.

The site was attractive, with rolling ground, but only a slight pitch at most places. Groups of houses could be arranged around courts without too much grading. There were some moderate hills that offered attractive locations for buildings of importance, such as the high school. Very little of the land was marshy. Most of it was good for economical large-scale building, with little rock that would require heavy blasting.

The property lent itself very well to the development of a new street system. Fairlawn Avenue, which appears on George Washington's military map, was the only existing road of importance. The large open areas to north and south we later connected by an overpass where the avenue dipped below the land at either side. The Borough of Fairlawn, then mainly a rural community, had not yet been sold an official road plan or a zoning ordinance. For this we offered thanks; we were free to design a functional town plan.

About two square miles of irregularly-shaped land on which to build Radburn was ultimately secured by the City Housing Corporation. There was an area sufficient for three neighborhoods, with a total population of about 25,000.

Not a Garden City

There was not, however, adequate area to surround the proposed town with a broad protecting greenbelt. This essential element of the garden city was sacrificed because of the greater emphasis on our other objectives. All that remained of green belt in the general plan was the proposed narrow parkway as northern boundary, and the recreation field along Saddle River to the east. That these would have been insufficient to give the essential protection was proved by what happened. The unrelated, badly conceived products of the speculative builder now hem it on every side. Fortunately, Radburn can still look into the center of its superblocks for peaceful green (Fig. 49).

Industrial opportunities seemed good, according to the rules that were generally followed. The town was served by the Erie Railroad; it was near Paterson, which had been one of the great silk industry centers; an express highway was planned to the great bridge which was being constructed to link New York with New Jersey.

We made our decisions quickly in those days. Our preliminary plans showed spacious sites for industry adjacent to the proposed express highway and the railroad. But the railroad was a secondary branch that went nowhere of importance. The Hudson River bridge to New York and the proposed through highway were both in the future; industry lives in the present, we found. Perhaps it was the bad times that kept factories away; but I think that section of New Jersey was on the downward trend, industrially. Certainly Paterson was losing its principal industry—the manufacture of silk (the fact that it has had an industrial revival since was of no help then). Most of the workers in the Paterson plants were too poorly paid to afford Radburn houses. This was only partially due to the quality of planning and building and the high standard of community facilities and organization at Radburn. At that time the provision of decent homes for low paid workers was an

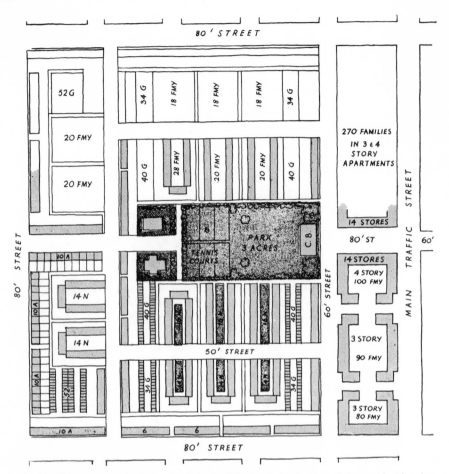

Fig. 18—Diagram reproducing a sketch in the "Study of Application of Sunnyside Planning Principles to a Larger City Area," a report prepared by Henry Wright in December 1924. The idea of the Radburn superblock with an inner park is emerging.

economic impossibility. It would still be so now, if there were no governmental subsidies, low rate loans or insured mortgages. Government aid in housing was non-existent at that time Radburn was built.

Thus two of the basic Garden City ideas, green belt and industry, were eliminated, and Radburn had to accept the role of a suburb. Though some engineers· and executives of New Jersey public utility companies and other corporations purchased houses, most of the inhabitants were, and still are,· 'white-collar' commuters from New York City.

At that period, access to Manhattan was difficult. The Erie Railroad service was poor and expensive; and the journey had to be completed by ferry and streetcar. By the time the George Washington Bridge and the connecting superhighway were completed, the depression had blighted all hope of success of Radburn, which required quick growth to balance carrying charges of land, plant and management organization.

CO-ORDINATION OF ECONOMIC WITH PHYSICAL AND SOCIAL PLANNING.—The failure of Radburn to become a Garden City, and its limitations as a suburb of New York, emphasize the dominant importance of the convenient and economic relation of working and living places in the choice of site of any new town. Generalizations are not sufficient. Good timing is essential to succesful New Town planning. Future transportation, or tomorrow's highways, do not market houses to workers now. It was not only at Radburn, but in the choice of sites for the three Greenbelt towns, that the economic and industrial studies were not sufficiently specific and realistic.

The Radburn Idea

Radburn's ultimate role was quite different from our original aim. It was not to be a Garden City. It did not become a complete, balanced New Town. Instead of proving the investment value of large-scale housing it became, as a result of the depression, a financial failure. Yet Radburn demonstrated for America a new form of city and community that fits the needs of present day urban living in America, and it is influencing city building throughout the world.

We did our best to follow Aristotle's recommen-

dation that 'a city should be built to give its inhabitants security and happiness.'

THE NEED FOR RADBURN.—American cities were certainly not places of security in the twenties. The automobile was a disrupting menace to city life in the U.S.A.—long before it was in Europe. In 1928 there were 21,308,159 automobiles registered (as compared with 5 in 1895). The flood of motors had already made the gridiron street pattern, which had formed the framework for urban real estate for over a century, as obsolete as a fortified town wall. Pedestrians risked a dangerous motor street crossing 20 times a mile. The roadbed was the children's main play space. Every year there were more Americans killed or injured in automobile accidents than the total of American war casualties in any year. The checkerboard pattern made all streets equally inviting to through traffic. Quiet and peaceful repose disappeared along with safety. Porches faced bedlams of motor throughways with blocked traffic, honking horns, noxious gases. Parked cars, hard grey roads and garages replaced gardens.

It was in answer to such conditions that the Radburn plan was evolved. For America it was a revolution in planning; a revolution, I regret to say, which is far from completed.

Elements of the Radburn Plan

'The Radburn Idea,' to answer the enigma 'How to live with the auto', or, if you will, 'How to live in spite of it,' met these difficulties with a radical revision of relation of houses, roads, paths, gardens, parks, blocks, and local neighborhoods (Figs. 19, 20 and 21). For this purpose it used the following elements:

1. THE SUPERBLOCK in place of the characteristic narrow, rectangular block.

2. SPECIALIZED ROADS PLANNED AND BUILT FOR ONE USE INSTEAD OF FOR ALL USES: service lanes for direct access to buildings; secondary collector roads around superblocks; main through roads, linking the traffic of various sections, neighborhoods and districts; express highways or parkways, for connection with outside communities. (Thus differentiating between movement, collection, service, parking, and visiting.)

3. COMPLETE SEPARATION OF PEDESTRIAN AND

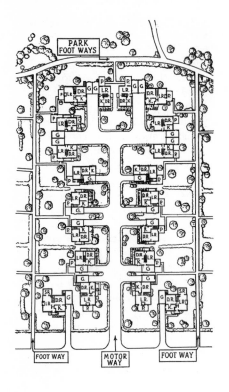

Fig. 19—Plan of a typical "lane" at Radburn. The park in the center of the superblock is shown at the top; the motor ways to the houses are at right angles to the park.

Fig. 20—Typical transverse section of a "lane" in the first unit of Radburn.

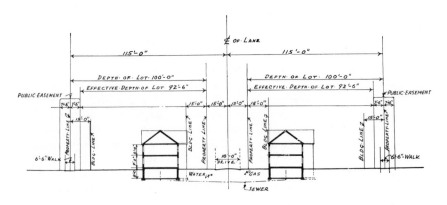

Fig. 21—Plan of the residential districts, dated November 1929.

AUTOMOBILE, or as complete separation as possible. Walks and paths routed at different places from roads and at different levels when they cross. For this purpose overpasses and underpasses were used.

4. HOUSES TURNED AROUND. Living and sleeping rooms facing toward gardens and parks; service rooms toward access roads.

5. PARK AS BACKBONE of the neighborhood. Large open areas in the center of superblocks, joined together as a continuous park.

Geddes Smith described Radburn compactly in 1929 as:[9]

'A town built to *live* in—today and tomorrow. A town "for the motor age." A town turned outside-in—without any backdoors. A town where roads and parks fit together like the fingers of your right and left hands. A town in which children need never dodge motor-trucks on their way to school. A *new* town—newer than the garden cities, and the first major innovation in town-planning since they were built.'

Precedents

None of the elements of the plan was completely new. The distinctive innovations of Radburn were the integrating superblocks, specialized and separated means of circulation, the park backbone, and the house with two fronts. Radburn interwove these to form a new unity, as a practical and attractive setting for the realities of today's living.

There were precedents for all the elements.

SUPERBLOCKS with great green interiors had been built in America. Before 1660, the Dutch in *Nieue Amsterdam* (New York) built their homes around the periphery of large blocks, with farms behind and sometimes with a great garden core (Fig. 22). However, throughout the nineteenth century and the early twentieth, most city growth was based on the repetitious geometric gridiron; a plan for facile plotting, surveying, legal recording—but not a plan for living. So Henry Wright and I went to Britain, on a special investigation to study superblocks with culs-de-sac, before we started planning Radburn. We concluded that, because of the greater use of the automobile in America, we were justified in increasing the size of superblocks over those at Welwyn, Letchworth and Hampstead Garden Suburb. The Radburn blocks were 30 to 50 acres in size. Their outlines were determined by their internal needs and by topography. Because of our heavier automobile traffic we faced fewer houses on main highways than most of the British examples. The English experiences helped us greatly, but if the superblock had not existed logic would have forced us to invent it. A rational escape from the limitations of the checker-board plan in which all streets are through-streets, with the possibility of a collision between auto and pedestrian every 250 feet, compelled it.

CULS-DE-SAC.—The dead-end lane had served in England for peacefulness and for economy of roads and utilities. Culs-de-sac had been used occasionally in our colonial villages. But the typical early American arrangement of houses was along the main, and sometimes only, road. This was more neighborly, and it was easier to shovel snow away in winter. The costliness of through street pavement and main line utilities was not yet a factor of economic importance. Later the extravagance was not understood. Real-estate and municipal engineering customs perpetuated obsolete forms.

I have already spoken of our experience with courts opening off streets at Sunnyside.

SEPARATION OF DIFFERENT MEANS OF COMMUNICATION had an excellent nearby precedent, Central Park in New York. Here, almost half a century before the invention of the automobile, Frederick Law Olmsted and Calvert Vaux planned and executed what they described in 1851 as:[10]

' . . . A system of independent ways; 1st, for carriages; 2nd, for horsemen . . .; 3rd, for footmen; and 4th, for common street traffic requiring to cross the Park. By this means it was made possible . . . to go on foot to any district of the Park . . . without crossing a line of wheels on the same level . . .' (Fig. 25).

The automobile has multiplied the need of separating antagonistic uses of streets. The need is

Fig. 22—Nieue Amsterdam in 1660. Redraft of the Castello Plan, by John Wolcott Adams and I. N. Phelps Stokes, 1916.

Fig. 23—Air view of Radburn. Photo taken in 1929.

recorded in the statistics of automobile accidents—
33,410 deaths in 1946, to say nothing of the million
or more cripples.[11] At Radburn we proposed to
unscramble the varied services of urban streets.
Each means of circulation would take care of its
special job and no other: through traffic only on
the main highways; with street intersections decreased about two-fold; most parking as well as
garages, delivery, and other services, on the lanes;
walks completely separated from autos by making
them part of a park instead of a street, and by
under- or over-passing the roads; finally, children's
play spaces in the nearby park instead of in busy
roads.

SPECIALIZED HIGHWAYS were in their infancy in
the U.S.A. at the time that Radburn was conceived.
There was not much more than the differentiation
of parkways and pseudo-expressways from the ordinary city or town street. To plan or build roads
for a particular use and no other use required a
predetermined decision to make specialized use
permanent or rather long-lived. That was contrary
to the fundamentals of American real estate gambling, to serve which the pattern of ordinary highways had become the basis of city planning. I say
this in spite of the fact that the 1920's were the
heyday of zoning. None of the realtors, and few
city planners who accepted zoning as their practical
religion, seemed to have faith enough in the perm-
anency of purely residential use to plan streets to
serve solely that use. No, not even when the economy of so doing was clearly proved by Henry
Wright and Raymond Unwin. Zone for dwellings?
Yes, but don't give up the hope that your lot may
be occupied some day by a store, gas station, or
other more profitable use.

The Radburn Plan proposed to protect the residents, 1st, by planning and building for proposed
use, and no other use; 2nd, by private restrictions
rather than by wishful zoning.

THE HOUSE TURNED ROUND.—The creation of
the Radburn Idea and of the Radburn Plan was a
group activity. It was not merely the conception of
its architect-planners. It took form out of actual
experience at Sunnyside. It was influenced by the
character and diversified abilities and experience
of the technicians and the staff of the City Housing
Corporation. But there can be no question that

Fig. 24—*The underpass is a safe way between home, recreation
ground, school, and swimming pool.*

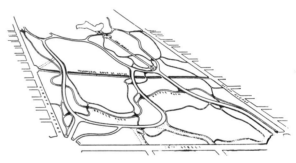

Fig. 25—*Perspective sketch showing the separation of routes for
vehicles, equestrians, pedestrians and outside traffic at the south
end of Central Park, New York City. Greater comfort and
safety is attained on all routes by the elimination of grade crossings, as planned by Frederick Law Olmsted a century ago.*

the seed from which the Radburn idea grew was conceived by that imaginative genius Henry Wright. Luckily we have in his own words 'The Autobiography of Another Idea'[12]—that is, the Radburn idea.

'In 1902, as an impressionable youth just out of architectural school . . . at Waterford . . . Ireland, . . . I passed through an archway in a blank house wall on the street to a beautiful villa fronting upon spacious interior gardens. That archway was a passage to new ideas. . . . I learned then that the comforts and privacy of family life are . . . to be found . . . in a house that judiciously relates living space to open space, the open space. . . being capable of enjoyment by many as well as by few.'

From that time on Henry started 'to face kitchens and service rooms toward the street, and living-rooms inward toward the garden.' At Sunnyside we both wanted to turn all the houses that way, as we ultimately did at Radburn, but conservative opposition only permitted placing some of the porches on the lovely garden side.

ECONOMY OF THE RADBURN PLAN.—The parks that formed the interior core of the Radburn superblocks were secured without additional cost. Or rather the savings in expenditure for roads and public utilities at Radburn, as contrasted with the normal subdivision, paid for the parks. The Radburn type of plan requires less area of street to secure the same amount of frontage. In addition, for direct access to most houses, it uses narrower roads of less expensive construction, as well as smaller sized utility lines.

The superblock of 35 to 50 acres is surrounded by wide streets, but it replaces the greater number of wide broad streets of the normal checkerboard plan with service roads only 18 to 20 feet wide. The use of these is limited to 15 or 20 families living on each cul-de-sac, and they carry no through traffic going elsewhere. Therefore they can be of lighter construction, and sewers and water lines are of lesser size and cost than the main lines on the through highways. In fact the area in streets and the length of utilities is 25 per cent less than in the typical American street plan.

The saving in cost of these not only paid for the 12 to 14 per cent of the total area that went into internal parks, but also covered the cost of grading and landscaping the play spaces and green links connecting the central block commons. The greater part of this expenditure was for improvement. The land itself—in spite of its value for spinach-growing —cost only six cents a square foot. What makes subdivided land costly, even with the financing, carrying charges, taxes, and profits, is not the land itself. It is the roads and walks, sewers, water lines, electric, gas and other utilities that surround it. This land in lots along streets or lanes costs 6 cents gross or 10 cents per square foot, but an additional 25 cents must be added to pay its share of the improvement that lead to it. A park or playground in a regular town surrounded directly by improved streets would cost as much as it would with houses as a frontage. But not at Radburn—there land is just land (except for surrounding walks). There are no streets. So before landscaping the land, the cost of the parks was less than a fifth of what it would have been had dangerous highways encircled it.

The Plan of Radburn

The time between the purchase of land in Fair-lawn and the starting of construction was too short to develop a plan of Radburn as a whole. This was vaguely in the back of our minds, to be given more definite form later. Our immediate problem was to relate the superblocks to the form of the land. We began with an area near the railroad station (Figs. 23, 26 and 49). As we did not want direct access to culs-de-sac from Fairlawn Avenue, which promised to become a main thoroughfare, we left a strip, an ordinary block wide (200 feet), between it and our first superblock. If we had had time to study our whole plan carefully before deciding on the first superblocks, we probably would have eliminated all of the old forms of block and separated the superblock from Fairlawn Avenue merely by a parallel service road. For these blocks have not lent themselves as well to practical development for modern living or shopping.

NEIGHBORHOODS.—At Radburn, I believe, the modern neighborhood conception was applied for the first time and, in part, realized in the form that is now generally accepted.

The neighborhoods were laid out with a radius of half a mile, centering on elementary schools and

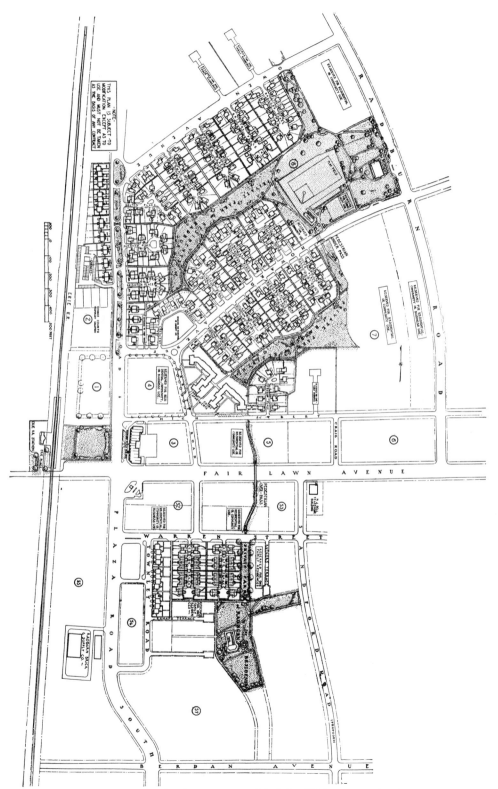

Fig. 26—Plan of the development completed by 1930.

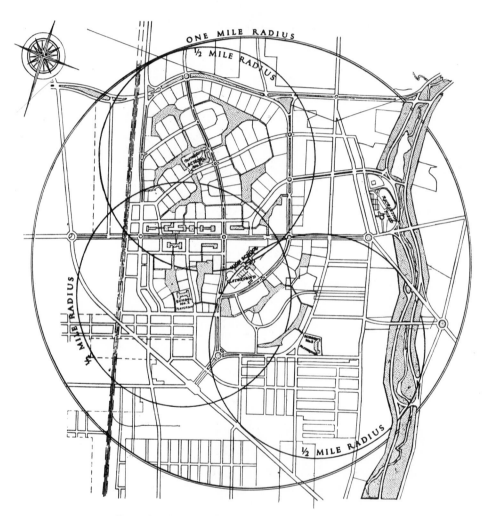

Fig. 27—General plan showing neighborhoods.

playgrounds. Each was to have its own shopping center. The size of the neighborhood was determined by the number of children cared for by a single school. So as to allow for flexibility in development, we tentatively overlapped our half-mile circles (Fig. 27). This left lee-way for somewhat greater concentration of population in apartments or row houses, where it would be found most advisable to place these as building progressed. All parts of each neighborhood were to be connected by over- and under-passes.

The neighborhoods were planned for 7,500 to 10,000—this to depend on the most desirable number of pupils in a school—a matter that was then, and I believe still is, open to a wide diversity of opinions. Although a start was made in the building of two of the neighborhoods, ultimately neither was completed.

TOWN PLAN: THE TOWN AS A WHOLE.—As a main educational and cultural center we chose a point nearly equidistant from the three proposed elementary schools, within a mile radius of all future houses. This was close to the intersection of the main north-south and east-west avenues. We planned to set the high school and town community building on a beautiful hill. Below was a low nearly marshy area. This, although not desirable for residential purposes, was excellent for the central recreational field, to serve both high school and town athletic needs.

The main commercial center might, we felt, serve as a regional market. So we located it close to the proposed state throughway at the main entrance to Radburn, rather than in the physical center. We assumed that most of the regional market's clients would come by automobile. Therefore we planned superblocks, with an interior area of some 400,000 square feet, to permit the parking of some 1,250 cars. This parking area was to be used in the evenings by the nearby Regional Theater.

For industry the section to the south of the State Highway was planned. This would have had direct access not only from the main entrance highways, but also from a spur from the railroad (Fig. 28).

How the Radburn Plan Worked

Those who live in Radburn and have lived there for any great length of time find that it has served its objective of making home and community life more reposeful, pleasant and safe—and particularly safe for children. The physical plan of central parks, superblocks without through traffic, safe walks, houses facing on gardens and parks along with the convenience of service have, they find, given them a quality of living that, as medium-income folks, they could not find elsewhere. My associates and I have observed the actions and reactions of the people. We have talked it over with a good many of them, and we have studied the investigations of others. We find that the general feeling, after twenty years of trial, is enthusiastic approval. This does not man that there are not adverse criticisms of details. But these are secondary in the minds of the people.

SAFETY FOR CHILDREN.—Radburn is above all a town for children. The safety features, the free safe life in the open, is what drew young parents to it in the beginning. The first forty families who moved into the town were young folks in their thirties with children of early or pre-school age. Although Radburn was affected by the national shifting of population during 1939-1945, stability has returned to the town. Old residents are re-appearing. Former Radburn children have married and have come back to bring up their own youngsters. Seventy-five per cent of the present Radburn men are veterans of the recent war. They are starting their married life in Radburn apparently because they want their families, and particularly their children, to have the same background for free living which they knew as youngsters.

In regard to safety, let us look at the figures. In Radburn's 20 years there have been only two road deaths. Both were on main highways, not in lanes. There has been only one serious accident on any lane, which resulted in a little girl's arm being broken.

That the small proportion of auto fatalities is due to the physical plan is indicated by the record of other towns that have followed in general the Radburn scheme. In 1949, when Greenbelt, Maryland, Greendale, Wisconsin, and Greenhills, Ohio, were all over ten years old, only one pedestrian had been killed by a car. The fatal accident was in Greenbelt. There had not even been a severe injury at Greendale, and only one at Greenhills—a boy who did not look round after getting off a bus—(and he is all right now). That is quite a good record for four towns of 2,500 to 7,500 population, compared with other towns of similar size. In 1945, there were 1,240 deaths in towns of 2,500 to 10,000 in the United States (a rate of one death per 100,000 population), and the ratio of injuries to fatalities is about 30-35 to 1.

This does not mean that pedestrians are kept 100 per cent apart from autos at Radburn. No, they are human—old habits stick—the sense of exploration and curiosity leads youngsters into forbidden places.

PLAY PLACES—The playgrounds, the central greens, and the swimming pools in summer, are the favorite recreation places for Radburn children. But the paved lanes are also used for playing. I have studied the reasons for this so that in the future we might keep children and autos apart to an even greater degree. We never will do so completely, nor do I think we should attempt to. The spirit of adventure should not be extinguished.

Young children play in the lanes because their mothers, who spend much of their time in the kitchen, want to keep them in sight. We put the kitchen on the service side of the house, because that was where things would be happening—delivery of goods and fuel, the coming of postman, husband, even visitors. But I think that in the future we should use (as we did in Burnham Place) a type of house with a combination kitchen-diningroom running through from garden to lane side. Then the mother can easily go from one side to the other, and keep a watchful eye on the kids on the quiet side as well as on the life of the cul-de-sac (Fig. 34).

There is another reason why children play in the lanes. They are paved, and so wheeled toys run better than in the grass, and with less objections from parents. They can use the walks, it is true, but these are crowded enough already. Even roller skates and bicycles are often found to be an inconvenience on the paths.

A solution might be wider paved areas for wheeled toys on the walk side of house groups—a couple of them, perhaps, one near the park and the other midway between main highway and park. For bicycles we should have special paths, as in

Central Park. This might lead to a greater use of bicycles and thus cause a decrease in the use of autos for trips to market and recreation places.

THE UNDERPASS.—The underpass permits safe passage from home to school, playground and swimming pool. The younger children religiously obey parents' injunctions to use it. When asked where they live they invariably say 'through the underpass and so many houses farther.' Cyclists find it convenient. Older children use it to a much lesser degree. A young Radburn boy, old enough to test his own judgment, scrambles up the hill beside the pass and braves the perils of traffic rather than walk a step out of his way. To be effective, such a pass must follow the shortest distance between two points, and the bank beside it must be steep and thickly planted.

The underpass is closer to the swimming pool than to the school, and therefore is used by most of those in bathing suits.

THE OVERPASS.—The overpass crossing the busiest highway, Fairlawn Avenue, and connecting the north and south sections of Radburn, was reached by a gradual slope on the north and easy steps on the other side. Both ways were much easier than climbing down steep slopes to the road. It was therefore much used.

SAFETY goes beyond the physical plan of pathways far from traffic, of underpasses and overpasses at crossings, and of playgrounds, even beyond the provision of recreation supervisors.

Paradoxically, the very position of some of these precautions for safety can encourage enough relaxing on the part of busy mothers in the supervision of their children to create some safety problems. The fact that there is a playground and supervised play, provided and paid for out of the community pocketbook, gives some parents a vague confidence that all is well with the children all the time—and family responsibility is lessened.

This kind of all-out care cannot be given in any community. Recreation staffs can take responsibility only for those children who come under their supervision voluntarily. Usually the children in Radburn and similar towns find so much of interest in school, home and playground that there is little need for concern. It is possible, however, for youngsters to fall between the relaxed parental attention

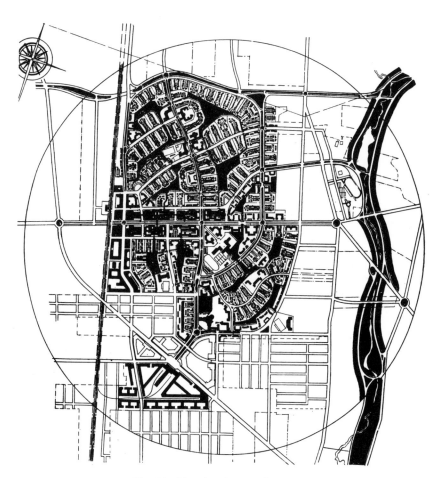

Fig. 28—Plan for the complete town.

Fig. 29—Typical plan of one of the early Radburn Houses. It has three separate entrances. Later houses had two.

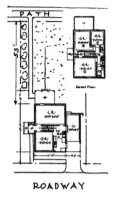

and the limited community control, leaving them more free for unconventional activity than the child in a traditional environment. Some parents feel that this is good, making for independence and self-reliance, and for some children this is probably true. Others think that it is an unsafe situation conducive to destructiveness and a lack of consideration for others. These thoughts are based on disturbing experience through the years, of broken street lamps and school windows, and of automobiles mischievously rolled down hill.

Unit Plans

SINGLE FAMILY HOUSE.—The development of the first house with two fronts, one for convenient service, the other for peaceful living, took much time and study. Customary planning habits had to be suppressed and replaced. The house interior had to be reorganized, so that it would fit naturally into the whole Radburn pattern. Changes in the relation between house, garden, path and highway were not to seem extraordinary if the logic of our answer to auto-age requirements was to be accepted by the prospective owner and his future visitors. Plan requirements were: living room, porch and as many bedrooms as possible facing the garden; kitchen and garage and cellar storage easily accessible from service lane; the main entrance door leading directly by corridor or stairs to all rooms. These were satisfied in the early plan, with the exception of that affecting the kitchen (Fig. 29). Experience and use showed that the principal entrance should be most conveniently accessible to both public path and service road, as visitors might park their car in the latter or walk from a main road across the inner park. The three exterior doors in the early plans were afterwards cut to two for economy and simplicity.

The disorderly loose appearance of the free-standing houses in relation to each other, and the insufficient space left on either side of the small buildings, lead us to join houses by coupling garages— the most interesting grouping of two houses was that in which garages and houses were joined by porches, through which summer breezes could play.

Cheaper houses were later designed by attaching two or three houses to each other as in Burnham Place (Fig. 34). These compact units have a com-

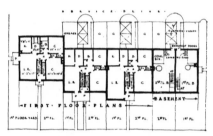

Fig. 30—An experimental plan of four attached two-family houses used in one place only. The eight families have separate stairs to their own basements and their own gardens.

Fig. 31—An inner park, beautiful as the estate of an 18th century country gentleman.

Fig. 32—Small children play in safety on the footpath adjacent to the brick and clapboard houses.

Fig. 33—The turning circle at the end of the service lane in Burnham Place, showing the additional space gained by a grouping of houses.

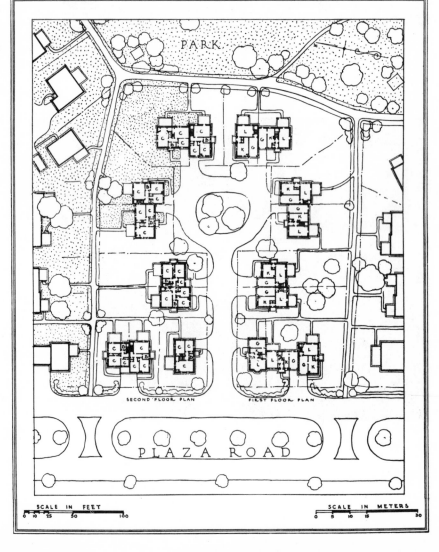

Fig. 34—Plan of Burnham Place. This, with its grouped houses and turning circle, is the most spacious cul-de-sac at Radburn. The turning circle allows vehicles to turn and get away more easily, and it provides an island for planting.

PARK

SECOND FLOOR PLAN   FIRST FLOOR PLAN

PLAZA ROAD

SCALE IN FEET
0 10 25   50   100

SCALE IN METERS
0   5   10   15   30

bined kitchen and dining space running through the house. This gives the mother in the kitchen an opportunity to watch the children playing in the garden, an advantage I have already indicated.

Longer rows of single family houses were ultimately built on Randolph and Reading Terrace in what was to have been the second neighborhood. The topography and soil were such that we could cut the service roads a story below the main entrance on the garden side. Thus the garage, service entrance and laundry are in the basement. The two fronts of the houses are connected externally by stairs at the ends of each group of four (Fig. 48).

THE ECONOMY OF SPACIOUS PLANS.—Habits of economy of space in house planning, developed at Sunnyside, were carried over to the early days of Radburn. The bathrooms and kitchens in particular were tightly planned, though they held the required fixtures in an orderly manner and there was room for essential and convenient movement. Experience has taught me that though this kind of careful planning does save some original capital cost, it does not adequately take into account the factors of time and progress—or new requirements. It is not flexible enough to meet technical or style changes. For instance, the standard size of stoves was increased after we had started to build Radburn. When some original installations wore out there was not enough space for the new models. The same inflexible tightness has made many garages inadequate since some types of American autos were increased in size.

The time factor is not always sufficiently considered in economical planning. As residential financing is based on long-term amortization over the useful life of the house, and not on the immediate payment of all capital costs, there must be adequate space for change and for various arrangements of equipment. Good business sense, as well as a desire to make our homes as livable and attractive as possible over their long future life, requires not only enough space for now, but sufficient room to allow for growth and change.

Spacious planning of this kind is equally—perhaps even more—essential in site and group planning. Inadequate space for parking or garaging causes increasing difficulties in America as the proportion of automobiles to families goes up. Shopping districts without spacious parking areas

are losing trade to new centers, where the planners have foreseen the need for ample parking space to serve an increasing number of people using cars. In California, it is generally advocatd that car parks should be three times greater in area than selling space.

In many new housing developments there is a tendency to omit garages—and thus reduce building costs. This is understandable during a period of high construction costs. But where inadequate or inappropriate space is left for future garages, or for parking of many more cars for tenants and visitors than may be immediately needed, the development is likely ultimately to lose occupants and to be a poor paying investment.

Spaciousness in planning, with an eye to unforeseeable future needs and developments, is particularly important in public centers. None of us can actually prophesy just what activities will be required by a community as time goes on. The space requirements for recreation, education, and entertainment have a tendency to expand continuously. The number of community facilities that are first desirable, then essential, are increasing; there are, for example, health centers, youth centers, nurseries—and who knows what next?

All of this is an argument for openness—for leaving plenty of uncovered ground while the land is still cheap, and while it can be planned and developed at a minimum cost of utilities and highways. On the whole we did show this kind of foresight at Radburn, particularly in the interior parks and the recreation spaces.

The Building of Radburn

During the first few years at Radburn we were able to draw on the experience gained at Sunnyside, of large-scale building operations in which the installation of streets, parks and utilities keeps pace with the construction of houses.

The problems which faced us at Radburn were made more difficult as the main utility lines and framework of municipal services did not exist. We had to plan and construct a sewage disposal plant as well as main sewers. All had to be arranged within a long-term development program and in co-ordination with different governmental authorities and public utility corporations. The staff of

Fig. 35—A hedge-lined path leading from the houses to an inner park.

Fig. 36—The service lane to houses in Burnham Place. This is used for garages, parking, deliveries, the drying of laundry and as an outdoor workplace.

the City Housing Corporation included members with the many technical skills required.

Louis Brownlow, who had been the chief officer of the municipal government of Washington, was invaluable in all civic affairs and, particularly, in establishing diplomatic relations with the Borough of Fairlawn and the New Jersey State agencies.

Ralph Eberlin, who had been civil engineer at Sunnyside, grew and developed with his varied responsibilities at Radburn. He laid out and supervised the construction of roads and utilities as well as buildings, and he was responsible for site engineering in relation to all structures. Later, after Herbert Emmerich went to Washington, he became General Manager as well as Superintendent of Construction—a big job—but he was a doer, not merely an administrator.

In the busy days of construction, Ralph Eberlin would drive over to Radburn in his old Ford, the rear seat piled high with boots, surveying instruments and blue prints of architectural and engineering drawings. On the way we would discuss the next construction job, and would stop to search for the working drawings roughly filed in Ralph's office on wheels.

Eberlin in the Second World War was Colonel in charge of most U.S.A. construction in Eastern India and up to China. He is now the outstanding American site engineer—at least I think so. We have worked together on many jobs since Radburn.

Life in the Community

The early residents, approximately 400 families during the first few years, established the character of the town. They were mostly young people of medium income and almost exclusively from New York and New Jersey. They came to Radburn mainly because of their children. Seventy per cent of the men worked in New York City, and to live in Radburn meant commuting. But it was an economical place in which to live. It was suburban and it offered unusual advantages.

Although a few owned their own businesses, the great majority of men were employees with annual

Fig. 37—The private life of the family is in the home and private garden, close to, but independent of, the community life in the inner parks.

incomes between $2,000 and $5,000. Their occupations, in 1933, were mainly 'whitecollar'; salesmen, engineers, teachers, 'junior executives,' etc.

The educational and religious background was also more or less the same. About 86 per cent of the men and 75 per cent of the women had received their education in American colleges. Seventy-seven per cent belonged to Protestant churches and about 16 per cent were Roman Catholic.

These elements of similarity, added to the novel setting, promised a full community life. The promise was more than fulfilled. The formation of a citizen's organization was only the beginning of a close association of friends and neighbors. The community and what happened in it was soon the chief leisure interest of Radburn people.

Home and community as sources of recreation and culture became very important in America in the years, 1929 to 1935, when the family allowance for these interests was practically nil. At Radburn this partially accounts for the widespread, enthusiastic participation in community life that took place. Ninety-seven per cent of the adult population joined other members of the community in some form of activity. Approximately half the community worked in the Parent-Teacher Association, in Citizens' Association committees, or in the Radburn Citizens' Association.

By 1937 the depression was over but it had left its serious effects in Radburn. Numerous young families had to give up their homes. Some had gone away. Others remained as renters. Many bided the time when they might return and start over again.

Curtailment of expenditures had been exercised in the community program as well as the family budgets. The City Housing Corporation could no longer assist. The financial status of Radburn people called for elimination of those parts of their program which were not essential.

In November 1937, the Citizens' Association appointed a committee to re-evaluate the community program. This committee in its report reviewing the life and spirit of Radburn eight years after its inception, concluded:[13]

'We look forward with confidence to the future of Radburn as a desirable place in which to live and raise our children, not to a city of 25,000 people as originally conceived, but to a community assured of an orderly growth, retaining the virtues of smallness but at the same time reaching a size which will assist us to have the civic values we all desire.'

Then came World War II.

The great shifting of population throughout the country, affected by war industry, war preparation, and war itself, caused a tremendous turnover in Radburn families from 1939 to 1945. But stability has returned.

Wandering about the town today, one is conscious of a sense of the stability of an old community with a definite character and roots. But there is also a spirit of youth and a feeling of revived energy and ambition. Just below the surface, one finds all about the town an awareness of neighbors and their interests, of their abilities, their ambitions and their needs.

You are told about it by an elderly man who is a cripple and can't get about easily. According to him, after eleven years in the town, 'No one needs to be in a jam here—all he needs to do is to call for help.'

Doing things together is an everyday indication of happy family life. This grows out of the physical plan and the plan for living. Mother and children can spend the afternoon together at a swimming pool by strolling across their park; father and daughter can play tennis on Sunday morning— within easy call of the dinner bell. When the Players perform just down at the Plaza, and one of those glamorous people beyond the footlights is a member of the family, the whole clan turns out.

The twenty-five per cent of the population who are 'ol'timers' have weathered the almost overwhelming storms of eighteen difficult years and have carried on the traditions of friendliness, neighborliness, and civic responsibility.

The informal relationship of houses, the ease with which one can cross a couple of lawns and call out 'Who's home?' has affected the social and civic expression of the people. Neighbors can see each other frequently and with little effort. Pooling of interest and effort follows.

Radburn's plan has resulted in well-kept parks and common areas even through years of depression and war. The activity observed in yards and gardens, the friendly atmosphere, the relaxed tempo of the community, speak of pleasure in living. Moreover, the basic requirement at Radburn that residents share in the cost of the social program has resulted in continuing responsibility for what happens in the community. Inability of Radburn to expand after the depression created obstacles to the town's progress, but the physical layout and the original plan for sharing responsibility retained unity in the town.

Undesirable social tendencies as well as commendable ones are related to the physical plan. Experience at Radburn is a pretty convincing argument for the theory that it is not wise to undertake the development of a town until the fulfillment of the complete physical plan can be assured.

Radburn has never been a separate governmental entity, but from the start has been a part of the Borough of Fairlawn. Friction seems to have existed between Radburn and the rest of Fairlawn. The inability of Radburn to expand in an orderly fashion, as planned, created a very small town, with exceptional facilities, in the midst of people for whom the Borough could not afford similar advantages. Whether or not the attitudes were fair, it is understandable that the people of the new town were not popular with their less privileged neighbors and that a social chasm should develop very quickly. The matter of Fairlawn votes snowing under the projected high school in 1935 was the culminating episode of several years of friction between Fairlawn and Radburn residents. Almost before Radburn was built, Fairlawn people feared that the new community of 25,000 might control the old Borough of Fairlawn, with its 5,000 population.

Years of working together and real effort on the part of wise Radburn people and those from outside the town perhaps bridged the gap in time, but the bad situation of the early years planted seeds far from democratic in nature.

If a town cannot be large enough to include a normal cross-section of American people or to serve with its facilities the entire population of a political unit, the bad social effects might easily outweigh the benefits.

GOVERNMENTAL COMMUNITY ORGANIZATION.—Radburn was better planned for an integrated community life than Sunnyside. The wide-spread parks, the safe footpaths for pedestrians, giving easy access to the homes of neighbors, all led the way to friendliness and neighborliness.

The City Housing Corporation devised a plan for maintaining property and for a shared responsibility based on the experience gained at Sunnyside. This was developed under the able leadership of Louis Brownlow and Major John Walker. At Radburn restrictions to protect architectural harmony were made part of the purchase deed. These restrictive covenants provided for public services required in an urban community, but not yet adequately provided in the local semi-rural Borough of Fairlawn. These included sewage disposal, garbage collection, street lighting, policing and operation of the large park areas, playgrounds and recreation facilities.[14]

As the local tax rate of Fairlawn would not cover the cost of these extra services, the Radburn Association was empowered to impose an additional annual charge which could never exceed one-half the current Borough taxes.

RADBURN ASSOCIATION.—The Radburn Association was incorporated as a non-profit, non-stock corporation to fix, collect, and disburse the annual charges, to maintain the necessary community services, parks and recreation facilities, and to interpret and apply the protective restrictions.

The Association was governed by a self-perpetuating Board of Trustees. The first nine trustees were civic leaders of New Jersey or officers of the City Housing Corporation. The 1929 report of the City Housing Corporation stated:

'The powers and responsibilities of the Radburn Association will devolve upon the residents of Radburn, but we have not attempted to say in advance exactly when or in precisely what manner.'

In short, the Radburn Association was to have the power and functions of a municipal government, including taxation. An American government without public representation! Luckily it was well-administered for the good of the Radburn people by one of the ablest town managers in America, John Walker, chosen by the Trustees.

The Municipal services for the first few years consisted of sewerage, garbage and ash removal, and street cleaning, street lighting, police, fire and

Fig. 38—There is space for every kind of recreation within easy reach of every home.

health, as well as care of parks. Some of these functions have now been taken over by the Borough. Some were eliminated because of the decrease of financial resources. The only services of this type, now provided for by the Radburn Association, are the care of parks and walks, and the Radburn Volunteer Fire Department.

In the early years, the Radburn Association provided gymnasium instruction in the elementary school. But since the expense was all carried by Radburn people and this service was given to all children who attended the school, it was eliminated in 1941. The school now conducts its own physical education program with a Borough physical education supervisor visiting weekly.

THE FIRST RADBURN CITIZENS' ASSOCIATION.— The Radburn Citizens' Association was formed two months after the first family moved in. The purposes of the organization were to discuss questions of community interest, to formulate and express community opinion, and to co-operate in creating a community life. The Association had no real power.

The Citizens' Association was extremely active during the early years when enthusiasm was high and residents were getting acquainted. It then sponsored a great variety of activities through its numerous committees: educational and civic as well as recreational and religious.[15] Need for the association's participation decreased as the basic program of community activities became routine. Financial difficulties of the nineteen-thirties also caused curtailment. Throughout the war Radburn, like other American communities, was involved in a program of war work, and the Citizens' Association found little need either to supplement or implement the work of the Radburn Association. The Citizens' Association has continued to function to the present time, but mainly as a forum open to all Radburnites on matters of interest to the neighborhood.

As many Radburn people felt that the Radburn Association has not progressed sufficiently toward a democratic state, the Citizens' Association, after a thorough study in 1938, recommended plans for reorganization of the Radburn Association which would give the residents more direct representation,

Fig. 39—One of Radburn's two swimming pools, which form centers of outdoor life in the summer.

more democratic control, and more responsibility.

EDUCATION.—The general community plan of Radburn with three elementary schools and one combined junior and senior high school as the center of educational, cultural, and recreational life of the town, was destroyed by the depression. Only one school had been built. As Radburn and the surrounding area became more densely populated, in 1941 a wing was added, which includes a pleasant, large auditorium with a stage, dressing-room, lavatories, and a kitchen. However, the Radburn Players continue to use a small hall and stage in the Plaza building because of the inadequate stage lighting and make-up rooms, the small size of the stage and, above all, the fees for rental and janitor in the school auditorium.

In 1943 a high school was operated in Fairlawn. It is within walking distance of Radburn, but on the opposite side of the railroad; about 350 Radburn young people attend.

RECREATION.—Radburn was above all else planned for children. Facilities for their play are dispersed throughout the community. The two play-grounds, located in the north and south centers of Radburn, are primarily for the use of the elementary school children. They are supervised during the summer months, and instruction is given in a variety of sports and other playground activities. 'Tot-lots,' equipped for the little ones under four, and supervised by trained leaders, are also at either end of town and are open all summer. The two swimming pools and the wading pool, where there is instruction in swimming as well as safety assured by experienced life guards, are so popular that the guest privileges once possible for residents are increasingly difficult to grant. There is no fee for the use of the pools by residents. The operating expenses are paid by the Radburn Association.

The tennis courts are restricted to the use of residents and guests when accompanied by a resident. There is no charge for the use of the courts. Nearby is the athletic field, six and three-quarter acres in size—an extremely popular spot in summer and winter for football, softball and other games.

An existing small two-story building on the grounds, popularly known as 'The Grange,' was

Fig. 40—Children ride their
bicycles on the park paths.
There is no danger from automobiles. A further separation
of functions should lead to the
provision of separate bicycle
paths. In recent years these
have been added in Central
Park, New York.

Fig. 41—The family at work on the house
and in the garden.

Fig. 42—A first view of an inner park.

early equipped as a gymnasium. It also houses a large 'quiet' games room. In the absence of a real gymnasium in the Radburn school building, this has been used by men, women and children as the community gym. Here the children gather for music, drama, scouting, games, dancing, and other social activities.

The Plaza Building, opposite the railroad, accommodates all of Radburn's stores. Since this was built we have learned much about neighborhood shopping centers and their relation to the economic, social, and architectural plan of a community. A study of shopping centers, with particular reference to Radburn, was made by Catherine Bauer and myself, but too late to be of use there. It served later as basis of Greenbelt's delightful and successful commercial center.[16]

The upper floors of the Plaza building are used as Radburn's Community Center. Besides the offices of the Radburn Association, the study of the 'Church in Radburn' minister, and the Radburn Library, there are several rooms for recreation. One of these, with a stage and raised floor, has made the theater one of the popular interests of the community. Another large room, with a kitchen adjoining, has served a wide variety of social functions.

These rooms are all used daily by children and in the evenings by adults for educational, recreational, or civic gatherings. Saturday evening open forums are held. On Sunday the rooms accommodate religious classes.

The opportunities for the young people, in addition to the extensive parks and open areas, the paths safe for wheeled toys, the safety of access to school and play areas, have contributed in a large measure to the popularity of Radburn as a place for growing families. A survey among the new residents in 1937, made by the Radburn Citizens' Association, indicated that 85 per cent of them moved to Radburn because of the recreation facilities.

ADULT CULTURAL LIFE.—The energy of the early days at Radburn was spontaneous and tremendous and within the first year there were formed important cultural groups such as the Radburn Singers, the Radburn Players, the Friends of Music, and the Garden Club. A library was started and various sports were organized.

The combination of physical plan, community plan, and the youth of the residents—the majority of whom were college-graduates—offered an unusual opportunity for cultural and social activity. It led to experimentation in the field of Adult Education. With the aid of a grant from the Carnegie Foundation in 1931-33, Mr. Robert Hudson studied the activities of this lively young community and developed a broad program of Education and Recreation. His report was appropriately called 'Radburn—a Plan of Living.'

Forced leisure of the partially unemployed during the depression gave time for continued community activity. This gradually dried up as many of the 'old-timers' lost their homes and moved away—and as defense and war activities filled everyone's time.

The adult community activities of today are primarily recreational; golf, bowling, and softball—eight teams of it. The Garden Club continues, ending the season with its annual Flower Show.

A few cultural organizations carry on. The Radburn Players are still active on their 20th anniversary, and the Radburn Singers will probably be revived in the near future. The Community Forum, now in its 12th year, about ten times a year discusses vital problems of the day. Speakers and topics are liberal in character. The usual audience of 40 or 50 is entirely of Radburn people. Although all Fairlawn has been invited—in the hope of breaking the feeling of exclusion—few have come.

RADBURN REVISITED.—The impressive feature of Radburn superblocks are the inner parks (Fig. 31). You enter from the highway by a path between hedges (Fig. 35). These are of varied height. Some partially hide, others disclose, the gardens beyond; well-cared-for, very personal gardens, many of them gay with early flowers and shaded by varied trees—a quarter of a century old or more. They partly conceal the two-story houses of brick and wood (Fig. 37).

It is late spring; people are burning off old paint and putting on a new white coat, or trimming hedges or spading gardens (Fig. 41).

Then at the path's end the park opens up to you. An apparently endless grassy lawn, with groups of trees (Fig. 42). Around the edges are the paths, alive with children on bicycles and velocipedes (Fig. 40). Beyond the hedge's border are the private gardens of the end houses of the lanes. There is only limited composition of the buildings— their harmony comes mainly from similarity of materials —common brick and white clapboards (Fig. 32). They are unified also by the simple good taste of Fred Ackerman, the architect of this group. But above all it is the natural green that dominates and controls the picture. Your architecture cannot look bad when time makes it part of the bigger composition of landscape. Radburn has come of age architecturally because time has mellowed it into a oneness. Harsh lines are subdued and enveloped by the verdure. It is almost what happens in primeval forest to rock and tree bark when they have lived together for a long time—they seem to reflect each other's color and texture (Fig. 15).

The picture constantly goes through kaleidoscopic changes of planting and distant structures as one walks up the center of the broad lawn. It is so spaciously open that one thinks of a lordly estate, but it is filled with democratic life. Little girls playing tag; boys playing baseball or on their backs looking up through the leaves at the blue, their bicycles at their sides; and here comes a whole family in dripping bathing suits (Fig. 45).

The outdoor swimming pool is the real center of Radburn's summer life. During the long hours after work it is gay with youthful color and movement (Fig. 39). Next to it is the wading pool for the little ones (Fig. 51). Beyond is the large field for baseball or other big games, and enclosed nearby is the playground for the younger ones, with slides and other apparatus. On our way we have passed sand-boxes for the tots, at the end of each block, each enclosed by a little fence and hidden by bushes (Fig. 43). Beyond the pool and playground is the elementary school (Fig. 44).

We go through an underpass to the next superblock (Fig. 24). If we look up we may see an automobile against the sky. We had forgotten that our civilization is dominated by motors. Nowhere within the peaceful superblocks are you reminded of their existence. In early June the rosebushes dominate the landscape in the passage between the two superblocks (Fig. 45).

The second inner park is different in form, in topography, in planting. There is a small unobtrusive natural theater, and on the higher ground

a rustic pavilion. The lawns again are spacious and broad. The trees and bushes are massed so as to leave large open spaces, easy for machine mowing (Fig. 42).

At the end of the park are two low but massive apartment buildings (Fig. 46).

Another inner park was partially completed at the other side of Fairlawn Avenue. It was intended that it should be the center of the second neighborhood. Another swimming pool was built there— close to the playground which forms part of the inner park. The school which we proposed should be built at the further end of the park was never erected (Figs. 27, 47, 48 and 50).

The function of the auto side of the houses is the reverse of that facing parks and gardens. The two sides are as different as night and day. The dead-end lanes are some 400 feet in depth. On most of them houses stand out, perhaps too strongly, for lack of green foreground and hiding foliage. Some of the earlier buildings seem crowded: we architects had planned for short rows intermingled with single units. We were finally restricted to free-standing units. Our sense of economy in paving and utilities led to some tightness. It creates annoyance where there are semi-public paths connecting lanes and walks, and people pass close to windows. Later, with houses attached in twos or threes, as in Burnham Place, we achieved a greater sense of spaciousness (Fig. 34).

On the service side the washing is festooned— and I recollect that in the days when houses were first opened to public inspection the dominant problem was where to hang the laundry. Mr. Bing and his associates had gone with us in our American planning revolution; street and walk divorced, house faced round, superblocks. But here the salesmen rebelled. They could not sell houses to good Americans if the week's washing was to be displayed on the public side. So, on the days when the houses were first shown, we tried the drying lines on different sides of various houses. The public decided that laundry naturally belonged with other services, and not in the park or garden. And there it has remained (Fig. 36).

The garages are set back far enough to allow for a parked car for visitors between them and the road. Perhaps with the latest, longer machines they

Fig. 43—At the point where each group of houses joins
the inner park, there are sand boxes.

Fig. 44—The formal playground in the inner park,
between the swimming pool and the school.

are crowded now. As time goes on I am convinced
that we architects must always plan spaciously—
allowing for the growth and change of all equipment.

The ends of the lanes, where the cars must turn,
are particularly tight. We planned for U-turns.
Backing to turn, especially with big cars, is a clumsy
process. It takes too much time—particularly when
the delivery boy has entered the wrong lane. It
leads to improper language!

We built some culs-de-sac with circles, which
when large enough, make a turn and get-away
easy. Burnham Place, which is illustrated, is an
example (Figs. 33 and 34). And it shows how
much more attractively attached or triple houses
can be grouped.

Radburn: Success or Failure?

Radburn was never completed. Only a small portion of the new town was built before the operation
was engulfed by the depression. On the surface
Radburn may appear a failure. But essentially it
was a great success. It was a splendid adventure:
a voyage of discovery in search of a new and practical form of urban environment to meet the actual
requirements of today. This exploration opened up
and charted the way—no matter how limited the
settlement that remains. The two superblocks that
were built, and in which people have lived happily
and safely for twenty years, have demonstrated the
essentials of the new form of city, that is increasingly accepted as the basis of planning urban residential areas in Europe and America. With this
in mind let us examine and evaluate its apparent
shortcomings.

Radburn did not become a Garden City. It
lacked a complete greenbelt. It did not succeed in
securing industry. Its underlying land, excepting
the inner block parks, was not retained in single
ownership for or by the community. All this is true
—but the fact remains that in spite of the avowed
intention of the Corporation to create a Garden
City, eventually the pressing need of demonstrating
the Radburn Idea overshadowed the Garden City
idea. In large part it superseded it. For instance,
our thoughts, as planners, were concentrated on
the value of the living green close to homes in the
midst of the superblocks: it seemed more essential

than greenbelts. The retention of the ownership of the underlying land was not part of the program of Mr. Bing and his associates on the Board of the City Housing Corporation. They considered this impractical in the New York region at that time, because of the difficulty of mortgaging leaseholds, and of selling property when the ownership of the land did not go with the house. As to industry: we planned for it physically, but our timing was bad. This was probably due less to bad judgment than to the unforeseen breakdown of the national economy.

The financial vicissitudes of Radburn were due to matters beyond the control of those who conceived, planned, developed or operated it. They did not result from the novel form of the Radburn plan. Nor were they caused by its community organization and operation, or the charges for these. Why Radburn was not completed and the City Housing Corporation went into bankruptcy is shown on the diagram that faces page 19 (Fig. 1). The graphic indication of business failure, unemployment, national deflation, which was reflected in the loss of jobs and the impoverishment of the people of Radburn and ultimately in the bankruptcy of the City Housing Corporation, came from causes that could not be controlled by any individual or private corporation. A depression, when it comes, is like a tornado; no human being can then stop it. It cuts down all in its path— it leaves destruction behind.

When Radburn was conceived in 1928, all the economic trends were upward—the sky was the limit. But the first inhabitants had hardly put their houses in order when the stock exchange broke: the depression was under way. However, construction continued at Radburn as elsewhere in the New York area for a while, though at a continuously decreasing rate. In 1933 only twelve houses were erected at Radburn.

Continuous, large-scale development is essential to the financial success of a new town such as Radburn. Otherwise the carrying charges on land, main highways, and utilities will soon devour possible profit and force the operating company deeper and deeper into debt. This is what happened at Radburn. At Sunnyside large-scale development had been continued during five years, with the construction of roads and the installation of utili-

Fig. 45—Rosebushes flank the footway to the underpass.

Fig. 46—The apartment buildings overlook an inner park. Andrew J. Thomas, Architect.

Fig. 47—The inner park which would have formed the center of the second neighborhood had it been completed. The second swimming pool is beyond the bicycles in the background.

ties paralleling the building of complete blocks of houses, all of which were marketed as soon as they were finished. The Corporation was confident of equaling or bettering this record at Radburn. No one believed the deflation would last long. So the Corporation, advised by its planners, continued to buy land, until it had acquired some two square miles at a total cost of approximately three and a third million dollars. Most of this was purchased at a high price for rural land. Only a small portion of it was improved before the depression engulfed the Corporation. During the following ten years the land decreased in value until it reached a low of 10 per cent of the purchase price. Other investments that had been made on the presumption of a rapid and continuous growth of population were for many years carried at a loss. Examples are the large sewage disposal plant and the Radburn Building planned as a shopping and community center. To add to these financial difficulties, the returns from houses already sold decreased. Purchasers out of employment could no longer pay all —or, in many cases, any—of their monthly charges. The City Housing Corporation had the junior interest in the mortgages at Sunnyside and Radburn. Ultimately a good many of the houses were returned to the Corporation. They could not be resold—at that time; there was no market. The houses were gradually rented. But the return on them, as on all of the investment, was far too little to pay operation expenses and carrying charges. The City Housing Corporation which had guaranteed the Sunnyside notes as well as the Radburn bonds was forced into bankruptcy. As a result it had to give up or sell the greater part of the land. The reorganized Corporation later was able to continue building, but only at a slow rate on the small portion of the land that remained. The dream of a complete new town for 25,000 people had been destroyed by the depression.

The Radburn experience indicates that a private corporation has only a gambling chance to carry through to completion the building of a city. There are too many valleys, as well as hills, on those graphs—too many unforeseeable and uncontrollable factors (Fig. 1). If we are to build New Towns in America—or rather when we build them—for I am convinced we will—there must be a certain

Fig. 48—The reverse side of the houses shown in Fig. 50. The topography of the site with some judicious grading made it possible to place the garages below the living quarters.

*Fig. 49 — Air view of Radburn. Photo taken in 1955.
(Litton Industries — Aero Service Division)*

Fig. 50—Row houses facing the park leading into the
second neighborhood, which was never completed. The
steps in the foreground are from the inner park. James
Renwick Thomson, Architect.

amount of government co-operation. Of this I will speak later. None of the forms of governmental financial assistance that exist now in connection with housing or redevelopment was available in the nineteen-thirties. The City Housing Corporation was on its own when it started to build a new city. It did a good job—within the economic limitations. True, mistakes in judgment were made in timing and in other regards. But Alexander Bing's purpose and the method he chose of carrying it through were fundamentally sound: *large scale,* orderly and continuous building development according to a logical plan that met the requirements of sensible good living, individual and community, no matter how the plans and development might upset conventional method and form.

That was twenty years ago. The Radburn idea is now accepted as a fundamental basis of urban residential planning in many lands. I visited Sweden this summer. In Stockholm, I found that the basic form for the remainder of that beautiful city—which is to be completed in about ten years for an additional 100,000 people—will be derived in large part from the Radburn plan. It will consist of green communities, made up of superblocks with central parks, and the separation of walks and roads. Gothenburg's growth will follow a similar general pattern. Other countries are planning variations on the Radburn Idea. Warsaw intends to reconstruct on that basis. Radburn is influencing the plans for New Towns in England. Back in America, the Greenbelt Towns and wartime housing developments are direct or indirct descendants. The redevelopment plans for Los Angeles and other cities show similar derivation. And so, though the seeds that Alexander Bing and his associates planted in the Borough of Fairlawn had a limited growth at Radburn, they are germinating, developing and flowering in varied forms throughout the world.

Conclusions

I. THE RADBURN PLAN serves present day requirements of good living in a more practical and pleasant way than does the conventional American city pattern.

It is safer.

It is more orderly and convenient.

It is more spacious and peaceful.

Fig. 51—The wading pool for small children next to one of the swimming pools.

It brings people closer to nature.

It costs less than other types of development with an equivalent amount of open spaces.

Most people who live in Radburn prefer it. They enjoy the expansive nearby verdure; they appreciate the freedom from worry about their childrens' safety.

Radburn works in practice as it was intended to function when it was only the Radburn Idea, twenty years ago.

II. A PLAN FOR LIVING, in addition to an appropriate, flexible physical setting, requires an organization with vision, capable leaders and adequate finance for the operation of the physical plant.

Until there are competent and well-financed governmental agencies for this purpose, a private association is essential.

To be effective such an organization should:

1. Start to function when the New Town opens.
2. Include in its membership all families in the community—both tenants and home-owners. All must pay for its services just as they pay rent and taxes.
3. Be a single central organization rather than a group of separate sectional block associations.

III. A SEPARATE POLITICAL ENTITY is required by a New Town with a new form and advanced objectives, so that it may freely and clearly carry out its purposes.

A private government within the borders of a political entity, which gives special services and privileges to its members which are not available to the entire urban area, causes resentment and leads to disunion.

All services for which people are taxed should be directed and operated by their elected representatives.

IV. THE BUILDING OF A NEW TOWN requires large capital investment in land, utilities, highways and public buildings on which there can be little, if any, financial return for many years. Lacking governmental assistance, a private corporation (with the exception of organizations with large aggregates of capital such as insurance companies or endowed foundations) have small chance of more than temporary success under economic conditions such as those illustrated on the graph in Fig. 1.

Governmental co-operation is required, at least in the following:

1. Taking land—all the land that will be needed to complete the New Town.
2. Holding the land until needed for construction; or financing the land cost at low rates for long periods.
3. Financing the cost of main lines and central works of essential utilities and main highways, on low and long financial terms.
4. Assisting the local government authorities in the construction of essential public buildings such as schools.
5. Financial aid similar to that given to existing municipalities, including subsidies, for housing low income workers.

V. CONTINUOUS RAPID GROWTH of a New Town is imperative in the early years, so that overhead expenses do not devour all earnings.

VI. CONVENIENTLY PLACED AND VARIED INDUSTRY is an essential requirement of a New Town. Therefore industrial plans must be specific and realistic. Generalizations are valueless.

Timing of industrial development must be synchronized with that of the building of homes and community equipment.

3 CHATHAM VILLAGE

Ingham and Boyd, Architects

Clarence S. Stein and Henry Wright,

Site Planners and Consultant Architects

In 1929, when Henry Buhl, Jr., left 13 million dollars to a foundation for the welfare of the people of Pittsburgh, business was booming. At the proposal of the socially-minded director, Dr. Charles F. Lewis, the foundation determined to make some of this money do double service: 1st, pioneering in community housing for those of limited income; 2nd, demonstrating the security of 100 per cent investment in good large-scale housing development. In Chatham Village he did both. For 17 years it has been one of America's most attractive low-rental communities ($11.35 per room per month rental, during hard times reduced to $9). It blazed new trails in hillside site planning of row houses in America. There have been no vacancies except while one tenant replaced another. As investment it has paid as well as the Foundation's sound securities; 4.32 per cent net return in addition to a depreciation fund which, in 31 years (more than half of which have already passed), will pay back the whole original investment in buildings.

Preliminary Research and Study

The success of Chatham Village was in large part due to two years of preliminary study. First, in 1930, Dr. Lewis investigated the work of limited dividend companies such as the City Housing Corporation. Then a survey was made, by the Bureau of Business Research of the University of Pitts-

burgh, of housing needs and markets. Meanwhile a large low-cost site within easy transportation distance of the central business district was sought. Sociological, economic, and civic studies were made of the surroundings of the most desirable sites.

Henry Wright and I were then asked to make preliminary studies of houses to be sold to clerical workers as a safe investment. The houses were to be built according to a community plan and a hilly site was tentatively chosen.[17]

The Buhl Foundation desired to investigate the soundness of selling homes and, because of local habits, considered free-standing houses essential for sale. But we found that all our schemes using individual structures were too costly for those who were to be served. On the other hand, row houses, based on the Sunnyside experience, could be built for about two thousand dollars less per house. It was just cheap enough. This scheme was finally accepted on the basis that houses must be rented, not sold. That proved to be a fortunate decision—as Chatham Village has demonstrated the advantages, to both landlord and to occupants, of a rental policy (Fig. 53).

The Site and the Plan

THE SITE chosen was a wooded hillside of 45 acres looking down on a public park. It was two miles from the 'Golden Triangle,' where the clerical workers who were to be housed were working. The grounds had hardly been changed since William Penn retired it as a manor farm. Nearby were schools, churches, a library, and other facilities for the surrounding single-family houses.

GENERAL PLAN.—Only 16 (30 per cent) of the 45 acres have been used in the two developments for purely housing purposes. The rest are in open spaces that form a miniature greenbelt surrounding three sides: four acres are playground, 25 acres are forest with a picnic ground and two miles of pedestrian trails. The old manor house serves as a club (Fig. 55).

Chatham Village was naturally influenced by our experience at Radburn and Sunnyside, with superblocks, paths and roads separated, houses fronting on inner greens. The single superblock proposed in early studies of the first unit was ultimately divided in two by the purely local Sulgrave Road—because as a dead-end street it seemed too long. (Figs. 53, 55 and 59).

The garage compounds were used to group the garages for the houses that could not easily be arranged with basement garage. They were far better than the Sunnyside group garages, both in construction and in convenience. They have been found satisfactory in spite of the American habit of keeping a car in the house as some European farmers keep their cattle. The compound is unquestionably the economical solution of the garage problem in a closely-knit community.

SITE PLAN.—Chatham Village is one of the outstanding American examples of housing and site planning. I feel free to say this because the site plan was mainly the work of my associate Henry Wright. He had a feeling for the shape of the ground and what could be done to mold it to the practical needs of home and community that seemed superhuman. He appeared to sense the site possibilities long before surveys were made. Besides this he had an analytical mind that went to the roots of the basic problems of development costs.

The form of Chatham Village in relation to the ground gives one the pleasure that comes from visiting the best of the site planning work in England, such as Raymond Unwin's Hampstead Garden Suburb (Fig. 52).

SITE TOPOGRAPHY dominated the general plan far more than at Radburn and Sunnyside. Careful study, with builders' estimates, indicated that the hilly ground could be more economically molded to our need by using large-scale machinery, that would form a series of wide terraces, rather than by detailed handwork around individual houses. The large terraces were carefully graded, so there is a minimum of easy garden steps.

Row houses were found advantageous on the hillsides (Figs. 57, 60, 61 and 66). Their foundations served as economical retaining walls. By running most groups with the contours we were able to secure a well-lighted basement one-half above ground. Those basements which faced roads were

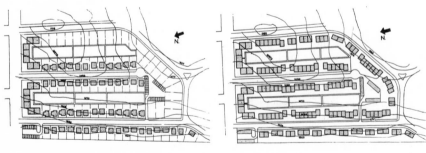

Fig. 53—Two of the preliminary studies made for part of the Chatham Village site. The one solution provided 80 six-room detached houses to sell, on the average, at about $10,500. The other provided 128 row houses to sell for prices between $7,860 and $9,042.

Fig. 54—The greenbelt surrounding Chatham Village has two miles of pedestrian trails.

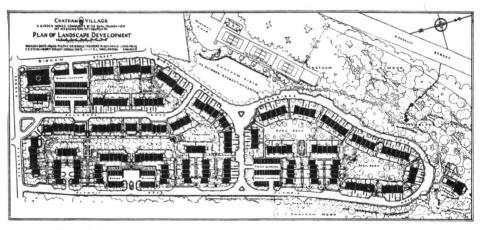

Fig. 55—General plan of the development showing the final layout, the landscape design and the club house.

used as garages, having direct stairs to livingroom and kitchen. On the other side where, thanks to topography, they faced west there were sunrooms for recreation (Fig. 57).

HOUSES are all two-story single-family dwellings. There are two basic types that have been developed out of the Sunnyside row houses as a result of the information derived from the detailed cost studies made there (Fig. 56).

The three-bedroom house has been widened to 20½ feet. These two extra feet added only moderately to th total cost on cheap land. As a result the smaller bedroom becomes more than an infant's room and the lower floor is no longer cramped. In the houses above garages there is space for a vestibule leading from both livingroom and kitchen by the stairs to laundry and garage.

The two-bedroom house is 26 feet deep, 2 feet less than the Sunnyside houses. It is also slightly narrower. There are two types of ground floor, one with typical kitchen and dining-nook, the other with compact kitchenette, purely working space, but with a larger eating place. Livingroom and diningroom in both cases form one space. These small houses were used instead of the two-family house, as at Sunnyside and elsewhere. The latter were objected to because the lower apartment was noisy and the upper floor tenants too far removed from the garden. The expense of two Chatham small units totalling 26-ft. x 35-ft. (910 sq. ft.) was only slightly more than the other 28-ft. x 25-ft. (700 sq. ft.).[18] Mechanical equipment was practically the same. Land was cheap. The Sunnyside two-family houses were more likely to have vacancies—as contrasted with 100 per cent use of the Chatham dwellings

Another matter in which our experience dictated building for time use, rather than on a basis of original cost, was in regard to exterior materials. At Chatham Village these were chosen as far as poslsible to save maintenance costs. Therefore stone doorways and slate roofs were used with brick exterior walls. The architectural richness and variety was achieved by Ingham and Boyd, the architects, by the use of very simple means: the massing of the buildings and the rhythmic location of unornamented doors, windows, balconies and stairs. The harmonious landscape was designed by Griswold and Kohankie, Landscape Architects.

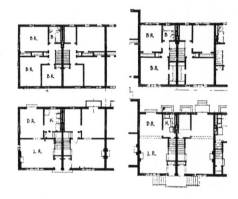

Fig. 56—The two basic type plans—the one for a six-room house. Both types were improvement of those built at Sunnyside.

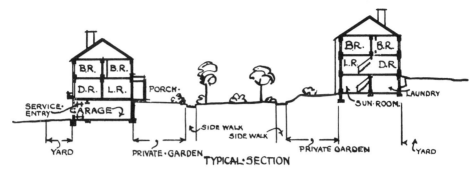

TYPICAL·SECTION

Fig. 57—Cross-section through a hillside block at Chatham Village. Garages in lower houses are at basement level. Upper houses have basement sun rooms facing the garden.

Fig. 58—Winter in Chatham Village.

Fig. 59—Final plan of the first unit of Chatham Village showing the interior park, the walk systems and streets with parking bays and the garage compounds.

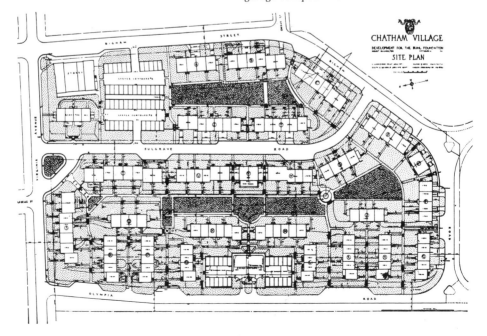

CHATHAM VILLAGE

Investment Financing

ECONOMICS.—The first decade in the history of Chatham Village was, economically, the hardest the U.S.A. has known. It included the depression, mortgage panic, readjustment, war, frozen rents and soaring operation costs. These did not affect the Foundation's 100 per cent investment, which was all their own funds, free and clear. The City Housing Corporation was ruined by the lending institutions and striking 'home-owners' of Sunnyside, who refused to pay. Meanwhile Chatham Village was over 99 per cent full of tenants who paid regularly. There has been less than 7/100 of 1 per cent uncollected rent. Although rentals were reduced temporarily during the hard years, from $11.35 to $9.65, net returns, after depreciation was taken into account, have dropped below 4 per cent for only one year—and have averaged over 4 per cent.

When building work reached a low ebb in 1932 the Foundation built the first 129 houses at near bottom costs. Prices were higher, but still low, in 1935 when the second unit of 68 houses was added.

Charles Lewis, who is primarily responsible for the conception and realization of Chatham Village, said of it:[19]

Fig. 60—Approach up a hill to a central green in 1953.

'A part of the success of the Village was in its timing. However, a greater element of success was the fact that the Village was based upon exceedingly thorough and careful social, economic, site planning, and architectural studies over a period of more than two years before ground was broken. Nor was the timing a greater factor, in our opinion, than the Foundation's financial policy with respect to management, based on faith to build well, confident in the soundness of the investment.'

Home Ownership or Rental

THE INHABITANTS.—Chatham Village was built for moderate-income clerical workers. Most of its inhabitants have come from the office buildings in Pittsburgh's 'Golden Triangle.' Some were from wealthier families. But young married people were all hard up during the depression. Some have risen to junior executive positions, but they stay on in Chatham Village. Teachers, research workers and other professionals form 20 per cent.

Apparently, they like Chatham Village. The

Fig. 61—A view of houses in the first unit of Chatham Village. Photo taken in the spring of 1938.

1955   *Figs. 62 and 63—Seasonal changes in Chatham Village.*   *1937*

Fig. 64—Air view of the first unit of Chatham Village. Photo taken soon after completion in 1932. (McLaughlin Aerial Surveys, New York)

Fig. 65—The William Penn Oak, which was growing when the Penn family owned the property, was preserved.

Fig. 66—Row houses at different levels, to fit the hillside site.

Fig. 67—A central green in 1955.

turnover of tenants is very low. The average tenancy was for 7 years during the first 15 years. At least half of those who moved did so because of business transfers to other cities.

Luckily for them they were tenants, not 'homeowners.' When they had to move the Foundation freed them of their lease as quickly as possible, sometimes in 24 hours. There was always a long waiting list.

The American people are still pioneering. A great many of them are nomads and tend to migrate, particularly in their youth. Families expand and then disperse. So a house seldom serves the family for the mortgage period.

Experience at Chatham Village demonstrated, as compared with Sunnyside, the fallacy of the American faith, almost a religious belief, in what is called 'home ownership.'

The Sunnyside people—and a good many of those at Radburn—found that when they could no longer pay interest on their mortgage, owning your own home was merely another form of tenancy. They had the minority holding in their dwelling; voting power was held by the lending institutions. They discovered that they had actually been the janitor, caring for the mortgagee's property. They found that all their savings which had gone into the maintenance of their home, the years of payment to reduce the mortgage, the interest they had regularly paid, were cancelled when the depression deprived them of job, income, and savings. They rebelled. They attacked the City Housing Corporation with whom they had direct dealings. But this Corporation, as far as mortgages were concerned, had become by this time only the agent of the lending institutions. Mr. Bing and his associates gave the owners as much time as they could to pay. But they were powerless; the lending institutions were in command. Ultimately a great many of the Sunnyside 'owners' lost their homes. The City Housing Corporation went bankrupt. Alexander Bing, who had made such a valiant and unselfish fight for constructive housing and community planning, was vehemently attacked.

A well-managed rental policy in a large-scale, planned community appears to pay the landlord better than does a sales policy—10 per cent down and collect the rest if—! The City Housing Corporation made a return on its rental apartments and lost on most that it sold at both Sunnyside and Radburn. The 4.2 per cent average net return on investment, with half that investment paid off out of earnings in 15 years at Chatham Village, seems adequate evidence of the advantage in renting to the proprietor of a well-planned and well-operated housing community.

Conclusions

Chatham Village, with less than 200 homes, has made an astoundingly large contribution to American community housing. A community such as Chatham Village demonstrated:

1. *The security of 100 per cent investment.* Charles Lewis said:[20]

'The secret of the investment success of any large-scale neighborhood held in one ownership is that it is planned, that it is managed as an investment, and that it is large-scale.'

Insurance companies in America are tending to follow this policy, particularly the Metropolitan Life and the New York Life Insurance Company.

2. *A greenbelt,* even one as small as that of Chatham, insulates a community from neighborhood depreciation and external annoyance.

3. *A rental* rather than sale policy is likely to be a better long-time investment. It also offers more security and freedom to most American families of moderate means.

4. *A hillside site* is a challenging problem for economical planning, but it offers unique possibilities for beauty, variety and convenience.

5. *Time*—plenty of it—for the study of economic, social, civic, and above all physical planning is well invested in a project that may live a half-century.

6. *Row houses and group garages* in a community have many advantages, aesthetic as well as economic. They can be made very livable.

Fig. 68—The great central court of the first unit (1930) of Phipps Garden Apartments.

4

PHIPPS GARDEN APARTMENTS (I)

Clarence S. Stein, Architect

The Phipps Garden Apartments were erected on a portion of the property originally purchased for Sunnyside (Fig. 3).

The Society of Phipps Houses, the promoter, was no more affected by the depression than was the Buhl Foundation. Formed by the steel magnate Henry Phipps 'to provide . . . housing accommodation for the working classes,' it built new projects when it had accumulated adequate earnings for the 4 per cent or so net return on its past developments to make a 100 per cent capital investment. It proposed at Sunnyside to house white-collar clerical workers in place of the lower-income manual workers it cared for in its compact Manhattan tenements. Therefore more spacious rooms and courts were required.

THE SITE was one of those few at Sunnyside near the railroad where we had succeeded in having useless streets closed. Therefore it was 460 feet wide. It was practically square, with a depth of 400 feet. The location was some 600 yards from the rapid transit and other means of transportation. Too far, we had thought, when we were completing Sunnyside, for anything but small houses. So we had made a number of studies of row house groups, taking advantage of the unusually broad square block. By 1931 a large number of apartment buildings had been built around Sunnyside.

The new owner decided that apartments were required to give adequate return on the valuation of the land, which had increased between the time the City Housing Corporation bought the land in

1924 and sold it to Phipps Houses. Because of the distance from transportation it seemed the development must be made unusually attractive.

Planned Around a Great Court

THE ARCHITECT'S PROBLEM was to (1) plan buildings with enough families to distribute the land cost sufficiently to keep down rents, at the same time (2) preserve attractive openness and spaciousness so as to minimize vacancies, and (3) minimize as far as possible depreciation from obsolescence, structural, functional, or economic. All studies of plan and mass we tested by comparative estimate, not only of capital but also of maintenance costs.

The Phipps family were liberal clients. They wanted a sound job—and an attractive one. Although they required a certain yet limited monetary return, they were liberal in expenditures that served to make the buildings sound in construction and attractive in appearance. They wanted exteriors less severe in appearance than the Sunnyside houses. So I am afraid I was somewhat too exuberant in the use of brick pattern. The vari-colored special brick was attractive, but my puritanical sense of economy has since led me back to our local common Hudson River brick.

One thing for which I am everlastingly thankful —the Phipps family loved rich foliage, and approved of the expenditure of $2,900 on six large elm trees. These made the great court a living green place from the beginning.

PHIPPS GARDEN APARTMENTS (I)

The southern 250-ft. portion of the plot was studied to see how many families could be well housed without losing the sense of spacious openness. The advantages of four-story walkups and six-story elevator buildings was compared in various arrangements around a single central court.

The final group plan consisted of six six-story units and sixteen walk-up units (Fig. 73). In spite of the fact that 43 per cent of the site was covered with building and the central open area was divided into four bays, there is a real sense of openness. The contrast of height of the buildings adds greatly to its interest, but I would have preferred to have a still more spacious foreground from which to view them (Fig. 68).

The site work was studied with care and affection. The landscape gardening by Marjorie S. Cautley was rich, varied, and imaginative. The planting has been well cared for by the able manager, Ernest Schofield. We even sank a private well so as to be sure the gardens would be watered in case the city's supply should be inadequate at any time.

The life of the community focuses on the great court or central park. (Fig. 68). All units are entered from it, most livingrooms face it, balconies are turned toward it. Careful grading of the sloping terrain permitted the use of some space, below the first floor but above the ground, as apartments with their own private terraces and enclosed gardens (Fig. 70).

The great court was intended as a place of restful natural beauty, as a park, not a playground. Arrangements were made to give the tenants the privileges of the Sunnyside Park, with its playground, across the street. At first they made little use of it, as they did not consider themselves a part of the existing Sunnyside Community. But time has changed that. Now, 259 of the Phipps families belong to the Park Association and, during the last few years all of the elected officers have been Phipps tenants. For the young children, a playground was set up in a large lot purchased by Phipps Houses, across Middleburg Avenue. This is attended by most of the 150 children between 8 and 14 years old. In addition, the Social Hall and other basement space serves for the activities of boys in the groups of 6 to 9 and 9 to 11 years of age, as well as for Girl Scouts, Brownies and two groups of dancers. There is a nursery school and

Fig. 69—Two units combined in a six-story elevator apartment building. Because of the semi-fireproof construction, each apartment was required to have access to two stairways. In this design there is a fire stair well between the central apartments and indented stair wells at the bottom of the T's.

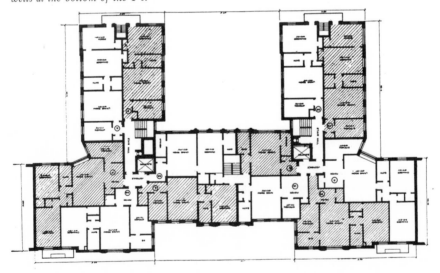

a large community room in the basement, in the space above ground but not available for apartments. But the architect must admit that the nursery was not perfectly orientated: that at Hillside was much better (Fig. 73).

Walk-up or Elevator Apartment Buildings

UNIT PLANS.—A further development of the simple, compact, I-shaped unit of Sunnyside was used for most of the four-story walk-up apartments (Fig. 97). To increase room sizes the depth of the structure was deepened but the width remained 50-ft. as it had been through the history of Sunnyside. It continued all the good qualities of directness, simplicity, good light and ventilation. Also it repeated the defect of access to other rooms through the livingroom. This still seemed the most economical way of securing maximum livable space. That it has been acceptable is indicated by the fact that the Phipps Apartments have been almost 100 per cent occupied for nineteen years (Fig. 72).

The apartments in the taller buildings were far less satisfactory from the point of view of ventilation, directness of circulation, and economical use of space. This was in spite of endless study. It was because we calculated that an elevator in a moderate rental apartment requires about 100 rooms to pay for installation and maintenance costs. Self-service elevators were the type chosen. Seventeen rooms to a floor demands a complicated plan form —at least a T with dark centers and long wings (Fig. 69).

I think it is safe to generalize from our experience. The elevator apartment building cannot economically be made as livable as the walk-up. Without wastefulness, which is unacceptable in public housing and inexcusable in housing for those of moderate means, the taller apartment building must sacrifice the best ventilation, limit sunlight, and restrict privacy.

In the Phipps Apartments the costs of the elevator units were greater than those of the walk-ups. According to our estimates the former were approximately 42 cents, the other 39 cents per cubic foot. As there was more usable space and less corridor and foyer in the walk-ups, the actual difference for equivalent rooms was still greater.

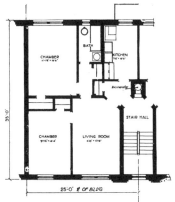

Fig. 71—The four-room walk-up apartment is the element from which the other units were developed.

Fig. 72—Balconies leading to a fire-escape required by law. The balconies were painted light green, the fire-escapes brick color.

PHIPPS GARDEN APARTMENTS (I)

Operation and maintenance of elevators adds to the cost of the taller buildings. The addition for this factor in 1938 was about 75 cents per room per month.

The rents charged in the four-room apartments are one to two dollars more per room for the elevator buildings, making a difference of about 8 per cent—more for the small-sized apartments.

The tendency in New York at present is toward apartment buildings of 12 to 14 stories, even for those of limited income. The law requires these tall buildings to have two elevators and two stairs for each unit. This requires the organization of about 40 rooms per floor, and results in long public or private corridors or lack of privacy. Cross-ventilation is at a minimum and there are other sacrifices of comfort, convenience or livability.

The 12 to 14 story apartment buildings which are being erected in large numbers in New York by the Municipal Housing Authority, and by insurance companies as investments, are ingeniously planned and in many cases elaborately equipped. None the less, practically all are far more deficient from the point of view of livability than if they were less high. The principal excuse given for crowding of over 300 persons per acre in these skyscrapers is the so-called 'land value.' But the present tendency in America is to try to wipe out this artificial or imaginary dam to sensible housing progress by governmental subsidy under the redevelopment laws.

Building Technology

TECHNOLOGICAL PROGRESS affected the plan of Phipps Apartments in various ways. Push-button elevators, during the planning, had been made completely safe after a few serious accidents to children. Their installation eliminated the cost of attendants.

Dumb-waiters had been used in all our Sunnyside apartment buildings. These were objectionable because of the space required and the dangers of a service passage in the basement, and they also transmitted domestic noises and conversation. They had been needed for deliveries, particularly of ice, and for the disposal of refuse. Mechanical refrigera-

Fig. 73—*Plot plan of Phipps Garden Apartmnts (I) showing general arrangement at basement level. Included are management offices, nursery, community social room, perambulator stores (note ramps to these). Stippled buildings are six stories high, all others are four stories. There are six private gardens to basement apartments, as well as an enclosed play space for the nursery. Two units on ground level, in buildings N and Q, have terraces.*

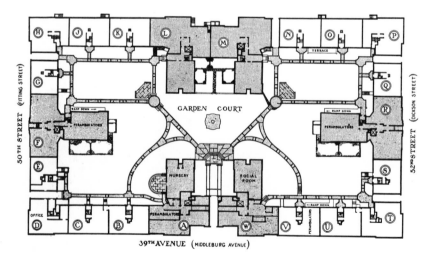

tion was to be installed in Phipps, and incinerators with access at each floor were just coming into use. Therefore, I advised against dumb-waiters.

Although the directors of Phipps Houses approved my suggestion to install incinerators they at first decided to play safe and also have dumb-waiters. These ultimately were eliminated — they have not been missed. However, in the case of fuel for the boilers, the directors insisted, in addition to oil tanks, that a large bin for coal be installed. This was good judgment as war conditions made oil difficult to secure, and the use of coal was advisable, if not essential.

CONSTRUCTION was sound because the owner was going to manage the development, which was built as a long term investment, and not as a commercial speculation. Exterior walls and fire walls separating apartments are of solid brick masonry. Salt-glazed brick walls were used around stairways, wood-trim on exteriors and public interiors was minimized. Door frames are of metal. The roofs are slated instead of the typical tar and gravel finish.

Staircases, fire-walls, and the slabs under the lower floors are the only parts of the buildings completely fireproof. This is in accordance with building law requirements. At Hillside we were to learn the financial advantages of complete fire protection that led to its use in the second part of Phipps to be built in 1935.

Conclusions

I. *Walk-up apartment buildings* compared with equivalent unit-plan elevator buildings are:

  1. Cheaper to construct.

  2. Less costly to operate and maintain.

  3. More livable: they have better ventilation, more sunshine, less reflection of noise and heat from walls at right angles, and they are more accessible to the ground.

II. *Good landscaping,* including the planting of well grown trees in the beginning, is a sound investment—financially as well as in good living.

III. *Private gardens* or terraces are desirable for tenants on the ground floor of apartment houses.

Fig. 74—A typical apartment building entrance seen through an archway on the main axis.

5 HILLSIDE HOMES

Clarence S. Stein, Architect

In 1932, at the depth of the depression, the idea that was to be realized in Hillside took shape. In the beginning it was only an architect's abstract conception. There was no site, no client, no local precedent, no available financing—just an idea.

The Idea

Direct governmental housing, or credit for housing, did not exist in the U.S.A. Most of the building industry had been unemployed for years. President Roosevelt's New Deal promised large scale financing. How could that be used to build a complete, integrated neighborhood within the larger framework of our cities? In New York City, custom dictated mostly communities of apartment houses. These could not then be built for the very poor—housing subsidies were still in the future. However, an untried New York State law offered partial tax exemption to dwellings renting from $11 a room per month.

I decided to develop diagrammatically the basic conception of a self-contained, integrated residential neighborhood in New York, for desirable community living in apartment buildings at $11 per room rental (Fig. 75).

Phipps Garden Apartments was the basis of the first studies. The object was to secure the same advantages of apartments with cross-ventilation, surrounding garden courts, but at a third less rental.

Continued study, with comparative estimates by the builders, Starrett Brothers and Eken, indicated that the required result necessitated:

1. Land costing one dollar per square foot or less.
2. A building operation four times as large as the one at Phipps.
3. The use of over one-half of the basements for apartments.
4. A simplification of exterior and of interior equipment, and smaller room sizes than Phipps.
5. Financing at low interest and with long amortization.
6. Tax exemption of the buildings.

Meanwhile the city was combed for large low-cost sites fitting the following requirements:

1. Adequate for a community of 5,000 (at 250 persons per acre, about 20 acres).
2. Improved land at one dollar per square foot or less.
3. Possibility of closing streets to eliminate through traffic.
4. Adjacent to an elementary school.
5. Attractive site without undue construction difficulties such as rocks and swamps.

The Site

The property finally selected was a 26-acre undeveloped piece of land owned by Nathan Straus. Fortunately, he was deeply interested in housing those with limited incomes, and later, he was to become Administrator of the U. S. Housing Authority. The price of the land was 70 cents per square foot, exclusive of the area mapped for streets. This site, by reason of its slope, permitted

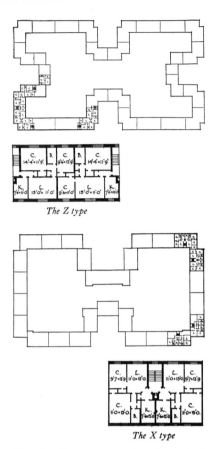

The Z type

The X type

Fig. 75—Above are two plot plans which were in the early studies. A plot of 460 feet by 260 feet was assumed for convenience in comparison with the Phipps Garden Apartments. Various apartment type plans were developed in the studies. The X type uses the same layout as the Phipps scheme, but with smaller rooms. In the Z type the span was decreased to 29 feet, as compared with 33 feet for the X type and 35 feet for Phipps Garden Apartments (I).

maximum utilization of the basements for apartments (Fig. 78).

Planning Hillside

Once the site was determined, we applied our theoretical buildings and courts to it (Fig. 79). Every change in the drawing was paralleled by study on the three-dimensional model, in relation to the site and topography (Fig. 83). Finally, a full-sized four-room unit was built and furnished. Thus various construction methods and materials were tested. Here the two-inch solid plaster partitions which we afterwards used were tried out. Complete units of plumbing and other mechanical equipment were studied in detail to find ways of cutting costs, securing greater efficiency, and saving time in erection. And here I discovered that by moving one closet it would be possible to reach all rooms in the apartment without passing through the livingroom.

As a result of judicious grading of the hilly site we were able to utilize one half of the basement area for apartments. They could be placed one step above grade on the garden court side and thus have a door leading directly out to a private terrace—on the other side they are entered from the public stairs by going down a half flight, and they have cross ventilation. I had experimented with this arrangement at Phipps. At Hillside we were able to secure 188 garden apartments. They have been very popular and particularly convenient for old people, who are thus saved the necessity of climbing stairs. They can have a good view of the life going on in the court and can be near, without always being with, their family (Fig. 92).

But if one-half of the basement was to be utilized for rental apartments it was necessary to find out the space requirements of all other essential demands upon basement space: storage space for trunks, screens, perambulators, rooms for gas and electric meters; administration and maintenance of buildings and grounds; community social facilities such as nursery school, assembly room, clubrooms; boiler room and fuel storage (Figs. 76 and 77). So during the year in which we waited for governmental loans, a detailed survey of the adequacy and size of these facilities in existing hous-

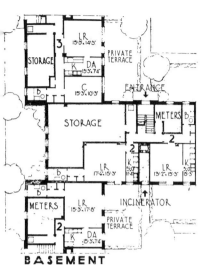

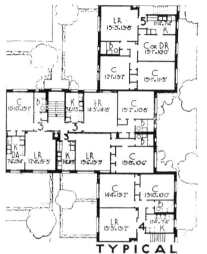

BASEMENT

TYPICAL

Fig. 76—Typical apartments in I units arranged as a T, and characteristic basement plan showing a combination of apartments and utility rooms. Although typical units were used throughout (without variation), the basement layouts were varied according to site conditions and the requirements for utilities, storage, and communal facilities.

ing developments was made for our office by Catherine Bauer and Margaret Morgan.

Meanwhile, so as to encourage building, Federal financing was offered at increasingly easy terms (Fig. 85). Finally, in September, 1933, the Public Works Administration approved a loan of 85 per cent of the cost at 4 per cent interest (Fig. 81). A long amortization was allowed on the basis of fireproof construction.

The general plan, as approved, was carried out. It included the central playground and the grouping of standard units around great courts (Figs. 80 and 86).

Only one main feature of the earlier plans was lost; and this, to me, was an important one. Hillside had been designed as a neighborhood within a superblock. Only one street was to have cut through—and the central pedestrian way was to have passed under it. After a fight lasting two years we were unable to eliminate mapped streets.

The elderly Superintendent of Highways said that he had devoted a lifetime to planning the streets on the map—and there they must stay! And there they are, even those that go nowhere. As a result of children hit by autos, Seymour Avenue has been made a 'play-street' and so closed to through traffic.

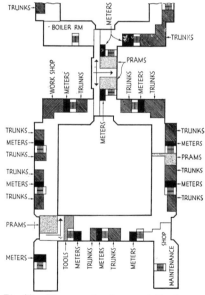

Fig. 77—Diagram showing carefully determined and conveniently located basement services. White portions indicate spaces used for garden court apartments.

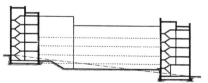

Fig. 78—A section showing how the natural slope was used to create garden court apartments at different levels.

The stores and movie theater that fringe Boston Road would, I believe, have served the community better and been more successful financially and as civic design, if they had been unified in a group around a green, as was afterwards done at Greenbelt.

UNIT PLANS.—The unit plans of Hillside grew out of experience at Sunnyside and Phipps (Fig. 97). The predominating type of apartment with two bedrooms added greatly to privacy and efficiency. All rooms are accessible from a small central entrance passage. Despite the need of economizing to remain within the $11 rental, the room sizes were increased and proportions improved. This and the change to fireproof construction, which has lessened maintenance costs, were the results of continuous united study and research by builder and architect.

The advantage of the simple I unit, for economy of space and cost as well as increased light and ventilation, the development of the T composed of three I units, led to the elimination of L, T, or U forms in walk-up apartments (Figs. 76 and 82). Livability is therefore superior in these as compared with the six-story elevator buildings in which the construction and maintenance costs of elevators required many rooms around each elevator shaft. On the other hand, the taller buildings, located on the crest of the Hillside site, have certain advantages. From them one gets a broad view in every direction and, in the general composition, the larger mass adds interest and variety.

Most American housing reformers claim that walk-up apartments of more than three stories are objectionable. Tenants at Phipps and Hillside seem to disagree. There have been practically no vacancies in the top floor at either place. Perhaps this is partially due to the fact that we put our balconies on the upper story, and the management charges about one dollar less per room each month (Figs. 80 and 86).

Building Hillside

When construction started on Hillside, most of the building industry had been out of employment for two years or more. There was a long queue of bricklayers waiting outside the enclosure. They were hungry for work: but they were out of the habit.

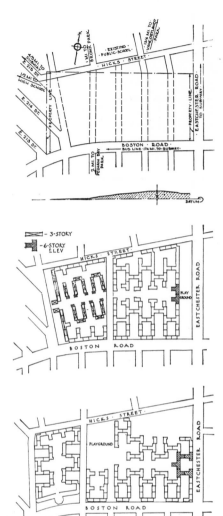

Fig. 79—The site selected was a 26-acre undeveloped piece of land. Its section facilitated the development of garden apartments one-half story below street entrance level. Two of a series of preliminary layouts are shown. The first included some three-story two-family buildings. The second has a 2½-acre playground for elementary school children. This was later moved to the southern side of the plot.

Fig. 80—Air view of the Hillside Homes development. The main traffic artery, the Boston Post Road, is on the right, the public school on the left. The distant part of the site is 55-ft. above the nearer.

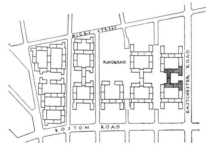

Fig. 81—In September, 1933, the new Public Works Administration approved a loan of 85 per cent, subject to a satisfactory contract, based on this plan. This loan allowed a 4 per cent interest rate as compared with the 5 per cent required by R.F.C. A change to fireproof construction throughout ensured a longer period of

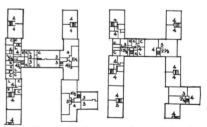

Fig. 82—A further step forward in the architectural studies was made when it was decided to replace the old T units (left) by I units joined together in T form (right) with less waste and cost.

amortization. At this stage it was apparent that closing streets would be a lengthy business. So no buildings were shown covering mapped streets.

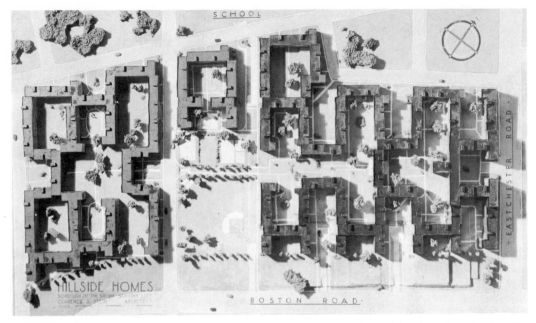

Fig. 83—The model used for three-dimensional studies.

Fig. 84—A court on the central axis.

HILLSIDE HOMES

At first they each laid only some 750 bricks a day. But as they got the swing of the work their pace increased; and, before long, they were laying 1,100 a day. It was a lovely sight to see the long line of men in rhythmic motion on the scaffolds, following the gang leaders. They seemed to draw a curtain of beautifully textured brick up from the ground toward the sky. It was good to see homes being erected once more.

Starrett Brothers and Eken had the great job completely and superbly organized. One trade methodically followed another from footings to roof—and then moved on to the next block. The strong competition of the trades, as building started again, along with the organization of the work, did much to keep down costs. This made it possible to build larger rooms than those of Phipps, and still keep within the limits of the maximum $11 average room rental. But much of the economy of construction was due to the long period devoted to the study of plans and construction in which the staff of architect and builder co-operated. I wish I could give credit to the various talented people who worked with me and Andrew Eken, the builder, in the production of Hillside. One I cannot neglect, my associate Frank Vitolo, because of the outstanding part he played at Hillside and Phipps. He formed the essential link between architect and builder. For Frank was an architect who understood the ways and the nature of the various construction trades as thoroughly as a builder did. Moreover, he knew all the intricacies of the complicated legal framework of building and housing laws, more thoroughly even than the building department officials. What is more they knew he knew. So therefore, when Frank Vitolo presented one of my unorthodox plan arrangements, they felt sure that Frank was on sound legal ground. The unorthodox plans were generally approved. Frank Vitolo got things done, not only because he so completely understood the practice and law of building, but because he understood the people he dealt with. He was a fine person, and we all respected and loved him.

Life in Hillside

The 1400 families that moved into Hillside in 1935 came mainly from the surrounding Borough of the Bronx. The wage-earners were white-collar workers, predominantly salesmen, with average annual salaries of about $2500.

The playground, nursery school, clubrooms, and the safe green courts drew families with children. Almost a third of the population was below 21 years (3,000 adults, 1,430 children). A good many of those children, now grown up, have returned from the war to bring up their own youngsters in Hillside.

In the typical Bronx apartment, from which the tenants of Hillside came, there is no sense of community ties or neighborliness. You may live for years on the same floor with families who remain strangers. Not so in Hillside. Hillside for twelve years has been a neighborly community, buzzing with activity. This was the result of the combination of the physical plan and the development of community activities.

The two and a half acre playground is the central feature (Fig. 89). Here, for all ages, is everything from ballgames to wading pool. Here, on summer evenings, the whole community, some 4,500 strong, gather, or lean out of surrounding windows, to enjoy pageants, festivals, or dramatic productions. A shelter built in the hillside offers protection from sun and rain, with toilets at either side.

The main community rooms are in the basement of the building to the north. This space, as a result of the natural slope, is above ground level. Here are the office of the community consultant (note: in the democracy of Hillside, 'consultant,' not director), various club and game rooms, and finally the assembly room. Here dance and music classes, calisthenics, plays, women's clubs, and festivals follow each other from early morning to late night.

The main community rooms have served well in their present central location. However, I think it would have been better to put them in a separate structure. This could have very well been an enlargement of the shelter in the park, with rooms on both upper and playground level. Apart from other advantages it would separate the meeting-rooms exit from the apartment houses, where it is sometimes disturbing at night when crowds depart.

The Assembly Room, of some 375 seats, is too

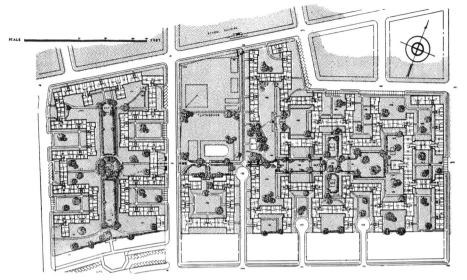

Fig. 85—Preliminary site plan, dated July 1932. All the mapped through streets had been eliminated with one exception. This was used as the basis for the application made to the Reconstruction Finance Corporation, a Federal government agency. By this time the owner had decided to retain a 100-ft. strip along the main traffic road; incidentally, this decreased the cost of the land by eliminating the part that would be most heavily taxed, and the project lost merely that portion of land least desirable for residential purposes because of its proximity to noisy traffic. On November 1, 1932, the R.F.C. approved a loan on this layout, which had been previously approved by the New York State Housing Board. The loan was to consist of two-thirds of the estimated cost of land and buildings at 5 per cent interest, with an amortization of 2 per cent. 5,378 rooms were provided in semi-fireproof construction.

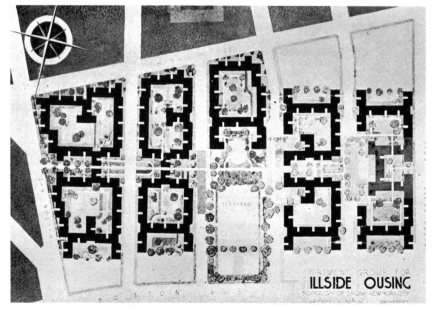

Fig. 86—The final site plan of Hillside Homes, dated September 1933.

Fig. 87—The interior of one of the workshops, in which both children and adults may pursue their hobbies in groups.

Fig. 88—One of the two nursery school rooms.

Fig. 89—The two-and-half-acre playground forms the central feature of Hillside Homes.

Fig. 90—The central axis showing the rising ground.

Fig. 91—A gravelled play area for small children, one of several in the inner courts. Note the apartments with private gardens on two sides of the court.

Fig. 92—Garden apartments are particularly convenient for old people.

small for gatherings of the whole Hillside Community. But the public school across the street has an auditorium large enough to serve such assemblies, although the Hillside residents feel freer and more at home in their own large community room. There they can sit around after meetings, talk, eat and drink, and, if they like, dance.

The workshops were distributed one in each court, where we found well-lighted space in basements not practicable for apartments. They are spacious, unplastered but painted, with a sink and toilet in each. No specific use was determined in advance. As those interested in a special activity such as painting, handicrafts, modeling, or other hobby, got together, these rooms were made available (Fig. 87). Some activities were temporary, such as painting and sculpture. Others were longer-lived, such as the camera club, which equipped its own workshop with darkroom, elaborate lighting, and a comfortable clubroom in which to discuss its techniques and carry on an educational program.

In the beginning most of the Hillside tenants were young parents. Their first activity was organization of a nursery school. The management offered free space and basic equipment for the carefully-planned nursery school facilities, and guidance of an expert teacher (Fig. 88). Teachers' College, Columbia University, provided student teachers. The mothers whose children did not attend the nursery, either because of the expense or because of its limited space, organized group care in each court. They took turns supervising the gravelled play areas, each of which included a sandbox, under the guidance of the nursery school director, and so actually served as an extension of the nursery school into the community as a whole (Fig. 91).

In the same way there were requests from groups of residents who had like interests to use all available space. The management gave heat and a limited amount of janitorial service free, as well as help and guidance, when it was required, from one of America's ables recreation leaders, Louise P. Blackham.

A community council, representing all clubs, developed in time, and has assumed sponsorship of projects of general community-wide interest.

The setting and the social organization of Hillside have for over twelve years created a real neighborhood community in which at least half the families have actively participated. As a result, the potentialities of personality and citizenship, too often stifled by city apartment life, here grew through association and experience in civic life.

Vacancy figures provide a good indication of what people think of home and community life. In most New York City apartment buildings, the number of vacant dwelling units increases as time goes on—and rises to between 10 and 15 per cent in hard times. This is not so at Hillside. In fourteen years there has never at any time been more than one quarter of one per cent vacancy or bad debt. Buildings which are more than ninety-nine per cent occupied make possible low rentals and an adequate return on the investment.

For eleven years Hillside Homes paid its full six per cent interest on the capital investment and, in addition, all operation and maintenance costs and the amortization of mortgages were fully covered. The greatly increased costs of operation, and the freezing of rents due to the war and its after effects, made it necessary to postpone the payment of interest on the capital investment for a period of two years. Since then, permission has been secured to raise rentals from $11 a room per month to $12.32. This has allowed the payment not merely of current dividends but also the paying up of previous unpaid dividends. So, for many years to come, Hillside Homes promises to continue its success as a financial investment. Its success as a neighborhood community has always been well assured.

PHIPPS GARDEN APARTMENTS (II)

Clarence S. Stein, Architect

By 1935 Phipps Houses had put aside sufficient from earnings to complete that development. The addition was to use the remaining portion of the site—460 x 200 ft. (Fig. 95). Its design was influenced both by management experience in the first Phipps Apartments and my experience at Hillside Homes. It was therefore decided that:

1. Fireproof construction should be used throughout. The owner expected to operate the building throughout its life, which we hoped and expected would be long. The expenses were therefore figured on a time basis, that is, operation and maintenance expense had more weight than original capital costs. There was an additional advantage that fireproof apartments in New York do not require exterior fire-escapes, which made design easier and more attractive.

2. Four-story walk-up buildings rather than elevator apartment structures should be used for reasons I gave in discussing the first construction. Lengthy study of Hillside Homes had confirmed my opinion that far more livable dwellings, and somewhat lower costs, could be attained in the walk-up buildings. After figuring the difference in costs and returns on buildings of three usable floors instead of four, it was decided that we would stick to the taller buildings. This was because tenants had shown their satisfaction by keeping the upper floor apartments full most of the time. We

estimated that the three-story building would have cost $1,186 instead of $1,149 per room for the four-story one.

A large number of small units that might serve for bachelors or newly-weds or, on the lower floors, for old folks, were used. These single large rooms, with a special niche for dining near the compact kitchenette and with windows on two sides, have been found very comfortable. The single bedroom apartment, with all rooms directly accessible to the compact entrance corridor, has worked very well.

Further development of these two types of units for small families would be useful in some future building of towns in which families with children would be housed in single family dwellings with gardens, and newcomers, or those without youngsters, might have the convenience of apartments cared for by the management.

A further development of the T composed of three I buildings, tried at Hillside, gives all apartments windows on two or three sides (Fig. 98). In the four-room unit, as a result of moving the kitchen to the end, the livingroom has been arranged with its long side parallel to the outer wall. This is an improvement that Wright and I had long desired—but we had not wanted to unduly increase street frontage.

Exteriors are less elaborate than in the first

PHIPPS GARDEN APARTMENTS (II)

Phipps. Harmony was secured by use of the same brick and similar but simpler patterns (Fig. 94).

There were advantages and economies in adding to the size of the Phipps development. The manager, Ernest Schofield, needed little addition to the staff for operating the buildings. The heating plant in the old building was connected to the new structure.

The general plan was determined somewhat by the long narrow form of the remaining plot. It was affected by my desire to continue the use of the effective T-grouping of buildings. The result was a series of open courts facing the older structure (Fig. 93). The greater part of the apartments face it rather than the outside. Each court has an individual type of garden (Fig. 96).

These courts with one side open appear on plan to have great advantages over the completely enclosed central green. They work well here because they turn toward and form part of the group building. There is no traffic between the buildings, excepting on the few occasions when deliveries of oil and other supplies must be made. If the open courts had faced toward a street they might have been objectionable because of traffic noises and their echo. The court enclosed on four sides, as in the first section, has, if it is large enough, a sense of spacious privacy and unity. Large entrance passages and the low buildings let in the summer breezes (Figs. 73 and 95).

Fig. 94—A typical entrance to an apartment stair hall. The lighting fixture indicates the particular stairhall at night as well as in the daytime.

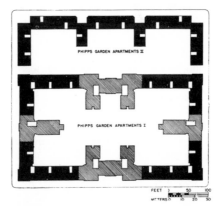

Fig. 95—Block plan showing the first and second units of development. The hatched portions are six-story elevator apartments; the solid portions are four-story walk-up apartments.

Fig. 96—The gardens in each court are varied in detail. This is known as the Dutch Garden.

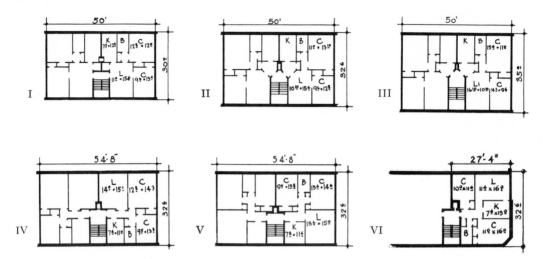

Fig. 97—EVOLUTION OF THE FOUR-ROOM APARTMENT 1926-36. The first apartments built at Sunnyside were similar to the two-family houses erected at the some time in 1924. Two apartments were behind a facade fifty feet in length. This length was used in each development until 1931, when the first unit of Phipps Garden Apartments was constructed. But the depth was increased from year to year. The gross area per room was increased from 181 square feet in 1924 to 219 square feet in 1931.

I. 1926, SUNNYSIDE, MONROE COURT, 187 SQ. FT. GROSS PER ROOM. The compact Sunnyside plan has little corridor and no foyer. All other rooms are entered from the living room. Plumbing is concentrated and the location of structural walls is determined by the length of standard wooden joists. In spite of the lack of privacy in the living room, this type has always been popular. There is good cross-ventilation and the plan is most economical.

II. 1927, SUNNYSIDE, 203 SQ. FT. GROSS PER ROOM. The convenience of the plan was greatly increased by adding a foyer with direct access from it to the kitchen.

III. 1931, PHIPPS GARDEN APARTMENTS (I), 187 SQ. FT. GROSS PER ROOM. The plan and method of construction were similar but the depth of the apartments was increased.

IV and V. 1932, HILLSIDE HOMES, 223 SQ. FT. GROSS PER ROOM. At Hillside there was direct access from the entrance hall to every room. This was secured by moving a closet. The additional 4-ft. 8-in. in the length permitted great internal flexibility and, in particular, it allowed an arrangement with the kitchen and bathroom on the same side. There were two alternative plans. The living room could be placed on either side to face a garden court or the sun. Where an apartment was on a corner, it was possible to have windows on two sides of the living room. The additional cost of fireproof construction (employing reinforced concrete) was balanced by the lower interest rates on the mortgage and the longer life allowed for in the amortization.

VI. 1935, PHIPPS GARDEN APARTMENTS (II), 223 SQ. FT. GROSS PER ROOM. In the second unit of Phipps Garden Apartments, fireproof construction was again employed and the four-room apartment units had a third external wall. Together, they allowed greater freedom in design. The long side of the living room is on the main external wall and there is a door from it to the kitchen. The extra cost involved in the separation of bathroom and kitchen is fully recompensed by the advantage of having direct access between the kitchen and living room, and a kitchen deep enough to allow a comfortable dining space.

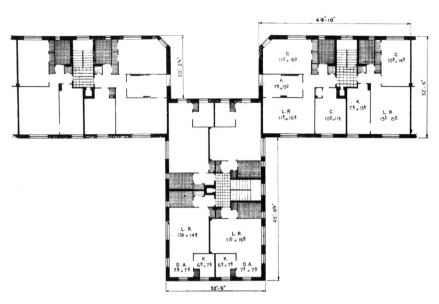

Fig. 98—*Typical apartment plans in three I units arranged as a T. This is a further improvement of the Hillside Homes arrangement. The four-room apartment has light and ventilation on three sides, the smaller apartments on two sides. The smallest apartments can be grouped four to a stair.*

7 VALLEY STREAM PROJECT
and Clarence S. Stein, Charles Butler, Frank Vitolo, Architects Associated

By 1935 a vast number of workers in the United States were unemployed and receiving assistance from the government. Building had practically ceased. Housing construction around New York, for instance, declined 95 per cent between 1928 and 1932—and 85 per cent of the building workers were unemployed.

The construction industry is one of the largest in the country. Its activity affects not only structural work but numerous other occupations in factories, forests and mines, and also, indirectly, many services and commerce. Therefore much thought was given at Washington to ending the depression by getting the building industry going again. This came to be called 'priming the pump.' Everyone talked about it—but nobody did anything about it. Valley Stream and a group of other communities, planned to be built throughout the country near industrial or business centers, were intended as a first step toward 'priming the industrial pump.'

Dwellings for 18,000

Valley Stream was to provide dwellings for 18,000 people and it was to be built, together with the other large, integrated communities, to fulfil a primary objective of giving employment.

Secondly, families were to live in these towns in sound and decent houses at low rentals, and there were to be community facilities to provide oppor-

tunities for the advantageous use of leisure time. The low rentals were to be maintained not only in times of depression, but at all times.

Thirdly, the towns were to demonstrate to the whole country a better way to design, build and manage communities to serve contemporary needs in an economical manner.

The proposal was made by a group, which besides having an interest in the purposes above, had individual interest. The heads of three of the largest corporations manufacturing building materials and apparatus were on the Board. They wanted to get their factories going again. The president of a large building company naturally desired to revive the dormant construction industry. Even one of the great airlines was represented. Here was an opportunity to dispose of airfields in various parts of the country which were being replaced by larger municipal fields.

We architects wanted to carry the Radburn Idea further—to see complete, modern, integrated communities planned, built and operated. We hoped this would be the next move toward New Towns.

CHOICE OF LOCATION. The first step was to choose the sites. Airfields throughout the country were examined from the point of view of physical conditions, including the availability of essential utilities, and future regional work opportunities. After a first selection had been made, a more detailed, but still a quick, study was made of social, economic, and governmental (including educational) conditions in nearby communities. This was carried out by Catherine Bauer and others. I went out to Los Angeles and San Francisco to investigate conditions there. It is interesting that the site on which we afterwards developed Baldwin Hills Village was suggested to me at that time. Its advantages were apparent although it, and the vast area around, were still vacant and undeveloped.

It was finally decided that the preliminary drawings and estimates be prepared for developments in or near Milwaukee, Wisconsin; Los Angeles and San Francisco, California; and Valley Stream in Nassau County—just outside New York City.

In the end these projects were not built. A large government is slow of action and its machinery complicated. So the building of communities was postponed until, to relieve unemployment, the Greenbelt Towns were constructed by workers mainly unskilled in building. The opportunity to use the vast number of unemployed building craftsmen to create economical homes at low rentals in pleasant modern communities was lost in 1933. At that time work was most needed in the construction industry (see frontispiece).

I will speak of one of the developments only, Valley Stream, which is characteristic in general

of the design of all four. Even though it was only a project, I think its plans formed an important step toward the development of the Greenbelt Towns, and ultimately toward New Towns in America.

THE SITE consisted of 350 acres of flat land just beyond the New York City border. It was well drained, and its sand and gravel soil could be economically used for large-scale building. The property was surrounded on three sides by well built-up areas.

THE TOWN PLAN followed the Radburn pattern with superblocks, underpasses, central parks, and an even more complete separation of pedestrian and auto (Fig. 99). We proposed that the groups of houses be protected from the noises and odors of passing motor cars by placing them, in general, sixty feet away from the highways. This space was to be used for garages, grouped in this location for the following reasons:

1. So as to concentrate the paved surfaces and thus cut down the cost of highways, and
2. to make practical use of the space along the highways, and screen the houses in the group from dust and noise (Figs. 100 and 101).

This arrangement, as is apparent, would give utmost economy in roads and walks. It was open to the criticism that an American wants to leave his auto just outside his door. But, as many of the

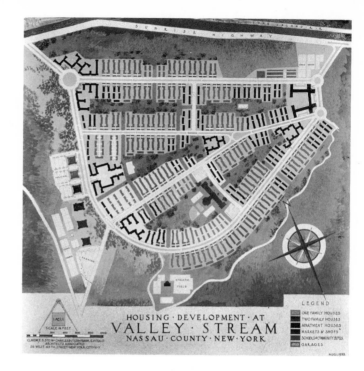

Fig. 99—General plan of Valley Stream Project.

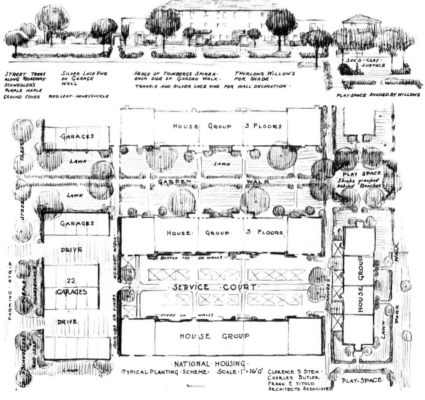

Fig. 100—A service and garden court study showing proposed planting.

tenants in Phipps Garden Apartments walked 200 feet or more to their stair entrance, I believed that they would do it in row houses or flats if the inducement of low rentals were great enough. Although we were not able to try out this idea at Valley Stream, we used it successfully at Greenbelt, Md. Since then it has been further developed at various places—finally at Baldwin Hills Village.

HOUSES were to be built in rows for economy, and thus to assure low rentals. In addition to two-family houses two stories in height, we proposed three-floor buildings with one family using the lower and another the two upper floors. There was to be housing for 4,500 families, at thirteen to the acre.

COMMUNITY FACILITIES. A greenbelt of limited width was proposed to surround the development. In this was to be the athletic field. Seven acres in the center of the development were to be given to Nassau County for school and playground. The existing hangars were to have been turned into markets and garages with surrounding parking space.

COST STUDIES which our office made included, in addition to estimates of construction and utilities made by the builder, a financial statement of annual income and expenses. We had learned from experience that the costs which counted in the long run were the operation-maintenance costs and carrying charges, rather than the original capital costs. In this connection there was a new problem. Valley Stream we proposed as an independent municipality. Therefore, the costs of government would have to be calculated as part of the annual expenses of the inhabitants. Whether it was charged to them as taxes or as rent did not matter in determining their living costs.

The cost of government must be added to that of operating, maintaining and financing buildings and grounds. So I made a study of the costs of government of small communities in this part of America as a basis for the budget of Valley Stream. I was aided by one of America's ablest town managers, John Walker, who had managd Radburn and other places. Our studies for Valley Stream served as basis for my future recommendations to the Resettlement Administration that were to be used in the Greenbelt Towns.

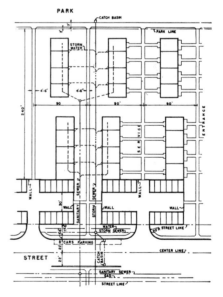

Fig. 101—Proposed layout of utilities by Ralph Eberlin.

8 GREENBELT

**Douglas D. Ellington and R. J. Wadsworth,
Chief Architects
Hale Walker, Town Planner**

When Franklin D. Roosevelt became President of the United States in March, 1933, ten million American workers were unemployed. The summer before a demonstration 'Bonus Army' of veterans had marched on Washington. Some of the unemployed settled down at the capital and built 'Hoovervilles.' The New Deal's first attempts to reverse Hoover's policy of leaving the jobless to local care succeeded in giving employment, but were in the main unproductive 'boondoggling.'

There were two outstanding exceptions: the first was the Tennessee Valley Authority, the fame of which is world-wide. Only second in importance as a demonstration of future possibilities was the building of the so-called Greenbelt Towns. Here the seed of future city development was planted. For in these towns for the first time were amalgamated the three basic conceptions from which new towns are being evolved: the Garden City, the Radburn Idea, and the Neighborhood Unit.

THE PURPOSES as officially stated were:

1. To give useful work to men on unemployment relief.
2. To demonstrate in practice the soundness of planning and operating towns according to certain garden city principles.
3. To provide low-rent housing in healthful surroundings, both physical and social, for

families that are in the low-income bracket.

The creation of the Greenbelt Towns was made possible by the Emergency Relief Appropriation Act and the National Industrial Recovery Act, both of 1935. By executive order of September of that year the President established the Resettlement Administration and prescribed its functions in regard to the Greenbelt Towns. Since then the administration of these communities has been successively transferred to various federal agencies: in December 1936 to the Secretary of Agriculture, under whom it operated as a separate unit of the Department, the name of which was afterwards changed to Farm Security Administration; in February 1942 the President transferred all housing developments which did not relate chiefly to farming to the National Housing Agency, afterward the National Public Housing Authority, and now the Public Housing Administration. In 1949, as a result of special legislation for that purpose (Senate No. 351), the towns were to be disposed of by sale, with first preference to veterans' and present tenants' groups organized on a non-profit basis. Negotiations were put under way for that purpose.

Organization for Production of the Towns

To return to that 'Never-Never' land of the New Deal: President Roosevelt appointed Rexford

GREENBELT

Guy Tugwell, one of his brain-trusters who fervently believed in Ebenezer Howard's Garden City, as Administrator of the Resettlement Administration. To produce the proposed new communities Tugwell set up, as part of the administration, the Suburban Resettlement Division under John Lansill as Director.

The Federal Governmental officials and employees multiplied and multiplied during 1935. All office buildings in Washington were overcrowded. The Suburban Division of Resettlement was finally lodged in the extravagant mansion of a former multi-millionaire, Senator MacLane. The drafting rooms, in which the homes of the poor were to be designed, surrounded a monumental marble stairway which was said to simulate the *rococo* central hall of the Atlantic liner on which the Senator had made his first trip abroad. On the landing half-way up the stairs one collided with a monstrous sculptural group of naked figures, so bulky and heavy that the government could not afford to resettle it.

In these surroundings the architects, engineers and other technicians planned homes and communities for families with incomes of $1,250 a year. It was no easy task for designers, to whom residential architecture had meant individually tailored mansions for those who could afford conspicuous waste, to limit themselves to bare essentials. Some of the early studies looked as though they were meant for the Westchester villas of young bankers. But, ultimately, the architects created a great and unified beauty out of essential requirements and simple designs.

The technicians were wisely divided into teams, each responsible for a single town—and working as though they were separate and distinct offices. Each group was headed by one or two senior planners, architects, engineers and a co-ordinator. Assisting were a staff of younger technicians and draftsmen. The Chief of the Planning Staff, Frederick Bigger, under whom the groups worked, was broadminded. He had no decided formulas. He believed that each town should be a distinct experiment—that new ideas and new approaches should be given the maximum possible opportunity to develop. This method is in sharp contrast with that which afterwards developed in the various

governmental housing agencies. They so regulate and standardize housing that the essential abilities of the architects—imagination, invention and ingenuity—are dried up and negated.

Fred Bigger decided to let the technicians be on their own as far as possible, so that they would take risks, so that they would explore and experiment. As a result they worked with enthusiasm, and gave their utmost. All the towns consequently have characterful individuality.

However, so that the planners and architects should not lose sight of the objective, this statement of the functions of the organization was given them as guide:

'To obtain a large tract of land, and thus avoid the complications due to diverse ownerships; in this tract to create a community, protected by an encircling green belt; the community to be designed for families of predominantly modest income, and arranged and administered (managed) so as to encourage that kind of family and community life which will be better than they now enjoy, but which will not involve subjecting them to coercion or theoretical and untested discipline; the dwellings and the land upon which they are located to be held in one ownership, preferably a corporated entity to which the federal government will transfer title, and which entity or corporation will rent or lease the dwellings but will not sell them; a municipal government to be set up, in character with such governments now existing or possible in that region; co-ordination to be established, in relation to the local and state governments, so that there may be provided those public services of educational and other character which the community will require; and finally, to accomplish these purposes in such a way that the community may be a taxpaying participant in the region, that extravagant outlays from the individual family income will not be a necessity, and that the rent will be suitable to families of modest income.

'To develop a land-use plan for the entire tract; to devise, under the direction of the Administrator, a system of rural economy co-ordinated with the land-use plan for the rural portions of the tract surrounding the suburban community; and to integrate both the physical plans and the economies of the rural area and the suburban community.'

Among the first problems of the new agency were how many new communities to build and where to place them. The number would be limited by the funds available and the fact that, because unskilled labor must in large part be used, costs would be very high. On the other hand unemployment was nation-wide; work was needed everywhere and at once.

The location of the limited number of towns that could be built must be determined on the basis of the above-stated purposes that they were 'to demonstrate . . . garden city principles.' That, among other things, meant that the towns be placed convenient to industrial opportunity — in fact that the towns be planned both for work and living, as had been advocated by Ebenezer Howard. Therefore Warren Vinton, the chief economist, devoted himself to a painstaking study of the probable future industrial opportunities near various large cities.

Without waiting for the completion of this research an acute emergency — or, should I say, political embarrassment — led to the immediate locating of the first community near Washington. The 'Hoovervilles' left by the 'Bonus Army' on the doorstep of Congress was too much like hanging the nation's wash in the front yard of the Capitol. It had to be removed. And so plans and specifications for Greenbelt, Maryland, 13 miles from the center of the Capitol were rushed.

In the end only two other towns were constructed: Greendale, Wisconsin, seven miles from the business center of Milwaukee; and Greenhills, Ohio, five miles north of Cincinnati.

Although these three were among America's outstanding demonstrations of New Towns, it must be admitted that they all missed out on the score of industry. Cincinnati, Milwaukee, and Washington have grown as centers of industry, business or government. But the Greenbelt Towns have not yet drawn in factories or offices. They have continued in the role of suburbs, near but yet too expensively far from employment. All this shows the difficulty and the importance of co-ordinating broad physical planning with industrial planning.

In the location of the fourth project, Warren Vinton did prove to be an industrial prophet; the New Brunswick area of New Jersey has of late had a fantastic industrial growth. The town of Greenbrook, of which Henry Wright was planner and Albert Mayer and Henry Churchill the architects, would probably have been a complete garden city. But it was never built because of local opposition and the threat of court action.

John Lansill, Director of the Suburban Division, asked me to offer constructive criticism of the plans that were being developed. After studying them, I felt that the greatest danger was unnecessary wastefulness, not only in capital expenditure, but what was even more important in this case, in operation and maintenance. I therefore prepared a series of studies of the effect on both capital and operation-maintenance costs of various manners of grouping as well as planning houses. Finally I decided that to find the most economical means of securing good living in these new towns we would have to consider other elements than those that formed part of housing developments in an existing urban area. The Greenbelt Towns were to be independent municipalities. Therefore, economy of town management was quite as important as in housing development operation in making them financially successful. By financially successful I here mean run so that their operation and maintenance would be covered by their rentals. To do more—that is to pay off the exorbitant cost of their building or to pay interest on the federal government's investment—seemed hardly possible as the tenants were all to be chosen from low income groups. The effect of size of community on operation-maintenance costs therefore became a real, and in fact, a basic element in their success.

It was apparent that the construction cost of the Greenbelt Towns would be high because of use of unskilled labor: these capital costs therefore could and in fact must be written off as unemployment relief. But on the other hand I felt certain that Congress would not annually appropriate monies to pay for deficit. Therefore it was essential to plan and build and to organize management so as to minimize the operation-maintenance expenses. This does not mean that the original costs could be wasted on unnecessarily large, elaborate, or complicated construction or equipment. On the contrary, as the capital expenditure voted by Congress would be limited, it was important that it be used to house as many families as possible.

To assist the planners in determining their plan in such a manner as to minimize capital costs as well as operation-maintenance expenditures 'without jeopardizing the popularity, social success, and future influence of the development' I made two studies:

1. *A Report of Method of Appraising House*

Plans.[21] This did not use the customary method of allowing a given number of square feet for each type of room. Such procedure only by good luck produces livable homes with flexible use. The method followed stated—or rather illustrated in diagrams—the minimum requirements in terms of requisite furniture, space for human activity and movement, and varied possible location of doors, windows and clothes-closets. As far as possible the attempt was made to allow for a number of desirable arrangements, to serve as a method of developing or appraising plans on the basis of minimum cost for adequate and varied use.

2. *Studies of the Relative Improvement Costs of House Grouping.*[22] To appraise different arrangements of houses in relation to access from paths, roads, parking areas and parks, diagrammatic plans of 11 different groupings were made. The cost of each was carefully estimated as under normal conditions of construction as they existed at the time we were actively building Radburn.

The studies showed a difference of 100 per cent per family for its proportions of roads, walks, local utilities and landscaping between the normal method of placing houses along a main highway and an arrangement similar to the earlier studies for Valley Stream (See Fig. 100). This latter arrangement was tried out in various forms at Greenbelt, and I will report later as to their success.

Two studies were made that dealt primarily with cost of operation and maintenance. The one had to do with the projects as rental housing developments.[23] This followed the usual method of cost accounting to which we had become accustomed in making preliminary studies for Chatham Village, Hillside Homes, and other large-scale housing.

The other report, which dealt with local government cost, had less precedent.[24] The costs of government generally come to the house-owner or landlord in a package or lump sum as taxes—and as far as the tenant is concerned these costs are lost or hidden in his rent. The proposed Resettlement projects were to be unified, self-supporting communities in which a tenant's monthly charges must cover *all* costs of operation and maintenance, both as a town and as a housing operation.

I attempted to organize this study in such a way as to show the relative effect of change of policy or of cost of any single factor such as education, type of house, grouping of houses, manner of disposing of waste, income group to be housed, portion of income that can be afforded for rent, distance and cost of transportation, etc. Primarily, I was interested in finding out the effect of the change of the number of family units on the costs of both housing operation and government.

This study was restricted to municipalities of 3,000 to 7,000 population; these were the probable limits of the proposed towns, at least in the first stage of construction.

The comparative study of Operation-Maintenance Costs of Government and Housing indicated not only that the cost per unit (family or person) grew increasingly less as the population grew in size, but also that the charges required to pay these operation and maintenance costs, even without allowance for interest or amortization, were too high in the 3,000-population projects to be possible for the $1,250-income group that was to be housed. Both of these conclusions have been verified by the experience in the three towns during the past ten years. At Greenbelt the unit cost decreased very much in the proportion we had indicated when the number of inhabitants increased from about 3,000 to 7,000.

SHOPPING CENTERS. The final study dealt with shopping centers.[25] It attempted to determine the different requirements of towns of 3,000 to 7,000 population. It estimated the probable local expenditures if shops were properly designed; the types and size of stores that could be successfully supported; and the incomes that could be derived from the shopkeeper and by the landlord in the towns of various sizes. The actual experience at Greenbelt has in general tendency confirmed these predictions as explained later. (See p. 217).

Three Basic Planning Ideas

The Greenbelt Towns are the first experiments in the combined development of the three basic ideas of the modern community: the Garden City, the Radburn Idea, and the Neighborhood Unit. These three conceptions in greater or less degree form the essential basis of the plans for New Towns that are being discussed, planned, or constructed in various parts of the Western World.

In Sweden, in Poland, in Great Britain, the planners are starting out on the great voyage of discovery of the form and operation of new communities that will fit today's living, practically, economically, and at the same time spaciously, safely, and beautifully.

For over a decade Greendale, Greenhills, and Greenbelt have in embryo form been trying out the various elements of the evolving city. All too little is known of how these ideas really work. New conceptions of planning of communities are constantly discussed as pure theories, long after they have been tested in the solid form of actual building and community living. Again and again the same experiments are carried out at vast expense, without study or analysis of past experience. It is true that dissimilar places, peoples, times, customs and politics require different settings and forms of communities. It is true that we cannot take, in every detail, a type of community that fitted English life at the beginning of the century, or even one that fits it now, and expect it to operate successfully in America or Russia. But we should study the basic conceptions wherever they have had the test of time.

The analysis of the 11 to 12 years' experience in the Greenbelt Towns can be of the greatest practical value to planners, architects, and engineers, as well as to administrators, sociologists, economists, and leaders in recreation, education, and various other fields, if we can discover just to what extent and how the three basic conceptions have worked in practice. To what degree were the Garden City, the Radburn and the Neighborhood Ideas developed and carried out? How were they limited in application—by the size or the operation of the development; by its relations to the federal government; by costs or financial policy; by regional or local customs or by the nature of its inhabitants? How did its form or operation differ from the original conception of the idea, or its application elsewhere (The Garden City in England, the Radburn Idea where first tried out at Radburn, New Jersey, for example)? How did it differ from the manner in which the idea is now being used in creating New Communities in other countries? Finally, what do the people who have lived in the community think of the elements of

the ideas in practice? In short how do they work?

This last, an analysis of the human reactions to these new forms and conceptions, is of course the hardest to get at. The evolution of the form of the Garden City is too incomplete. The Neighborhood Idea is still somewhat nebulous. It is difficult to separate the elements. But it is important, even on the basis of a limited study or information, to try to analyze the application of the Garden City, Radburn and Neighborhood Ideas.

The three Greenbelt Towns all followed these basic conceptions—but they did so differently, in varying degrees, and often with contrasting emphases. This was due in part to the fact that the design and development of the three towns was wisely given into the hands of three separate teams of planners, architects, engineers and administrators, rather than being standardized by a single centralized office. Therefore there were three different conceptions of desirability for good living and broad economy, and of the extent to which Garden City, Radburn or Neighborhood Unit Ideas should be applied. The form these took was influenced not only by the planners' taste or experience, but also by the distinctive qualities of the site; the topography, soil, and climate; the regional character of the population, local customs and regulations, and politics. In operation and realization all of these elements have modified the application of the three basic conceptions. Their effectiveness has also been limited by the small size and gradual growth of the towns.

For these reasons a study or analysis of the elements of the three towns is of greater value if made separately for each. It would be too complicated for the reader—as well as the analyst—to describe the elements of the three at the same time. A more thorough investigation of one place with limited comparison with the others should be more valuable and more understandable.

Why Greenbelt, Maryland, Is Chosen as a Subject

I have selected Greenbelt, Maryland, as the principal subject of this study, rather than Greendale or Greenhills, for a number of reasons:

1. Greenbelt has grown from a town of less than 3,000 to about 7,500 population. Thus we can study the relation of size and distance as elements

N

Parkbelt

M. E. Church   Woodland   Way

Forestway Rd

Hillside Road

Northway

Ridge Road

Eastway

Crescent   Road

Garages

BRADEN FIELD

Parkway Road

Nursery School

Youth Center

Swimming Pool

COMMUNITY CENTER   Parking Area

Library

Parking Area

Elementary School

Crescent   Road

Gardenway

Ridge Road

Health Association

Southway

Ridge   Road

Community Gardens

Maintenance Buildings

Oldham Farm

Community Gardens

Community Gardens

Community Gardens

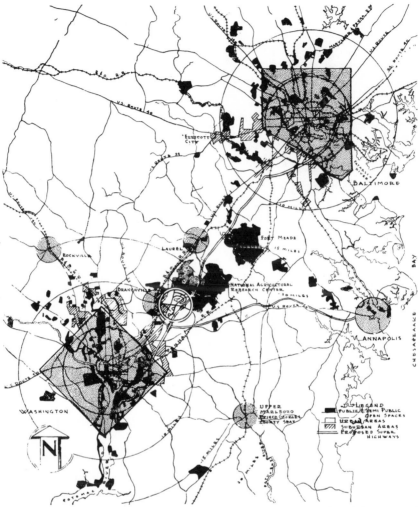

Fig. 104—Regional map showing relation of Greenbelt to outside urban influences, and proximity of National Agricultural Research Center.

Fig. 103 (previous spread)—Aerial view of Greenbelt compiled by G. T. Marts and G. Nichols.

of a neighborhood. Also we are able to compare two different methods of realizing the Radburn Idea in planning for a similar population and local conditions, but with a different approach on the part of the planners and builders.

2. Greenbelt, for various reasons, carried out and developed the Radburn Idea more fully and completely than either of the other towns. It applied all the elements full-heartedly and with fresh approach rather than partially as at the other towns. It revealed its possibilities in some ways more clearly than Radburn.

3. Greenbelt also allows one to compare the effect of two sizes of community on the cost of government and management and the various elements of these. Although this may not seem to relate directly to the three basic ideas, it is of great importance as indicating one of the means of determining the desirable size of a Garden City or New Town.

Before analyzing Greenbelt in relation to the three basic ideas, let us consider its site, the people for whom it was created, and the general plan that was dictated by these.

The Greenbelt Site

The site of Greenbelt is about 13 miles from the center of the National Capital (Fig. 104). When it was chosen in 1935, Prince George's County, Maryland, in which it was situated, was sparsely settled. Up to that time most of the overflow from the limiting ten-mile square of the District of Columbia had streamed toward Virginia, where standards of education were higher. But since the war there has been a building boom in Prince George's County— a boom of a disorderly, unorganized character. The main access from the north to Washington, U. S. Route No. 1, which passes through the Greenbelt property, is now a continuous strip development of ugly, unrelated stores and houses. The nearby municipalities of Hyattsville, Riverdale and Berwyn have been sprawling rapidly over the landscape toward Washington. But the 3,300 acres or so which the government purchased for this great experiment in city building in 1935 is still mainly open country.

The land for Greenbelt was gradually acquired from numerous owners, the family titles to the property of some going back to the original grants from the King of England. It was no longer of much agricultural value. It had been overworked as farm-land, especially for tobacco-growing, and had ceased to be used for this purpose. Therefore it was bought for an average of $90 an acre. Little if any of the extensive open land that surrounds the development has been used for agriculture since its purchase.

The southern 1,200 acres, separated by the Branchville-Glendale Road from the northern area in which the present development is located, is of a rougher topography, with pine-wood ravines and plateaus of oak and other hardwoods. In this section there are about 300 acres of pasture and grainfields. This might make an excellent and much needed National or State Park, and thus serve as an additional permanent protective greenbelt.

The General Plan

If you are fortunate you will first see Greenbelt from the air while flying between New York and Washington (Fig. 103). The town is formed in the shape of a graceful crescent set on a vast background of green. For a moment its attractive flowing curves remind you of the Crescent at Bath, England. But the Greenbelt crescent is much bigger and bolder; it is much freer — though no less rhythmic. It is not so monumentally formal. The Bath crescent is a closed wall of masonry with landscape foreground and background; at Greenbelt most of the principal buildings are at right angles rather than parallel to the great curve.

The Greenbelt crescent is marked mainly by the graceful sweep of the two main highways, and the shadow of lower land that surrounds the natural plateau that suggested and give its form.

The essential shape of the Greenbelt town plan was indicated by nature. Here, as in many other great plans, the planners' job was primarily to discover, not invent. As Benton MacKaye says:

'Planning is a scientific charting and picturing of the thing . . . which man desires and which the eternal forces will permit. The basic achievement of planning is to make potentialities visible . . . Planning is revelation.'[26]

The planners of Greenbelt revealed the potentialities of the great curved plateau as a beautiful place for good living. The plateau was roughly a thousand feet wide, more or less, at various places. The two main cross-town highways, Crescent and Ridge Road, although almost parallel, gradually open up the central area for some 5,000 feet then, to the north, they separate rapidly to take in the broadening of the plateau. They follow the curve of this highland but not always at the very ridge. The land in many places rises gradually and gracefully at one or both sides of the highways to form tree-clad backgrounds to the house groups, or to allow of their location at varying levels. The arched swings of the highways have great enough radii to permit safe visibility for auto driving. The driver's view is increased by the fact that buildings are either widely spaced and at right angles to the road, or have a liberal set-back.

The inner crescent sweeps round the spacious community center, some 1,500 feet wide and, including the athletic field, quite as deep. This forms the heart of Greenbelt. Here is the focus for the common life of the town, and here, in its physical center, are located in logical and beautiful arrangement the various elements for community activities. Here is the seat of government and management; the focus of cultural, religious, and educational life; the main recreational and entertainment center; and the market place.

The area between Crescent Road and Ridge Road is cut about every 1,000 feet by connecting traffic ways. The space is thus divided into superblocks of about 14 acres each.

The five superblocks south of Northway formed the main site of the houses built between the winter of 1935-36 and autumn of 1937 by the Resettlement Administration. In addition to this inner superblock area a few groups on the outside of Crescent Road and Ridge Road were completed, along with the apartment buildings on Parkway Road (Figs. 103 and 105). The other houses were built as part of the Defense Homes Development.

The People

The first settlers of Greenbelt moved in as the homes were completed between October 1937 and the summer of 1938. The demand for living places in the Washington area was limitless. It was therefore necessary for the government to set artificial limitation in choosing its tenants. Preference was given to poorly housed families whose incomes were limited but who could however afford the rentals which were set at $21.75 to $45.85 per month. In the row houses first choice was given to young married families with children. There was place for the smaller families, and even for bachelors, in the three-story apartment buildings. These small units were built to increase the number of families as much as possible when it was discovered that the $14 million or so—including $570,000 for land—that was being spent, would be insufficient, because of the use of unskilled labor, to build the 1,000 houses that had been set as a minimum. The apartment units consisted of one or two rooms and kitchenette (Fig. 118, E1-6). Thus of the first 885 families many were small in size and lived in apartments. Altogether there was a population of 2,831: an average of only 3.2 per family.

Greenbelt started as a young community in every way; fathers and mothers were practically all under 30, and most of the children, although two or three to a family, were still under school age.

An effort was made to populate the town with an average cross-section of residents. Proportions found in the nearby District of Columbia were applied. Among the first residents, therefore, 70 per cent of the wage-earners were government workers, 30 per cent non-government; 30 per cent were Catholic, 7 per cent Jewish, and 63 per cent Protestant.

The families were fairly homogeneous in respect to education. Most were high-school graduates, a small percentage professionally trained, and a small proportion had had little schooling. The government workers represented the white-collar clerical group; the other 30 per cent were professional or manual workers.

During over a decade of life Greenbelt, Maryland, is the only one of the Towns that had any decided increase in population. The original construction was undertaken in an emergency, and the second was again the result of an emergency. As a prelude to America's entry into the Second World War, during the so-called Defense period, factories again opened wide their doors, industrial employment shot up, and Washington became a beehive filled with administrative and clerical paper-work. Congress, through the Lanham Act, set aside funds to

Fig. 105—General plan of Greenbelt prepared to show outdoor recreational facilities in housing areas. Note the location of play areas for groups of various ages.

build homes and finance community facilities for workers in 'essential defense industry.' As a result 1,000 homes were added to Greenbelt at the end of 1941.

The make-up of the new group was different from that of the original Greenbelt people. Families were older and larger. The average family size, which had been 3.2 in 1941, before Defense Homes were built, was 3.7 in 1943. War-time incomes were higher. No income limits could be established, since essential workers had to be housed. In 1940 the median family income was $1,599, in 1943 it was about $2,900.

By and large the groups merged. They meet at the stores; they work and play together in varied social and recreational activities; they are represented on the council and, at election time, they vote on the same local issues.

Greenbelt as a Garden City

Rex Tugwell and his associates were apparently more deeply influenced by Ebenezer Howard's Garden City than any other idea in their conception of the New Towns they proposed to create. To what extent was Howard's program realized? What were the causes and what the effects of the variations from Howard's conception?

The accepted definition of a Garden City is:

'A garden city is a town planned for industry and healthy living, of a size that makes possible a full measure of social life, but no larger, surrounded by a permanent rural belt, the whole of the land being in public ownership, or held in trust for the community.'

PLANNED FOR LIVING. All of the Greenbelt Towns are exceptionally well planned for healthy living. They meet the requirements of good living in these days, and they do it at a moderate cost, so that people of limited means can secure these advantages. That they enjoy them is attested by the inquiry that we made at Greenbelt and by similar investigations in the other two towns.

PLANNED FOR INDUSTRY they have not been— and none of the three towns have had any industry worth considering within its boundaries. Although all of them were located in regions in which employment has grown, they have all had serious difficulties because of travel to work—caused by time consumed and the cost of transportation.

Let us consider Greenbelt. It is true that there is about 2,500 feet frontage on the Baltimore and Ohio Railroad toward the western boundaries of Greenbelt which would not require much grading or fill to prepare it for industry. But there are many and various considerations other than railroad frontage that determine the location of new factories in a district that has little heavy or related industries. They might or might not be induced to come. The Washington area is not an industrial region in the usual sense—even though George Washington in locating the Capital thought it would be. The predominating occupation is government: most Greenbelt workers are employed by the Federal Government. The basic problem is not to find new types of employment but to bring some of the predominating work closer to or within the boundaries of Greenbelt.

Federal agencies are crowded in Washington; their employees are forced to make long, tiresome journeys to and from work; the streets of the capital are congested; traffic is blocked, parking space scarce; if there is danger from atomic warfare anywhere in this country it is the concentrated governmental focus of federal administration. If agencies, or those portions of agencies which need not be in the executive nerve center in Washington, should be decentralized, no better nearby place than Greenbelt could be found. There is plenty of space for office or laboratory buildings and for outdoor experimentation, as at the Agricultural Research Center, as well as for a largely increased number of homes in Greenbelt, with all its combined country and city attractions.

The Census Bureau has already started to decentralize by setting up a branch at Suitland in Maryland. But this was apparently chosen without adequate investigation as to possibilities of securing housing for employees. Most of them must travel to and from Washington or beyond.

Greenbelt has had at its very door from the beginning what on the surface appears a natural source of employment. That is the National Agricultural Research Center at Beltsville[27] (see Fig. 104). This is the largest experimental station of the kind in the U.S.A., occupying 12,000 acres. It borders Greenbelt to the north, and employs over 2,100 workers (including 875 in the Plant Industry Section). These workers, a great part of them scientific specialists and other technicians, would make ideal inhabitants of Greenbelt. And yet up to a short time ago none of them lived in the town; even now there are only 83 of the 1,236 employees of the Center itself who are inhabitants of Greenbelt, and most of these lived in the town before they got their jobs.

C. A. Logan, the Chief of the Center, had a careful survey made some time ago and found that the average distance travelled was 10 to 15 miles each way. Many of the employees lived at the other side of Washington, in Arlington, Virginia. Twice a day in their travel they passed the Greenbelt inhabitants bound for Washington, and quite a number of them who work in the colossal Pentagon Building near Arlington.

Now a good many of the Agricultural Center workers have moved out to the houses built since the war at Beltsville, Silvertown, and other Maryland towns. But a great many still spend 50 minutes each way on the special buses to and from Washington.

Workers at the Center have not lived in Greenbelt for two different reasons. In the beginning only low-income workers were admitted to the Development, and most employees of the Research Center earned too much. Second, although there was no income limit in the Defense Homes, eligibility was restricted to workers who came to metropolitan Washington after July, 1941, and who were employed by agencies having priority ratings as essential war work. Most Agricultural Center work was not considered essential. This excluded some 95 per cent of the employees of the center.

Because Greenbelt is purely a dormitory city serving Washington, its workers are forced to make lengthy trips back and forth daily, many of them slowly through congested Washington streets. The majority, who travel by buses and streetcars, must change once or twice and spend about an hour each way. Weekly passes are $2.25. That means $117 for yearly transportation, or, with allowance for the travel of members of the family, about $140 per family. In budgeting cost of family living in the studies for the Resettlement Administration I allowed $45 to $60 a year for travel.

Cost of transportation by automobile, even when used by a group cooperatively, costs even more

than by buses and streetcars. The trip to Washington can be made in half an hour or so. But during the rush hours at the beginning and end of the day the main highways are blocked by traffic—and this is just when the Greenbelt workers use them.

The proposed express highway between Baltimore and Washington will cut travel time from Greenbelt. There will be a clover-leaf permitting entrance to the superhighways at the eastern border of Greenbelt. It is uncertain whether public buses will be permitted on the highway. If not, most of the Greenbelt workers will still devote the equivalent of over a tenth of their working hours to the journey to and from work.

PERMANENT GREENBELT. Greenbelts have continued to form an essential part of the three towns since the beginning. ' . . . In this tract to create a community, protected by an encircling greenbelt . . . ' formed part of the statement of the objectives of the Resettlement program, which also proposed 'a system of rural economy co-ordinate with the land use plan for the rural portions of the tract surrounding the suburban community.' The importance of the greenbelts was accentuated by the names of the towns. In all three towns there is still a predominance of open land; the developed areas form a very small part of the total tracts.

In Greenbelt the land has not been used for agricultural purposes, unless you call the allotment gardens agriculture. These have been located in five places, more or less near the residential areas. Here 500 families have grown food on 50-feet x 50-feet plots. Up to a short time ago these were ploughed and fertilized by the town for a charge of $1 each (Fig. 103).

The two other towns have been much more successful in using their open land for farming. At Greenhills about 4,000 acres are in agricultural use. There are 34 old farms used as suburban residences with one to 20 acres each, but the greater part of the land is occupied by 28 full-time farmers, whose products are chiefly dairy. Although a farmers' market was originally proposed, the dairymen have tended almost entirely to market their milk, eggs, poultry, and vegetables in the bigger center at Cincinnati.

At Greendale there are about 3,000 acres in 18 farms or dairies of 100 to 240 acres each, as well

Fig. 106—An aerial view showing the Resettlement Development at Greenbelt.

Fig. 107—Greenbelt from the air, showing the Resettlement Development shortly after completion. Left center is the community center, community-school, swimming pool, shopping center with parking area at either end, and the underpass below Crescent Road. (Library of Congress photo by Fairchild Aerial Surveys Inc., New York)

as rural homes and 25 acres of allotment gardens.

In Greendale and Greenhills the unity of town and country has been of mutual advantage to the urban and rural population. Farms, dairies, and forests form a familiar part of the daily life of the town children and their parents. Town and farm folks have come to know each other as neighbors, friends and associates. They gather together in town meetings, at church, social parties, and lectures, at the movies, the co-operative stores, or, in Greendale, at the tavern. This association has broken down barriers of misunderstanding between farmer and factory workers at Greendale, and in Greenhills.

At Greenbelt the great open area that surrounds it has served for recreation and free contact with the out-of-doors, rather than agriculture. Groups of little ones explore it without restraint; they are pioneers and Indians in their own wilderness. In the picturesque rugged section to the south, areas have been set aside for both Boy Scouts and Girl Scouts. On weekends the whole family is united in hiking and picnicking in the woods. At the side of the lake are picnic tables and benches as well as fireplaces on which to prepare hot meals. At the lake, young and old fish for striped bass. From the lake can be heard the crack of rifles from nearby Greenbelt Gun Club. Although swimming in the lake has been temporarily prohibited because of lack of sufficient town funds to pay guards, sunbathing and boating are favorite forms of relaxation. There is horseback riding also, for a more limited number who rent their horses from nearby stables.

Large portions of the surrounding greenbelt at Greendale and Greenhills have been dedicated to permanent use as parks and recreation areas, by putting them in the hands of the County Park Departments. At Greenbelt this method of perpetuating the protection is not yet accomplished. However, the National Capital Park and Planning Commission is considering a large tract in the southern portion as a regional park. This land, which is in large part rough and well-wooded, and cut by a meandering brook some 50 feet below the higher plateaus, would make an excellent semi-wilderness recreation area. As a public park it would be a permanent protective greenbelt to the

south, as the National Agricultural Center is along the northern boundary. The narrow green natural wall along the future Washington-Baltimore Superhighway, with only one point of access to Greenbelt, will protect the eastern boundary. Only a park to the west is required to complete the greenbelt.

The Congress, when it passed legislation at a recent session for the purpose of disposing of the three towns, signified its desire to preserve the greenbelt by authorizing the Public Housing Commissioner to transfer 'streets, roads, public buildings, federally owned utilities, playgrounds, swimming pools, and parks, including adequate open land surrounding or adjacent to each project, to the appropriate non-Federal governmental agency.'[28]

To clarify the meaning of this section, the report of the Senate Subcommittee, written by Senator Paul H. Douglas, stated:

'The particular portion of the amendment relating to adequate open land is intended to preserve as far as practicable the original design of having each of these projects protected by a green belt of park and forest land surrounding such a community. In fact the committee deems it desirable that the Commissioner exercise his authority in such a manner as to retain the essential character of the entire original development in any disposal of these projects.'[29]

PUBLIC OWNERSHIP. 'The whole of the land being in public ownership, or held in trust for the community'—this last section of the definition of a Garden City has been followed—at least up to the present. The Federal Government has remained in possession of all of the three towns, with the exception of comparatively small areas. For example, in the three towns churches have lately purchased plots, and in Greenhills, two moderate-sized groups of houses for sale have been developed by private builders: the latter cannot, in my opinion, be called 'an improvement.' On a smaller scale a limited number of lots at Greendale have been sold and covered with inharmonious houses.

Of the future I cannot as yet report.[30] In the sale of the towns, which will be consummated in the near future, Congress has stated that preference be given to 'veteran groups organized on a non-profit basis (provided that any such group shall accept as a member . . . any tenant occupying a

Fig. 108—An airview of Greenbelt. In the center East-way crosses from Ridge Road to Crescent Road. Photographed before the Defense Homes to the east of Ridge Road were built. (Fairchild Aerial Surveys Inc., New York)

Fig. 109—The shores and the lake are used for picnicking and play. Swimming, which was popular, is not permitted now because of the lack of funds to pay guards.

136

GREENBELT

dwelling unit) . . .' But whether this will serve as a means of preserving single ownership for the good of the community is questionable: the 'home ownership' idea has been well sold in America in spite of its apparent weaknesses.

LIMITED SIZE. 'Of a size that makes possible a full measure of social life, but no larger'—this is the only section of the Garden City definition that remains. Unquestionably the people of Greenbelt have had a very full measure of community life. There are features that can be added as the population of Greenbelt grows.

The important element concerning size, about which we know altogether too little, is its effect on the cost of operating government. We do know that when a town grows beyond a certain size the cost per family or per person tends to augment for many services. This may be due to the increased complexity or increased administrative expenses of operating a gigantic undertaking of any kind—whether commercial, industrial or governmental. We have also judged that the costs of operating government in a smaller municipality decreased as the town increased in size up to a certain point. However, there has been very little definite study of this subject that is of much value. At Greenbelt we have been able, I think, to gather some important facts in this almost unexplored field. Of this later.

The Radburn Idea

Although the Garden City was the inspiration for the general conception of Greenbelt, in detailed form it followed the elements of the Radburn Idea. So here is another opportunity to find out how it works, with its superblocks with central greens, and streets and paths insulated from each other, and with different kinds of roads for different purposes. Here again is a chance to see what the people think of it; people who had been accustomed to living in a conventional type of American city with houses facing on busy thoroughfares, and with schools, parks, playgrounds and stores accessible only by crossing one or many streets. So from time to time during this last 10 years I have visited the town and community managers, the director of the stores and various other friends at Greenbelt. I learnt much from O. Kline Fulmer, the architect,

who after working on the plans and helping to supervise the construction was assistant manager. I saw his three children grow up happily and freely at Greenbelt, and Mrs. Fulmer told me about the busy life one spent at Greenbelt keeping up with its many activities. To get an up-to-date impression of the reaction of the people who live there now, a short time ago with the aid of Kate Edelman, we questioned some 21 of the inhabitants in regard to their attitude toward certain features of the plan—and particularly those that were influenced by the Radburn Idea. The people interviewed lived in different sections of the town; some in the older, some in the newer development; some dwelt in apartments, the others in houses of various sizes. Some of them had had homes in Greenbelt ever since it was started; most had been there over three years. The majority had lived previously on the outskirts of a large city; a few had never before lived outside a big city. All those interviewed were married, and with two exceptions had one to four children. Six were men; all of the women did their own housework, although several had other employment.

The attitude of the people interviewed was favorable on most points, but opinions ranged from uncritical enthusiasm to the unqualified disapproval of 'everything about Greenbelt' on the part of one woman.

STREET AND PARKING PATTERN. Everyone—including the woman who dislikes Greenbelt—agreed that the street lay-out is convenient for traffic. As to convenience for various kinds of deliveries: no one reported any complaint from milkmen, grocery-truck men, drivers of furniture trucks, moving-vans, expressmen or anyone making deliveries of any kind.

The original Resettlement Development carried out the theories and practices evolved at Radburn more thoroughly than the later Defense Homes Development. This included superblocks with parks as backbone; specialized means of circulation, each planned and built for one and only one special purpose; complete separation of pedestrian and automobile; houses with two fronts, one for service, the other for reposeful living. In fact in some ways the Radburn Idea was carried a step further, for instance, in experimentation in various ways of relating and distinguishing automobile and pedestrian access and also, of the greatest importance, in the complete separation of pedestrians and motor vehicles in the Community Center.

Although the Radburn Idea served as model for the plans of the Defense Homes as well as for the earlier development, the actual execution was quite different. This seems to have been due in part to the financial limitations in the latter development. The cost of the 1,000 units was only $4,500,000 excluding the land, which had already been paid for.

The difference, I believe, was mainly the result of the manner in which the work was carried out. I have spoken of the spirit of enthusiastic dedication to the discovery and development of new communities, with which the groups of architects and planners worked in the MacLane residence in the Resettlement days.

The job of producing the required drawings and specifications for the Defense addition was dumped into the factory-like office of the Public Works Agency along with innumerable other projects, and supervision was from the center. Work was shot through the draftingroom efficiently and speedily, and was followed by economical and quick construction.

Fortunately, the general plan for the location of the new houses had been in the main determined in the inspired days of the Resettlement Administration. As you see them from the sky the two developments seem to be a single united design. The Defense Development in the main was intended to follow the principles of the Radburn Idea in harmony with the early Greenbelt plan. Advantage was taken of the existing main utility lines by constructing some groups to the south and east of Ridge Road. But the greater part of the addition was constructed beyond Northway, where the earlier development ended.

GARAGES. For the earlier development of 885 dwelling units, 475 garages were built. As no garages were added for the Defense Development these 475 garages are all there are now for the 1,885 Greenbelt families, who in 1949 had 1,374 passenger automobiles. There is a strong competition for the existing garages, and a continued demand for more garages. Although in the original development more garages were planned for than were built, not enough space was set aside there or in the Defense Homes to meet the present need. This is another example of the need for allowing plenty of land for future change and growth.

PARKING. According to people questioned, parking space at the town center is adequate and accessible. Parking arrangements for cars of residents themselves are generally found convenient. But parking space for the cars of visitors is too limited, according to several residents who have found their own spaces taken up by people visiting in the neighborhood and who have been forced to leave their own cars on the street. In the Defense Homes sections, however, where overnight parking in the street is allowed, many of the residents prefer to leave their cars on the street rather than in the parking lot, in order to avoid the danger of running into the children who use these parking areas for play.

In the Resettlement Development the auto approach to houses is, in most cases, from paved areas permitting no through passage. Some of these are dead-end lanes leading to all the houses served. But, in the main, the cul-de-sac went through a logical change, resulting in a service court. This, which was further developed at Baldwin Hills Village in all its various forms, differed distinctly from the Radburn service road, which gives direct motor access to all houses. The best of these were arranged so that the automobiles maneuvered and in many cases remained in a forecourt, and the houses faced on and are served from a path, some at a hundred feet or so distance from the forecourt. Others are separated from the paved area by rows of garages. This disposition permits easier use of sloping land. It gives greater privacy. It completely protects the entrance and the surroundings of the houses from the annoyance of automobiles. It is safer than the Raburn type of cul-de-sac or the paved courts surrounded by and directly accessible to dwellings as used in the later Defense Development at Greenbelt (Fig. 108).

The original purpose in using this type of service forecourt, similar to that suggested for Valley Stream (See Fig. 100) was primarily economy. The studies which I made of the relative improvement costs of various schemes of house grouping for the

Fig. 110—Typical row house built of cinderblocks and painted. Brick is used as a decoration.

Fig. 111—Bungalow forming end of row of houses; most of these so-called "Honeymoon Cottages" are inhabited by elderly couples.

Resettlement Administration, before the final planning of the towns, had shown that the normal cost per family of utilities, roads and paths, as well as grading and planting of house lots for the typical American arrangement of houses facing a traffic street could be decreased to a minimum by use of such garage and parking compounds. Thus a saving of approximately 54 per cent in the improvement costs could be made. This I noted in my report to Mr. John Lansill on November 19, 1935:

'The cheapest arrangement as affecting improvement costs, is that of row houses on lanes without vehicular roads in the lanes, but with garages grouped at the entrance to lanes. This arrangement has great advantages from the point of view of good living. It offers increased safety and quiet on the service side of the houses and at the same time it permits complete privacy on the garden side. On the other hand, some planners may prefer to sacrifice these advantages for the convenience of direct access to each house by automobile and greater ease in the delivery of bulky goods and fuel, and easier fire protection.'

The automobile access to the Defense Homes follows the same general planning as did the earlier development. It was based on stereotyped formulae that had the general objective of concentrating the parking of, and the servicing by, automobiles in a compact court off the street. But it was done crudely, without adequate consideration of appearance, either from the inside or the outside of houses, and—what is more important—without sufficient precaution against danger to children.

As in the Resettlement Development, the Defense Homes consisted of simple row houses grouped around dead-end automobile lanes or courts. All principal rooms looked away from the service side. The unit plans were particularly good for use in connection with the Radburn Idea of livingroom and bedroom facing and opening out to safe and peaceful green (Figs. 118 and 119). The main doorways were properly located. But they are seldom used—for they lead to unfinished open spaces. The paths on the 'garden' side were never constructed. In fact there is not only no incentive to planting a garden, but sufficient top soil was never supplied to make gardening successful. There are few trees and therefore little shade. Not enough trees were

planted around the houses to invite the use of these open spaces for playing or loafing. The members of the families or their friends seldom approach this side, for most of the inner block connections of the main framework of paths were never realized. Even where they exist, the houses are separated from them by barren fields or mud. Underpasses were entirely omitted. So at most places the roads are used by the pedestrians. In a few of the more used or dangerous places the sidewalks have since been added.

The outstanding difference between the two developments is in the location and surroundings of the automobile courts. The typical Defense houses face directly on the dreary concrete pavement of the courts. In many cases the service door, which is by necessity used also as the main entrance, is but a short distance away (Fig. 115). No hedges or fences were included in the original work. None have been added since, except a few rough fences built by tenants, in spite of regulations forbidding such variations in the prevailing monotony. The uninspired design of the wooden houses would not have been objectionable in a setting of trees and gardens. The external environment of the Defense Homes is illkept and disorderly. In these slumlike surroundings there is little incentive to exercise the loving care that the earlier tenants give to gardens and hedges.

The difference goes deeper than appearance. Safety for children has been decreased as has outdoor comfort and repose for adults. Underpasses near schools have been replaced by policing of road crossings (Figs. 112 and 113); the inner block paths are missing; the park play areas were not developed on the safer side of the house. The little child has no choice but the paved court, with the constant danger of moving vehicles, as children's playground. In questioning tenants in regard to their observations on the safety of the plan it was mainly those living in the Defense Homes that were apprehensive of danger. And rightly, as illustrated by a tragic incident that occurred lately. A child was killed by an automobile in one of the service courts in the Defense Development. I went out to Greenbelt from Washington as soon as I heard of it, to see how it happened. The City Manager showed me

Fig. 112—A Greenbelt underpass leading directly to the community-school.

Fig. 113—Because of lack of inner block paths and underpasses, children must be policed at road crossings in the Greenbelt Defense Development.

where the municipal refuse-collecting truck had turned to drive out of the court, and how the little girl had run out from the house and directly under the rear wheel of the truck. The yard between the paved auto space and the house was narrow; there was no fence or hedge to enclose the yard; the other side, where there should have been a garden and a walk, was uninviting.

The probability of a fatal accident of the kind described above is less in most of the courts of the Resettlement Development. In a great number of these the houses do not open directly on the paved court; they are served by forecourts such as I have described above, or the house rows do not run parallel with the court but are at an angle to it, or the residences are separated from the courts by garages. It is true that some of the groups face the paved lanes. They are the exception. Moreover, in most of the Resettlement houses, the yards are enclosed by hedges (Figs. 114 and 116) and the other side of the house is attractive for playing. Danger has been greatly lessened by thoughtful planning and planting in the early development. But even these are by no means 100 per cent effective for keeping children out of danger.

Parents in all parts of the town report that small children play in the parking courts. The paved surface is a little uneven for wheeltoys, but handy, being so near the house. Mothers dislike the use of the parking areas for play for all of the reasons that attract the children: they do not like the sand or the mud the children track into the house. They worry, too, about the danger from cars entering or backing out of the parking lots.

People living in houses adjoining the courts do not like the noise. Car-owners also complained that cars were scratched and dented by the play of the children.

The problem of parking-lot play in the original part of the town is very minor, compared with that in the Defense Homes sections. Here many of the parking lots were said to have been given over almost entirely to the children, who find these the only sizeable areas for play in the immediate vicinity. 'My heart is in my mouth every time I drive into one of these areas,' said one woman, who parks her car on the street a hundred feet away, rather than take the risk of running over a child on the parking area.

In an attempt to lure the children away from the parking areas, a number of pieces of play equipment have been installed this past summer in areas between groups of buildings. Apparently children play in the auto courts first for easy use of their wheeled toys and vehicles, and secondly, to get out of the damp and muddy soil after it has rained. In connection with Radburn, I observed that there should be adequate paved area solely for play—completely separated from the paved areas for vehicles, and therefore on the opposite side of the house. A number of the house plans are arranged so that the livingroom and sometimes also the kitchen-dining-room and the main bedroom run through the house (Fig. 118, C2-2 and C3-6). Thus the mother can more easily keep an eye on the youngsters at either side of the house.

Several people reported that some children—not their own— play in the streets. The principal reason for this is the lack of open space in which the little ones can play ball. The only other important recreational use made of the streets is for sledding in winter; the children prefer the streets to sledruns provided for their use away from the street.

No one mentioned the use of the streets for bicycling, which is evidently considered quite safe even for small children seven or eight years of age along the side of the streets. Except for bicycling, the number of children found playing on the street

Fig. 114—Garage court on service side of Resettlement Development houses. Note protection of hedges.

Fig. 115—Parking court on service side of Defense Development houses. There is no protection for children leaving the house. They play mostly on these courts, as paths and gardens are lacking on the other side of the houses.

Fig. 116—Laundry on the service side of Resettlement Development houses. Orderly separation of play and work.

Fig. 117—Laundry on the service side of Greenbelt Defense Development houses. Disorderly use of same space for drying, auto parking, and children's play.

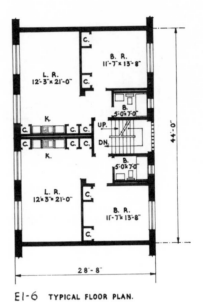

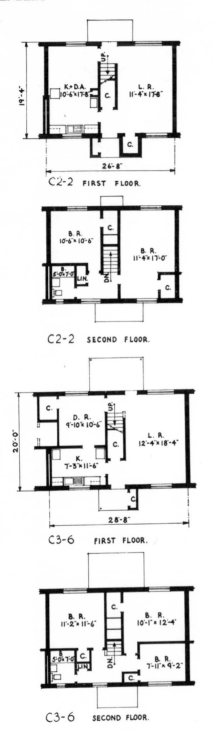

Fig. 118—Some Resettlement Development living units. C2 and C3 are typical two-story houses with living rooms from front to rear. The maximum amount of living space is on the garden side. E1 is one of the apartment types for small families in three-story walk-ups. A1 is a three-room bungalow. These are mainly occupied by old folk but were known as "Honeymoon Homes."

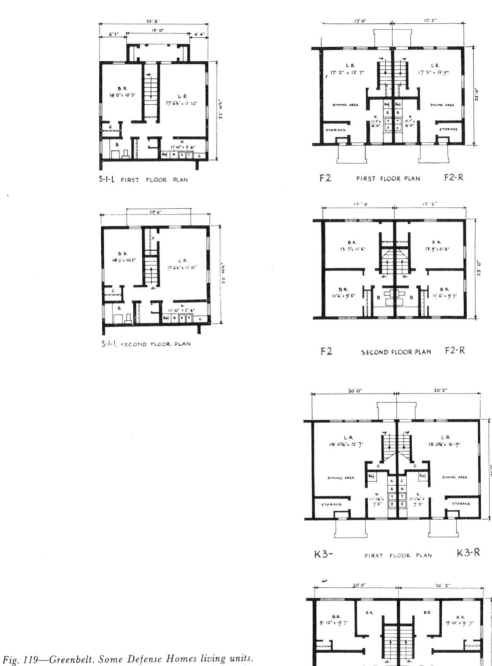

Fig. 119—Greenbelt. Some Defense Homes living units. S1 shows typical small flats which occur one above the other as end units. F2 and K3 are two- and three-bedroom two-story houses. Tenants find there is a shortage of storage space despite provision made. The houses were planned to face garden side, but paths were never built and there are few gardens.

Fig. 120—Family life at Greenbelt.

Fig. 121—Life in the open around apartment houses.

Fig. 122—*Private gardens along a path leading to the woods.*

Fig. 123—*Everyone trims his own hedge.*

at any time is negligible, compared with the number that can be seen in almost any conventionally-planned suburban development.

WALK SYSTEM AT GREENBELT. The main framework of walks is completely separated from roads The backbone of pedestrian circulation passes through the center of the superblocks, gracefully following the crescent dictated by the form of the land. Through each garden court it is connected to the highways by collecting paths. From these the private walks sprout. It is all like the orderly growth of a tree—or the human nerve system.

This describes the walk pattern in the Resettlement Section where the system was completed There it works very well and is generally satisfactory. Everyone we interviewed there agreed that the routes to the town center and to the various parts of the village were direct and convenient It is quite a different matter in the Defense Section where some one told us 'It's a wonderful system —or would be if we had it.' Not only were the paths to the garden side of the house omitted there, but also many of the main paths. Here if the paths are indirect or steeply sloped people sometimes make a short-cut by crossing or following roads. This is particularly apparent where, because of economy, walks which tenants really need were sometimes omitted. In some cases their persistent direct promenading makes a path where it should have been planned.

No one can claim that the 'Safety System' of separating pedestrians and autos works 100 per cent, even where the planning is carefully and sanely carried out. Humans are human. They will take the short cut when in a hurry to save time. Excepting where youngsters consistently crossed traffic there are no sidewalks along the edges of the streets. Outsiders and newcomers miss these, and sometimes walk in the roads. Even old inhabitants do so if they find it more direct. Two women said they occasionally use the street instead of the walks when pushing a load of groceries plus a baby, because the connecting walk to their homes is difficult to climb. The highways are used more at night than in daytime, particularly in the Defense Section where the walks often follow circuitous routes. Even in the older parts some said they followed the road because of lack of sufficient central lighting on the inner block

paths. The lights, which were placed low, are attractive and economical in original cost, but have not proved practical (see Fig. 102). This is because ingenious children who delight in destroying bulbs can easily get at them.

Despite the corner-cutting indulged in by most of the people interviewed, all of them prefer the center-block walk plan to the conventional scheme. They appreciate particularly the added safety for children, and even the elders, who admitted taking short-cuts along the streets, instruct their small children to use the center-block paths on their way to and from school, just as the parents do at Radburn.

UNDERPASSES. Parents take particular care to train the little ones to walk through the underpasses connecting the main central walk system with the shopping center and school. Most of them do so, even when it takes longer than if they crossed the highways. Use by adults and older children depends on comparative convenience. Where access is direct and by easy sloping paths practically everyone goes through the underpass. The underpass leading to the center of the marketplace is almost always used by women on the way to the center, but on their return they sometimes use the highway, as I have said, to avoid the grade. Where grades do not gradually and easily lead to the underpass, or where the path as it approaches the road is at its level, older children and others in a hurry by-pass it and cut across streets. But even at such places I have noted that shoppers with full bags or loaded baby-carriages take the longer way passing below the highway. One under-pass is found hazardous by pedestrians because children on bicycles use its long curving walk and grade as a speedway. As a whole the people of Greenbelt find that the underpasses serve their purpose. They strongly favor them.

THE USE OF OPEN SPACES in a logical way is one of the basic innovations of the Greenbelt, as of the Radburn plan.

A Service yard on the street or lane side is strange to tenants at first, but ultimately most of them see its advantages. 'Now that I'm used to it,' said one woman, 'I don't mind it a bit. And one thing that is nice about it is that you can sit out in your garden and not have the cars whizzing by.'

As long as they can hang their laundry out to dry, they are not fussy about its location—or its visibility. Sunshine directly on the clothes is considered important. 'Trees in the yard are nice, but they do interfere with drying clothes.' Several women who lived in the apartments referred to the lack of space for drying as a serious disadvantage—and felt that it should be provided.

INDIVIDUAL GARDENS. In the Resettlement Development, individual gardens are separated from each other and from the public paths and open areas by hedges. These enclosures are low. They do not give that complete privacy that the English require and secure by walls or tall hedges. But the Greenbelt hedges are sufficient to mark the limits of each family's own terrain, its little kingdom. This bounding seems to engender a proprietary pride in spite of the lack of actual ownership. You can observe its effect by comparing these earlier homes with the later Defense Homes which not only had no hedges or other lot enclosure, but also had inadequate top soil and planting in the beginning.

Many of the earlier settlers took full advantage of the fine natural background of varied trees and the careful initial landscape planting. A great number of the gardens are thoughtfully planted and well cared for—many, but not all, of course.

The interest in gardens in Greenbelt varies, as it does in all communities, so it was wise to differentiate the size of lots under tenants' care. I remember years ago, as I walked around Welwyn with Ebenezer Howard, the father of Garden Cities, that he pointed out how the large plots went to the tenants who wanted to do small-scale farming. Here in Greenbelt, it is to those who love floriculture. One end house is occupied by a worker whose every minute of spare time is devoted to making his surroundings an ever-changing prospect of brilliantly colored flowers. The interior of this house, planned for the utmost economy in space, might be criticized as tight, if it were not for the gay vistas of his own cultivated terrain that broaden his outlook on life.

ADVANTAGES OF OPEN SPACES. Since a bench or two or three chairs can be seen in practically every garden, one can assume that most of the people living in Greenbelt like to sit out in their yards at some time. Everyone interviewed said they

enjoyed it. On a sunny day in summer almost every tree in the central part of the town is used as shelter for a resting place. A number said they like to sit and gossip in the Town Center.

SPACES USED FOR PLAY. In the original part of the town, where yards are clearly defined by hedges, children of all ages use their yards for some kinds of play. Usually a playpen is provided for the baby, and several families have built a little fenced enclosure within the larger hedged area for youngsters just beginning to walk. A good many parents have put up swings, installed sandboxes and provided other attractions to encourage their children to play in their own yards. A few yards have trees well adapted for climbing. Shrubs in some make good hiding-places for traditional games.

In the Defense Homes sections, it is difficult to distinguish between play in their own yards and play in the neighbors' yards, but a good deal of play, especially by the small children up to say seven years, centers around the area close to their homes; this may be in green courts, in parking areas, in their own or neighbors' yards.

Children of all ages get together in small groups in each others' yards—some irritation was reported in connection with such gatherings, primarily from nearby families with no noisy children of their own.

Play areas within the superblocks are used, parents told us, only intermittently; the children tend to use them consistently only during the hours of supervision in the summer. However, a good many of them serve as centers for informal group play, as well as for activities involving the use of the equipment.

Shopping Center

The most important forward step made at Greenbelt toward the evolution of New Towns that fit the special problems of these times was in the creation of the shopping center and the related community center (Fig. 124). Here at last the modern market square was integrated into the plan for complete separation of walkers and motors. At Radburn, although educational and recreational places could be safely reached by foot from all homes, the commercial buildings were built on an island cut off by streaming auto traffic. At Hillside the stores were an unrelated piece-meal addition that turned its back on the residential community. Baldwin Hills Village shops later were also dissociated from the Village.

Here, at Greenbelt, even more than in the characteristic European medieval marketplaces, there is a definite exclusion of active flow of traffic from the areas for peaceful shopping. Around the quiet square are grouped the varied functions of one of the finest small town centers of these days. It is both thoroughly functional and architecturally of a simple, attractive unity.

The market place is set back from the main traffic way, Crescent Road, and is on a one-way service road, which leads to the end of, but not through, the shopping plaza. This is for pedestrians only; a place for leisurely marketing, for resting on the park benches and gossiping. There is direct access to the square for walkers by the underpass under Crescent Road. This ties into the main path system of the inner blocks.

At the further end of the plaza the ground falls abruptly to an old wood that shades a playground for young boys and girls. Beyond, past the swimming pool, is the recreation field for the older ones and their dads—for everyone. The broad view is but slightly hidden by the somewhat too massive statue that was left from the WPA days when we were all so hard up that even a sculptor could get a job in connection with public housing. The same sculptress did some excellent panels on the exterior of the school-community building.

The Co-op's splendid new food supermarket built in 1948 was fortunately prevented from cutting the view of open countryside because building costs necessitated cutting down the length of the structure. At its side, stairs lead down to the lower floor which is to house the bowling alleys, and a restaurant which will look out on broad views of open country. From here are convenient walks to the little ones' playground and to the Youth Center.

At the other end of the plaza, paths lead to the Elementary School-Community Building, to the Swimming Pool—the center of summer community life, and beyond it to the Braden Athletic Field for baseball, tennis, and other sports of the grown boys and their parents; still further through the woods and picnic grounds is Greenbelt Lake. This is a half-mile stroll from the market-place, a peaceful hike with no danger or disturbance from motor vehicles.

The automobiles of visitors to the shopping center are parked off the roads on areas to the light and left, well screened from the market square. These serve not only shoppers and visitors to the movies; they are also convenient to the Swimming Pool, to the Community School and its Library. At the same time they are close to the various municipal offices; those of the City Manager and his staff at the west end, and the Police-Fire-Department to the east; also that of the Community Manager, who represents the Federal Landlord, PHA, and that of the Greenbelt Consumer Services, Inc., the co-operative the organization that runs the stores and the moving-picture house. These offices are on the second floor at either side of the Square. The Bank and the Post Office complete the community facilities of the central group that forms the focal point for the nerve system of walks and roads that circulate through the whole town (Fig. 103).

The Neighborhood Unit

At the present time the neighborhood unit is generally accepted as a basis for the purposeful design of new communities. But the Neighborhood less consciously influenced the planning of the Greenbelt Towns than the Garden City or the Radburn Idea. Yet the three towns are among the best applications of the principles laid down by Clarence Perry, which we would have carried out at Radburn, had its growth not been stunted.

Each Greenbelt Town in the beginning was, in effect, a single neighborhood. The focus of each is a planned neighborhood center consisting of school, community buildings, shopping center, government and management offices, and principal recreation activities. They are each built around such a planned center. However, only in Greenbelt have we an opportunity to study the effect of growth and changing size on the neighborhood. Here we can get some idea of how many people form a neighborhood community for different activities of various age or interest groups, and how the size of neighborhood is affected not only by distance, topography, and means of getting to and from a center, but also by many special factors that can

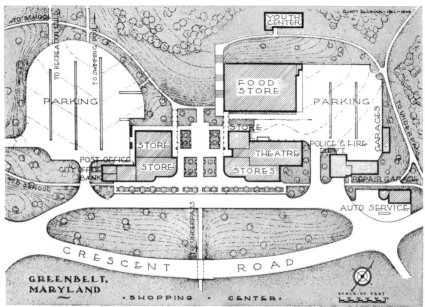

Fig. 124—Plan of the shopping center at Greenbelt showing the new food store and youth center.

Fig. 125—The movie theater and new supermarket in Greenbelt shopping center.

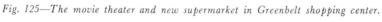

Fig. 126—*The shopping center, looking towards the swimming pool.*

not be broken down and classified quite so easily.

Greenbelt in the beginning had a population of 885 families, consisting of 2,831 people. All of the principal common activities were centered in a single well-planned and well-related group. Community center, elementary school, shopping center, town and management offices, police and fire station, automobile gas and service station, movie theater, swimming pool, recreation field: all these have a common related location that was central and was easily and safely reached by foot and by car.

The shopping center is the informal gathering place. Here is where one hears the news, discusses town politics, and here in the middle of the square or in the shade near the theater entrance, tickets are sold for town gatherings, dances, or lectures to support common town activities such as the Day Care Center. Townspeople of all ages come here. In the arcades at either side of the square, baby carriages are parked, and the youngsters, with little carts, waiting for their mothers, dart and play. Mothers with babies gossip in the sun; school children rush homeward; older boys and girls from the swimming pool are gaily bound for a five cent drink at the drug store (Figs. 125, 126).

The shopping center was so placed that all the residences built in 1936-37 by the Resettlement Administration were within one-half mile distance. The paths approaching this as well as the community-school building, all connected with the garden entrance of the houses, were as direct as the nature of the terrain and its park-like character permitted. They were protected from through auto traffic by underpasses (Figs. 103, 127, 128).

A neighborhood community is a group of people with common interests in which they actively participate. Greenbelt from the beginning was such a community. The children all went to the same school, with the exception of the few high school students and those who travelled to outside Catholic parochial institutions. At Greenbelt, school is an exciting place for the children, where they do things for the town as well as the school; in fact school is fun.

The elders gathered at the community building to attend the many and various social, cultural, or adult educational meetings. They came either in special groups to clubs or classes or as a community to the Auditorium-Gymnasium to attend lectures or basketball games, to the holiday festivals, or the country fair at which they exhibited the products of their allotment gardens in the autumn. The swimming pool and the athletic field and the movies were meeting-places for everyone. So were the stores. The fact that these stores were a co-operative undertaking was another bond of union. The fact that they were well run, and had an adequate supply and variety to fill daily needs at reasonable cost, added to their general popularity. But above all everyone bought at the Shopping Center because it was convenient, easily and safely reached and adjacent to the other facilities that drew the people of Greenbelt together.

The planning theorists differ vehemently not only in regard to the validity of the Neighborhood Unit but even as to its proper size. Let us see what really happened when the population of Greenbelt was increased from 885 to 1,885 families—and from 2,831 persons to a population of 7,000 and more.

THE SHOPPING CENTER. When the town was expanded, the shopping center increased its total sales from roughly $450,000 to over a million, but the sales per person decreased from $158.90 in 1941 to $143.10 in 1943. It is true that the purchases of the average family, which had increased in size, did rise from $508 in 1941 to $531 per year. But this was small in proportion to the increase in the average income of the new (Defense) families, which was not necessarily low, so that their purchasing power was greater than that of the earlier settlers. Apparently a larger part of the purchasing power was used elsewhere—possibly by the workers at Washington, or at some store on the way back. The maximum walking distance to the shopping center, which had been no more than a half-mile, was in the case of the more northern of the Defense homes almost a mile. This quite apparently had much to do with the fact that sales did not show a greater increase. But topography also affected the business of the center. The ground mounted up from the stores toward the north. Women objected to carrying heavy bundles or pushing carts filled with purchases and babies up the slope.

When the Defense Homes were built a site was

Fig. 127—Greenbelt shopping center is safe for pedestrians. Beyond the arcade automobiles are parked.

Fig. 128—The path from the shopping center to the swimming pool and the school beyond.

set aside about three-quarters of a mile from the main market center for a North End Shopping Center. But there were no funds available for these or other needed community facilities. Ultimately the Co-op set up a temporary grocery store, because of the demand of the more northern inhabitants to have at least these essentials nearby.

However, so as to bind the increased population to the old center, the Greenbelt Consumers Service Inc. has met the difficulties growing out of distance by:

1. *The Co-op Pantry* or travelling market—a store on wheels that makes the rounds of the town daily with a varied stock of groceries, fruits and other supplies, conveniently displayed for customers who walk through the truck. Refrigerators and deep-freezers carry a choice supply of meats and other cold or frozen foods. The driver also collects clothing for pressing or cleaning.

2. *The Bus Line,* established in 1945 by the Co-op, brings passengers from all parts of the town to the center. The bus-driver delivers prescriptions from the drug store.

3. The great *Food Super-Market,* two and a half times the size of the old food store, that was added to the shopping center in 1948, offers increased variety, service and attractions. The space vacated by the old food store made possible the expansion of the Variety Store into a so-called Junior Department Store.

4. Plans for the addition, when financing is available, of a ten-alley *Bowling Center.* (Bowling is one of the favorite sports of Greenbelt. There were 77 teams in the Town in 1949 which were forced to drive several miles to play.) Bowling is to be in the basement under the super-market, along with a bakery and restaurant. As a result of the sloping terrain the latter will be above ground, well-lighted, and have a delightful view toward the woods.

5. *A Nursery* for the children of parents who are shopping is also part of the co-operative's proposed program.

All this expansion promises to make Greenbelt's principal market-place more than a local affair. The exceptionally fine and commodious super-market along with the other facilities and attractions — of which the peaceful, harmonious architectural and natural setting is an important factor, should draw customers from a wider area, outside Greenbelt's boundaries. It is true that other large super-markets with other shops and amusements are appearing along the main highways to Washington. But they are of the obsolete strip type without any natural setting and—what is more important from the point of view of lasting success—with utterly inadequate space for parking automobiles. The Greenbelt shopping center was supplied with two conveniently placed parking lots in the beginning. These were adequate before the construction of the new super-market. Unfortunately, some of this area has been taken over by the new building. However, there is additional open ground adjacent that can be added to the parking grounds, and that this be done is essential to the success of the stores if it is to be more than a purely local or neighborhood marketplace.

Education

THE SCHOOL COMMUNITY BUILDING, built as part of the Resettlement Development, was centrally located within a half-mile distance of all houses, and close to the stores. It can also be reached directly by paths and underpasses protected from auto dangers. In the beginning the average family's size was only slightly over three as a result of the large percentage of small apartments. In 1939 there were only 385 children in the elementary grades, financed and run by the County. The Kindergarten, of 80 children, in the same building, is supported and its teachers are employed by the Town, but is under the supervision of the County.

In the School Community Building there are 12 classrooms as well as a music room, home-making room, arts and crafts workshop, health room, social room, and a large combined gymnasium-auditorium, and also the Town Library.

Without the high school children, 115 of them, the total of 465 did not crowd the schoolhouse. Up to the time the additional Defense Houses were built in 1941 the total number of children in the Elementary School remained much the same, although those in High School increased from 115 to 227. In 1943, after the new houses were constructed, there were 785 in the Elementary School,

175 in the kindergarten, and 283 in the High School.

No additional educational facilities were constructed with the 1,000 new houses in 1941, although a site was reserved opposite that for the North Shopping Center and about three-quarters of a mile from the old school. As a temporary measure classes were held, to the inconvenience of everybody, in residential buildings. It was not until 1946, after over three years of congestion and double sessions, that the North End Elementary School was opened with room for 500 children of the first to sixth grade, and for about 100 in the kindergarten. There is, in addition to the 12 classrooms, a multi-purpose assembly room.

The experience of Greenbelt's elementary schools' development seems to confirm the accepted neighborhood theory of one-half mile radius—at least for a community with houses at about seven or eight to the acre. The building of a new school was accepted as the practical thing to do when the town grew so that children would have to walk or be driven to the first school, a distance of three-quarters to one mile away. This in spite of the fact that ground space had been left so that the central building's size might be doubled.

In the Neighborhood Unit theory the high school building is generally considered the logical place for the district community center. But at Greenbelt the original central School Community Building has remained the unquestionable focus of community life. This was due to (1) its superior facilities for community purposes, (2) its more central location for Greenbelt people, (3) the fact that it is so closely related to the shopping and recreation-entertainment center and finally (4) habit on the part of the older inhabitants, and the fact that the later comers were absorbed into the established community life, whether they lived in the older section or the new north end portion of the town.

THE JUNIOR-SENIOR HIGH SCHOOL was placed near the western edge of the property, so that it might serve not only Greenbelt but also a surrounding area. It is about a mile and a half from the Community School. The High School building, in strong contrast to the older educational center, lacks any attraction architecturally or in regard to choice and treatment of site. The appropriation for the building was apparently cut to the bone—the architects had no opportunity to supply more than bare necessities. This is true both of the earlier structure, built in 1937, and the addition by the Federal Works Agency when they built the Defense Houses. There is accommodation for about 600 pupils in the six high school grades.

Prince George's County has for years been considering the erection of a large and adequately equipped senior high school that would care for a much greater area, and would probably be located near the University. Lack of funds, or rather increasing educational demands from various parts of the county, has led to the continuous postponement of this much needed improvement. Meanwhile, the Junior and Senior branches of the Greenbelt High School are forced to get along without adequate staff or modern equipment, which can only be afforded in a large institution. For a high school such facilities are naturally of far more importance than the distance that grown boys and girls must travel. This would indicate the advantage of solving education at high school level on a broad regional basis.

THE UNIVERSITY OF MARYLAND is within four miles of Greenbelt on the road to Washington. It can easily be reached by bus from the shopping center and by street-car. This makes higher education more convenient than it is in most parts of our larger cities. Residents of the State pay a very low tuition rate and veterans during the last few years received financial assistance under the G.I. Bill of Rights. Three hundred and twenty-five of the young people from Greenbelt were enrolled as regular students last year. In addition many of the townspeople take advantage of the University Extension Courses, not only cultural but practical. For instance, emergency or 'volunteer' fire fighters are obliged by the Protection Department of Greenbelt to take courses in fire protection at the University.

Community Activities

The school and the activities of the community are closely bound together at Greenbelt. It is not merely that the same building in the main center is used by all ages, all day and evening, and for all kinds of activity from dance to religion, from studying science or art to exhibiting one's own farming products in a country fair. There is no hard line between the use of the community-school as part of the regular County educational system and its service as town gathering place. The spirit of the town influences the school and the school plays an important part in forming that spirit.

The enthusiastic participation of parents in the school's work reflects the informal atmosphere of the town. The teachers and the building are as familiar to the parents as to the children, and so also is the program of the schools. The school program is difficult to label: no fashion of education is held up as a model of perfection, but rather a few basic purposes are kept in mind. At the Greenbelt schools the important thing is living—living successfully with others, rather than merely the individual himself—and the program grows out of this.

The children obviously love to go to school. They arrive on time and are happy while there. There is a contagious atmosphere, in the classrooms and out, of eagerness to learn and do things. Truancy is practically unheard of. The schools have enjoyed continuity of leadership, and their philosophy of education has had wide-spread influence on education in the surrounding community, and even throughout the county. The county is taking a leading position in the State in developing a more modern approach to education. The former principal of the school, Mrs. Reed, who made good use of the superior equipment of the Central School to influence the whole life of the community, is now supervisor of Prince George's County schools. As a result the other schools of the county are catching up to the higher standards of Greenbelt.

Community activities have not decentralized or started branches. This may be due to the fact that distance from the newly developed area is not too great, or that easy transportation is available by the Co-op bus which connects the whole town with the old center. It may also be because of the superior facilities of the Community-School Building which was planned and is operated to act as a Community Center. The North End School was not, and is not arranged or equipped to serve in this way. Only a very few special local activities

are held in its assembly rooms. The Boy and Girl Scouts meet there, and the Parents-Teachers group. The Community-School is an outstanding demonstration of what can be done through the multiple use of community facilities, and the cooperation of various agencies and different levels of government.

The Community Building is owned and operated by the Federal Public Housing Authority. The U.S. Government through FPHA merely loans the use of the building to Prince George's County as an elementary school. The County's Board of Education operates the school, furnishes textbooks and other supplies, and pays the teachers. Until 1949, the program of social activities was arranged through the office of the FPHA, but it now comes under the office of the City Manager. The town operates a public library and several kindergartens in the building. It also houses the town recreation department, which provides the physical education instruction for the elementary schools as part of the town recreation program. The Town Public Safety Officer promotes the program for safety, assisted by 40 school boys. Janitorial services, heat, water, light and maintenance of the building have been supplied under the direction of the FPHA Community Manager. They have been charged in part to the Town and in part to the Board of Education. By this means it has been possible to continue effectively the use of the building for the varied purposes for which it was designed.

In the North End Elementary School, where janitorial services and utilities are charged to the Board of Education only, it would be much more difficult to carry on a broad community program. School janitors are proverbially unco-operative, and County School Boards have inflexible rules that apply to all schools.

Adult Education is officially under the County School Board, which supplies teachers and pays most expenses. The program varies from year to year and includes classes in languages, arts and crafts, sewing, interior decorating, typing and shorthand, commercial law, public speaking, consumer education, and lectures and discussions on matters of general interest.

Facilities included in the original school that serve the general community, in addition to the classrooms and gym-auditorium, are the studios for arts and crafts, a music room, a social room—used also as a cafeteria—and the library. The social room is equipped with pingpong tables, radio-phonograph and games donated by the Town Council. The library although operated by the Town is used freely by the school.

RELIGION. For 11 years people have used the auditorium-gymnasium, social room and class-rooms of the Center School for religious services, their church organizations joining with all the othei groups in the struggle for dates on the busy calendar.

On Sunday morning the large hall has been given over to the religious services of the Com-munity Church, which represents in its congrega-tion 14 Protestant denominations. Lutherans and the Church of Jesus Christ of the Latter Day Saints hold their services in other rooms of the building. The Hebrews take over on Friday evening. Mass is celebrated for Catholics in the moving-picture theater.

In the fall of 1946 all church congregations joined in an effort to find out what the religious situation actually was in the Town so that they might proceed to provide appropriate facilities. A very careful survey gave the basis of facts needed for planning. Building campaigns were started. The Town Council approved the sites selected. Land has been purchased by three different churches. The construction of the Protestant Community Church is under way and the Catholic Church will probably soon be built.

The sites chosen seem attractive. They are, how-ever, widely distributed and have little relation, that I can see, to the community center or the general plan. In these days when so many people go to church by automobile, it would seem wise to locate a church, if possible, near enough to park-ing areas used on weekdays to serve the other build-ings, or else to group two or more churches close enough togther to use common auto parking.

The experience of the Greenbelt Towns is valu-able not only in showing the uses of multi-purpose educational-cultural buildings. It also indicates that, although some rooms serve adults as well as children, it is not always practical to use the same spaces and equipment for quite dissimilar purposes The County Colleges of Cambridgeshire, England,

have pointed the way to a fuller solution. Here under the brilliant leadership of the Educational Director, Henry Morris, buildings have been func-tionally designed for use not only as secondary schools, but also as community centers for all ages and varied groups; farmers as well as villagers and townspeople. The classrooms, studios, and labora-tories serve day and night for young or old, and so in various ways does the auditorium-theater-gymnasium. But in addition there are special club and meeting rooms that were specially designed for community gatherings rather than teaching. The billiards and games room, and lounges, for instance, are available to the oldsters at all hours.

The desire of groups to have a place of their own is indicated at Greenbelt by various organizations. The American Legion has its own building, an old farmhouse which has been rebuilt for its many and varied activities. The veterans even use the allotment gardens near the Legion's house, although there are others nearer their own homes. The Youth Center is provided in a separate building, acquired through the efforts of Greenbelt people young and old. It consists of a large social room, kitchen and snack bar, and is a general head-quarters for young peoples' activities.

GROUP CARE FOR SMALL CHILDREN. Although not housed in a school building, the nursery schools are both near the main community center. A co-operative nursery school was opened very early in Greenbelt's history. The federal government gave the use of a basement room in one of the apartment houses and some equipment. The parents engaged a director and the mothers shared responsibility for running the school, serving as assistants to the director. The school is still open.

Child care on a much larger scale was undertaken during the war when many Greenbelt mothers were employed. Under a special bill (The Lanham Act) the federal government provided funds to assist local communities in the care of children so that mothers might be released for war industry. Green-belt received such assistance, and a large child care center was operated.

FPHA provided a whole building consisting of 11 bachelor apartments and an enclosed play-ground for the exclusive use of the center. They also provided maintenance, light, and the original

Fig. 129—Children leaving the community-
school building.

Fig. 130—Play starts in the sandbox.

160

GREENBELT

equipment. Parents of children cared for at the center paid $3.00 per week for all the services rendered.

Since the Lanham Act funds were withdrawn in 1946, a number of Greenbelt mothers have continued to keep the center in operation on a smaller scale. The management has continued to co-operate in this.

OUTDOOR RECREATION at Greenbelt is the one activity in which the community unit is not limited to the town as a whole or to the neighborhood. For play in the open the unit of population and area is broken down to a variety of sizes to fit the needs and above all the traveling capacity of different ages. Greenbelt is particularly well supplied with play spaces convenient to the needs of everyone from babyhood to old age (Figs. 103 and 105). For the infant there is the private yard within hearing and sight of the mother. For the smaller children there are the enclosed equipped playspaces and sand-boxes and climbing apparatus. These are generally located so as to serve a number of groups of houses, in the superblock center or in the green beyond the groups on the outer edge of the town. They are supervised by high school girls during the summer months. For children of school age playgrounds with apparatus are limited to five, more widely spaced. They are in open areas not designated for any particular type of play but used for various kinds of sport, and mainly for ball games on a diminutive scale by boys under teen age. For big games of baseball or football the older boys use Braden Field, as do their fathers. Here the town as a whole gathers as audience. Close by are the various outdoor facilities, forming part of the town center, in which all ages participate. At one end is the 25-acre lake, at the other the outdoor swimming pool—which forms the principal summertime community center. The swimming pool is not only a great success from the point of view of health and fun; it actually pays its own way (Fig. 132).

Cooperation and the Shopping Centers

GREENBELT CONSUMER SERVICES INC. has had a greater influence in molding the life of Greenbelt and its people than anything but the federal landlord, PHA, and the American democratic process as exemplified by their City Council and Town or City Manager.

When the town and the shopping center were ready in 1937, the Consumer Distribution Corporation,[31] a national organization, at first operated the stores, until the people of Greenbelt could determine whether they wanted to own their own business co-operatively. The 1946 Annual Report of Greenbelt Consumer Services, Inc., gives their decision. 'By the end of 1939 about 500 Greenbelt citizens had set aside $4,000 as initial payment for purchasing the local enterprises. On January 9, 1940, Greenbelt took over the operation of the stores through their own newly organized co-operative, Greenbelt Consumer Services, Inc. In spite of the war, every year has been a successful one for the Co-operative.'

Two-thirds of the Greenbelt families now hold stock; a number of them have taken the limit of $1,000 per person. Those who do not hold stock are Greenbelt people (a) who feel that residence in Greenbelt is a very temporary arrangement with them and buying stocks suggests something too permanent or (b) who feel that Co-ops interfere with free enterprise and therefore do not wish to co-operate.

There are some who object to the monopoly of commercial facilities and to the dominant leadership of the Consumer Services. This has been an important issue not only at many Council meetings but at hard-fought elections. From these it is apparent that the majority of the people of Greenbelt are in favor of the Co-operative and of its very able general manager, Samuel F. Ashelman, Jr.

A new lease was entered into in 1946 by the Greenbelt Consumer Services, Inc. for the facilities it had been using, that is, the food store, variety store, general merchandise, drug store, beauty shop, barber shop, movie theater, filling station, valet shop, tobacco and news stand. The lease stipulates that until November 1956, the federal government will not permit its property within a one-half mile radius of the shopping center to be used for any of the purposes outlined above. In addition, the Greenbelt Consumer Services, Inc. had a long term lease on about 40,000 square feet of vacant area in the present commercial center upon which it has constructed the supermarket.

Fig. 131—There are many equipped play spaces for younger children in Greenbelt's inner blocks.

Fig. 132—In summer the swimming pool is the real social center of Greenbelt.

Therefore the first neighborhood will have a unified and a restricted shopping center until the end of 1956, no matter what may be the terms of sale of the residential buildings. Whether new stores built outside the half-mile limit will be able to compete with the well-entrenched and efficient Consumer Services is to be seen.

The central shopping center was planned on the basis of the requirements set up by the Special Report of 1935 to the Resettlement Administration.[32] This followed the method of determining commercial needs which had been developed in 'Store Buildings and Neighborhood Shopping Centers' by Cathrine Bauer and me in 1934.[33]

The fact that the principles and requirements formulated in the report to Mr. Lansill were followed in building and operating the Shopping Center with results very similar to those we predicted has convinced me that:

1. Shopping centers can be located and laid out to meet definite factual requirements in an orderly or attractive manner with every prospect— if not assurance—of financial success.

2. Commercial development, if left to the land speculators or individual shopkeepers, has a poor gambler's chance of success, financial or otherwise.

3. Limiting the number of and size of stores to the definite requirements best serves the interest of all concerned: the landlord, the shopkeepers, the buying public and finally the municipality.

4. The municipality can find one of its surest sources of income (either in taxes or rent) if development is properly limited, located and planned.

The basic principles followed in the planning of the commercial area of the three towns and particularly of Greenbelt are so concisely and succinctly stated in the Resettlement Report that I am going to copy it here:

SHOPPING CENTERS

The shopping centers of new towns built by the Suburban Resettlment Administration should be designed to give the inhabitants low prices, good quality, and convenient facilities, and at the same time, bring in the maximum possible revenue to the town.

For purposes of this preliminary study, we have assumed:

1. An average family income of $1,250 and an average family of four persons.
2. Rental of stores to commercial companies. (We are able to secure more definite information in regard to incomes and rentals paid by chain stores.) If the stores should be efficiently operated as co-operatives, lower living costs might be possible. The comparative advantage of such a step should be given further study.

The problem of providing adequate store facilities is affected by:

1. The degree to which the town will be used as a shopping center of the area.
2. The proportion of family expenditures made locally.
3. The family incomes.

1. *The town as a shopping center.*
It is unlikely that much outside business will be drawn to the new towns, since they will be off the main highways and the existing nearby industrial towns have established shopping centers.

2. *The proportion of family expenditures made locally.*
This is affected by the income group, the family size and family composition. Higher income groups are inclined to go to larger shopping centers for clothing, house furnishings, and certain other items which the low-income families must do without. The needs of small children will be met locally, whereas the needs of grown children are met better in the large center, where it is possible to shop for style and quality.

3. *The family income.*
Analysis of expenditure for various income groups, when related to local family expenditure and annual sales of different types of stores, gives us a fairly definite indication of the number and types of stores that might be supported.

The accompanying tables indicate—

1. Estimated local expenditures.
2. The types of stores that could be supported.
3. The income that could be derived from stores in towns of 3,000, 4,000, 6,000 and 7,000 population.

We are estimating rentals at 3 per cent of gross sales. These we believe are conservative as the number of stores will be restricted so as to increase as far as possible the gross sales of each store.

It is apparent that in towns of 1,000 families having incomes of $1,250, the estimated expenditure will provide adequately for food stores. One variety store which carries apparel and all sorts of household needs could exist on the expenditures for such items. There does not seem to be sufficient expenditure to maintain a typical chain drug store. However, independent stores are often operated on smaller margin and a drug store carrying on other types of business might be operated successfully.

Recreation needs outside of those supplied as part of the community facilities should be limited to a small movie house. A careful study should be made in regard to the possibility of successful operation in a small community and of the probability of increasing the patronage from outside of the town.

A combined filling station and auto accessory and repair shop could operate within the town independently of transient trade.

Expenditures for fuel would not maintain a commercial coal company. This could be bought through outside dealers or by setting up a co-operative.

A laundry service would probably be from a nearby town, although an agent might have space in the shopping center.

4. *General Policy in regard to stores.*

Store properties will be owned by the town and income from stores will be used to decrease dwelling rentals. The stores must therefore be efficient units, prices must be low and service at least as good as in neighboring communities. This will guarantee a large proportion of residents' expenditures to the local shopping center.

5. *Planning Requirements.*

One shopping center is sufficient for a 4,000 population town. This center ought to be within one-half mile of all dwellings. In larger towns of 6,000 or 7,000 population, there should either be two separate complete centers, or better still, one major center and several neighborhood food stores. The number of centers may be affected by topographical conditions.

6. *Location of shopping center.*

Locations are affected by the contours and the relation to the residence areas and the main approaches to the town—it is desirable that residents pass the center on the way in or out of the town. However, it is even more important that shopping centers be placed within easy and safe walking distance of all dwellings. As the approach usually should be through the park areas, access should be possible from park walks, without crossing vehicular roads. Adequate parking space for cars should also be provided.

7. *Store Areas and Layout.*

The layout and size of the stores is affected by the method of merchandising. The following estimates of space requirements for towns of 3,000—4,000 population are based on the experience of certain chain stores:

Store Areas.

Grocery and Meat (2 or 3 stores)	3,000-3,500 sq. ft.
Variety	6,000 sq. ft.
Drug	2,500 sq. ft.
Movie House	500-600 seats
Gas station and minor repairs	

So as to assist in determining the amount that low-income families would spend for various items the Bureau of Home Economics of the U.S. Department of Agriculture set up tentative budgets for families of four persons in annual income groups of $900, $1,250 and $1,600.

Item	Level A $900 yearly income	Level B $1,250 yearly income	Level C $1,600 yearly income
Food	400-475	475-520	560
Clothing	100-125	135-165	165-200
Housing	180	280	330
House operation (fuel, light, household supplies)	70-80	90-115	125-155
Furnishings and equipment (replacements)	20-35	35-55	35-75
Transportation	35-40	40-50	45-60
Recreation and education	20-30	35-60	55-75
Personal	10-25	20-30	30-45
Medical care	25-45	30-65	45-100
Community welfare (church, gifts, charity)	0-15	10-35	25-75
Savings	0-10	50-100	75-125
Total	860-1,060	1,200-1,475	1,490-1,800

TENTATIVE BUDGETS FOR A YEAR FOR FAMILIES OF FOUR PERSONS IN A SUBURBAN RESETTLEMENT COMMUNITY NOTE.—These budgets are based upon prevalent ways of spending as shown by studies of family expenditures. For food, adequacy as measured by nutritional standards is used as a basis for the suggested budget. For the remaining items of the budget, adequacy can be determined only by studies of the consumption habits and needs of families in each of the localities. These budgets suggest what may be the broad spending patterns of a group of families at each of the three income levels: they are not presented as examples of desirable spending plans for all families. A family budget, to be suited to a specific family, must be planned to meet its needs and desires under existing conditions. Each budget is set up with a range in expenditures for most items. Since the low total is in each case somewhat less than the suggested income level, there can be a little leeway in spending on some items. Obviously, a family cannot spend the top figure for many items without spending less than the bottom figure for others, if it is to keep within its income.

Family includes: husband, wife, boy aged 10, girl aged 8.

Suggestions for expenditure are based upon 1935 price levels.

GREENBELT

On the basis of this study we then estimated local store family expenditures.

ESTIMATED LOCAL STORE FAMILY EXPENDITURES

Based on $1,250 income budget for a family of 4 persons
NOTE on Transportation Expenditures. Amounts provided are only adequate where 5 cent fare transportation is available. The $45 transportation allowance plus the $50 provided for savings will be necessary to meet the extra costs of transportation in Suburban Resettlement Towns. Local conditions will have to be studied carefully in relation to this item. Further data on automobile expenditures is being prepared.
NOTE on Motion Picture Expenditures. Most of the recreation item will probably be spent in the local movie house. However this item is not included in the estimate of store expenditures as our shopping facilities are not affected by it. A town of 4,000 population can support a 500-600 seat movie house.

Then using the experience of chain stores as basis of the average sales required for a successful store in various categories we estimated the number of stores that might be supported by 1,000 families of four, with $1,250 incomes.

ESTIMATED ANNUAL STORE EXPENDITURES BY TYPES OF STORE
NUMBER OF STORES SUPPORTED BY 1,000 FAMILIES

Based on $1,250 income budget for a family of 4 persons
NOTE.—As the town grows and/or as higher income groups are accommodated, there will be need for other types as well as more stores. These would include service stores, e.g , tailor, laundry and cleaner, barber and beauty shop and, also such retail stores as shoe, millinery, electrical supply, hardware.

ESTIMATED LOCAL STORE FAMILY EXPENDITURES

Item		Total Annual Expenditure	Local Store Expenditure	Per Capita Expenditure
Food		$475-520	$475	$118.75
Clothing		145	50	12.50
House Operation		90	17	4.25
Coal	$53			
Oil	8			
Electricity	12			
Household Supplies	8			
Ice	9			
Furnishings and Equipment		35-55	45	11.25
Recreation and Education		35-60	10 (not inc movies)	2.50
School supplies	5			
Newspapers, etc.	8-10			
Recreation (movies, trips, children's toys)	22-45			
Personal		22 50	11	2.75
Tobacco, soft drinks, etc.	10			
Barber shop, toilet needs	12.50			
Medical Care		30-65	10	2.50
First aid supplies, medicines	15			
Services	15-35			
			$618	$154.50

ESTIMATED ANNUAL STORE EXPENDITURES BY TYPES OF STORE

Store	Item	Per Family	Per 1,000 Families	Average Sales per Chain Store 1921-1930 (Varies irregularly with size of Chain)	Approximate Number of Stores
Grocery and Meat	Food Household sup.	$475 8	$483	$483,000	$45,000-$170,000	3 large stores
Variety Dry Goods & Apparel	Clothing Furnishings and Equipment Barbering Personal Care School Supplies	50 40 4 1 5	100	100,000	50,000-250,000 30,000-150,000	1 combination
Drug	Medical care Books, newspapers, etc. Household appliances Tobacco Soft Drinks	10 5 5 3 3	26	26,000	60,000-150,000	A small independent drug store could operate
Filling Stations Accessories Repairs	Automobile		25	25,000		Would depend on number using autos for transportation to work.
Coal, oil	Fuel Ice	40 9	49	49,000		Would depend on policy.
Movie, etc.	Recreation		20	20,000		Further study required to determine if town can support a small theater.

GREENBELT

Viewed from the angle of the community and its people I was particularly interested to see how the increase in size of purchasing public would affect the returns to the town or to the individual purchasers and citizens. This return might be in—

1. *taxes* under normal form of tenancy
2. *rent* to the municipality or other public agent such as the PHA
3. *dividends* if co-operative stores were set up
4. a combination of these

ESTIMATED STORE INCOME
assuming $1,250 median income group
and local expenditures at $155, per capita
and local food expenditures at $118, per capita

Population	3,000	4,000	6,000	7,000
Gross annual income of stores at $155 per person	$465,000	$620,000	$930,000	$1,085,000
Rentals at 3% of gross income (all stores)	13,950	18,600	27,900	32,550
Maintenance cost of all stores	2,000	2,000	2,000	2,000
Net income from all stores	11,950	16,600	25,900	30,550
Gross annual income of food stores at $118 per person	354,000	472,000	708,000	826,000
Rentals of food stores at 2.5% of gross income	8,850	11,800	17,700	20,650
Maintenance cost of food stores	1,200	1,200	1,200	1,200
Net income from food stores	7,650	10,600	16,500	19,450
Per capita net income from all stores	4	4.15	4.30	4.35

The indication of the probable effect of size on the return to community or individual purchases is in the last line, the per capita net income from stores. Our estimates showed an increase from $4 per year for 3,000 population to $4.35 for the 7,000 population.

Let us compare what actually happened at Greenbelt, Maryland, with these generalized estimates. The store income at Greenbelt is shown below. In 1941 the population was approximately 3,000; and in 1943 and 1946 about 7,000.

INCOMES for the 1935 estimate were based on $1,250 median per family. Actually the incomes have always been higher than this; even in the beginning the average was between $1,800 and $2,000; and the limit of incomes was set at $2,100. By July 1947 the average in the Resettlement section had risen to over $3,674, with 35 per cent over $4,000. No records have been taken of the incomes of the Defense Homes occupants. There was no income limit. They were housed not because of their need, but the national need. However, their median income was somewhat higher than that of the earlier inhabitants. Therefore the average spending power of the 7,000 population town was greater than that of the 3,000. The decreased value of the dollar since this study was made must naturally be considered.

SIZE OF FAMILIES was estimated at four (based on husband, wife, and children of eight and ten years). The average was much smaller in the beginning—3.2 increasing to 3.7 when the Defense Homes were built.

SIZE OF STORES proposed in the report for 3,000-4,000 population was 11,500 to 12,000 square feet. Slightly over 13,000 square feet was built. (This does not include office space.)

The supermarket later added 10,000 square feet of main floor selling space and the equivalent in semi-basement to the main center.

The table Greenbelt Store Incomes should be compared with estimated Store Income (see page 216). The estimate was made in 1935. The records were made in 1941, with 3,000 population, in 1943, soon after the increase of the town to a population of 7,000, and then in 1946 before the new store was built, with population only slightly increased. The gross income of stores for the 3,000 town was estimated at $465,000 (page 216). In 1941 it was $499,867.91. For the 7,000 population the estimate was $1,085,000. In 1943 it came to $1,001,668.94.

RENTALS which we estimated conservatively at 3 per cent of gross income, were 4.2 per cent in

GREENBELT STORE SALES AND RENTALS

Year		Gross	Per-centage	Per Family	Per Person
1941	SALES	$449,867.91	100	$508.35	$158.90
	RENTS	19,078.13	4.2	21.55	6.74
1943	SALES	1,001,668.94	100	531.34	143.10
	RENTS	35,320.85	3.5	18.74	5.10
1946	SALES	1,414,741.00	100	755.30	202.11
	RENTS	48,215.00	3.4	25.58	6.89

STORE AREAS

Type of Store	Existing Footage	Proposed in Report
Food	4,200 sq. ft.	3,000-3,500 sq. ft.
Drug	2,160 sq. ft.	2,500 sq. ft.
Variety	3,600 sq. ft.	6,000 sq. ft.
Stationery and Magazine	500 sq. ft.	
Beauty Shop	670 sq. ft.	
Barber Shop	670 sq. ft.	
General Merchandise and Valet	1,350 sq. ft.	
TOTAL OF STORES	13,150 sq. ft.	11,500 to 12,000 sq. ft.
Office Space of Greenbelt Co-operative	2,600 sq. ft.	
Movie	590 seats	500-600 seats
Gas Station		

GREENBELT STORE INCOMES			
Date	1941	1943	1946
Population	3,000	7,000	7,000-plus
Gross Income from Sales	$449,867.91	$1,001,668.94	$1,414,741.00
Rents	19,078.13	35,320.85	48,215.00
Maintenance Cost	5,232.56	6,731.00	9,554.00
Taxes	4,000.00	6,492.00	7,605.00
Net Gain	9,845.57	22,097.85	31,056.00
% Rent/Income	4.2%	3.5%	3.4%
PER FAMILY STORE INCOME			
Sales	$508.35	$531.34	$755.30
Rents	21.55	18.74	25.58
Maintenance	5.91	3.57	5.07
Taxes	4.52	3.44	4.03
Net Gain	11.12	11.73	16.48
STORE INCOME PER CAPITA			
Sales	$158.90	$143.10	$202.11
Rents	6.74	5.10	6.89
Maintenance	1.85	.96	1.36
Taxes	1.41	.93	1.08
Net Gain	3.48	3.15	4.45

The gross income from sales for 1949 was about $2,200,000. It is apparent that outside business is being attracted, partly by the new supermarket, partly by better parking and shopping conditions, and partly by outside interest in the cooperative method.

1941 and, when the town grew to 7,000 population, 3.4 to 3.5 per cent. The rentals in dollars were higher than the estimate in the 3,000 person town ($19,000 as compared with $13,950), and were very close to the estimate in the larger town ($35,000 instead of $32,000).

MAINTENANCE COSTS were difficult to figure. The PHA (or its predecessors of varied other initials) as representative of the landlord, the U.S.A., kept accounts of the whole first development as a single unit. The maintenance costs for the stores as well as for the community schools, including heating, etc., were not allocated to residential, commercial, or educational buildings in the accounts. Instead they were taken as a whole, and then distributed as part of the expenses of the houses. The Community Manager has unscrambled these accounts for me with the greatest possible accuracy. His estimates, on which we have based our maintenance figures are, I believe, close enough to serve our purposes. They double or more than double our estimated figures.

NET INCOME in our estimate was intended to cover the return to the community. We had hoped that the store buildings would ultimately be owned by the town, and that the returns from them could be used to decrease rentals, or in a sense be a dividend to the people. In such a procedure there would be no real need to differentiate between taxes or rent to the community.

What we refer to in the estimated incomes as *per capita* net income from all stores is the proportion per person of the difference between rental and maintenance. In the figures of what actually happened the net-gain equals rents minus maintenance and taxes. This actually did not go directly to the community, but it served to decrease the cost per unit of housing expenses. So I have called it net gain per family or *per capita*. This net income or gain *per capita* was estimated as $4.00 for 3,000 population and $4.35 for 7,000. In 1941 it was approximately $3.48, and in 1943 it was $3.15 when the population was 7,000. In 1946 it was $4.45.

Government

The fact that the federal government has been the owner of Greenbelt and the landlord of practically all its citizens might give the impression that it is a 'freak' town. On the contrary, the citizens take at least as active a part in determining civic policies as in most small American municipalities. Their local government, the Town (now the City) Council is democratically elected. Administration is under a City Manager directly responsible to it and the Mayor. The only difference between it and other Maryland municipalities with managers is that all voters have been tenants of the single owner of all taxable property, the U.S.A.

Although there has been no serious difficulty so far, there have been indications from time to time of some sense of irresponsibility on the part of the local governing body. This is because the Federal Government foots the bill for all new installations and services through its payments in lieu of taxes. On the other hand the Council, on the advice of the Town Manager, determines the budget and expenditures. In spite of this I think that, as a whole, in budgeting and operation great care has been taken to give as complete service as economically possible. The good record has been due in large part to the technical efficiency and the dedication to public service of the town managers.

Greenbelt has been integrated into the pattern of Prince George's County and Maryland State governmental procedure in a manner similar to to other municipalities. Such was the intention of the Resettlement Administration as stated in its early memorandum of objectives:

'A municipal government to be set up, in character with such governments now existing or possible in that region; co-ordination to be established, in relation to the local and state governments, so that there may be provided those public services of educational and other character which the community will require; and finally, to accomplish these purposes in such a way that the community may be a taxpaying participant in the region, that extravagant outlays from the individual family income will not be a necessity, and that the rents will be suitable to families of modest income.'

So as to assist the Resettlement Administration in carrying out this statement of objective, and particularly the latter part of it, I made the study of operation-maintenance costs for the purpose of:—

1. Setting up minimum desirable standards of housing and community equipment.

2. Estimating the costs of operating and maintaining the facilities and services required.

3. Measuring these costs of operation-maintenance against the ability to pay of families at various income levels.

In regard to its scope and limitations the report said:[34]

'For the purpose of this study a median family income of $1,250, an average family of four (consisting of two adults, one child of 10, one child of eight), and occupancy at one person per room were assumed.

'The study deals only with operation-maintenance costs of government and housing. These costs are basic and must be met by the inhabitants. Additional amounts to be paid as amortization and as interest on capital invested are matters of policy to be determined by the administration. The study differs from statements of operating costs in existing communities in that it does not include the factors of payment on capital outlays or debt service.

'The study is organized in such a way as to show the relative effect of change of policy or of cost of any single factor such as education, type of house, grouping of houses, manner of disposing of waste, income group to be housed, portion of income that can be afforded for rent, distance and cost of transportation, etc.

'Certain matters that are self-evident from the studies are:

1. Education is the largest single factor in operation-maintenance cost. However, it is most subject to probable economies or reduction, and appears to be the pivotal point on which Suburban Resettlement communities will reach closer to or away from low income groups. The actual cost per pupil will vary in each project with:

(a) The standard of education in each state on which state assistance is based.

(b) Extent to which the program of education in each community exceeds the minimum standard.

(c) Extent of state aid.

'The transportation factor will be a most important item of cost in the family budget in Suburban Resettlement communities. A base figure of 10 cents per trip has been figured in these studies, which brings the total family expenditure for transportation at the $1,250 income level to double the customary amount. This cost should be considered an integral part of the rent, and no rents are comparable unless weighted with transportation costs.

'Unless radical savings can be made in the costs of education or transportation, the $1,250 income group can pay a rental equal only to the cost of operation-maintenance in towns of 4,000 population and over. For families below this level operation-maintenance costs exceed the ability to pay except at the expense of minimum requirements for food, clothing, etc.'

It was apparent at an early stage of the investigation that the size of the population greatly affected the costs of both housing and governmental operation. So we made a comparison of cost of operation-maintenance of well-organized municipalities of various sizes run by town managers in a businesslike way. We restricted our studies to communities of 3,000 to 7,000 population, as this was to be the size limits of these New Towns, at least in the first stage of construction. Most statistical data on this subject was based on generalities. There were too many variations to form scientific or factual conclusions. Costs of government in existing towns were too often affected by:

1. Debt.

2. Antiquated laws and customs.

3. Obsolete machinery and poor organization.

4. Low standards or limited services.

5. Motivations other than service, such as politics.

We proposed to, and in fact did, set up statistics relating to municipalities with as high as possible a standard of service, having:

No debt.

Town management form of government.

New equipment, and no old restrictions.

The budget of government cost was laid out as far as possible on the basis of what was to be done by each department or division, what employees and materials would be required, and how much the annual cost of these would be. In a few instances where we had had parallel experience (in parks at Radburn, for instance) I based probable cost on comparison with these. But in most cases

GREENBELT

we set up the work to be done just as one might in budgeting for a factory or, and this came closer to my own experience, for the operation-management of a housing development. This required judgment as to what services should be given and how carried out. I fortunately had the advice of one of our most expert small town government authorities, Major John O. Walker, who was afterward in charge of operating the Greenbelt Towns. We both hoped for a broadening of the local government expenditure in that department than was or is customary in small towns. Public health services have improved in the last decade in America but mainly at the expense of federal or state agencies.

The cost of the function of government that we found most difficult to predict was the most expensive of all, that is, education. The quality and therefore the expenditure for schooling differ greatly in various parts of the country. Greenbelt, Maryland, pays much less per child than do the other two Greenbelt Towns, which are in northern states with higher standards. The administrative and fiscal set-up for public education differs in various parts of the country. The functions of state, county, school district and local authority vary as do the portion of the costs paid by each of these, and the method of collecting and distributing monies for that purpose. For the time being in the comparative cost of government of the three towns, I have separated the costs of education from the other municipal expenditures, so that I may have an opportunity to analyze separately these later costs and services.

The estimated local government and community services' costs exclusive of education showed a continuous decrease in unit cost as the size of population increased from 3,000 to 7,000 persons(from $27.57 to $17.22). The actual figures, although they differed in detail, as was to be expected, show the tendencies we predicted. The cost of governing Greenbelt (exclusive of education), with a population of 2,831, was $23.61 per person in 1941. With a population of 7,000, in 1943, the cost had dropped to $14.57 per person.

The proportion of decline in operation-maintenance costs between the larger and smaller-sized town is somewhat less when taken on the basis of family rather than individual unit. This was because the size of family, which in 1941, was 3.2, due to the large percentage of small apartment units, had grown in 1943 to 3.7, whereas in our theoretical set-up we presumed an average family of four persons. These differences have only very slight effect on the relation; so the total cost per family of serving the larger and smaller communities with protection, public works, recreation, and the other typical governmental services, which we had estimated at $110.34 for the town of 3,000 population (with 750 families), and $68.84 for the 7,000 persons (or 1,750 families), was in Greenbelt in 1941 (with 885 families), $75.35, and in 1943 (with 1,885 families), $54.08. In short the trend downward followed much the direction we had indicated.

How long would that tendency continue as a town increases in size? We know that beyond a certain expansion, unit cost of operating municipalities increases. But where and why? Over-expansion, increased complication, greater amount of expenditure for 'administration' in place of 'doing,' changing degree of participation by the public— all of these and other factors have their influence. To take just one example. Small American towns such as the three Greenbelt Towns have volunteer firemen. When a municipality reaches a size where paid firemen replace the volunteers, the unit cost of administration goes up.

Astoundingly little factual investigation of the effect of size of governmental units on cost of operation has been made. Further research of this type is urgently required in determining policy and a plan for New Towns. This should serve as an important factor in deciding what is the desirable size.

The comparative cost of local government and community activities for communities of approximately 3,000 and 7,000 as estimated in 1935 and as realized at Greenbelt are summarized on Tables I and II. On Table III are shown the approximate breakdown of similar costs including Greendale and Greenhills. As cost accounting methods have been slightly different in the various towns, there may be some slight variations in the breakdown.

The cost accounting has special difficulties because of the unusual relation of the Federal Government to the Greenbelt Towns. It is, at the same time, the main taxpayer and the landlord of properties used by all levels of government and landlord of nearly all the residential property.

This is a particularly difficult time to describe the relation of the various levels of government at Greenbelt. The disposal of the town required by national legistlation (1949) is about to be negotiated. The Federal Government will, in all probability, shortly retire not only from ownership of the town, but also from the administration of certain functions normally carried on by the municipal or other levels of government. In fact during the past year or two certain of these have been handed over to the municipality in preparation for the retirement of the Public Housing Administration (which I will refer to hereafter as the PHA).

Another change that has taken place during the past year is the designation of Greenbelt, by the Maryland legislature, as a City instead of a Town. Apparently this does not give the municipality additional powers. Now that Greenbelt is about to be entirely on its own, the change was made so that it would be in a position of equal importance

TABLE I

PER PERSON

ESTIMATED AND ACTUAL COST

LOCAL GOVERNMENT AND COMMUNITY ACTIVITIES

	CSS est.	Green-belt	CSS est	Green-belt
Date	1935	1941	1935	1943
Units	750	885	1,750	1,885
Population	3,000	2,831	7,000	7,000
Administration	$2.66	$3.45	$1.43	$1 78
Recreation and Community Activities	7.00	5.06	4.50	2.94
Parks	1.33	2.00	1.04	.71
Public Works and Services	6.27	7.29	3.91	5.05
Repair Shop (Equipment)		.71		.31
Protection—Fire, Police	4.43	3.47	2.11	2.71
Health	3.33	1.20	2.25	.60
Cemetery		.01		.002
Civilian Defense				.09
Insurance	.17	.42	.09	.24
Contingency	2.38		1.89	.14
TOTAL	$27.57	$23.61	$17.22	$14.57
Education	22.50	17.05	22.50	14.76
GRAND TOTAL	$50.07	$40.66	$39.72	$29.33

TABLE II

PER FAMILY

ESTIMATED AND ACTUAL COST

LOCAL GOVERNMENT AND COMMUNITY ACTIVITIES

	CSS est.	Green-belt	CSS est.	Green-belt
Date	1935	1941	1935	1943
Units	750	885	1,750	1,885
Population	3,000	2,831	7,000	7,000
Administration	$10.66	$10.95	$5.71	$6.61
Recreation and Community Activities	28.00	16.19	18.00	10.91
Parks	5.35	6 39	4.14	2.63
Public Works and Services	25.07	23.32	15.64	18.74
Repair Shop (Equipment)		2.27		1.16
Protection—Fire, Police	17.73	10.99	8.44	10.05
Health	13.32	3.84	9.00	2.23
Cemetery		.05		.006
Civilian Defense				.33
Insurance	.67	1.35	.37	.88
Contingency	9.54		7.54	.53
TOTAL	$110.34	$75.35	$68.84	$54.08
Education	90.00	54.56	90.00	54.87
GRAND TOTAL	$200.34	$129.91	$158.84	$108.95
Omitting Contingency, TOTALS	$100.80	$75.35	$61.30	$53.55

TABLE III

LOCAL GOVERNMENT AND COMMUNITY ACTIVITIES
COMPARATIVE COSTS PER PERSON IN THE
GREENBELT TOWNS

		CSS est.	Green-belt	Green-dale	Green-hills
Date		1935	1941-1942	1943	1940-1944 av.
Units		750	885	572	676
Population		3,000	2,831	2,610	2,500
Person per family		4.0	3.2	4.5	3.7
I.	ADMINISTRATION	$2.66	$3.45	$4.09	$1.15
II.	RECREATION AND COM-MUNITY ACTIVITIES	7.00	5.06	2.54	6.89
III.	PARKS	1.33	2.00	.96	2.83
IV.	PUBLIC WORKS AND SERVICES	6.27	7.29	11.78	10.49
V.	REPAIR SHOP (EQUIPMENT)		.71	.99	2.98
VI.	PROTECTION, FIRE, POLICE	4.43	3.47	4.60	5.12
VII.	HEALTH	3.33	1.20	.50	.20
VIII.	INSURANCE	.17	.42		
IX.	CONTINGENCY	2.38	.01		
	TOTAL	$27.57	$23.61	$25.46	$29.66
X.	EDUCATION	22.50	17.05	35.95	33.37
	GRAND TOTAL	$50.07	$40.66	$61.41	$63.03

NOTE: The exact comparison of the actual cost of operation and maintenance of various services performed by local government with the figures in the estimate of 1935 is difficult because certain of the functions are distributed differently in Greendale, Greenhills and Greenbelt, not only from each other but from that presumed in the original set-up. In some cases, instead of the local government's taking financial responsibility, in part expenses have been covered by the federal government through PHA, FHA, etc., or through school boards, etc. One example of this is in regard to supplying water. In the estimate it was presumed that this would be a local function. In the case of Greenbelt this has been distributed by PHA as a service of housing management. Again, certain of the community activities, such as adult education or library have come under various agents of different levels of government.

with nearby small cities. From now on, the Town Manager will be titled City Manager, and the Council the City Council, and the people of Greenbelt will have the satisfaction of being citizens of a city.

As I am going to deal with the past in my summary description of governmental relations and functions, I may use past titles and speak of relations that have of late changed.

There have been two types of managers at Greenbelt, as well as the other Greenbelt Towns: the Community Manager, representing the PHA, and the Town (now City) Manager in charge of the administration of local government.

Under the Maryland State Legislation, by which Greenbelt was incorporated as a chartered town in Prince George's County in 1937, the charter created a town-manager form of government, acting under a municipal council of five members, elected for a term of two years. Until a few years ago the town council always elected as town manager the person who represented the Federal landlord as community manager under the Housing Agency.

There was a certain economy in the administration of the town in having these two functions carried out by one official. However, they have now been separated, for political or other reasons, in all three towns. In Greenbelt, after the change took place in 1948, the incumbent of the two offices was re-elected Town Manager. The present City Manager, Charles T. McDonald, has had a varied experience in connection with the operation of all three towns.

The PHA management collects rents and makes payment in lieu of taxes. As the Federal government is not permitted constitutionally to pay taxes to a lower level of government, it has made equivalent payments in lieu of taxes—or in many cases it has directly paid the costs of new installations and services.

EDUCATION. The PHA, in addition to payments made to the municipality, finances education by payments in lieu of taxes to Prince George's County. It is somewhat difficult to figure the exact cost of education, as these payments to the county are used in part for certain other county purposes. But the greater portion goes to the Board of Eudcation. The fact is that the school buildings were built by various federal agencies, and have been either operated in whole or part by PHA, or have been loaned to the Board of Education of Prince George's County. Of these relations I have already spoken.

The cost of education at Greenbelt has been not only lower than that which we estimated in 1935 at $90, but also much less than Greendale and Greenhills, due, as I have said, to the lower educational standards of Maryland.

The town has supplemented the education given by the County by directly financing adult education, the library, and the two kindergartens. Child care has been either a co-operative undertaking or a war-time federal expense. The county expenditures have also been supplemented by PHA in the form of janitorial and other services.

PROTECTION. The proposal to combine fire and police protection made in the studies for the Resettlement Administration has been followed successfully in all three towns. At Greenbelt the number of men permanently employed and the costs of operation have been very much as predicted. The Public Safety Department takes care of both fire and police protection. There is a staff of five full-time professional policemen who have also trained as firemen at a University of Maryland night course. When Greenbelt had a population of 2,831, there were four policemen. By 1943, there were five policemen for a population of about 7,000. In 1948, the staff consisted of a Director of Public Safety, an Assistant Director, three officers, and two part-time clerks, plus the help of two part-time relief officers for special occasions.

Police work consists of traffic control, and the inspection and registry of bicycles (at a charge of 25 cents, and children seem to enjoy having a license plate). Police perform other services, such as keeping the development's main switchboard open after regular working hours and on Saturdays, Sundays and holidays. They take messages for the doctors, and keep a list of those willing to be blood donors in emergencies.

FIRE PROTECTION. The staff of professional police-firemen is assisted in fire prevention by volunteers who receive 50 to 75 cents an hour for their participation in the fire-fighting and training program. During the war, under the Civil Defense Act the force consisted mainly of old men and high-school boys, but since the war there are 16 well-trained young men, many of them veterans. In emergencies they can be supplemented by 8 or 10 of the project employees — heating men, plumbers and electricians. These men have been trained in fire fighting, but the Department tries to call on them as little as possible. Actually there have been few fires in the dwellings, and the main concern of the department has been brush fires. This, combined with the prompt response of the volunteers to fire calls, has kept fire losses very low.

PUBLIC WORKS AND SERVICES. A number of services have been distributed or operated by the PHA and not the municipality—at least up to a short time ago. These include water, sewers (both sanitary and storm), and electricity. Water as well as electricity is purchased in bulk from an outside public utility corporation. Water is furnished by the Metropolitan (Washington) Sanitary Commission. It is delivered to a standpipe, of 2 million gallons capacity. The distribution system has been owned and operated by the PHA. Water was sold to the Town of Greenbelt for hydrants and other purposes, and to the Consumers Services, Inc. The water costs to the municipality have been far less than we etsimated, because it has paid only for what it used and has not had to operate and maintain the plant.

GARBAGE AND TRASH DISPOSAL. Although PHA owns the incinerator plant, it has been leased by the municipality, which operates large trucks for collection and disposal. This service is included in the payments in lieu of taxes, by PHA. These complicated relations may be simplified when the government sells the town.

THE SEWAGE SYSTEM remained in the possession of the Federal Government, but it is operated by the municipality. The disposal plant is large enough for 3,000 houses. The trunk sewers run through parks as well as streets. The cost of sewage disposal remained very much the same for the 7,000 population town as for the 3,000, as we had predicted. Costs were less as no assistant operator was needed.

PUBLIC WORKS. The 1935 Report proposed that all of the functions listed as Public Works and Services should be managed as one department with an efficient engineer at its head. Fewer skilled assistants could then have been put in charge of the various functions. In reality public works are all under one head, but municipal functions and housing functions are not under the same engineer. The volume of work was found to be too great for a single person to discharge both responsibilities.

HEALTH was one of the items for which our 1935 budget estimate was much higher than the ultimate costs in any of the three towns. Major John Walker and I both strongly believed in a municipal preventive program. We were apparently a little ahead of the time, and as the need of a program such as we suggested became a public policy the functions or costs of public health, in whole or part, were taken over by government at higher levels. We had proposed:

(a) medical inspection of school children
(b) immunization against small-pox
      and diphtheria
(c) school hygiene
(d) first aid in cases of emergency nature.

Thus, services in all cases were to be preliminary to reference to a physician when medical care was required.

The planned set-up also contemplated a first-aid station with a full-time nurse and doctor in attendance, preferably located in the school. We also said:

'It will probably be advantageous to place the nurse under the jurisdiction of the County Health Service, thereby permitting the Community to participate in the benefits of such service (laboratory facilities, sanitary officer, etc.). The cost of hospitalization is not included and is assumed to be contained in State or County levies. It is not proposed to erect a hospital in any of the towns as part of first construction.'

Strange as it may seem, the Town Council of Greenbelt did actually vote in 1940 to build a hospital, in spite of the fact that there were a dozen hospitals within as many miles of Greenbelt. Although the Town and Community Manager opposed it as financially unsound, in 1941, none the less, $16,607.60 was spent on changing some dwellings into a small hospital building. By 1943 the hospital had been abandoned, and the Greenbelt Health Association used the space.

GROUP HEALTH. The Greenbelt Health Association was active in the earlier years of Greenbelt's history. It provided a means of paying medical bills in advance. For a payment of $1.00 to $2.25 a month, depending on family size, members were allowed unlimited office visits and charged only 50 cents for the first home visit in each week of illness. Moreover, members obtained complete obstetrical care (exclusive of hospitalization) for the exceptionally low rate of $25.

In 1939, 130 families out of a total of 885 belonged to the association. In 1943, 375 families out of a total of 1,885 had joined. Greatly increased demand for public health service was to be expected under war conditions. The low number of families taking advantage of Group Health during the war years may have been partly due to the lack of sufficient doctors. Originally there had been three physicians, but during the war there was only one.

The Health Association, with its present staff of three full-time doctors and two nurses, seems to be overworked in spite of its reduced membership. The two other doctors and a dentist have busy private practices at Greenbelt.

PUBLIC HEALTH WORK has been confined to: (a) examination of school children, (b) operation of various adult clinics, and (c) immunization of young folks against contagious disease. The staff has consisted of one part-time health officer and one public health nurse.

The cost of public health service in 1941 was $3,399.00 for a population of 2,831. This included $500 for supplies. Space used was supplied free by the FHA. In 1943, for 7,000 people, the total cost was $4,214.00, including $3,260.00 for salaries, and $953.87 for supplies and services. By 1947 it had risen to $5,168, that is, $2.74 per family or about $0.75 for each person.

This is to be compared with our own 1935 Report's estimate, for the 7,000 population Town, of $15,000. However, there are additional health facilities made available by county and other governmental agencies. The latest of these is the Mental Hygiene Clinic of Prince George's County, which is housed in the University of Maryland, and the cost of which is in part paid for by the Federal Government. The services of the clinic are free.

RECREATION AND COMMUNITY ACTIVITIES have been discussed elsewhere. In carrying out the program there are varied parts, played by the PHA, in operation of the Community-School Building as well as the housing of the Child Care Center, of the Board of Education of Prince George's County in adult education, etc., and the private cooperation activities such as the nursery school.

This all naturally lessens the expenses that might otherwise have to be met by the municipality. The Recreation Department, which functions under the Town (now City) Manager, operated in 1941 (population 3,000), at a cost of $14,330 as compared with the 1935 estimate of $21,000. For the 7,000 person community the estimate was $31,500, the actual expenditures were in 1943 $20,564, in 1945, $37,108 and in 1947, $40,079. (The decreased buying power of the dollar in war and postwar years should be noted.)

The Recreation Department supervises the playgrounds, athletic fields, tennis courts, ice-skating rink, swimming pool, teen-age youth center, and all organised sports. During the summer months the program is very extensive, from baby playground programs to semi-professional baseball series. During the winter the recreational staff organizes and directs adult gym classes and teaches the elementary physical education classes in the two public schools.

The music program, which now consists of two elementary glee clubs and a children's string orchestra, is under the superision of the Recreation Department. There are several annual special community programs such as a Fourth of July celebration and a Christmas program. These are planned and carried out by the Recreation Department.

THE SWIMMING POOL has been operated as a separate feature by the municipality. It has required 20 half-time workers for a period of three months of the year. It now more than pays for itself. Expenses are $7,000 to $9,000 a year; income, $8,000 to $10,000. The extra income is used for other recreational expense. Charges are: Adults $.35, or 10 tickets for $2.00; children $.20, or 10 tickets for $.75. The pool did not pay during the first year, although it was crowded. It was opened only to Greenbelt people and their friends. Members of the community were able to purchase a pass for $6.00 a year for the family, $2.50 a year for individuals. The present rate schedule produces more revenue than the above system, thereby resulting in a successful financial operation.

Cost Accounting

There is much to be learnt from the decade of experience in Greenbelt, Greendale, and Greenhills that can help in the further development of functional contemporary towns. One of the difficulties I have found in trying to uncover the experiences is that results are not always clear.

It has been much like laboriously excavating archeological ruins. Many of the experiments that might be of great assistance in planning or running future communities have not been sufficiently observed or recorded. Often this is merely a matter of bookkeeping, or the method of setting up figures. Here is just one example.

In the heating of the houses a number of different methods have been used. In the Resettlement Development each row of houses has one boiler. As these were coal-burning, to tend the boiler and collect ashes a man had to travel from one group to another. This always has seemed an unnecessarily complicated system. So, when the Defense Homes were built, group heating for a number of rows was tried: some for as many as 200 units, others for lesser numbers. Here was an opportunity to get information that could be of much future value, not only as to practical experience with the number of units served by a single boiler, but also the difference in efficiency of using coal or oil. But the accounting records were set up so that the comparison could not be made between cost and efficiency of heating in units of 6 or of 200. This is due in part to the fact that the heating of all the buildings of the earlier development are accounted for together, and then divided by the number of house units. As the Community-School and shopping center were included, and their costs distributed among the 885 houses, the information as to heating costs is vague to say the least, and is of no use for purposes of comparison. I note that the British Mission to study District Heating in American Housing had similar difficulty in securing what might have been valuable information on heating at Greenbelt.[35]

GREENBELT

An Unfinished Story

The Greenbelt Towns are often referred to as *demonstrations*. Perhaps it would be better to say that they have been *indicators*. They have indicated that certain unusual policies and practices in the planning, organization and operation of communities are both attractive and highly practical. They have indicated very strongly that certain development methods and forms that have been followed in the past are obsolete, unnecessarily wasteful and ugly. One illustration is the contrast between the concentrated Greeenbelt shopping center and nearby roadside sprawl.

Perhaps the co-operative shopping center is the appropriate place to leave Greenbelt. For physically this marketplace, with the nearby related community buildings and recreation fields, is the heart of Greenbelt, and the dominant spirit of Greenbelt is that of doing things together—or co-operation.

This is an unfinished story because a town as vibrant with life as Greenbelt is constantly changing and its history can only be sketched in this limited space. I have tried, however, to indicate as adequately as possible how the three planning conceptions, the Garden City, the Radburn Idea, and the Neighborhood Unit, have actually worked.

This is written as one chapter of the history of Greenbelt is about to close and another to begin. Early in 1950 the Federal Government will end its guardianship of Greenbelt. The town will be sold, but on exactly what terms none of us know yet. However, the Congress has authorized the Public Housing Commissioner in the disposing of the Greenbelt Towns 'to give the first preference . . . to veteran groups organized on a non-profit basis (provided that any such group shall accept as a member . . . any tenant occupying a dwelling unit in such project . . .).'

It further permits the Commissioner to preserve the green belts by authorizing him to 'transfer . . . adequate open land surrounding or adjacent to each project to the appropriate non-federal governmental agency.'

We can only hope that these powers will be used in such a way that the spirit and form of Greenbelt will survive and that it will develop into a complete New Town.

Fig. 133—Double crescent roads encircle the community center for shopping, education, swimming and other recreation and community activities. This photo shows most of the Resettlement Development of 1937 as well as the lake in the distance. (Fairchild Aerial Surveys, Inc., New York)

GREENHILLS

**Justin R. Hartzog and William A. Strong,
Town Planners
Roland A. Wank and G. Frank Cordner,
Architects**

Fig. 134—Airview of Greenhills taken in 1949 toward the northeast. All houses shown were part of the original Federal government construction excepting a small number (121 lots) to the extreme right and on Gambier Circle at the top of the picture. These were finished in 1947.

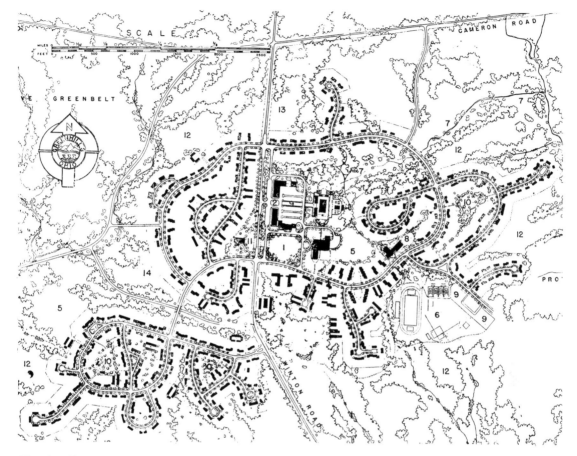

Fig. 135—Town plan showing (1) common; (2) shopping center (northern half not yet built); (3) community school; (4) swimming pool; (5) inner park; (6) playfield; (7) stream; (9) parking areas; (10) small children's play areas.

Fig. 136—Greenhills School, with the administration building in the background beyond the Common.

Greenhills is situated on an undulating, wooded site, five miles north of Cincinnati. The initial plan was for 676 dwelling units which were built in the first stage (Fig. 134). The form of the plan was suggested and limited by the rolling ground and many ravines. The latter have been preserved in the open space system as delightful and naturally wooded parks.

In Greenhills the Radburn Idea has been followed but not as completely as at Greenbelt. The turn-arounds of the dead end lanes are better than those at Greenbelt, Greendale or Radburn. Cars entering the lanes may easily return without backing or maneuvering. The arrangement of the elements in the Community Center is noteworthy (Fig. 137).

Of the 676 dwelling units there are 112 one-bedroom apartments, 40 two-bedroom apartments, 18 single-family detached four-bedroom dwellings, 6 single-family detached three-bedroom units; and, in row houses, 260 two-bedroom units, 208 three-bedroom units, and 32 four-bedroom units.

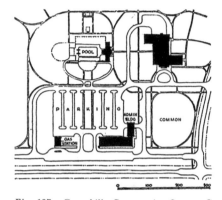

Fig. 137—Greenhills Community Center. Community school building and the administration building face the Common. The parking area lies between the shopping center and the swimming pool. The back of the pool shelter was designed to be used as an outdoor stage. The central part of the parking area was intended to be used as a farmer's market, but the farms in the area sell most of their products to the larger dealers in Cincinnati. The community building serves for gatherings of all kinds as well as for school. The auditorium-gymnasium is equipped for theatrical performances and the libraries and art studios are open in the evenings for adults. The large cafeteria in the basement is open day and night.

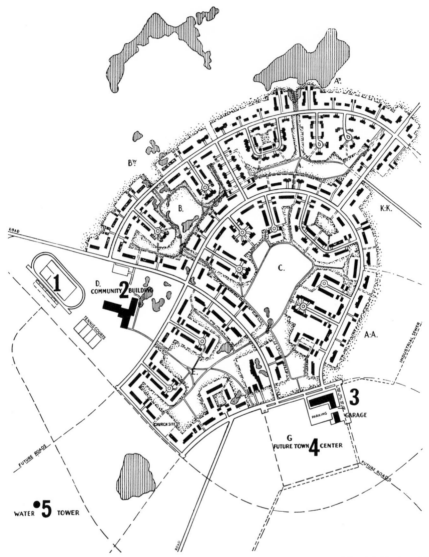

Fig. 138—Greenbrook, New Jersey. Initial project plan, showing the residential blocks with interior commons and walk systems and (1) athletic field; (2) community building; (3) shops and garage; (4) future town center; (5) water tower.

GREENBROOK

**Henry Wright and Allan Kamstra,
Town Planners**

**Albert Mayer and Henry S. Churchill,
Architects**

Greenbrook, the fourth of the Greenbelt Towns, was never carried out. Work on the project was begun in October, 1935, and ended in May, 1936, when legal controversies arose. Rather than risk holding up all four projects, the Resettlement Administration decided that the Greenbrook project, on which controversy centered, should be dropped.

Subsequent events have proved that the location of Greenbrook was well chosen. It was on the southwest edge of the rapidly growing New Jersey industrial belt, five miles west of New Brunswick, and adjacent to the main lines of communication between New York City and Philadelphia. Within 40 minutes of the site by motor there was employment for about 50,000 in industry, with an anticipated growth making 10,000 more jobs available in two to three years. There was also an abnormal shortage of low-rent housing in adjacent areas.

The site was to have been of between 3,800 and 4,200 acres, of which about 1,400 acres were for the ultimate built-up area. The initial project was for: 750 dwelling units, occupying 125 acres; a community center, commercial area and town common of about ten acres; with 25 acres in roads (Fig. 138). Of the dwellings, 3 per cent were to be detached houses, 20 per cent double houses; 70 per cent rows of 3 to 6 houses; and 7 per cent multi-family dwellings. Seventy per cent of the dwellings were to have had garages, 35 per cent to 40 per cent of that number as integral parts of the dwellings, and the balance in compounds located not over 200 feet from the farthest dwelling.

The final scheme for the ultimate town provided for 3,990 families at 4.9 families per net acre (exclusive of streets but including all interior open spaces, school areas and peripheral blocks, to the rear lot line). There was to have been an industrial area of 125 acres.

Fig. 139—The Community-School at Greendale. The school and community building contains thirty classrooms, an auditorium and gymnasium, recreation room and youth center, and the municipal library. It is surrounded by parks and is adjacent to the major playground.

GREENDALE

Jacob Crane and Elbert Peets, Town Planners

Harry H. Bentley and Walter G. Thomas, Architects

Greendale[36] is superby related to its natural site. The form of the land has indicated the location of roads paths, and buildings. Attractive features of nature have been preserved: for example, the stream that flows through the wooded park in the very center of the village.

Greendale was planned and built as a harmonious whole. It shows that regimentation and monotony are not necessarily the product of over-all design of the street pattern and buildings of a village. The buildings are harmonious in spite of the diversity of their form and placing. The care with which the planners related structures to site and to one another is the result of skilful practice and a real affection for the place they helped to create. The varied architectural beauty accentuates rather than overshadows its natural setting. A restful and gracious unity is the result.

SAFETY PLANNED AND ACHIEVED. Greendale is safe. There has not been a single automobile fatality, and not one serious accident during the ten years of its existence.

It is not by chance that Greendale has this remarkable record. Its streets are planned for through traffic or direct access. As a result, only the machines that are serving the houses on a lane or a street are likely to go there. Also, the pedestrian paths are in large part separated from highways.

BUILT FOR GOOD LIVING. Greendale is a spacious, comfortable, convenient place for living. The green breadth of Broad Street that leads to the Village Hall introduces the visitor to the roomy character of the village. The Central Park along Dale Creek at one side and the commercial buildings and theatre with their own service road, as well as the mall and tennis courts at the other, open broadly to the view. Around the houses are goodly private gardens—most of them beautifully kept, I observed. The houses were carefully located so that they are not cramped and crowded as most speculative housing is. This, in spite of the need of economizing on the length of utilities and roads, so that rent could be low.

PROTECTED BY ITS GREENBELT. Greendale is shielded from external dangers and encroachments as were medieval towns. But there is a great difference. The old communities were protected by gray fortifications: Greendale is secured by a belt of natural green.

A wide-open area is needed to prevent destruction from the spread of blight just as much as from forest fire.

That is what the greenbelt around Greendale does. It guarantees the integrity of the town.

It serves other purposes too. It brings country and semi-wilderness within walking distance of

Fig. 140—*View of pedestrian walk and garden court.*

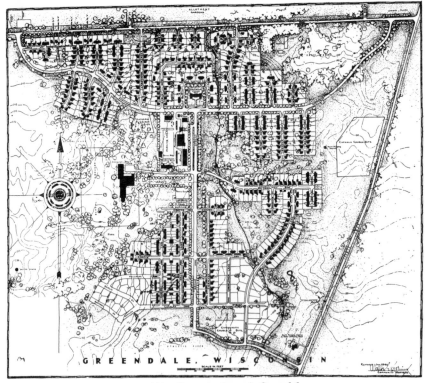

Fig. 141—*General plan of Greendale.*

homes. Farms and forests are familiar to kids from daily experiences, not merely from pictures in school books and movies. Picnics and hiking can be enjoyed by the family as a whole. The nature of changing seasons becomes a beautiful reality.

Town folks and farm folks know each other as neighbors, friends and associates. They come together in town meeting, churches, village and social affairs and at the co-operative, or the tavern. One more barrier that creates strangeness and misunderstanding among different groups of people is dissolved and broken down.

But the greatest advantage of the greenbelt is that it definitely limits the size and growth of the community. That is desirable, because only so can the neighborly character be sustained—and the common interest of all in their common affairs be kept alive.

GREENDALE A NEIGHBORLY COMMUNITY. The neighborhood community is now accepted as the basic unit of city building as well as planning. Small neighborhoods are essential for eye-to-eye democracy—and this is basic, not only for local contentment, but for national freedom and world-wide security.

It is just that kind of neighborly community life that makes Greendale such an important demonstration of the kind of towns we need all over America. All through the activities of Greendale one feels a spirit of fellowship—and as far as I could observe, it does not interfere with privacy or family life.

THE FUTURE. One of the fine qualities of Greendale is that it is small. But don't misunderstand me—I did not say Greendale was of a perfect size. In fact, I think it is apparent now that it has certain disadvantages because it is too small. A place that has a high standard of community and local-government services must spread the costs among an adequate group. Education and culture in Greendale require a large population to support them economically.

Greendale has plenty of space on which to grow. Less than 300 acres of the 3,140 acres (that originally were purchased by the Federal Government through the Resettlement Administration in 1936 as the site of Greendale) have been developed for houses and community facilities. So far, 525 acres of the greenbelt area have been dedicated to Milwaukee County for park and recreational purposes. It would be wise to deed permanently to the state or county the remaining greenbelt area surrounding the future expanded Greendale. Thus, the temptation to use portions of the protective belt for other than public or agricultural purposes might be done away with for all time. The smaller separation greens between the various neighborhood villiges should be owned and operated by Greendale itself. They should be permanently dedicated to public use as one of the first steps toward the development of the future of the village of Greendale.

NO UTOPIA. Strangers who read my description in praise of Greendale may think that I am writing about Utopia. But those who live there know that Greendale is not a phantom, but a fact. It is a living, growing reality.

It has had more luck than most villages. First, the conception of a community planned in orderly fashion for the motor age and increased leisure time, with its character and integrity protected by its greenbelt, was a great step forward. Then the detailed planning and development a decade ago was a very able job—thanks to the ability of the planners, Jacob Crane and Elbert Peets—their skill and more than that, the love that they put into the work. Then, there has been exceptional leadership on the part of one of America's ablest town managers, Walter Kroening. Here again has been a case of devotion as well as unusual understanding and skill. But none of these things would matter if it were not for the fact that Greendale has gathered together a lot of folks that appreciated its physical qualities and have made it a living community.

9   BALDWIN HILLS VILLAGE

**Reginald D. Johnson and Wilson, Merrill,
and Alexander, Associated Architects
Clarence S. Stein, Consulting Architect**

Fig. 142—View of garden and garage courts, looking toward the village green.

At Baldwin Hills Village in 1941 the Radburn Idea was given its most complete and most characteristic expression. There, in Los Angeles, with an average of over one automobile per family, was needed—perhaps more than anywhere else in the world—the combination of complete convenience in the use of the automobile and a peaceful escape from its dangers. And so at Baldwin Hills all the original elements of Radburn reappear—superblock, specialized means of circulation, complete separation of pedestrian and auto, park as community heart and backbone faced by all houses. They were freshly developed in a comprehensive, straightforward manner without compromise or indecision. Here, these basic elements have been clearly expressed and crystallized into more functional unity.

Economic Background

Baldwin Hills Village was another child of the long depression. During its final stage a forward-looking group of Los Angeles architects devoted three years to the development of plans for a new community, inspired by Radburn, but essentially local in character, to be built on a great empty ranch bordering Los Angeles. Too much of these three years was spent in securing approval, loans and mortgage insurance from cautious government officials in the Federal Housing Agency and the Reconstruction Finance Corporation. The bureaucrats, although they vaunted their progressive planning viewpoint, delayed and postponed all action that would result in any but 'safe' commonplace form or plan. Because of this procrastination there was time for the original conception of 1938 to be thoroughly studied and refined; about fifty plot plans were developed and the buildings were redrawn in detail some ten times. Yet it is remarkable how fresh and simple and straightforward the project was, when it was realized at last in 1941.

Pearl Harbor closely followed the arrival of the first of the 627 tenants. Rents, which had been set low, averaging $12.27 per room per month, were frozen. Financial plans, which had been figured tightly to keep rentals low, were disrupted as a result of unforeseen restrictions caused by wartime conditions. For instance, the proposed public omnibus that was to have carried tenants to the nearest transportation line was forbidden by the local authorities, and one had to be run by the Housing Company at a financial loss. Also no private direct telephone lines were permitted. So the company had the added unexpected expense of running a telephone central. In addition all operation and maintenance costs rose far above the estimated figures on which the fixed rentals were based.

In spite of this (due largely to the fact that it has continuously been 100 per cent occupied and not 90 per cent full as figured in the financial setup insisted on by FHA) Baldwin Hills Village has always paid its way; for eight years rentals have covered all operation and maintenance costs as well as debt services on mortgages and loans. In short, the only debts that were postponed were the interest and amortization of the equity, which had all been invested by the owner of the land, the architects and the builder. Now their investment has been returned with all back interest. This is the result of the sale of Baldwin Hills Village in 1949, to the New England Mutual Life Insurance Company of Boston, at a price sufficiently above its original cost to more than repay all equity and interest for eight years. And yet this wise company, I understand, knows that it has made a shrewd long-time investment.

The Site

The site consisted of some eighty acres of almost flat vacant land, with nothing on it higher than a blade of grass. It was part of an immense ranch that had changed hands only twice; first when the King of Spain deeded it to a conquistador; second when 'Lucky' Baldwin purchased it from his descendants over seventy years ago. It sloped slightly up to the low barren hills on which grow oil towers in place of foliage. The site is between Baldwin Hills and Beverly Hills, which create a 'draw' for cooling summer breezes from the nearby Pacific.

I had been shown this property by a broad-minded local builder, Joshua Marks, when I was looking for sites in 1935 for the group of communities of the Valley Stream type. I had recommended its use, in spite of the prevalent opinion that the peat in the soil of this valley made it undesirable for building. In the Baldwin Hills Village this difficulty was overcome by the use of floating foundations.

During the postwar boom the surrounding miles which had been empty were covered with speculators' disorderly housing. Baldwin Hills is now the population as well as the geographic center of the Los Angeles metropolitan area. It is within twenty minutes' auto ride of the business center, universities, airport, the beaches and other public recreation resorts, as well as the business centers of Los Angeles, Hollywood, and Beverly Hills.

The Objective

The purpose of Baldwin Hills Village was to demonstrate the practical possibilities of spacious homes and surroundings in an orderly community at low rentals, using the basic features of the Radburn Idea: superblock, homes facing central greens — twenty acres of green parks — pedestrian and auto completely separated.

The difficulties of carrying out these objectives in the Los Angeles area were twofold:

1. *The dominance of the automobile.* Nowhere else in the world are the problems of man's relation to his individual little railroad as acute. In Los Angeles there is an average of one automobile for every two-and-a-half persons—that is, more than one per family.

2. *The past control of housing by speculative subdividers and speculative builders* throughout Los Angeles. The old conventional type of street pattern and land subdivision best served their purposes of rapid sale. This gridiron pattern was adopted in spite of costly waste and its dangers to pedestrians.

The system of continuous through-streets had official recognition and legal backing. Municipal engineers had nailed down the typical pattern of streets in the official maps. They recognized no other arrangement. Change meant work — and making up one's mind — and possibly courting disapproval of superiors. In fact they looked upon new-fangled arrangements such as cul-de-sacs as dangerously revolutionary—or just the crazy idea of impractical architects.

Even where no streets had as yet been put on the city map the form of the circulation pattern was predetermined as though by command of the Almighty. The property that was to be Baldwin Hills Village was annexed to the city at the request of the architects so as to obtain city utilities, and

Fig. 143—Aerial view of Baldwin Hills Village showing the contrast between the development according to the Radburn Idea and the typical speculative development to the north and south. Baldwin Hills are at the south (bottom of the picture).

192

BALDWIN HILLS VILLAGE

at that time had no mapped streets. Nonetheless the plan to dispense with through highways between La Brea Avenue and Hauser Street—a distance of about three thousand feet, was disapproved repeatedly by City Engineer and City Planning Board. The intermediate streets to the north they insisted must be extended through the 1100-feet width of the project. It was the same struggle between the past and the future city pattern that we had fought at Sunnyside and Hillside.

It looked for some time as though the city engineer would be as obstinate as his professional brothers in the Boroughs of the Bronx and Queens. The City Planning Board was, however, finally induced to eliminate the streets that were to have dissected the residential area on the plea that these roads would be dead-ended by the hills beyond Coliseum Street and so might as well end at Rodeo Road.

In this eighty-acre superblock, therefore, we were free to work out a commonsense, logical and functional plan. However, the highway that separated this area from that which was zoned as business, they decreed must create an island to be surrounded by roads. We had hoped to design a market-place here with direct safe entrance from the residential park area of Baldwin Hills Village, in much the same way that I had indicated in the diagram illustrating the Neighborhood Shopping Center article.[37] The dismemberment of the superblock by cutting through Sycamore Avenue made this impossible. Natives of the Village, I understand, speak of this as a 'death trap.' Although I do not believe there have been any fatalities as yet, people are constantly dodging trucks and the bus which turns there. There have been a number of serious accidents, and recently the elderly guard of the theater building was injured for life.

The complete difference of the realtors' street pattern and the community pattern stands out in the air-view (Fig. 143). Below Baldwin Hills Village (to the north), built about the same time as the Village, a few meaningless curves are added to the typical gridiron. The through streets do not tie into any scheme of circulation—they go from nowhere to nowhere. The southern subdivision is more liberal of space than most of such wholesale developments. It was built only a few years ago,

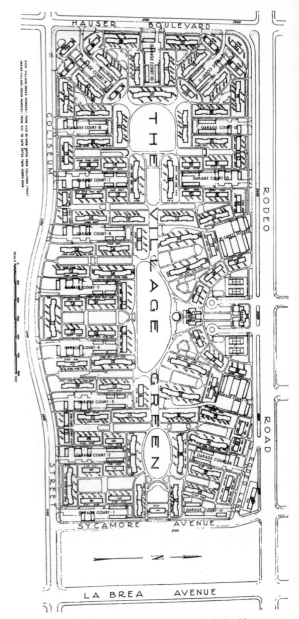

Fig. 144—Plan of Baldwin Hills Village. Only 15 per cent of the 80 acres of the site is covered by buildings, including the garages.

where we architects had hoped to locate an addition to Baldwin Hills Village that would have made it large enough to support a centrally located public school. It climbs the hill in a purposeless way. The outstanding feature of both these subdivisions is the undue importance and comparative spaciousness of streets. There is no concentration of green open spaces. Yet there are only 3.5 to 4 houses to the acre as against 7.8 dwelling units per acre in Baldwin Hills Village, with its spacious, verdant openness. The dissecting divisions of wide gray paved bands characterize, and dismember, these typical subdivisions to north and south.

The Village Plan

'Very pretty' says the Californian as he flies over, 'but is it practical? Where are the streets to take autos to the houses, and where do folks park and garage their machines?' There is no parking or storing of autos on public streets—in fact there are no streets within the 1100-feet by 2750-feet superblock. The highways that surround it are exclusively for movement—as they should be everywhere in all our cities. Rodeo Road, the one heavily used thoroughfare, is relieved of local traffic by the secondary roadway that parallels it on the Village property. This gives a safe approach to parking areas and auto courts. The two functions of through flow and access to groups are thereby separated and channeled, with entrances to Rodeo Road at only a limited number of points. On the periphery of the other surrounding highways there is off street parking space with indented curbs.

Not only are there no streets within the eighty acres of the Village, but even the dead-end of the Radburn type has been replaced. It has here been changed into a concentrated but adequate garage court. A new form has developed and come of age. Here is realistic modern functionalism replacing outworn traditionalism. Within the court is one garage for each home around it; also parking space for one car per family or its visitor. There remains adequate space for maneuvering, turning, backing into garages (Fig. 147 and 149). The automobile —arriving, departing, at rest, in storage—has all the room needed. Its local functions are not interfered with by through circulation.

Within each court are also the public group laundries with washing machines and out-door, but enclosed, drying yards. These were given increased space to meet war-time conditions. Now that wash can be sent out again, the additional drying enclosure is once more being devoted to parking.

There are less than four dozen families served by a garage court. Their houses surround it. This is similar to the location of the courts in the second (Defense) development at Greenbelt. But here the likeness ends. The dangers of too direct access to the paved courts by pedestrians do not exist at Baldwin Hills. There are only a limited number of entrances. A child running out of the house will be stopped by a high wire fence or planting. The view of cars is hidden, or at least lessened by the vines that overgrow the fences, as well as by the intervening planting (Fig. 146). This also serves to decrease the annoyances of auto sounds and smells.

Patios offer additional reposeful retreat on the garage court side of the houses. The patio is the indigenous private outdoor livingroom, dating back in California to the Spanish conquest. Although small, these six-foot redwood walled garden spaces, directly accessible to diningroom or kitchen, serve for sun-bathing, children's play and outdoor dining and lounging, as well as limited gardening during the lengthy mild sunny season. All ground floor dwellings and even some upper apartments have patios. Other second-floor tenants were compensated for lack of private grounds by private balconies. The new owner is so impressed by the advantages of these private enclosed courts that he is now building additional patios for those upstairs families that now have none. These will surround the entrance doors giving access to the second-floor apartments. Thus every one of the 627 families will have its own outdoor privacy (Fig. 146).

Another improvement planned by the insurance company is the building of additional garages. There are now 100 per cent garages, 100 per cent parking in courts, and about 100 per cent parking space in indented curbs—and yet more is needed! Where but in Southern California could this happen?

The orderly concentration of automobiles and servicing on one side of the houses leaves the other side free for pedestrians, play, and peaceful loafing. Here is another, a different, urban world; a world

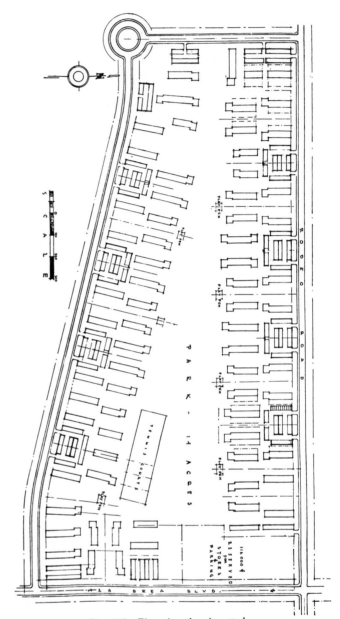

Fig. 145—First site planning study.

of quiet tranquility within the framework of per-
petual, congested movement. It is toward this calm
and restful verdant space that all livingrooms and
main bedrooms face.

About one-quarter of the area of Baldwin Hills
Village is devoted to green commons consisting of
inner parks and garden courts. The central park,
first planned as a single unbroken area, was afterward broken into three main bodies of different
shapes and sizes. The narrow connecting links
give scale and increased interest to the larger open
areas. The central green, although its maximum
width is only 250 feet, has a surprising sense of am-
pleness. This is due partly to the limited two-story
height of the long horizontal buildings. The central
greens serve for strolling, children's unorganized
play or romping, or even for informal ball games
by their elders. But above all their main function
is visual—or perhaps I should say spiritual. The
calm, long, orderly lines of the row houses and contrasting sweep of the brown hills behind—low hills
though they are, they seem to tower above the
domestic human scale of the homes—give the
feeling of spreading spaciousness. A tenant said to
me 'When I can't sleep nights I walk down the
length of the three central greens. I can hardly
believe I am in the heart of a great industrial me-
tropolis. The quiet sense of security and peace is only
broken by an occasional song of a night-singing
mockingbird.'

Although the Management leaves the great
central parks freely open for recreational use, they
look empty much of the time. Many of the youngsters seem to find the smaller proportions of the
garden courts, which form bays off the central
greens, more congenial. They are nearer home,
and the little ones love to use shrubs as hiding
places. Other causes for the sense of vacancy or
only partial use of the parks may be the omission
of benches which the planners proposed, and also
the insufficient shade of young trees. At the moment
the parks serve, above all, to form a visual foreground and spacious center of the architectural
composition (Figs. 151 and 164).

THE GARDEN COURTS are 100 feet or more wide.
Contrasted with the long horizontals of the row
houses less than twenty feet high, they have an
appearance of generous spaciousness. The homes

*Fig. 146—The enclosure of patios facing the garage
court. The serpentine brick wall has been added so that
the second-floor tenants might have privacy in their
patios. The ivy-covered wood walls surround the original
patios for the occupants of the first floor.*

Fig. 147—A garage court entered from Coliseum Street.

Fig. 148—View toward Baldwin Hills from garden court with entrance from Coliseum Street.

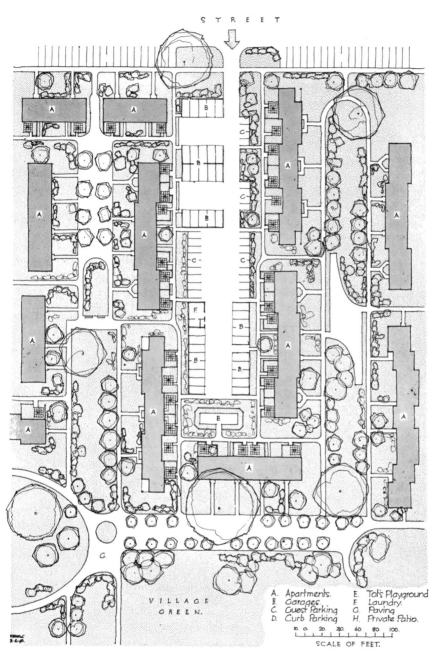

Fig. 149—Details of a garage court and two garden courts.

A. Apartments.
B. Garages.
C. Guest Parking
D. Curb Parking

E. Tot's Playground
F. Laundry.
G. Paving
H. Private Patio.

SCALE OF FEET.

197

BALDWIN HILLS VILLAGE

have a certain privacy as the public paths are twenty feet away and the intermediate space is planted with ivy or other ground cover. But there is no fence or hedge to make this space into a private yard, where one may plant one's own flowers or enclose one's baby. (That type of retreat is left to the patio on the other side of the houses.) These vine-covered foregrounds, along with the broad central lawns and the parks, are all part of the general landscape picture. They are very attractive, very orderly, very harmonious, with pleasing variety, like the buildings that surround the courts.

Baldwin Hills is so satisfying to the eye, and to the soul, of the visitor, that I hesitate to suggest ways in which it might possibly be improved. But let us look at it from the point of view of the people who live in the houses. They are all enthusiastic about the patios because of the privacy they give them. A good many of them, I imagine, want more of this. So I propose that when we take the next step in the evolution of the Radburn Idea we might increase in depth the individual space in front of each house, at the expense of the central part of the green courts, and then hedge them in, just as at Radburn or at Greenbelt. Look at the pictures of these two places (Fig. 37 and Fig. 123) and see what pleasure the people get out of having their own little outdoor kingdoms. The actual ownership of the land is not, I believe, the thing that matters. The man with the beautiful flower garden at Greenbelt has as much love for it and pride in it as any one in the subdivisions to the north or south of Baldwin Hills Village. He has much use of it and pleasure out of it, and as much sense of it being his own.

The maintenance of these private yards by the tenants would be a great advantage to the management. It could mean a decided saving in landscape upkeep—which is an important item in an open green community. Greendale, where a large portion of the open spaces are in enclosed yards, as compared with the other Greenbelt Towns, showed the economic advantage of increased tenant maintenance. The costs chargeable to management for gardening were far lower. Greendale's experience seems also to answer the question of whether a tenant will care for his garden as would an owner. This they emphatically—and proudly—do.

I do not believe the hedging in of varied gardens need spoil the orderly urban sense of openness in the courts—the big harmonious picture. It would make the Village what we at first proposed to call it: *Thousand Gardens.*

Do not let this thought for the future lead you to think that my enthusiasm about Baldwin Hills Village is diminishing. I will leave it to a more disinterested as well as a better critic to evaluate its design. Lewis Mumford said of Baldwin Hills Village: 'Here every part of the design speaks the same robust vernacular: simple, direct, intelligible. I know of no other recent community that lends itself so fully to strict scrutiny, simply because every aspect of its physical development has been thought through.

'The site plan represents a further development of the Radburn Idea, made possible by the use of the row house, with the removal of the garage to the service road. One of the most important facts about this plan is its clarity and readability; the buildings all form a comprehensible whole, which can be taken in at a glance; the stranger is not puzzled or led astray by any mere jugglery of the structures for the sake of achieving specious aesthetic effects or pinchpenny economies. Such order is a vital attribute of a modern urban environment.'[38]

Form, Mass and Pattern

The general design of Baldwin Hills Village differs in various ways from the other developments; Sunnyside, Radburn, Chatham Village and the Greenbelt Towns.

Baldwin Hills has an organized unity of overall pattern; a more formal grouping that suggests the balanced treatment of the squares of eighteenth-century London or of the *Places* built by Stanislas in Nancy. This is in large part the result of its being conceived and built as a single related operation with adequate time for thorough study, simplification and integration of the varous parts. Sunnyside and Radburn or the other hand show the effect of a continuous process of development from year to year, in which the original conception persisted as guide, but the detailed grouping and relations of parts altered on the basis of experience and changing requirements. There was no complete

Fig. 150—View from the Baldwins Hills to the south, showing part of the western section of the village. This photo was taken in 1956. Note how the trees have grown since the early photos were taken.

Fig. 151—A ballgame on the village green.

Fig. 152—Plan and site of a garden court and garage courts.

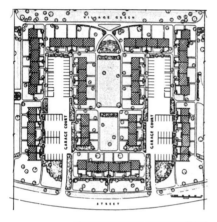

Fig. 153—Summertime in a garden court.

design of Sunnyside or Radburn at any time. They grew. The fundamental Sunnyside and Radburn Ideas were strong enough to unite them.

Chatham Village and Greenbelt's first development have much of the homogeneous architectural quality of Baldwin Hills, but in quite different ways. Greenbelt has more of the thorough, conscientiously studied simplicity of external treatment—perhaps slightly less polished—Chatham Village is more romantic. The hilly topography and the existing trees in both cases guided the architects in the location of buildings and dictated the picturesque variety of grouping. The almost flat site of Baldwin Hills on the other hand required that the over-all pattern be set entirely by the planners.

The architects in all three designs had the advantage of using row or terraced houses as the minimum unit. These are long enough and sufficiently varied in length to permit freedom of composition and adequate scale as part of the design of a large development. The typical American small freestanding dwelling is too spotty to count as a related part of a general picture. Radburn illustrates this in spite of continued architectural controls to preserve architectural unity. Most of the early freestanding houses were somewhat awkwardly cramped until the foliage had time to unite them by dominating them. It is true that the planners of Greendale composed some of their individual cottages so that they make interesting street pictures by contrasting one roof shape with the repetition of another form and by facing the structures on a gradually winding street. But even this type of design would be monotonous if it were not relieved by the long horizontals of the row houses.

Chatham Village and Baldwin Hills both illustrate excellent but dissimilar methods of composing long rows. The differences are the results of topography, climate, soil, external materials, and the local habits as well as taste, both of the architects and of the place and time. At Chatham Village the sloping land and its ultimate terracing suggested a more picturesque architecture and a more broken roof line. The desert-like soil of Los Angeles lacked the natural verdant background and foreground of the great old trees in the rich ground of Penn's ancient manor. The trees at Baldwin Hills, even after eight years, are mostly too small

BALDWIN HILLS VILLAGE

to be dominant. There are charming landscaped courts, some with spaced olive trees shading the gravel-covered spaces for walking and children's play. But it will be years before trees in the central parks or courts are large enough to form an important, rather than a minor, natural decorative element of the big composition. Local custom and economy in building material dictated brick walls, cast stone doorways, slate roofs, in Pittsburgh, contrasted with the painted stucco over wood frame predominant in Baldwin Hills. Climate—and particularly snow—required steeper sloping roofs at Chatham Village.

The shape of the land, the weather, local taste and habits, regional architectural customs — all played a part in forming the external design of Baldwin Hills Village. But the architect planners had unusual freedom of opportunity to fix form, mass and pattern. They set the borders of the project (the Baldwin Estate owned the surrounding land) and even determined the location and form of Coliseum Street. At their request the county moved the boundary of the city so that all the development might be within the Los Angeles municipality. There were no bisecting streets to prevent the free development of the 80-acre superblock, and each road and path was located where, in the architects' opinion, it would best serve firstly for convenience, secondly for good living, and thirdly for the beauty of the community.

The resulting design of Baldwin Hills Village is dominated by long restful horizontal lines and planes; long green courts paralleled by long low buildings. This horizontality is accentuated by the unbroken line of the delicate cornice and the deep shadow cast by its overhang, which is sometimes three feet wide. The horizontality is emphasized by the thin parallel line of porch and entrance roofs and the flat surface of balcony fronts (Fig. 165).

The forms of the buildings are all simple. There is no extraneous ornament or moldings. Adequate and rhythmic pattern is secured by means of the organization and grouping of the simple, straightforward essentials: windows, doors, balconies. There are contrasts in mass of different lengths of buildings consisting of two to six houses, and of heights of one and two stories. Additional variety comes from the different direction in which the

structures run, resulting in varied play of light, shade and shadow. Add to this the contrasts of pastel coloring — bluish green, suede grey, dark tobacco brown, grey blue—and holding these together large masses of white, slightly greyed, reminiscent of the house rows of Denmark and Sweden. There is added diversity in the individual landscape treatment of different courts (Figs. 159 and 161).

In spite of the harmonious unity of its horizontal treatment Baldwin Hills is never monotonous. It has a simple, decided rhythm. The big composition, that follows the dominating line of the flat ground, is relieved by the contrast of the long curves of the brown hills that form a background.

There is no waste motion, no pretence about the design. It is straightforward and entirely serviceable (which word is used to replace that overworked term: functional). The individual house plans are integral parts of the community plan. They all open out to its expansive beauty; livingrooms and principal bedrooms face towards the greens, while kitchens, though convenient to the service side, open to the patios. In these houses and the surrounding open spaces it is easy to live the kind of life people in Southern California seek in the present time. This, it seems to me, makes the buildings contemporary architecture far more than could any veneer of stylized 'modern.'

The House Units

The individual houses are so integrated into the whole scheme that I have already told much about them in speaking of the Village plan. They are extraordinarily commodious for rental houses—far more so than is required by the building code or by the FHA which, in insuring the loans on most builders' housing, fixes minimum standards of space and quality; and of course minimum standards really become maximum attainment. The Baldwin Hills houses are far more spacious and better built and equipped than houses 'normally' approved.

The size and openness of the rooms can best be read in the plans (Figs. 156 and 157). Note that they are all unusually well supplied with storage space; every bedroom has either two closets or a long closet with double doors. There is additional storage room under stairs, in the rear of garages,

Fig. 154—The center green.

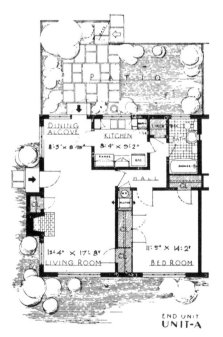

Fig. 155—Plan of Unit A.

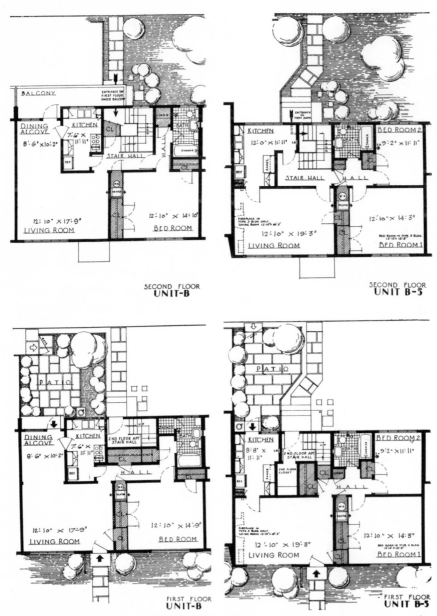

Fig. 156—Unit B is a two-family house. The entrance to the upper apartment is on the garden court, though family and many guests use the patio entrance. Unit B-5 has two bedrooms in each apartment. Note the large ground floor closet for the upper apartment at foot of stairs. Unit A (see Fig. 155) is of one story and used either at the end of a two-story row or as one of three attached bungalows. Gas-fired heater and water heater are centrally located in small closet. Bathrooms have electric heater. There are 55 one-story units.

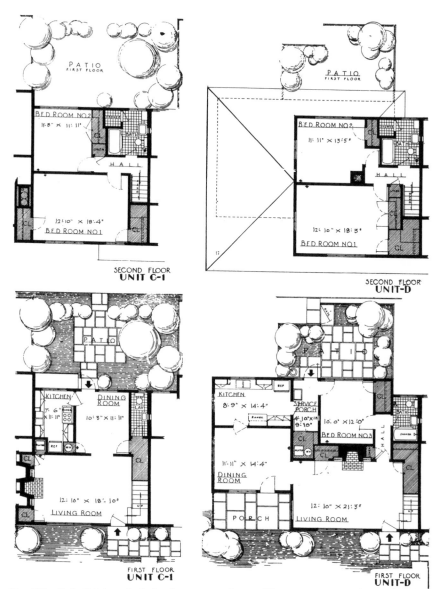

Fig. 157—Unit C-1 is a single-family two-story house. There are entrance doors on either side; thus circulation through living rooms is minimized. The ground-floor lavatory and bathrooms, with walls of ceramic tiles, have shower stalls as well as bath tubs. Unit D is the largest house. The ground-floor bedroom, with patio entrance, may be used for guests or servant. The dining room, with entrance from the porch, may be used as study, and the kitchen is large enough for children to dine. Doors of second-floor bedrooms are placed to allow varied arrangements of furniture and long closets. Dwellings of all kinds number 627. Of these, 55 are one-story bungalows, 216 are two-story houses, and 356 are flats in two-story units. There are dining-rooms in 356, dining alcoves in 143, and in 128 the family eat in the livingroom; there are 40 dwellings with 3 bedrooms, 312 with two, and 275 with one.

Fig. 158—A single-family house (Unit A) at the end of a row of two-family houses.

Fig. 159—Entrance side of row houses.

and elsewhere. There are wood-burning fireplaces in one-third of the homes. The bathrooms have tiled floors and wainscots and about two-thirds of them have additional separate shower stalls tiled to the ceilings. In the larger houses there are supplementary bathrooms or toilets on the ground floor. The floors are oak. Those on the lower stories are 3/16-inches parquet in mastic above full-floating slag foundations, with a membrane below the parquet.

There are three types of house: one-story bungalows—as the Californian calls them—fifty-five of them in groups of three or at the ends of rows of taller buildings; two-story houses—216. of them; and the flats, with one family above the other.

About half of these units have two bedrooms each and forty have three sleeping rooms. There are diningrooms in over half the units and dining alcoves in over a quarter, which means that only 128 families in houses or flats have to eat in a livingroom or, if they prefer, in the open on balcony or patio, or even in the convenient kitchen. Just a word about the kitchens. It is difficult to get visitors from abroad to go anywhere else—even out to see the green—when they discover the stainless steel drainboards, large divided sinks, and much cupboard space.

The flats, along with all the other units, are always full. They have many advantages over the typical two-family house. Each upstairs unit has its own entrance and private hall, distinctly separated from the tenant below. This entrance faces the garage court, which is the point at which almost everyone arrives. The ground-floor tenant can come in from either front. The upper-floor families all have large balconies—and in the future they are each promised their own patios.

In spite of all these advantages, I have a preference for single-family houses. This comes from our experience at Sunnyside, Radburn and elsewhere, where there was much dissatisfaction on the part of people on the lower floor who claimed to be disturbed by the movement or voices of people above. I do not know why tenants of apartment houses complain so much less about such annoyances; perhaps because they accept apartments at first as a temporary way of life, and then get accustomed to their annoyances and accept

Fig. 160—The entrance to an upper story apartment before the addition of the serpentine brick wall shown in Fig. 146.

BALDWIN HILLS VILLAGE

them as part and parcel of urban living.

In trying to think of the exceptional ways in which Baldwin Hills might be improved the next time that type of development is projected, I would propose fewer — many fewer — families on the second floor. Two-story houses, similar to those at Chatham Village, might provide more suitable accommodation. An even better solution for Southern California might be to use a larger number of bungalows, which are customary and popular there.

GARAGES—which were built in rows for about ten cars—have end walls of shiplap, but no separation between stalls. They have floors of asphalt concrete, continuing the paving of driveways and motorcourts. In the back of each stall is a storage closet for the use of each tenant. As a whole these economically built garages have stood up very well. There was only one main criticism: that there were no doors in the beginning. The omission of these was one of the exceptional and unwise economies in a job that was unusually liberal in expenditures. As a result the experience of Greenbelt was repeated; the garages became one of the favorite play and hiding places for children—and both cars and children were in danger. But now at Baldwin Hills overhead doors have been installed in the greater part of the garages—with an additional rent charge.

The Architects

It is impossible to divide credit for Baldwin Hills Village among its architects. Lewis Wilson and his associates did a splendid job in connection with the conception and development of plans. Reginald D. Johnson, in his simple, delicate, but dignified designs, surpassed even the great mansions for which he is justly famous.

An indication that the architects approve of their own work is that most of them have lived in the village. The Alexanders brought up their children there, and he has his office in the shopping center. The Johnsons and Lewis Wilson have both for a time given up their large dwellings for the simpler life of the Village.

The Village as a Community

The general plan and the air view may suggest

that the central axis is over-emphasized and out of harmony with the unpretentious urban quality of the rest. This apparent formal monumentality is more evident in the drawing or as viewed from the air than in reality. The individual on the ground sees only a small picture at a time, and he is not likely to observe the main axis, excepting in the relation of the two community buildings at either end of the charming formal garden court (Fig. 152).

The community group consists of the Administration Building and the Community Club. The former serves for contact between tenant and landlord. It is the center for information and complaints and for receiving packages. It was the telephone center for the Village, with extensions to houses from its large switchboard, during the war when direct wires could not be secured. The office also supplies maids on an hourly basis.

The Club House is used for various community activities. It consists of a great room some ninety feet long, that can be divided into three sections; also an adjoining kitchen, space for a darkroom, and a small lending library. There are weekly dances. Until just recently, when a church was built nearby, non-sectarian services were held there every Sunday morning. On weekdays it is used for parties, gatherings, committee meetings and general loafing. On its large terrace, shaded by awnings, badminton and other games are played.

A Child Center was originally designed to occupy what is now the Club House. But the little ones, to make room for their elders, have been located in two remodeled houses close by, containing room for thirty children. It has a spacious, well-equipped play space. Just outside, there is a large, wire-fenced enclosed play space with sandboxes, swings and other apparatus next to the nursery school (Fig. 149).

For little children who do not go to the Child Center there are a dozen or more small fenced and equipped play areas. These are generally placed just outside the ends of the enclosed motor courts, within sight, or at least hearing of mothers in their kitchens.

Convenient tennis courts are at either side of the Administration Building. Not far from the Village are public golf courses. There is also a 30-

acre public playground; but this is at the other side of two busy streets, La Brea Avenue and Rodeo Road.

A well-equipped playground for boys and girls of all ages, in easy safe walking distance, preferably within the superblock, is needed. This could be added now, possibly in the Western Central Park. It would be of great value even though it would have to be a little restricted in area. The next time it should be planned as an essential part of the development. Surrounding houses should be mainly those for families with children; though there should be some for old folks, as they like to be within sight of the activities of the younger members of a community.

The idea of devoting certain portions of the development to families with boisterous children— or any children for that matter—has been tried out at Baldwin Hills Village. Those without youngsters claim to have more peace and quiet as a result. This age zoning was the idea of the management; the architects did not plan for it. It would be wise to study carefully its success and the pros and cons of this kind of segregation, so that houses may be planned and grouped to meet special requirements —if this is found advisable.

A swimming pool is another addition that would probably have been very welcome at Baldwin Hills. The fact is, if I remember rightly, a swimming pool was suggested at one time, to be placed directly in front of the Community House. Los Angeles with its long warm season would be an ideal place for this. That a swimming pool makes a popular center for a community is vouched for by the experience of Radburn, Greenbelt and Greenhills. And they show that it can be run so as to pay its way. An adequate swimming pool might be difficult to add now—but the next time there should be one.

A wading pool was installed in front of the Village's Community House. For some reason it was decided that babies would not be safe in the pool. Now it is a flower garden (Fig. 154). I wonder if the pool was thought too small to make it worth while to have a guardian or some mother in charge when it is used. Experience elsewhere, at Hillside for instance, where a second one was later installed, is that these pools are extremely popular and need not be dangerous.

The Cost of Spacious Housing

Catherine Bauer wrote a splendid description and criticism of Baldwin Hills Village (for *Pencil Points,* September, 1944) which she speaks of as 'the most seriously progressive experiment in home building by private enterprise since Radburn, New Jersey, . . . probably the most spacious urban rental housing ever built in the United States . . .

'If Baldwin Hills Village is in many ways the most attractive, livable rental community in the country, how much does this extra degree of amenity cost? Some of it comes from good modern planning techniques, of course, and costs nothing but sense and sensibility on the part of the planner and entrepreneur. And cheap land facilitated great openness. But a lot of the attractiveness of the Village derives from standards of space, facilities, and equipment measurably higher than those in other large-scale housing, public or private.'

She then analyses and compares the costs of Baldwin Hills and the costs of subsidized public housing developments in the same city, Los Angeles, and built at about the same time. I am repeating here the analysis of Cost of Dwelling Unit, which I know has been carefully checked, as Catherine Bauer's facts and figures always are. Here is a condensation of some of her conclusions.

'All housing costs are subject to varied conditions dependent on time and place. And in the early 1940's other fluctuating conditions entered the picture which make any rigid comparison difficult if not impossible. Nevertheless the Los Angeles City Housing Authority, an efficient agency which employs good architects and has achieved about the highest local level of public housing quality in the country, did build a number of projects at about the same time as Baldwin Village. It may be worthwhile to set down a few figures on some of these projects next to the figures for the Village (see Table).

'The over-all cost per dwelling unit for Baldwin Village is $4911, and the average for the five public projects is $4385—11 per cent lower, or a difference of $526 per family. This is not a fair comparison, however, due to the high cost of central sites and slum clearance for three of the public projects . . . For a closer comparison it seems desirable to eliminate the land factor and also,

Project	Baldwin Hills Village	Pico Gardens	Aliso Village	Rose Hill Courts	Hacienda Village	Channel Heights	Average Cost for Public Projects
Sponsorship	Private FHA Insured	Los Angeles City Housing Authority; mostly for war workers, but all 'permanent,' all but Channel Heights built under U.S. Housing Act.					
No. Units	627	260	802	100	184	600	
Construction	Stucco, wood frame (ex. 9% masonry)	Stucco, wood frame	Some masonry; some stucco, wood frame	Stucco, wood frame	Wood, stucco wood frame	Wood, stucco, wood frame	
Families per gross acre	7	16	19	16	19	9	
Height	2 story some 1	2 story	2 and 3 story	1 and 2 story	1 story	1 and 2 story	
Rooms per unit	4.3 (FHA count)	5.2 (FPHA)	4.3 (FPHA)	4.4 (FPHA)	4.3 (FPHA)	4.2 (FPHA)	
Contract awarded	Feb. '41	Jan. '42	Feb. '42	Dec. '41	Nov. '41	May '42	
Completed[1]	Oct. '42	Aug. '42	Mar. '43	June '42	July '42	July '43	
COSTS: Land	$314	$1311[2]	$1022[2]	$796[2]	$279	$103	
Site impvmt.[3]	637	407	437	357	412	1163[4]	
Dwelling construction[5]	3730	2977	3441	2912	2704	2825	
Garages	138	none	none	none	none	none	
Community buildings	926	107	132	165	138	236	
TOTAL PHYSICAL COST PER UNIT	$4911	$4802	$5032	$4230	$3533	$4327	$4385
TOTAL EXCLUDING LAND	$4597	$3491	$4010	$3434	$3254	—	$3547[7]

COSTS PER DWELLING UNIT

NOTES: Figures include: Contractor's, architect's, engineer's fees; supervision. Excluded are carrying charges, pre-occupancy, administrative, or financial expenses. 1, occupancy often earlier. 2, including slum clearance. 3, including utilities and landscaping. 4, extremely rough site. 5, including equipment. 6, including administration, club and laundry buildings, but not dwellings now used for nursery school, etc. 7, excluding Channel Heights.

Fig. 161—Approach to a garden court from Coliseum Street.

Fig. 162—Looking across West Green.

because its peculiar site resulted in abnormal land development costs, to exclude Channel Heights entirely. Excluding land the cost per unit of Baldwin Village is $4597, and the average for the four public projects is $3547 . . . 23 per cent lower, or a difference of $1050 per family.

'No resounding generalizations should be drawn from these figures . . . But perhaps it would be reasonable to claim some evidence that, excluding the land and location factor, permanent community housing of "decent, safe, and sanitary" but minimum standards costs 20 to 25 per cent less than community housing of luxury standards in Los Angeles in the early 1940's. What does one get for this extra $1000?

'Landscaping and outdoor recreational and service areas much more highly developed than in public projects, and covering about twice as much open space per family;

'Garages; lawn sprinkler system; laundries with enclosed drying yards; enclosed playgrounds; athletic facilities;

'Private patios and balconies;

'Much larger rooms, particularly living-dining areas; luxurious storage space;

'Better heating and hot water systems, plumbing and electric installations;

'Oak floors, tile baths, stainless steel drainboards, Venetian blinds, etc.;

'Many fireplaces, some extra bathrooms.

'This is a lot . . . there is evidence that even 10 per cent more leeway in the costs and standards of "minimum" modern housing might bring a social return much greater than 10 per cent in more space, more amenity, more convenience.

'Perhaps the most significant single item is the cost of site improvements, landscaping, and utilities. The cost per unit for Baldwin Hills Village is $637, for the public projects (excluding Channel Heights) $403 . . . only $234 difference, although the Village has only half the density of population, and open space far more highly developed for varied use and beauty than do the public projects.'[39]

New Towns: 1766 and 1941

The closest historical parallel to Baldwin Hills Village is the New Town of Edinburgh, built in 1766 from the design of James Craig. Both layouts were reversals of the past planning practices of their city. The formal, balanced Georgian development of Edinburgh contrasted as sharply with the picturesque medieval congestion that herringboned from the High Street ridge as does the open orderliness of the Village, united around its expansive greens, differ from the repetitive monotony of the road-sliced subdivisions of Los Angeles.

Both developments were on open areas, unrestricted by existing streets and buildings — the planners worked out both patterns freely on clear, and approximately flat, land. The similarity in the size of the Edinburgh and the Los Angeles New Towns is remarkable—both are one thousand feet wide (Figs. 163 and 164).

The people for whom the developments were built were in each case united by social and family customs and taste, as well as by economic standards. The Scots were the prosperous burghers, in large part merchants, impressed with their own importance, who desired more spacious living, and greater opportunity for display and entertainment than was possible in the cramped quarters of the old town.

To Baldwin Hills Village came the typical mid-income Californians; lovers of informal life in the sunshine and open spaces, they sought freedom from care and worry for their children's safety, in spite of lack of servants to guard them.

In both cases land was in single united ownership; there was a definite clear conception of purpose, and the means of attaining the objective was fresh and new for its city; there was concentrated leadership; a unified design of which the whole development and each detailed unit all formed parts of a comprehensive picture, including the pattern of circulation and of open spaces. The street facades, from the massing and grouping of the building down to the last detail of windows, doors, projections, coloring and planting—all contributed to the unity of the single compositions.

The houses in both places were built according to standardized plans, and individualized by the variety of the family life and taste in interior decoration. They were constructed as a single or continuous operation. In all this the two developments closely paralleled each other.

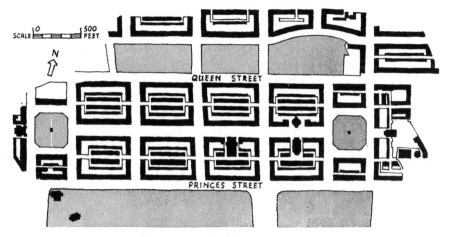

SCALE 0 500 FEET

N

QUEEN STREET

PRINCES STREET

Fig. 163—Plan of first section of the New Town, Edinburgh. George Street in the center links the two squares.

Fig. 164—Plan of Baldwin Hills Village to the scale of the plan of New Town, Edinburgh.

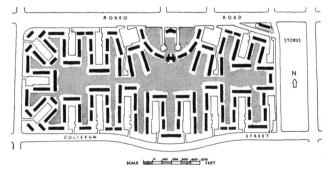

RODEO ROAD

STORES

N

COLISEUM STREET

SCALE 0 100 200 300 400 500 FEET

BALDWIN HILLS VILLAGE

Fig. 165—Typical row of houses.

Fig. 166—Entrance side of row houses.

But here the similarity ends — and the much greater dissimilarity that grew out of time, place, climate, the way of life, and the status of technology differentiate the two.

Of the social and cultural life of Edinburgh in 1766 for which the New Town was created and which served as its stage, E. J. MacCrae says:[40]

'The keynote of society was elegance, whether in dress, the dance, social recreation or buildings and furniture. The tempo of life was the easy speed of horse-drawn vehicles. This was reflected in the dignified orderliness of society and the literature of the Golden Age. Naturally, the adjustments of life to the new were revolutionary in their social implications. In the characteristic words of Lord Cockburn, "It was the rise of the New Town that obliterated our old peculiarities with the greatest rapidity and effect. It not only changed our scenes and habits of life but, by the mere inundation of modern population, broke up and, as was then thought, vulgarized our prescriptive gentilities".'

Cold winds and mists, predominating most of the year in Edinburgh, gave emphasis to indoor life. The sunny temperate clime of Los Angeles invites outdoor living. This dictates closer contact between the inside and outside of the houses. As a result, clothing, homes and living are freer and more informal.

Let us now see how the two physical plans crystallized the differences of period, place and people.

The dominant framework of the New Town of 1766 is rigid straight avenues; that of Baldwin Hills is flowing parks. Edinburgh's George Street, a broad and imposing corridor connecting two formal squares, was intended primarily to be viewed from moving vehicles or by the man on horseback. Straight broad avenues facilitated movement of horse and coach, and offered a stage for display of this symbol of social or commercial standing. From the moving vehicle it is the perspective that counts; one wants orderly regularity, repetition, the horizontality of uniform roof and cornice lines, in short, regimentation. Finally, and at not too great a distance, the perspective of the corridor should terminate in points of interest, and so George Street leads to the tall dome of St. George's Church at one end beyond the green of Charlotte Square; at

the other it approaches the graceful Excise House facing St. Andrew's Square.

The more leisurely, less tense rhythm of walking or loafing in the parks of Baldwin Hills calls for a greater variety and for a less rigid setting. Flowing paths; variety of width of open greens, of direction and length of building masses, of color and of planting; even the calm repose of long horizontal lines which unifies and gives repose to this variety is softened by the trees and the background of rolling hills.

There is one architecturally composed front to the Edinburgh houses, that on the avenues approached by the master's vehicle. The backs of the houses, for servants only, are of haphazard and unorganized design. At Baldwin Hills all sides are equally important. They are all approached by the tenants or their friends. So all facades were studied with similar care.

Edinburgh's New Town was built in the Grand Manner, which was best expressed by the Renaissance regal palace. This degree of external importance could only be attained by uniting groups of houses in a single external design. The style chosen was the graceful refined baroque, similar to that used by John Wood in Bath, and in the Squares of the Bedford Estate in London.

Life now in every way is more informal—and so is dress. As a result, so is architectural expression: patios and balconies for sunbathing; open green spaces close to the doors. Baldwin Hills is quite as orderly but the architectural composition is based on simple, more utilitarian motives such as windows, doors and balconies. Its stucco or brick exteriors, although by no means plebeian, are certainly less formal as well as less reminiscent than the typical Edinburgh stone facades.

Both developments were for communities of one class. But in Georgian Edinburgh that class was given distinction and supported in its luxury by many servants. Therefore it was possible to devote spacious halls and salons solely to entertainment and conspicuous display. These and the great stairways rising through many floors could be cared for by the many servants who inhabited the basements and attics.

This almost servantless age must be more economical of space and of labor. This means no nonessential space or projections to collect dust, fewer stairs, the same rooms for entertainment, generally informal, as for family use. The mother-cook in the kitchen must be where she can easily see and hear the children without devoting herself to their constant care. The lack of servants calls for few stories and closeness to the ground, and so does the informal Los Angeles life in the open. It is the unity of indoors and out that characterizes the California home life of today—the easy imperceptible flow from one to the other. And this is why the Radburn type of plan with its center of safe verdant openness fits so well the requirements of present-day Los Angeles.

Parks also form part of the New Town of Edinburgh. To the north and south are large open spaces that were landscaped as parks after the buildings were erected. The gardens to the north are enclosed for the use of the surrounding dwellings—but both are separated from the houses by busy streets—and so children must be guarded.

After almost two hundred years much of the monumental grandeur and beauty of George Street and its terminating squares, as well as Queen Street, still remain. But the invasions of commerce have destroyed the design of the Princes Street facades, and attacked the symmetry of the other street fronts. The plan was too static to bridge the change of two centuries. I wonder if the Baldwin Hills Village arrangement is flexible enough to weather the more rapid changes of the times in which we live. The fact that the buildings are cut off from the flow of traffic, and so are not likely to invite other than residential use, gives hope. The open spaciousness between buildings toward the greens offers opportunities for progressive and harmonious changes such as enclosed gardens,

organized or unequipped play spaces of varied kinds, and even a fairly large playground or a swimming pool. The greatest weakness is a certain incompleteness as a neighborhood. There should be a closer coordination between the residential super-block, its shopping center and its community facilities. This lack of adequate unity that requires an even larger, more comprehensive neighborhood plan and control is particularly apparent in the relation to the elementary school. If Baldwin Hills Village had been about twice its size it could have had a school located near its center. The architects had hoped that the land that climbed the hill south of Coliseum Street would be reserved for an addition that would have given the Village some 1250 families, and that the school and its playground might have been located on or near the center axis. But it was not to be. And so the children of the Village must risk their lives daily in crossing Rodeo Road, a busy highway.

If Baldwin Hills Village has not answered all of the physical problems of modern community development, it has found a saner and more progressive solution to certain basic difficulties in making city planning realistic and contemporary—of really making it work. We must recognize that to break all the chains that bind us to obsolete forms and procedures of past city building is a complicated task. We apparently must progress step by step. At Baldwin Hills Village the problem of co-ordinating full, direct, convenient service by automobile with spacious, peaceful, harmonious living came closer to solution than ever before. In its plan today's problems were frankly faced and answered both logically and beautifully. And so another step has been taken Toward New Towns for America.

INDICATIONS OF THE FORM OF THE FUTURE

This book has been called *Toward New Towns for America* because I have told the story of new communities at Sunnyside, Radburn, Chatham Village, Phipps Gardens, Hillside, Greenbelt, and Baldwin Hills Village primarily to see what could be found to help us in successfully conceiving, planning, constructing and operating New Towns. Although the developments described are not New Towns, they are steps toward creating New Towns. Each is limited but rich in suggestions. Note that I do not call them solutions. That is too final a word: at least they point the way. They contain many new ideas and are living experiences, not blue prints. I have reviewed them to see what might be regarded as warnings against errors, or might form the basis of future work.

Each of the developments has its own distinct individuality. Built in a period of twenty years of unprecedented technical progress, they are in different metropolitan areas, spread from the eastern to the western coast. The schemes differ in size and contain many types of residential buildings: apartments, row and free-standing houses. They have been constructed and operated by private corporations, foundations, or the Federal government for diverse income groups, and the dwellings have been for sale or rent.

In spite of these differences they are unified by common objectives, by the spirit in which these were pursued as well as by the three basic conceptions, the Garden City, the Radburn Idea, and the Neighborhood Unit, that served as guides in planning. Each heralds progress, some in one of the fields of organization, promotion, design, construction, or operation—some in another, but all are experiments leading toward New Towns.

Contemporary Towns

What do I mean by New Towns? Not merely that they are newly created. Many towns have been and are being built that are immediately obsolete and out-dated. They may have been fitted to an age long past; but they have nothing whatsoever to do with the life people now want to live, or would if they thought it were attainable.

New Towns are contemporary. This does not necessarily mean that they should have any particular type of 'New Look,' a different architectural style or veneer. By contemporary I mean towns that are planned, built, and operated to serve present day needs and conditions. During the past half-century or more we have rushed through history as never before. As a result our requirements for living, here and now, are utterly different from those met by the cities in which most of us live. This is apparent if we consider only a few of the main requirements of the period which New Towns are to serve:

1. *Increasing Leisure Time* means a shorter working day, and more hours for recreation. It allows evenings on playgrounds, in swimming pools, and loafing on the green, or for community affairs, lectures, clubs, and workshops. Free Saturdays as well as Sundays offer opportunities for hiking on a green belt, for long excursions, for keeping house and garden spic and span.

2. *Increasing Equality of Opportunity* to enjoy the goods of the world is available to an ever-larger proportion of American workers, together with some form of insurance schemes for unemployment, health, and old age. Sanitary and mechanical facilities are becoming standard equipment in the homes of those with moderate incomes and—thanks to public housing—even in those of the poor. Bathrooms, central heating, mechanical refrigerators, and even television are becoming universal. Community facilities, such as schools, cinema, outdoor and indoor recreation, libraries, are fundamentally the same for employer and employee, and for all groups. The opportunity for a good life is con-

stantly broadening. What is needed is a better community setting and organization, and it is these which New Towns can provide.

3. *Mechanization.* The form and organization of our New Towns will to a large degree determine whether the machine shall serve, command or destroy our civilization.

4. *Disappearing Domestic Service.* In comparing Baldwin Hills Village and the 18th century New Town of Edinburgh (see pp. 212-216), I indicated how the lack of servants was leading to simplification of planning and an organization of house and community pattern that would lighten the mother's care of home and children. Nursery schools are only a first step toward organized or associated care of little ones to allow more freedom for parents. Central kitchens and laundries are a few of the indications of increasing simplification through mechanization or organization to replace the maids and cooks of yesteryear.

The Present Period of Growth and Change—technical, social, economic and political—is unprecedented. It is leading, through changing phases, to a different and, we hope, more stable economy. It demands new town forms and environment, a new stage and direction—and the possibility of revising the setting to keep in harmony with the changing show.

From Obsolete Cities to New Towns

To serve the evolving culture and civilization of which I have mentioned only a few principal characteristics, New Towns are essential. This is because the existing cities cannot fit the needs of this age without a complete rebuilding. It is not merely that the elements and the details of plan and mass urgently require new forms, but that the relation of these to each other, must be radically revised. For this, one must begin with a clean slate and a large one. Therefore it seems to me that the sane policy is first to direct our energy toward building new and complete communities from the ground up: that is to say on open land outside developed urban areas. This we should do until such time as we have adequately demonstrated, by contrast, how unworkable and wasteful are the obsolete patterns of the old cities, and how completely they demand replacement. It is futile to

attempt this in a small, piecemeal manner. Meanwhile, where attempts are made to redevelop our old cities it must be on an adequate scale to form New Towns or at least modern neighborhoods within the old cities, but to a pattern far different from the old. Each redevelopment project should be a further exploration of the new patterns that we have, at least in part, evolved through our trials and demonstrations, from Radburn to Baldwin Hills Village. Redevelopment will be useless unless each scheme is part of a coordinated process that will ultimately make the old cities into New Cities—modern cities.

Here are some of the basic evils and limitations of the old cities which New Towns and worthwhile redevelopment of existing urban areas must eliminate:

Dangers to Health and Life: The strained nerves, tension, physical disabilities, declining birthrate, breakdown, and madness, resulting from 'normal' urban life. Death at every street crossing perpetually haunting parents. Sunless, insanitary, filthy, congested slums spreading blight throughout the towns. The constant threat of catastrophic breakdown of water, food, fuel, machines, movement, all dependent on long tenuous supply lines, is ever present and horribly intensified by the menace of atomic war.

Congestion: Life and movement is imprisoned by gridiron streets forming an archaic pattern within which houses, factories, shops, and offices are crammed. Sunlight and breezes are blocked; privacy and effective working conditions are lacking. Buses and subways are packed tight with human indignity; 100 m.p.h. machines crawl snaillike as traffic is congealed.

Loneliness: Man is submerged in the colossal human swarm, his individuality overwhelmed, his personality negated, his essential dignity is lost in crowds without a sense of community.

Lack of Nature: In the canyons of the city, nature is obliterated by the hard masonry. Man is lost in the stony urban desert, with increasing distances between him and his natural abode of fields and woods, free-flowing breezes, and the sight of sky, sea, mountains, and wilderness.

Waste of Time, Money, Energy: In the city people are always going somewhere instead of doing things. The everlasting journeys to work and to play consume the hours and wealth that should go into productive, worthwhile, enjoyable occupations. The growing costliness of great cities absorbs an ever-larger share of the incomes of individuals and municipalities.

Ugliness: Monotony is produced by the endless repetition of similar rectangular blocks and the decaying wreckage of past disorder. Vision is limited by confining ugly walls. There is monotonous regimentation, smoke, and dirt.

The grave faults of the obsolete urban environment inevitably lead one to seek physical patterns more in harmony with present-day culture. The developments described in the preceding chapters have been proving grounds, and partial demonstrations of the evolving form of the future, in which:

Safety will take the place of danger when pedestrian and automobile traffic are entirely separated by the use of properly designed superblocks and specialized means of circulation throughout our cities.

Spaciousness will banish congestion when an orderly relationship is established amongst circulation, buildings, and open spaces, including open greenbelts and expansive block centers.

Nature will dominate, and all cities will be green cities, with parks in the heart of each block and encircling belts of agriculture, natural playgrounds and wilderness. Man's desire for a good life and his love of nature will determine the form of the town.

The Neighborhood, which will have a limited area and a central meeting place, will provide a setting for neighborly friendship and co-operative participation in common activities.

Beauty will be derived from the composition of building groups, their color and texture, and their relation to each other and to nature.

Economy of money, time, and energy will permit creative and recreative leisure activity and will come from:

1. Efficient planning for use, in place of speculative sale.
2. Large scale building and operation.
3. More efficient government and community organization, made possible by a well designed town of limited size.
4. The related location of homes, community facilities and work places to facilitate safe convenient walking and bicycling.
5. The decrease in the journey to work and other unproductive travel. (Over 10 per cent of America's consumption expenditure is for transportation, much of which would be unnecessary if industry and business were located within convenient distance of workers' homes.) [41]

In the distribution of industry in relation to living quarters we have made little progress. Solutions are to be found not only in terms of individual Garden Cities but also in regional constellations of varied types of New Towns set in a broad background of agricultural land and regional parks.

A Different Technique

New Towns mean new plans and different physical arrangements, with green belts and inner block parks, neighborhoods and superblocks, community centers, and the separation of roads and walks. These modern urban forms are bound to replace the obsolete, socially repellent, barren real-estate gamblers' checkerboard. But communities fitted to the life of today—and fit to live in now—will neither come into being nor have any lasting existence merely because the plan is modern. Creating New Towns implies more than designing new forms. A new technique is required, and this will involve a different procedure all the way from raw land to the neighborhood built and lived in.

The New Town technique must differ from the customary process of city growth in every element: its promotion and organization for development, its design, its construction, its marketing and its operation. It even requires another kind of legislative background and different ownership or control—at least control of land if not of building. These differences grow out of a fundamental contrast in objectives. The purposes of New Towns are basically opposed to the influences responsible for the growth of our old cities.

THE OBJECTIVE of New Towns is fundamentally social rather than commercial. Bluntly, the distinction is that between building for people or building for profit. Whereas the customary motive is primarily that of trade in real estate in whatever form and manner is most profitable, New Towns will be created for use as communities, vital and contemporary, to encourage and foster present-day good living.

THE PROMOTER creating New Towns or communities must differ in his methods and procedure from the speculator. Quick profit requires rapid sale, whether it be in the subdivider's lots or the promoter-builder's houses. This is a game made for irresponsible traders. For long-time investment quite a different type of promotion is essential. This demands large-scale finance for a long period. It is the field for limited dividend corporations, for companies with large capital to invest such as insurance companies and foundations. It is likely to be increasingly carried out by co-operatives and unions. It is more and more bound to be an activity of government, either as principal or as assistant, of co-operative or private group endeavor.

This type of promotion brings no quick profits as does the speculators'. But as in the cases of Hillside and Chatham Village, where the homes were on a rental basis, it has already proved a very sound investment. They both paid their way, amortized their capital costs and paid regular dividends. Because they are for lasting investment they were built soundly and spaciously planned, as communities, so that they would remain full of satisfied tenants—and they do. Under an economy illustrated by the valleys as well as hills pictured in the graph at the beginning of this volume, it seems the only way to make housing and New Town building a safe and sound investment (Fig. 1).

The New Town promoter naturally tends to be progressive: his purpose is to serve the public, to demonstrate a finer and more fitting background for community and family life. He and his architect and builder, and the other technicians, because they are in search of new and better ways of planning, constructing, and operating, do work that is both imaginative and scientific. They are pioneering. Not so the speculative builder. He takes the minimum risk and plays safe: that is the easiest way to get a loan. As a result his plans, exteriors, even the relation of his houses to each other and to their surroundings, are dull and conservative. They are just as near as possible like something

that has already been done. He repeats even his own past blunders. And so his products are, as likely as not, conventional and nearly always obsolescent before they are occupied.

BUILDING, both in its character and in its quality, is largely determined by its objective. The New Town investor counts costs on a long-term basis. The yearly expenses of operation and maintenance are more important to him than the original capital investment. So he constructs soundly. At Hillside the buildings were fireproof throughout, instead of the less expensive semi-fireproof the law permitted —and yet the annual cost, that is, the carrying charges on the investment, was decreased as the loan charges on the safer construction were less and for a longer term. At Chatham Village wood was eliminated as far as possible from exteriors because brick required less care.

Keeping all buildings full during depressions, as well as in periods of housing scarcity, is essential to moderate rental housing. No vacancies, no bad debts, over the period of years in which the original investment is paid off, more than balance higher original costs for sound construction, spacious greens and gardens, as Hillside, Chatham Village and Phipps so well testify. At Baldwin Hills Village the large rooms, the many closets, the well-equipped kitchens and bathrooms not only spell good living but sound investment. In short, in New Town building the time factor is the prime consideration in counting costs.

This is not so in speculative building. The only time that interests the speculative builder is the short period between securing his mortgage and unloading his product. The speculator is more likely to put his money in gadgets, in advertisements, selling force and ballyhoo than in sound lasting qualities or in livability or neighborhood features. There are exceptional speculative builders such as the builders of Levittown, but most of them give no more in size and quality than the scant requirements for FHA insurance.

City Planning New and Old

To build a substantial setting for neighborhood and family life, rather than to control and regulate, requires a completely different kind of planning. That is why I intend to call it community development or *New Town Planning* to differentiate it from the procedure that is generally called city planning in America. There is actually an antithesis between the two procedures. The prime objective of one is to assist in the marketing and protection of property, of the other to create communities. The latter deals with the realities of living rather than with trading. The two are at cross-purposes: preserve and protect in contrast with devise and produce.

New Town planning is an integral part of a co-ordinated procedure for building communities that will be both contemporary and dynamic. Note:

CO-ORDINATED, not disorganized
BUILDING, not delineating
COMMUNITIES, not lots or streets
CONTEMPORARY, not obsolete
DYNAMIC, not static.

New Town planning is not a separate function; it is an integral part of a procedure that creates a complete, solid, living community. It is an essential link in the chain of related and interdependent processes that actually turn open country land into complete, vibrant towns—good places to live in.

City planning is too often an afterthought; in other words it is no more than city patching. It is not the work of a creator, but of a surgeon called in too late to operate on a decaying carcass. Such city patching deals with *means* rather than ends. It creates superhighways, supercomplicated intersections or other gargantuan minutiae while neglecting the causes and sources of congestion. Thus it often fans the flame instead of extinguishing the fire. It is so fully concerned with mechanical or engineering feats that it loses sight of the ultimate goal of planned development—better living.

The New Town planner requires a broad understanding of aims and objectives, and of all the related functions with which he must work to realize them. As his technical work is part of a larger process of creating a community background, that is to say of building, and not mapping or drawing, he must work as part of a team. That was one of the great and and inspiring features of the work of the City Housing Corporation under the leadership of Alexander M. Bing in building Sunnyside and Radburn—the teamwork of a group with such varied knowledge and ability as had Herbert

Emmerich, Louis Brownlow, Henry Wright, John O. Walker, Frederick L. Ackerman, Charles S. Ascher, Ralph Eberlin, Marjorie Cautley and myself.

The old type of city planning is merely one of a disorganized series of unrelated activities that produce chaotic cities, including land speculation, lot subdivision, skeleton highway plans, individual house plans, regulations, spotty location of public buildings, and ultimately rebuilding unrelated structures one after the other, when zoning inevitably surrenders to the greed of individual lot owners.

In all this the city planner plays but a minor role. It is not his detailed factual surveys, his traffic counts, his calculations of population growth, his clever graphs, his many colored diagrams of use and heights, nor his superbly presented reports that determine the ultimate form and substance of our cities. Look at the ugly, dangerous, irrational, chaotic messes we call cities: certainly these are not the result of a purposeful plan for good living or even for efficient industry and trade. The essential reality of these cities has not been conceived, devised, pre-determined.

This present kind of city planning does not deal with substantial realities; but with phantom cities, outlines of cities. It delineates bodiless skeletons instead of creating habitable, solid cities. Its subject is primarily a framework for saleable lots, not a community. It is concerned with separate and limited units: lots, individual houses, a single road, not community building. Because city planning outlines and regulates, and does not relate these units in a composed group or neighborhood, it must generalize. This requires stereotyped, conservative, easily classified, standardized objects; these are more easily marketed and regulated.

The present city form is not molded by the planner. It is the random consequence of the separate and unrelated decisions of subdivider, municipal engineer, zoning board, speculative builder, aided and abetted by the FHA and the lending institutions.

Finally, the shape and appearance of things, and the relation of the parts that make the chaotic accidents called cities, are the summation of the haphazard, independent whims of a multitude of

INDICATIONS OF THE FORM OF THE FUTURE

individuals. They ultimately determine the pattern for living by filling in the cubby-holes marketed by the subdivider; and for the individual there seems to be no alternative.

To fill in the form, the body, the reality of the town, city planning proceeds not by positive action but by negations. It restricts and regulates, and limits use, height and bulk by zoning laws.

These regulations are usually commonplace generalizations. They result in monotonous similarity of use, height, coverage and outline of neighboring buildings. Predetermined related variety of mass, height, and a common pooling of open spaces is found in our cities only in such exceptional large-scale unified developments as Rockefeller Center. This kind of purposeful organized design that produces architectural and civic beauty as well as better lighting and ventilation is never attainable by the old highway-framework-subdivision process of city planning, even with the addition of the best-intentioned and most expert zoning. Nor can the special community facilities be grouped in a serviceable or attractive manner by this type of wishful negation.

The kind of city planning of which I have just spoken was not helpful in creating the communities described in these articles. It was foreign to their objectives: they would have been hampered, not aided, by its use. Experiments such as the Radburn Idea never could have been realized within the framework both legal and physical, that has circumscribed the city planners' thinking and activities. At Radburn we were able to work on a clear slate because we got there before the zoners and the subdividers and the municipal highway engineers. Their immovable framework would have held up progress there and, afterwards, at Chatham Village, the Greenbelt Towns and Baldwin Hills Village.

The full realization of the economic as well as the living advantages of the Radburn Plan cannot be attained by the ordinary piecemeal process of city planning for lot subdivision. It must be built in—houses, roads, walks, parks, gardens—and a definitely determined reality must be created that will fit a desired way of living long enough to pay off its capital, maintenance and operational costs. It must furthermore be arranged to allow the changes required to keep it in harmony with this changing world.

To attain the economies that the Radburn type of planning officers, the gambling chance of increased monetary values of a lot must be given up. If the less costly types of specialized means of communication, such as the cul-de-sac at Radburn or garage court at Baldwin Hills Village, are to be used, there is little opportunity of finding a better paying future use for an individual piece of property, for example, for a commercial purpose. Therefore zoning would be only reiteration. The future use is more purposefully and lastingly set by group buildings than by regulations open to constant change.

The green inner core of the superblock is the cheapest as well as the most satisfactory way of securing nearby verdant openness. But the unusual location of the inner block commons requires an unusual form of community organization or of legal framework to maintain and organize it.

In creating New Towns, planning and building go hand in hand. They must be united as two inseparable parts of one process. Just as architecture is concerned with the solid realities of structures, so New Town planners must deal in terms of three-dimensional actuality. As city architect or civic designer he must mold form and mass as well as predetermine city plan or outline. A beautiful and livable urban environment requires a comprehensive design embracing the site, the form, the mass and the detail of every building and the relation of each building to the whole site and neighboring structures — in short all the visual surroundings.

Civic design is foreign to the methods of the old city planning. It cannot be clamped within the confines of lots or of the conventional gridiron. It requires the unified design of a portion of the city at least large enough to form a complete visual picture. This picture the New Town planner must paint on a broad canvas, a canvas large enough to comprise all that the human eye can envisage at a time. The developments which are illustrated in this book have done this in different ways. In every case the landscape and the structures have been blended into a unified composition, with great foregrounds of lawns and related verdure, and the mass and color of buildings composing pleasantly together and with this background. In Baldwin Hills Village the long horizontal lines of the houses contrast with the rounded slopes of the surrounding hills (Figs. 142-148); in Chatham Village the houses climb up the hills (Figs. 57, 61) and in Greenbelt the simple rows are arranged one above the other on the rising ground. In each one of them the great mass of spacious green around which they are set unifies and dominates the composition. At Radburn the broad lawns and spreading trees are the center of visual beauty just as they are the center of the community (See Figs. 17, 31, 38, 40). It is this spaciousness that is the keynote of the wholesome, good living of these places. And the comprehensive views of grouped buildings are dependent on the openness of the central greens, around which each one is composed in a different way. Even the greens of Sunnyside, in spite of the more restricted gridiron frame, give a natural charm and beauty to the simple rows of brick buildings (Fig. 12).

The contrast between the massing of open spaces at Baldwin Hills Village and the spotty, disorderly distribution in the typical lot unit development, with half the number of homes per acre, is apparent in the airview (Fig. 142). The spacious green inner park within the superblock, protected and insulated from auto traffic, has been applied only to limited neighborhood communities, as at Radburn, Greenbelt, and Baldwin Hills Village. It is still to be applied to a *city as a whole* (although Mayer and Whittlesey propose to do just that in the plan they are making for the New Capital City of East Punjab in India).

But it seems to me that the few examples in this book should indicate why and how the principles of New Towns should and can be applied to the planning and replanning of whole cities. So let me repeat, with somewhat greater emphasis on the City as a work of art, some of the reasons for the Radburn type of planning.

GOING PLACES and ENJOYING THE USE OF PLACES are quite distinct and different functions. What serves one is antagonistic to the other. Therefore a circulatory plan and a plan for a maximum practical and aesthetic use of the building and spaces of a city must be kept separate.

The same forms or means cannot serve the two at one time or at one place. Although they complement each other, they require different locations and forms, diametrically contrary in use. To coordinate these two is a basic problem of contemporary planned city development. That is the purpose of the Radburn type of plan.

CIVIC DESIGN for inspiring delight, and CITY TRAFFIC PLANNING for safe, easy, quick flow of modern traffic must be harmonized if a modern city is to be completely practical for circulation and use, and at the same time, full of beauty. Although these are by nature antagonistic, they must be integrated into a practical beauty. They will cripple or destroy each other unless they are functionally and spaciously separated and at the same time mutually serve each other.

Let us examine and compare the requirements of City Traffic Planning and Civic Design.

A CITY TRAFFIC PLAN requires for speed, safety and maximum steady flow:

1. Straight roads or long sweeps with clear visibility at crossings and of approaching traffic.
2. As few crossings as possible.
3. No access to or from buildings on primary roads.
4. Minimum visual distraction—the auto driver's attention should be kept on the road.

The objective of such planning is to allow vehicles to move from one place to another as safely, quickly, directly and easily as possible.

CIVIC DESIGN, on the other hand, deals with the presentation of a city's buildings and open spaces so that they give the greatest pleasure and enjoyment. That each individual building should have beauty of form, mass and color is not sufficient.

The display of a building as part of civic design has much in common with display of the treasures in a well-designed museum. Buildings, like art objects, must be placed so that they will be observed, examined, appreciated and enjoyed. This is impossible in a formal monumental museum and equally so in a gridiron-patterned city.

The automobile has made obsolete the classical monumental type of city plan, dominated by highway axes leading from one important structure to

INDICATIONS OF THE FORM OF THE FUTURE

another. Terminal vistas are not for the auto driver; he has not time to enjoy them while keeping on the move; and even if he did, his attention should not be distracted. In Edinburgh's Georgian 'New Town' the man on horseback, or in a horse-drawn carriage, had an opportunity to observe and enjoy the street composition while approaching its terminal of church, monuments or government building. This met the requirements of the Eighteenth Century. But it is meaningless in a Twentieth-Century city. Vistas of dominant buildings there should be for leisurely enjoyment. Therefore they should face parks or public places from which vehicular traffic is excluded.

Even less appropriate to the needs of a contemporary New Town than the Worlds' Fair kind of city plan is the typical gridiron plan, in which all buildings are filed away in cubby-holes at either side of a highway, so that one passes them by no matter how significant they may be. The architectural masterpieces might as well not exist for any citizen or visitor of a gridiron-planned city. He passes good and bad alike, with merely a hasty glance to right or left. His mind and eye are on the traffic and the distant perspective. He is going somewhere—he has neither the time nor the desire for visual enjoyment. Before him, if he is in an automobile, he sees and observes only flashing green and red lights, traffic police and congested highway. If he is on foot his attention is concentrated on the danger of street crossings, while he battles with the crowds. A striking group of buildings or a monument terminating a busy highway would be wasted on either pedestrian or driver. But in the typical gridiron city neither walker nor motorist approaches a building or an architectural group of structures in an attractive setting. If he did see them the composition, no matter how attractive, would be lost on him. His attention is elsewhere. He is not in the spirit for beauty, grandeur, inspiration.

The setting in which interesting buildings or groups of buildings are to be viewed must be separated from the massed flow of machines or people. It is not enough for one to give them a passing glance and be momentarily attracted, one must remain long enough for the beauty to become part of one's consciousness. This is not possible in the midst of rushing activity. Peaceful surroundings, away from the movement and uproar of the streets, is the proper setting for civic design. Here buildings can be enjoyed in relation to open places or in natural surroundings, across water or gardens. One should be able to remain long and comfortably to discover varied beauties, as the light changes. One should approach the great monument or group reverently, slowly, by foot. And there should be several approaches, so that one can see it at various angles, in different compositions of landscape and architecture.

Dynamic Cities

A new town must remain contemporary for a very long period. Only thus can we afford it. It must last long enough to allow its original cost to be amortized. That on the face of it may seem impossible, for the main characteristic of the present time is change—change in our way of living, in our thinking, even our objectives; and above all in our technical facilities and ability to make changes.

New Towns must not only be the flowering of today's life and civilization, but they must have in them the seed of the future—or at least the facility of growing and changing to fit it. They must be dynamic. Therefore our New Towns, if they are not quickly to become our Old Towns, must be flexible. We must plan so as to limit the difficulties we now face in the redevelopment of our old cities, which require extravagant destruction and the rebuilding of vast areas.

To make this possible we need:

1. A community of completely integrated neighborhoods.

2. A minimum original investment in buildings or equipment which are costly to alter or replace.

3. Plentiful open space in which the community form and pattern can be set and developed.

The cause of blight in the old sections of cities is due largely to the fact that they were built not as the living-working place of an interrelated, interdependent community, but as a conglomeration of crowded, unrelated units or cells. These are so packed together that there is no room for the individual house or workplace to stretch, expand or change. There is no space in which the community form or pattern can be modified or re-organized without complete destruction.

If revision to meet gradual and continuous change is not to be wastefully extravagant, we need the smallest possible investment in big buildings with complicated mechanical equipment and therefore high first costs. It is practically impossible to amortize such investment in either skyscraper office or residential buildings before they are functionally obsolete, or before the congestion they foster blocks city transit and transportation and makes their servicing and use unbearably slow and costly.

Large sections of New York are now being rebuilt with massed, regimented apartment houses, both by the Municipal Housing Authority and by large insurance companies. This tendency is being followed in various other cities in America and even in Europe. Here the basic living requirement of easy access to adequate natural green surroundings is neglected. If the life of these buildings were figured less on the basis of structural and more on that of social obsolescence in a changing world, I think the policy would be different.

Spacious planning with large areas left open for future change is the surest method of preparing for flexible growth. That is one of the principal advantages of Green Cities, with great open space surrounding them as greenbelts and in the centers of superblocks. There is room for change and for the growth of present requirements without complete destruction and rebuilding.

Many elements of the existing communities tend to grow and to demand more space, without having adequate room for expansion. The present trend to build one-story schools is an example. The increased acreage needs of play spaces for all ages is another. Additional community requirements, such as Health Centers, Nursery Schools, Youth Centers, are continually being recognized. As these new functions develop and need buildings, there should be room to place them in proper relation to other elements of the Neighborhood or District Center. Flexibility calls for, above all else, space—more space than is needed to compass the original requirements.

Parking space for motor cars is the type of unforeseen change that requires flexible spaciousness.

We now know that we must have immense parking space—far more than for building—if we are not to tie up all movement by filling our highways with parked cars. Yet old habits persist and many housing developments are still built with scant room for parking one car per family and no space for garaging.

These changes we have already seen. Others are sure to follow—for instance in transportation. If individual air traffic by helicopter or other means should replace or at least surpass the use of the automobile some day, nearby open areas either surrounding a town or neighborhood as green belts or in the middle of a superblock can be used advantageously to keep these towns contemporary.

The Basis of New Town Planning

THE UNIT OF DESIGN in New Towns is no longer each separate lot, street or building; it is a whole community; a co-ordinated entity. This means that the framework of the community and every detail down to the last house and the view from the windows must be conceived, planned and built as a related part of a great setting for convenient, wholesome, and beautiful contemporary living and working. In this way every house gains from its relation to the buildings around it. Beauty as well as convenience is produced by the rational relationship of the individual parts.

The planning of every house and every room in that house is part of the process which gives the superblock its ultimate shape and character. Thus, the size and specific requirements of inner green and private yard, of cul-de-sac or auto court, help mold the superblock in relation to good living in home, community and town.

As he designs, the New Town planner envisages the future home life of the individual and the family, and their life as part of the community. He sees it not only in terms of house and garden but in the grouping of houses in relation to each other so as to take the utmost advantage of sun and wind for every residence, and to open up pleasant, spacious and varied views from every house and, as far as possible, in every direction. He will in part be guided by the form and nature of the land, and how its trees and streams and rocks can best be used or preserved for the common use and enjoyment of the people who are going to form the community, and whose life, from birth to old age, will be molded by the place.

New Town planning deals with the fundamental realities of living in a contemporary community, and, since we cannot foresee tomorrow's needs, it must take the future into account and allow for flexibility. The town plan must be molded to the life people wish to lead, and to fit the special needs of this twentieth century with all its differences—mechanical and other—from the past. The form of the home and its surroundings and the whole city must fulfil the requirements and aspirations of those who are to live in them. What these needs and aspirations are the planner cannot learn from most books—certainly not from technical works that deal with merely spiritless forms. He generally cannot determine them by surveys of existing conditions and of past performance. That is more often the way to find out what not to do, because so much of the present-day form, structure, equipment and practice is outdated and obsolete, and unrelated to the needs of the day.

The planner cannot discover the needs of people merely by asking them what kinds of home and town or community they want to live in. They do not know beyond their experience. However, with their assistance—not their guidance—he must discover their requirements. He must explore patiently, realistically, imaginatively. He should live in the places he helps to create, as Raymond Unwin did at Hampstead Garden Suburb and Henry Wright did at Sunnyside and Radburn. If he does not become an active part of the community he should know the people and managers and storekeepers. He should visit them often and come to see the life there both through their eyes and his own. That is what I have tried to do, so that I might progress from one experience and experiment to the next, on the basis of the realities of living communities.

The guiding motive for the New Town planner in molding the whole and its part is this: he is creating a stage, a theater for the good life. Yes, the planner's work is in many ways surprisingly like that of the skilled scenic designer. Lee Simonson, who was trained as a painter, at first designed his sets as pictures that would surprise and delight

the audience and draw their first applause. But, he has told me, he soon found that did not serve the need throughout the play: the actors did not seem to fit into the place. So he carefully studied the text. In his mind's eye he followed each character as he would enter, move, stand and relate himself to other actors. He saw the life of the play, and as he followed this *it* set the stage; it determined the location of every door and piece of furniture. The shape of stage-set and the background became inevitable. The rest was easy.

That is just what the good planner does. He creates a setting in which people—the kind of people that will live there—will fit, where they will live a varied life, a convenient life, a beautiful life; where they will grow and change, and their surroundings can also change with them. The planner's subject, then, is man. It is his fellows and their reaction to their environment which he must study and understand.

I do not mean to suggest that taste and imagination and a feeling for good and great design in form and color are not essential requirements of community planner and architect. But they are not enough. New Town planning as well as architecture is an art, a great art, but it differs fundamentally from painting. The resulting work is not merely a form or pattern that the artist evolves out of his inner consciousness and projects on the canvas. Community planning starts not with aesthetic conception but with exploration, discovery, unveiling. It facilitates growth and leaves a record of human ideals and purposes that may last beyond its time.

THE SPIRIT in which the communities illustrated in this book were conceived, planned, developed, and in which most of them were operated, was that of exploration. From the days of Sunnyside to those of Baldwin Hills Village we have been in search of new or revised solutions of the setting for communities as well as for family and individual living. We have sought ways of bringing peaceful life in spacious green surroundings to ordinary people in this mechanical age. We have tried to simplify the complexity of needs and desire as contrasted with means, and thus to make changes, from the obsolete methods of the dead past, economically feasible.

Investigation and research has been an important

guide in our progress. In this the economic study always paralleled the social or architectural, as illustrated by my studies for the Resettlement Administration and Henry Wright's analysis of building operations at Sunnyside.

It has been my experience that one can never accept a planning or architectural solution as final. Every problem seems to require fresh analysis, a new approach, a different angle. As soon as an idea has become formalized into a rule of procedure, and as soon as designers give up the adventurous search, the solution used in the past seems to dry up and lose its quality and clarity.

Perhaps this tendency for ideas, that have bloomed, flowered and been accepted, to wither and petrify when given administrative sanction, has led me to be suspicious of all accepted formulas, even when I have sown the seed from which they grew. When an idea becomes conventional it is time to think it through again. Never-ending exploration and the charting of new ways is the life-force of the architect and the New Town planner, whose shield of battle should bear the simple device —a question mark.

APPENDIX

The Appendix includes some of the Reports which formed a series prepared for the Resettlement Administration in 1935 while the Greenbelt Towns were being planned. The Reports are described on pages 121-2 and are referred to throughout the article on Greenbelt. They dealt with:

Appraisal of plans

Studies of the relative improvement costs of various schemes of house grouping

> *Appraisal of group plans: relative cost of improvements of various schemes of house grouping*
>
> *Outline of specification used for estimating purposes*
>
> *Details of schemes*

Studies of relative cost of construction and improvements of various schemes of house grouping

> *Brief outline specification for houses (omitted here)*
>
> *Relative cost of construction of various schemes of house grouping*

Studies of operation-maintenance costs in Suburban Resettlement Communities

Operation-maintenance costs of local government and community activity

> *Operation-maintenance costs of houses*
>
> *Shopping centers*
>
> *Analysis of family budgets*
>
> *Rents, amortization charges and interest*

Parts of some of the above appear in the text and therefore are not repeated in the appendix: These include; *Shopping centers*, pp. 162-3, 164-6; *Analysis of family budgets*, p. 163; *Studies of operation-maintenance costs of local government and community activity in Suburban Resettlement communities*, pp. 168-9, 174.

The purpose of the studies was to indicate a broad and practical method of approach to the inter-related problems of social, economic and physical planning. It was felt that they were needed because the conception and design of a complete town to be built quickly were new subjects to most of the technicians involved. Previously they had been dealing with unrelated parts of a process: the architects with individual buildings, the city planners with the mapping of streets, zoning and restrictions. The effective relationship of buildings to each other and to the community had hardly been considered.

Many of the controlling factors have changed since the Reports were made. To give examples; the value of the dollar has decreased and specifications have in some ways changed as have size and character of equipment. Again, experience has since taught me that plans should be more spacious in many ways.

Therefore, the diagrams and tables are included to illustrate a method of approach rather than to be copied or slavishly followed. Both Gordon Stephenson and I felt the method is of importance and that the material is of value if it suggests a comprehensive and practical approach to the planning of community development.

The last two tables, page 243, give the comparative costs of the *lane* in relative values and not in dollars and cents. In general terms both apply to present day conditions despite the fact that the cost of all operations has greatly increased in the last fifteen years and, as a consequence, money values are different.

Some of the Reports made for the Resettlement Administration

and contained in Memoranda to John S. Lansill

APPRAISAL OF PLANS

The considerations in appraising plans, in order of importance, are:—

1. Standard of living offered.
2. Operation-maintenance cost.
3. Capital cost.

Method of Appraising Standard of Living Offered

As a measuring stick, set up plans of adequate minimum space and equipment requirements for various functions connected with living in house. These will consist of kitchen, bathroom, stairs, dining and living space, bedroom for one or two persons, space for heating and storage.

Consider relation of units, i.e. rooms to each other for purposes of spacious family living, individual privacy, light, ventilation, sanitation, cleanliness (convenience in cleaning and protection from vermin).

These should be considered for varied sizes of families and varied types of families to be served on the basis of:—

1. Their habits of living.
2. Better habits that they might find desirable, or at least acceptable.
3. Their economic ability to pay for the operation-maintenance and furnishings of the required space and equipment.

Method of Appraising Operation-Maintenance Cost

Make tentative house plans and grouping of houses that will fulfil standard of living requirements at minimum cost. All increase in space, equipment, and structural standards beyond these must be justified in terms of cost.

In considering cost, operation-maintenance cost should be considered first.

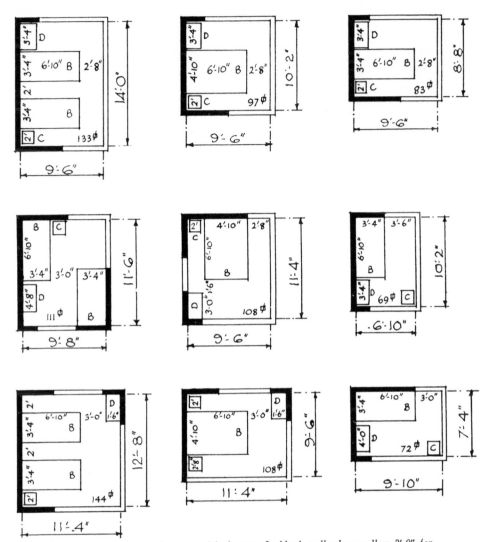

Fig. 167—Minimum space requirements of bedrooms. In blank walls shown allow 3'-0" for entrance door, 2'-6" for closet door, and space for windows. Add 6" to size of room where radiators and visers occur.

Operation-maintenance measuring stick must be cost of each factor of operation-maintenance of a given size and type of house grouped in a specified manner and of a specified type of construction.

In considering each proposed plan, measure the effect of change from standard of heating, painting, repairs, etc. as a result of:—

1. Change in size.
2. Increase or decrease of exterior wall.
3. Change in specifications.

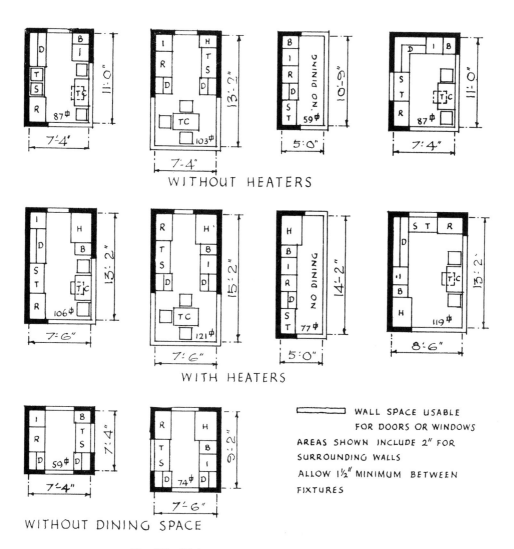

Fig. 168—Minimum space requirements of kitchens.

D	Dresser	2′ 0″ × 4′ 0″	L	H	Heater	2′ 6″ × 3′ 6″ W
B	Brooms	1′ 10″ × 1′ 4″ W		T	Tub	
I	Refrigerator	2′ 0″ × 2′ 0″		S	Sink	1′ 10″ × 3′ 6″
R	Range	2′ 0″ × 3′ 0″		TC	Table	2′ 0″ × 3′ 0″
	Range	1′ 0″ × 1′ 10″			Chairs	1′ 6″ × 1′ 6″

4. Changes in equipment such as refrigeration, heating, etc.

5. Relation to other buildings (grouping as affecting utility and road costs as well as house costs).

6. Relation to ground (site planning).

APPENDIX

Method of Appraising Capital Cost

Capital cost should be measured by comparison of breakdown of all costs of each proposed plan as compared with the tentative plans. This must consist not only of the cost of all material, labor, and equipment required for the house itself, but also of the utilities, roads, walks, and gardens required to serve the house when arranged in proposed typical grouping.

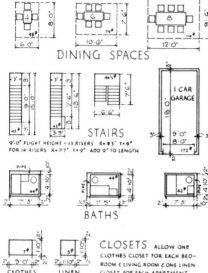

Fig. 169—Minimum space requirements.

Additional capital cost beyond that required for adequate standard can only be justified by the fact that it will decrease operation-maintenance costs. Even if capital cost is not charged to tenant, it must be kept to a minimum so as to:—

1. Take care of as many families and persons as possible within the appropriation.

2. Set standards of planning and building that will be sufficiently economical to serve as a guide to others in building in the near future.

Clarence S. Stein.
November 23rd, 1935

Memorandum to Mr. John S. Lansill

From Clarence S. Stein

Subject: *Studies of the relative improvement costs of various schemes of house grouping.*

The purpose of these studies is to measure the comparative efficiency of various methods of grouping houses as affecting street, yard, and park improvement costs. The same type of house has been used throughout. We have compared: houses facing on main roads and on lanes with and without vehicular roads; similar lanes of different lengths; houses in groups of different lengths with and without garages attached, as well as free-standing houses; houses with long and with narrow side towards the road.

The attached table showing cost per family, indicates that improvement costs may vary as much as approximately 54 per cent in Schemes 4 and 11. This would make a difference of approximately $457,000 for a development of 1,000 houses. These figures naturally do not take into consideration the possible differences of contour and soil conditions. They are based on approximate costs in the New York region at the present time under normal building conditions. They indicate, however, the relative—if not actual—difference in costs. Bearing this in mind, a few of the conclusions that may be drawn from these studies are:

1. The cost of improvements per house is greatest when houses are built facing on main roads. (Houses on main traffic ways are also probably the least desirable for good living). Schemes 10 and 11 show similar arrangement of houses, the one on a lane and the other on a main road. The estimates of these two indicate that conditions of soil and contour being equal, the latter will cost about 38 per cent more than the former.

2. Improvement costs of houses on lanes are increasingly cheaper per house as the length of lane increases. (See comparison of Schemes 2 and 3). It is apparent that a super-block of 1,000-ft. in width offers economic advantages over a block of half this width unless there are site conditions that over-balance the saving from decreased length of main highway and main lines of utilities per house.

3. The cheapest arrangement as affecting improvement costs, is that of row houses on lanes without vehicular roads in the lanes, but with garages grouped at entrance to lanes. (See Schemes 1 and 4). This arrangement has great advantages from the point of view of good living. It offers increased safety and quiet on the service side of the houses and at the same time, it permits complete privacy on the garden side. On the other hand, some Planners may prefer to sacrifice these advantages for the convenience of direct access to each house by automobile and greater ease in the delivery of bulky goods and fuel, and easier fire protection.

The lanes without roads show a cost advantage of about 18 per cent over those with roads (see Schemes 1 and 2). However, the length of lanes without

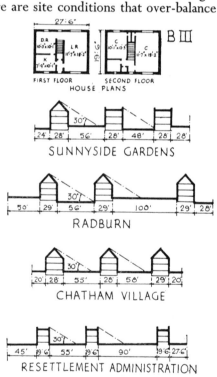

Fig. 170—Cross sections of lanes. House type B-III.

vehicular roads must be limited to facilitate delivery of heavy and bulky goods

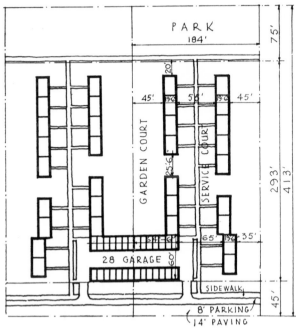

and of fuel. The proportionate difference of cost is greatly decreased when lanes with roads are increased to the greater length that their arrangement makes practical and acceptable (See Scheme 3). But, the economic advantage of the lane without roads will be increased on hilly sites where road construction is difficult and expensive.

This study has been made with the assistance of Ralph Eberlin and of Albert Lueders.

CLARENCE S. STEIN.

November 19th, 1935.

Fig. 171—House group. Scheme 1.

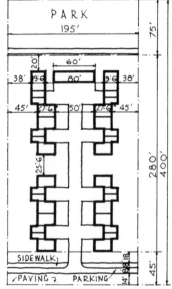

Fig. 172—House group. Scheme 2.

APPRAISAL OF GROUP PLANS
Relative cost of improvement of various schemes of

House Grouping

The diagrams are made for the purpose of measuring the comparative cost efficiency of various methods of grouping houses as affecting street, yard, and park improvements. The diagrams are not intended to be used as site plans. Site plans must be modelled to fit actual conditions of ground and the varied needs of those to be housed.

Costs will vary in accordance with wage rates, material costs, and organization of job operation in different locations. The costs here given were all arrived at on the basis of similar unit costs. They indicate the relative costs at the present time in the New York region. They are based on the theoretical use of approximately flat land and do not allow for grading. Actual costs will be modified by varied conditions of the contours and soil.

House Type B-III (See Fig. 170) has been used in all the diagrams. This type of house permits entrance to both kitchen and living room from a single vestibule at one side of the house. As a result, public passages at the garden side of the houses may be eliminated as in Schemes 1, 6, 8, 9. However, where there is a vehicular road on the service lane, a public path on the garden side is needed for the purpose of separating pedestrian and vehicular traffic. This principle of the 'Radburn Plan' has been adhered to excepting in Scheme 2.

The distance between houses, both on the service and garden side of houses is adequate, and if anything, liberal for moderate cost houses. Fig. 170 shows sections through lanes in Sunnyside, Radburn and Chatham Village for purposes of comparison with those used in these studies.

Parks are indicated in the diagrams as 150-ft. wide with houses set back 20-ft. from park line, making a total of 190-ft. between houses. This is the approximate average distance at Radburn. The amount of park land per family varies in accordance with the width of lanes and number of houses on each lane. Costs are given inclusive and exclusive of parks.

Where there is no lane and houses face on the main street, the park is indicated as only 50-ft. wide.

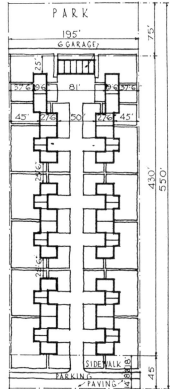

Fig. 173—(top right) House group. Scheme 3.

Fig. 174—(bottom) House group. Scheme 4.

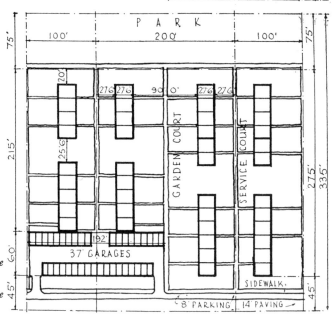

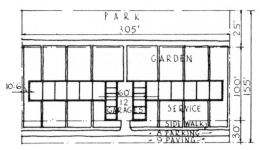

Fig. 175—House group. Scheme 5.

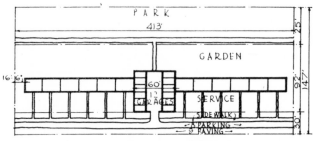

Fig. 176—House group. Scheme 6.

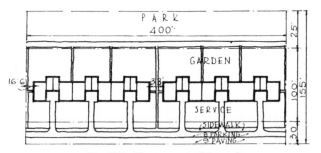

Fig. 177—House group. Scheme 7.

The depth of lanes is restricted in the case of those without vehicular roads directly to houses (Schemes 1, 4, 8, and 9) by limitations in delivery of fuel and in moving. A maximum distance of 225-ft. from road to house entrance has been used. This is not much greater than in large apartment groups such as Phipps and Hillside where furniture is carried from 180-ft. to 200-ft. It is presumed that there will be very little moving because of low rental charges for desirable houses. If coal is used rather than oil or gas for heating, it can be delivered in small quantities in hand carts with rubber wheels from municipal or co-operative centers.

In the case of lanes having direct road access to houses, the depth of the lane is limited by the distance from main road for delivery of fire protection and by the need of preventing congestion. Schemes 3 and 10 have approximately the same length as some of the longer lanes in Radburn. In Scheme 2, the lane was made shorter for the purpose of comparing with Scheme 1 which has the same number of houses, and with Scheme 3 which has similar arrangement of houses, but a longer lane.

CLARENCE S. STEIN.

November 19th, 1935.

APPRAISAL OF GROUP PLANS

Relative Cost of Various Schemes of House Grouping

In all studies one type of house has been used: a single-family, two-story, five-room house, 19-ft. 6-in. x 27-ft. 6-in.

Costs have been divided as follows:—

(*a*) MAIN STREET

Includes the following elements normally installed there even though some of the utilities may be actually located in areas other than in the main street and also some of the utilities that may be installed by the public utility corporation at its expense:—

Sidewalk—
   both sides of street.
Curb— ,,   ,,   ,,   ,,
Grass area—unpaved areas between curb and property line.
Main sanitary sewer.
Main storm sewer.
Main water main.
Main gas main.
Main electric and telephone pole line.
Paving—between curbs.

In computing the cost of installing these elements, consideration is given to the fact that some of these utilities serve both sides of the main street and therefore one-half of the actual quantities are charged to one side of the street.

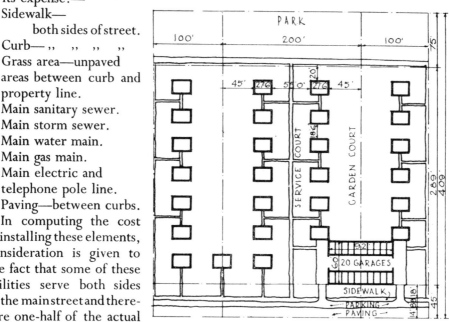

Fig. 178—House group. Scheme 8.

(*b*) GARAGE AND SERVICE ROADS
   Includes where they apply:—
   Garage driveways from curb.   Garage driveways from service road.
   Parking areas within service road and lane paving.
   Curb at parking area within service road and lane paving.
   Service road and lane paving from curb.

(*c*) PUBLIC SERVICES EXCLUSIVE OF (*a*) AND (*b*)
   Includes where they apply:—
   Common footways.
   Park footways.
   Park lighting.

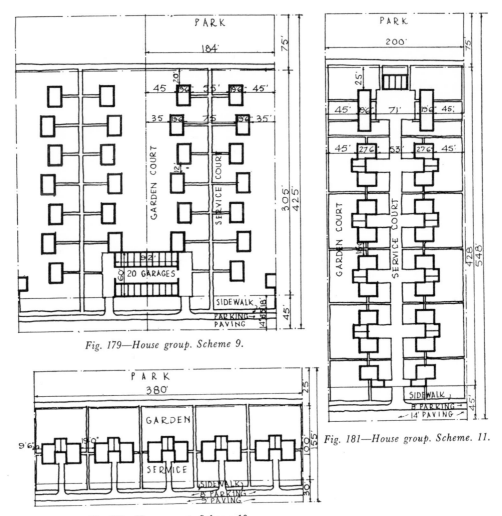

Fig. 179—House group. Scheme 9.

Fig. 181—House group. Scheme. 11.

Fig. 180—House group. Scheme 10.

Storm drain which serves for drainage of the park area and receives roof drainage service lines.

Lane sanitary sewer—where an independent sewer line is installed in the service lane to receive the house services.

Lane electric and telephone pole line—where an independent pole line is installed in the service lane to receive the house services.

Lane water main—where an independent water main is installed in the service lane to receive the house services.

Lane gas main—where an independent gas main is installed in the service lane to receive the house services.

(*d*) HOUSE SERVICES

Includes where they apply:—

Walks to buildings.

House sanitary sewer connections where these connections are made direct to an independent sewer.

Gas service where gas main is run through the length of the buildings and finally connects with one connection to the main gas main.

House gas service connections which are made direct to an independent gas main are considered as being installed free by the Gas Company.

Water service connections, where these connections are made direct to an independent water main.

House sanitary sewers where a common sewer is run through the length of the buildings and finally connects with one sewer connection to the main sewer.

Water service connections where a common water main is run through the length of the buildings and finally connects with one water connection to the main water main.

Roof drainage house connections from the roof leaders to the storm drain in (*c*).

(*e*) HOUSE YARDS EXCLUSIVE OF WALKS

Areas to be landscaped in yards, i.e. finished with top soil, seeding and planting or other surfacing.

(*f*) PARK LANDSCAPING

Areas to be landscaped in park, i.e. finished with top soil, seeding, planting, or other surfacing.

OUTLINE SPECIFICATION
USED FOR ESTIMATING PURPOSES

The Specification is based on the premise that operation-maintenance is the first cost consideration. Increase in capita cost, beyond that needed for adequate service, is justified on by decrease in operation-maintenance cost.

1. Paving of main street service roads and garage driveways—concrete, 6-in. thick, with wire mesh reinforcing, broom finish.

2. Curbs—concrete, 6-in. thick at top, 8-in. at bottom, 18-in. deep with steel nosings.

3. All walks—concrete, 4-in. thick, monolithic finish: street sidewalks 5-ft. wide: house walks 3-ft. wide: common footways 4-ft. 6-in., and footway along perimeter of park 7-ft. wide.

4. Park light—ornamental standard fed by park cable.

5. Sanitary sewers in service roads where they apply—8-in. diameter vitrified tile pipe and house service connections to these independent sewers 6-in. diameter vitrified tile pipe. These house service connections twinned for two houses wherever possible. Where houses are planned in a row without attached garages, house sewer lines run in cast iron pipes along the length of the groups and then finally twinned together in one main tile pipe service connection to the sewer in the main street.

6. Water mains in service roads where they apply—6-in. diameter pipe with one hydrant and house service connections twinned for two houses wherever possible with a service line. Where houses are planned in a row without attached garages, house service lines run along the length of the groups and then finally twinned together in one main connection to the water main in the main street.

7. Gas mains in service roads where they apply—4-in. diameter pipe and house service connections are twinned for two houses wherever possible. Where houses are planned in a row without attached garages, house service lines run through the length of the groups and then finally twinned together in one main connection to the gas main in the main street.

8. Storm and sanitary sewers—based on a separate system. These, together with water and gas in main highways, of course vary in size depending on their location within the town. Therefore an average unit price was used for the estimates for storm and sanitary sewers, water, and gas mains. A hydrant was allowed for approximately every 400-ft.

9. Landscaping includes top soil, seeding, and planting.

Comparison of Various Schemes of House Groups

B-III Single Family, Two Story, Five Room House, 19-ft. 6-in. x 27-ft. 6in.

SCHEME	1	2	3	4	5	6	7	8	9	10	11
Number of Houses	16	16	26	21	12	12	12	13½	13½	22	10
Number of Garages	14	16	26	18½	12	12	12	10	10	22	10
Gross Area of Plot	75,992 sq. ft. 1.75 acres	78,000 sq. ft. 1.79 acres	107,250 sq. ft. 2.46 acres	79,000 sq. ft. 1.81 acres	47,275 sq. ft. 1.09 acres	60,711 sq. ft. 1.39 acres	62,000 sq. ft. 1.42 acres	81,800 sq. ft. 1.88 acres	78,200 sq. ft. 1.79 acres	109,600 sq. ft. 2.51 acres	58,900 sq. ft. 1.352 acres
Area of Park	13,800 sq. ft.	14,625 sq. ft.	14,625 sq. ft.	15,000 sq. ft.	7,625 sq. ft.	10,325 sq. ft.	10,000 sq. ft.	15,000 sq. ft.	13,800 sq. ft.	15,000 sq. ft.	9,500 sq. ft.
Area of Houses	8,356 sq. ft.	8,450 sq. ft.	13,943 sq. ft.	10,904 sq. ft.	6,160 sq. ft.	6,241 sq. ft.	6,325 sq. ft.	7,240 sq. ft.	7,240 sq. ft.	11,763 sq. ft.	5,362.5 sq. ft.
Area of Garages	2,322 sq. ft.	2,592 sq. ft.	4,212 sq. ft.	2,997 sq. ft.	1,944 sq. ft.	1,944 sq. ft.	1,944 sq. ft.	1,620 sq. ft.	1,620 sq. ft.	3,564 sq. ft.	1,620 sq. ft.
Paved Areas	Sq. ft.	Sq. ft.	Sq. ft.	Sq. ft.	Sq. ft.	Sq. ft.	Sq. ft.	Sq. ft.	Sq. ft.	Sq. ft.	Sq. ft.
(a) Main Road	4,048	4,290	4,290	—	—	7,021	6,800	—	4,048	4,400	6,460
(b) Service and Garage Driveways	3,032	10,702	14,886	—	—	1,646	5,046	—	2,614	14,630	4,205
(c) Walks	4,790	2,275	7,177	—	—	6,722	5,683	—	4,811	6,836	5,867
Number of Families per Acre	9	9	10.5	11.6	11	8.6	8.5	7.19	7.5	8.83	7.4
Gross Land Area per Family	4,749 sq. ft.	4,875 sq. ft.	4,125 sq. ft.	3,762 sq. ft.	3,940 sq. ft.	5,059 sq. ft.	5,167 sq. ft.	6,059 sq. ft.	5,793 sq. ft.	4,982 sq. ft.	5,890 sq. ft.
Park Area per Family	863 sq. ft.	914 sq. ft.	562 sq. ft.	714 sq. ft.	635 sq. ft.	860 sq. ft.	833 sq. ft.	1,111 sq. ft.	1,022 sq. ft.	682 sq. ft.	950 sq. ft.
Front Footage of One-half Main Street per Family	11.5 ft.	12.19 ft.	7.5 ft.	9.5 ft.	25.41 ft.	34.42 ft.	33.3 ft.	14.8 ft.	13.6 ft.	9.09 ft.	38 ft.

Relative Improvement Costs of Various Schemes of House Groups

B-III Single Family, Two Story, Five Room House, 19-ft. 6-in. x 27-ft. 6-in.

TOTAL COSTS

SCHEME	1	2	3	4	5	6	7	8	9	10	11
(a) Main Street	$2,233	$2,328	$2,321	$2,419	$3,172	$4,274	$4,007	$2,417	$2,232	$2,397	$3,829
(b) Garage and Service Roads	667	2,400	3,275	653	362	362	1,110	575	575	3,219	925
(c) Public Services exclusive of (a) and (b)	1,183	2,093	3,300	1,319	865	975	1,038	2,278	2,334	3,314	837
(d) House Services	1,660	823	1,732	1,952	1,106	1,106	1,185	1,229	1,345	1,986	1,568
(e) House Yards exclusive of Walks	1,533	1,351	1,902	1,366	761	1,068	1,067	1,763	1,691	2,037	1,068
(f) Park Landscaping	500	530	530	544	218	297	287	544	500	544	273
GRAND TOTAL	$7,776	$9,525	$13,060	$8,253	$6,484	$8,144	$8,694	$8,806	$8,589	$13,497	$8,500
Total Exclusive of Park Landscaping	$7,276	$8,995	$12,530	$7,709	$6,266	$7,847	$8,407	$8,262	$8,089	$12,953	$8,227

COST PER FAMILY

SCHEME	1	2	3	4	5	6	7	8	9	10	11
(a) Main Street	$139.56	$145.50	$89.26	$115.19	$264.33	$356.17	$333.91	$179.00	$165.33	$108.95	$382.90
(b) Garage and Service Roads	41.69	150.00	125.96	31.10	30.17	30.16	92.50	42.59	42.59	146.32	92.50
(c) Public Services exclusive of (a) and (b)	73.94	130.81	126.92	62.81	72.08	81.25	86.50	168.74	172.89	150.63	83.70
(d) House Services	103.75	51.44	66.62	93.00	92.17	92.17	98.75	91.04	99.63	90.27	156.80
(e) House Yards exclusive of Walks	95.81	84.44	73.22	65.00	63.42	89.00	88.91	130.59	125.16	92.59	106.80
(f) Park Landscaping	31.25	33.12	20.38	25.90	18.16	24.75	23.92	40.30	37.04	24.73	27.30
GRAND TOTAL	$486.00	$595.31	$502.36	$393.00	$540.33	$673.50	$724.42	$662.26	$642.64	$613.49	$850.00
Total Exclusive of Park Landscaping	$454.75	$562.19	$481.98	$367.10	$522.17	$653.91	$700.50	$611.96	$599.18	$588.76	$822.70

Comparative Costs of Various Schemes of House Groups

B-III Single Family, Two Story, Five Room House, 19-ft. 6-ins x 27-ft. 6-in.

TOTAL COSTS

SCHEME	1	2	3	4	5	6	7	8	9	10	11
(a) Main Street	5.68	5.92	5.90	6.15	8.07	10.87	10.20	6.15	5.68	6.10	9.74
(b) Garage and Service Roads	1.70	6.11	8.33	1.66	0.92	0.92	2.82	1.46	1.46	8.19	2.35
(c) Public Services exclusive of (a) and (b)	3.01	5.33	8.40	3.36	2.20	2.48	2.64	5.80	5.94	8.43	2.13
(d) House Services	4.22	2.09	4.41	4.97	2.81	2.81	3.01	3.13	3.42	5.05	3.99
(e) House Yards exclusive of Walks	3.90	3.44	4.84	3.48	1.94	2.72	2.72	4.49	4.30	5.18	2.72
(f) Park Landscaping	1.27	1.35	1.35	1.38	0.56	0.76	0.73	1.38	1.27	1.38	0.70
GRAND TOTAL	19.78	24.24	33.23	21.00	16.50	20.56	22.12	22.41	22.07	34.33	21.63
TOTAL Exclusive of Park Landscaping	18.51	22.89	31.58	19.62	15.94	19.80	21.39	21.03	20.81	32.95	20.93

COST PER FAMILY

	1	2	3	4	5	6	7	8	9	10	11
(a) Main Street	0.36	0.37	0.23	0.29	0.67	0.91	0.85	0.46	0.42	0.28	0.97
(b) Garage and Service Roads	0.11	0.38	0.32	0.08	0.08	0.08	0.23	0.11	0.11	0.37	0.24
(c) Public Services exclusive of (a) and (b)	0.19	0.33	0.32	0.16	0.18	0.21	0.22	0.43	0.44	0.38	0.21
(d) House Services	0.26	0.13	0.17	0.24	0.23	0.23	0.25	0.23	0.25	0.23	0.40
(e) House Yards exclusive of Walks	0.24	0.22	0.19	0.16	0.16	0.23	0.23	0.33	0.32	0.24	0.27
(f) Park Landscaping	0.08	0.08	0.05	0.07	0.05	0.06	0.06	0.10	0.09	0.06	0.07
GRAND TOTAL	1.24	1.51	1.28	1.00	1.37	1.72	1.84	1.66	1.63	1.56	2.16
TOTAL Exclusive of Park Landscaping	1.16	1.43	1.23	0.93	1.32	1.66	1.78	1.56	1.54	1.50	2.09

This table was not included in the original Report. It was set up later to show costs in comparative terms rather than in terms of actual prices. Scheme 4, the most economical, was taken as the base and the grand total cost per family was assigned the value of 1.00.

APPENDIX

These detailed estimates of cost were made in 1935. They are now out of date. They are included only to show method of estimating.

Estimate of Scheme 1

16 houses and garage group of 14 garages.
Gross size of plot—184-ft. x 415-ft.—76,360 sq. ft.—1.75 acres.

(a) MAIN STREET

Main street sidewalk		780 at 18c	$	140
Curb		196 at 75c		147
Main Street paving		4,048 at 22c		890
Grass area		2,875 at 4c		115
Main sanitary sewer	92-ft. at 2.70	½ M.H. at 70		283
Main storm sewer	92-ft. at 3.00	½ M.H. at 70 and ¼ C.B. at 100		336
Water main	92-ft. at 1.45	½ Hydrant at 70		168
Gas Main	92-ft. at 1.25			115
Pole Line	92-ft. at 42c			39
				$2,233

(b) GARAGE AND SERVICE ROAD

Garage driveway (curb to P.L.)	402 at 22c		88
Garage and service roads	2,630 at 22c		579
			667

(c) PUBLIC SERVICE EXCLUSIVE OF (a) AND (b)

Common footway	1,411 at 18c		254
Park footway	1,288 at 18c		232
Park lighting—one standard			125
Storm drain connecting roof and park drains	348-ft. at 1.50 } 1.P.L. at 50 }		572
			1,183

(d) HOUSE SERVICES

Walks to buildings	1,311 at 18c		236
House sanitary sewer (through length of buildings)			568
Gas service	,, ,, ,, ,,		254
Water service	,, ,, ,, ,,		476
Roof drainage house connections (twinned)	252-ft. at 50c		126
			1,660

(e) LANDSCAPE—PARKS AND YARDS—grass area

Parks	12,509 at 4c	500	
Yards	38,330 at 4c	1,533	2,033

For 16 houses	$7,776
For 1 house	$486

Estimate of Scheme 2

16 houses—attached through garages.

Gross size of plot	195-ft. x 400-ft.—78,000 sq. ft.—1.79 acres.
Park	195-ft. x 75-ft.—14,625 sq. ft.
Main Street	195-ft. x 45-ft.— 8,775 sq. ft.

(a) MAIN STREET

Main street sidewalk	159-ft. x 5	795 at 18c	$	143
Curb		199 at 75c		149
Main street paving	195-ft. x 22	4,290 at 22c		944
Grass area—main highway		3,000 at 4c		120
Main sanitary sewer	97.5-ft. at 2.70 ½ M.H. at 70			298
Main storm sewer	97.5-ft. at 3.00 ½ M.H. at 70 ¼ C.B. at 100			352
Water main	97.5-ft. at 1.45 ½ Hydrant at 70			159
Gas main	97.5-ft. at 1.25			122
Pole line	97.5-ft. at 42c			41
				$2,328

(b) GARAGE AND SERVICE ROAD

Curb in lane parking			60 at 75c	45.
Lane paving—curb to P.L.	18-ft. x 23-ft	414 }		
	splays	172 } 6,886 at 22c	1,515	
18-ft. roadway	200-ft. x 18-ft.	3,600		
Dead-end	60-ft. x 45-ft.	2,700		
Garage driveways	18-ft. x 32-ft. x 6	3,456 } 3,816 at 22c	840	
	18-ft. x 10-ft. x 2	360 }		
				$2,400

(c) PUBLIC SERVICE EXCLUSIVE OF (a) AND (b)

Common footway	23-ft. x 5—115 at 18c	21
Park footway	195 x 7—1,365 at 18c	246
Park lighting		125
Storm drain connecting roof and park drainage	333-ft. at 1.50 ⎱	
	1.P.I. at 50 ⎰	550
Lane sanitary sewer—262-ft. (8-in.) at 1.50 1 M.H. at 70		463
Lane Pole Line—245-ft. at 42c		103
Lane water main—245-ft. (6-in.) at 1.35 1 Hydrant at 70		401
Lane gas main (4-in.)—245-ft. at 75c		184

$2,093

(d) HOUSE SERVICES

Roof drainage house connections (twinned) 30-ft. a 2—60 ⎱ 510 at 50c		255
45-ft. x 10—450 ⎰		
House sewer connections (6-in.) (twinned) 40-ft. x 5—200) ⎱ 270 at 1.25		338
70 x 1—70 ⎰		
Lane water connection (1-in.) (twinned) 270-ft. at 85c		230

$823

(e) LANDSCAPE—PARKS AND YARDS—grass area

Parks 13,255 at 4c		530
Yards 33,769 at 4c		1,351

$1,881

For 16 houses	..	..	..	..	..	..	..	$9,525
For 1 house	..	..	..	..	..	..	..	$595

Estimate of Scheme 3

26 houses.

Gross size of plot   195-ft. x 555-ft.   108,225 sq. ft.—2.48 acres.
Park   195-ft. x   75-ft.   14,625 sq. ft.
Main Street   195-ft. x   45-ft.   8,775 sq. ft.

(a) MAIN STREET As Scheme 2 except—

Grass area	2,816 sq. ft. at 4c	113

$2,321

(b) GARAGE AND SERVICE ROAD

Lane paving—curb to P.L.—As Scheme 2	586 ⎱		
18-ft. roadway—350 x 18	6,300 ⎰ 9,126 at 22c	2,008	
dead-end—56 x 40	2,240 ⎰		
Garage driveways—18 x 32 x 10	5,760 at 22c	1,267	

$3,275

(c) PUBLIC SERVICE EXCLUSIVE OF (a) AND (b)

Common footway	2,169 at 18c	390
Park footway	1,365 at 18c	246
Park lighting		125
Storm drain connecting roof and park drainage	488-ft. at 1.50 ⎱	
	1.P.I. at 50 ⎰	782
Lane sanitary sewer	415 at 1.50 1 M.H. at 70	692
Lane Pole Line	395 at 42c	166
Lane water main	395 at 1.35 1 Hydrant at 70	603
Lane gas main	395 at 75c	296

$3,300

(d) HOUSE SERVICES

Roof drainage house connections (twinned)	795 at 50c	398
House sewer connections (twinned)	391 at 1.25	489
House water connections (twinned)	391 at 85c	332
Walks to buildings	2,848 at 18c	513

$1,732

(e) LANDSCAPE—PARKS AND YARDS—grass area.

Park 13,255 sq. ft. at 4c		530
Yards 47,550 sq. ft. at 4c		1,902

$2,432

26 Houses	..	..	..	..	..	..	..	$13,060
1 House ..	..	..	..	..	..	..	..	$502

These detailed estimates of cost were made in 1935. They are now out of date. They are included only to show method of estimating.

APPENDIX

Memorandum to Mr. John S. Lansill

From Clarence S. Stein

Subject: *Studies of relative cost of construction of various schemes of house grouping.*

This is a continuation of the study which I submitted to you on November 19, 1935. The first report dealt exclusively with the cost of street, yard, and park improvements. In the attached study, the relative construction costs of the lanes already analyzed are compared. The same type of house has again been used.

We do not know exactly the type of construction that will be used. We have taken as basis, for estimating purposes, the type of construction of small houses that is used commonly in the New York region, i.e. brick veneer on wood frame.

Costs will naturally vary not only in accordance with type of construction used, but in method of organizing work. The costs given are approximately those in northern New Jersey at the present time under normal building conditions. The figures are intended to indicate the relative—if not the actual—difference in costs of construction of house type B-III grouped in different ways.

The findings of this study and of the earlier one are summed up on the table ' Relative Costs of Construction and Improvements of Various Schemes of House Grouping,' below.

In the preparation of this study I have been assisted by C. S. Carlson, F. E. Vitolo, and Albert Lueders.

RELATIVE COST OF CONSTRUCTION

OF HOUSES IN VARIOUS GROUPS

(All estimates are based on the use of house type B-III, see page 233)

(Costs do not include professional fees—or design and drafting; builder's fees—or supervision; insurance: or any charges for the use of money during construction)

COST PER UNIT	SCHEME 1		
$3,512 per family	16 houses at $3,432 each	$54,912	
	8½ end walls at $130 each	1,105	
	17 windows at $10 each (in end walls)	170	
			$56,187
$225 per garage	14 car garage		3,150
	TOTAL		$59,337

247

COST PER UNIT	SCHEME 3		
$3,502 per family	26 houses at $3,432 each	$89,232	
	12 end walls at $130 each	1,560	
	24 windows at $10 each (in end walls)	240	
			$91,032
$275 per garage	10 two-car garage units at $568	5,680	
	1 six-car garage unit at $1,450	1,450	
			$7,130
	TOTAL		$98,162
COST PER UNIT	SCHEME 4		
$3,432 per family	21 houses at $3,432 each	$72,072	
	No end wall required because this portion is included in the above price		
			$72,072
$225 per garage	18½ garages at $225 each	4,163	
			4,163
	TOTAL		$76,235
COST PER UNIT	SCHEME 10		
$3,588 per family	22 houses at $3,432 each	$75,504	
	22 end walls at $130 each	2,860	
	55 windows at $10 each (in end walls)	550	
			$78,914
$270 per garage	8 two-car garage units at $566	4,644	
	1 four-car garage unit at $1,000	1,000	
	2 one-car garage units at $300	600	
			6,244
	TOTAL		$85,158

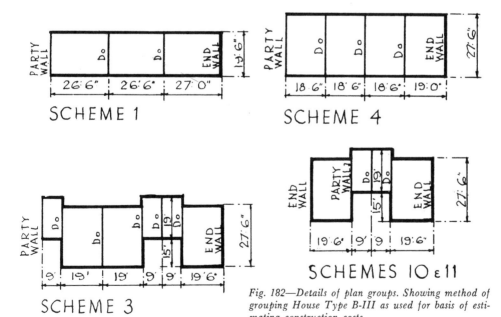

Fig. 182—Details of plan groups. Showing method of grouping House Type B-III as used for basis of estimating construction costs.

APPENDIX

RELATIVE COST OF CONSTRUCTION AND IMPROVEMENTS OF VARIOUS SCHEMES OF HOUSE GROUPING USING HOUSE TYPE B-III

(In regard to the cost of construction of houses, see page 246)
(In regard to the cost of improvements, see report of November 19, 1935—'Study of Relative Improvement Costs of House Grouping')
(The cost of land is not included in this study)

TOTAL COSTS					
SCHEMES	I	3	4	10	11
Construction of Houses	$56,187	$91,032	$72,072	$77,914	$35,870
Construction of Garages	3,150	7,130	4,163	7,244	2,840
Construction Total	59,337	98,162	76,235	85,158	38,710
Improvements exclusive of Park Landscaping	7,276	12,530	7,709	12,953	8,227
Total	66,613	110,692	83,944	98,111	46,937
Park Landscaping	500	530	544	544	273
GRAND TOTAL	$67,113	$111,222	$84,488	$98,655	$47,210
COST PER FAMILY					
Construction of House	3,511.69	3,501.21	3,432.00	3,587.00	3,587.00
Construction of Garage	196.87	274.24	198.24	283.83	284.00
Construction Total	3,708.56	3,775.45	3,630.24	3,870.83	3,871.00
Improvements exclusive of Park Landscaping	454.75	481.98	367.10	588.76	822.70
Total	4,163.31	4,257.43	3,997.34	4,459.59	4,693.70
Park Landscaping	31.25	20.38	25.90	24.73	27.30
GRAND TOTAL	$4,194.56	$4,277.71	$4,023.24	$4,484.32	$4,721.00

BIBLIOGRAPHY

GENERAL REFERENCES

Bing, Alexander M., Henry Wright, and Clarence S. Stein, *Preliminary Study of a Proposed Garden Community in the New York City Region.* 1923. 43 pp. Typescript with illustrations.

Dahir, James, *The Neighborhood Unit Plan: Its Spread and Acceptance.* A Selected Bibliography with Interpretive Comments. New York, Russell Sage Foundation. 1947. 91 pp.

Feiss, Carl, 'New Towns in the United States.' In *Town and Country Planning,* Jan. 1955, vol. 23:129, pp. 37-41.

Stein, Clarence S., 'City Patterns, Past and Future.' In *New Pencil Points,* June 1942.

Wright, Henry, *Rehousing Urban America.* New York, Columbia University. 1935. 173 pp.

Wright, Henry, *Some Principles Relating to the Economics of Land Subdivision.* New York, American City Planning Institute, 1930. 20 pp.

1. SUNNYSIDE

Annual Reports to Stockholders of the City Housing Corporation. 1924-1929.

Ascher, Charles S., 'The Enforcement of Deed Restrictions.' In *City Planning,* Oct. 1932, vol. 8:4.

Bing, Aleanxder M., 'American Garden Colonies' (Sunnyside Gardens and Radburn). In *Housing and Building,* May-June 1930.

Bing, Alexander M., 'Sunnyside Gardens: A Successful Experiment in Good Housing at a Moderate Price.' In *Municipal Review,* June 1926.

Bing, Alexander M., 'A New Limited-Dividend Housing Company.' Reprinted from *Housing Betterment,* May 1924.

Bing, Alexander M., 'Minimum Costs for Low-Rental Apts.' In *The Journal of Land and Public Utility Economics,* May 1929.

City Housing Corporation, *Sunnyside Gardens, a Home Community.* New York, the Corporation. Undated.

City Housing Corporation, *Sunnyside and the Housing Problem.*

Friederick, Anton H., 'Case History of a Community of Mortgaged Home Owners.' In *Survey Graphic,* June 1933.

Ginzburg, Benjamin, and Alexander M. Bing, 'Sunnyside Back and Forth.' In *Survey Graphic,* Aug. 1936, vol. 25:8.

Larsen, C. Theodore, 'Play Areas for Apartment Houses.' In *The Architectural Record,* March 1931.

Lasker, Loula D., 'Sunnyside Up and Down.' In *Survey-Graphic,* July 1936.

Mumford, Lewis, *Green Memories.* New York, Harcourt Brace Co. 1947. pp. 30, 31.

Mumford, Lewis, 'Houses—Sunnyside Up.' In *The Nation,* Feb. 4, 1925.

Reports of the Commission of Housing and Regional Planning. Legislative Documents, 1923, No. 43; 1924, No. 78; 1925, No. 91; 1926, No. 40; 1926, No. 66.

Roosevelt, Mrs. Franklin D., 'The Vanishing "Vine and Fig Tree." ' In *The Woman's Viewpoint,* October 1925.

Tough, Rosalind, Part I: 'Production Costs of Urban Land in Sunnyside, Long Island.' Part II: 'Building Costs and Total Costs at Sunnyside Gardens, Long Island.' In *Journal of Land and Public Utility Economics,* Feb. 1932, vol. 8:1; May 1932, vol. 8:2.

Wright, Henry, 'Housing. V. The Case for Group Housing. Sunnyside Garden Beginnings.' In *Architecture,* Aug. 1932, vol. 68:2. Afterwards part of the book *Rehousing Urban America.*

Wright, Henry, 'The Modern Apartment House.' In *The Architectural Record,* March 1929. Afterwards part of the book *Rehousing Urban America.*

Wright, Henry, 'An Account of Sunnyside Gardens in Relation to Problems and Development of Design and Site Planning and the Value of Same as an Experiment Directed towards an American Garden City.' 1926 Ms.

Wright, Henry, 'The Architect and Small House Costs.' In *The Architectural Record,* December

BIBLIOGRAPHY

1932, pp. 389-394.

Wright, Henry, 'Study of Application of Sunnyside Planning Principles to a Larger City Area.' Ms.

Wright, Henry, and D. M. Kendall, 'Investigation of the Present Speculative Building Operations Now in Progress in Brooklyn and Long Island.' May 1924. Ms.

Wright, Henry, E. S. Palmer and J. G. Hutton, 'Sunnyside Gardens: General Report on Cost Accounting.' December 1925. Ms.

II. RADBURN

Ascher, Charles S., 'Government by Contract in Radburn, New Jersey.' In 'Private Covenants in Urban Redevelopment,' Part 3 of *Urban Redevelopment: Problems and Practices* (Woodbury, Coleman, ed.). Chicago, University of Chicago Press. 1953. pp. 278-309. See also pp. 233-234.

Augur, Tracy B., 'Radburn, the Challenge of a New Town.' In *Michigan Municipal Review,* Feb., Mar. 1931, vol. 4: 2-3.

Bing, Alexander M., 'Community Planning for the Motor Age: How the City Housing Corporation Separates Pedestrian and Motor Traffic in Its Unique Experiment at Radburn.' In *National Association of Real Estate Boards. Annals of Real Estate Practice,* 1929. Address before National Association of Real Estate Boards, June 27, 1929.

Brownlow, Louis, 'Radburn: a New Town Planned for the Motor Age.' In *International Housing and Town Planning Bulletin,* Feb. 1930, no. 21.

Brownlow, Louis, 'Some Problems in New Planning.' In *Proceedings of 21st National Conference on City Planning,* 1929. Refers to Radburn. Also reprinted as Bulletin no. 4, National Conference on City Planning.

Cautley, Marjorie Sewell, 'Planting at Radburn.' In *Landscape Architecture,* Oct. 1930, vol. 21 No. 1, pp. 23-29. By the landscape architect.

City Housing Corporation, *Radburn Garden Homes.* New York, the Corporation. 1929.

City Housing Corporation, *Regarding Radburn.* New York, the author. 1928.

City Housing Corporation, Leaflets descriptive of Radburn as an industrial town. New York, the author. 1928. Plans.

City Housing Corporation, Leaflets entitled: *A Town Planned for Modern Industry; The Way Out; Light on Labor.*

City Housing Corporation, *Radburn, Protective Restrictions and Community Administration.* New York, the Corporation. 1929.

City Housing Corporation, annual reports. 1928-1933.

Comey, Arthur C., and Max S. Wehrly, 'Radburn, Bergen County, N. J.' In U.S. National Resources Committee. Urbanism Committee. Supplementary report, *Planned Communities.* 1939; vol. 2.

'Evaluation of the Town of Radburn, New Jersey.' A study by students in the Department of Architecture, Columbia University; Ronnie Chelouche, Alfred Mercado, and Bert Whinston. Ms. with photographs by the authors.

Hudson, Robert B., *Radburn: a Plan of Living.* A study made for the American Association for Adult Education, under the supervision of John O. Walker. New York, the Association. C. 1934.

Olmsted, Frederick Law, *Forty-eight Years of Architecture.* Vol. 2: *Central Park.*

Radburn Management Corporation, *Radburn, Protective Restrictions and Community Administration,* n.d. 40 pp. 'Declaration of Restrictions No. 1: Certificate of Incorporation and By-laws of the Radburn Association.'

Rosenfeld, Isadore, *Memorandum Re First School District of Radburn.* March 20, 1929. Typewritten report made for the office of Henry Wright and C. S. Stein.

Smith, Geddes, 'A Town for the Motor Age.' *Survey Graphic* reprint for the City Housing Corporation. C. 1930.

Stein, Clarence S., *Radburn and the Radburn Idea* —Encyclopædia of Housing 1949-50. This contains some material used in the article above.

Stein, Clarence S., and Catherine Bauer, 'Store Buildings and Neighborhood Shopping Centers.' In *The Architectural Record,* Feb. 1934.

Urban Planning and Land Policies. Vol. II of *Supplementary Report of the Urbanism Committee to the National Resources Committee.* United States Government Printing Office. 1939. pp. 97-101.

Whitten, Robert, and Thomas Adams, *Neighbor-*

hoods of Small Homes. Cambridge, Harvard University Press. 1931. Harvard City Planning Studies, Vol. III.

Wright, Henry, 'The Autobiography of Another Idea.' Reprinted from *The Western Architect,* September 1930, by the Regional Planning Association of America. 8 pp.

Wright, Henry, 'Housing—Why, When, and How!' Part II. *Architecture.* August 1933. pp. 79-110.

Wright, Henry, 'The Radburn Plan.' In *National Real Estate Journal,* Sept. 30, 1929. pp. 74-76.

Wright, Henry, *Rehousing Urban America.* New York, Columbia University Press.

Wright, Henry, *Some Principles Relating to the Economics of Land Subdivision.* New York, American City Planning Institute. 1930. 20 pp.

III. CHATHAM VILLAGE

Bigger, Frederick, 'More Limited Dividend Housing: the Buhl Foundation Project in Pittsburgh.' In *Octagon,* Oct. 1931, vol. 3: 10.

'Buhl Foundation Housing Project in Pittsburgh, Pa.' In *Architectural Record,* Oct. 1931.

The Buhl Foundation, 'Chatham Village, a Modern Community of Garden Homes Combining Architectural Charm with Security and Cultured Living.' *The Foundation,* Jan. 1932.

The Buhl Foundation, 'Facts about Chatham Village. Pittsburgh, Pa.' *The Foundation,* Oct. 1943.

Comey, Arthur C., and Max S. Wehrly, 'Chatham Village, Pittsburgh, Pa.' In U.S. National Resources Committee. Urbanism committee. Supplementary report, *Planned Communities.* 1939, vol. 2, pt. 1.

Lewis, Dr. Charles (Director, The Buhl Foundation), 'The Large-Scale Planned Community as an Investment.' Speech given at 41st Annual Meeting of the American Life Convention, Chicago, Illinois. Oct. 1946.

Mather, Alan, 'The variation of roofs and imaginative planning on a hill-side site are distinctive of Chatham Village . . . Wright and Stein as Consultants on site plan,' in article: 'Henry Wright.' In *Pencil Points,* Jan. 1940, vol. 21:1.

Report of the Buhl Foundation. 1942.

Wright, Henry, 'Housing. V. The Case for Group Housing. Chatham Village.' In *Architecture,* Aug. 1933, vol. 68: 2.

IV. PHIPPS GARDEN APARTMENTS (1)

Rosenfeld, Isadore, 'Phipps Garden Apartments.' In *Architectural Forum,* Feb. 1932, vol. 56, pp. 111-124, 183-187; with photos, plans, tables.

V. HILLSIDE HOMES

'A Comparison of Two Ways of Housing 5,000 People.' In *The Architectural Forum,* February 1933.

Blackham, Louise P., *Community Service at Hillside Homes.* A four-year report, June 1935 to June 1939. Report to the Hillside Housing Corporation. Mimeographed. Hillside Homes, Bronx, N. Y. July 1939.

Blackham, Louise P., *Community Service at Hillside Homes.* A Review of Eight Years of Community Life at Hillside Homes, June 1935 to July 1943. Mimeographed. Hillside Homes, Bronx, N. Y. July 1943.

'Hillside Group Housing.' In *Architectural Record,* Oct. 1932, vol. 72: 4.

Saylor, Henry, 'The Hillside Housing Development: The Case History of an Idea from Its Birth in the Mind of Clarence S. Stein, Architect, to Its Material Realization in the Bronx, New York.' In *Architecture,* May 1935, vol. 71: 5.

Stein, Clarence S., 'Hillside Homes.' In *American Architect,* Feb., 1936, vol. 148. No. 2542.

VIII. GREENBELT TOWNS

Casseres, J. M. de, 'Amerikaansche reiservaringen op stedebouwkundig gebied.' In *Tijdschrift voor volkshuisvesting en stedebouw,* Feb. 1939, vol. 20:2, pp. 41-51; with photos, maps.

'Greenbelt Towns.' In *Architectural Record,* Sept. 1936, vol. 80:3, pp. 215-234; with photos, plans, sketch. Also reprinted.

'Greentowns All Sold by Federal Government.' In *American City,* March 1953, vol. 68:3, p. 113.

Mayer, Albert, 'Greenbelt Towns for the Machine Age. The government's plan to build four in this country directs notice to the successful ventures abroad.' In *New York Times* magazine, Feb. 2, 1936, pp. 8-9, 18; with photos, plans, sketches.

Mumford, Lewis, 'City and Region: . . . Greenbelt Towns.' In his *The Culture of Cities.* C. 1938. p. 452; with photos.

BIBLIOGRAPHY

Reiss, R. L., 'American Greenbelt Towns.' In *Town and Country Planning*, Jan. 1938, vol. 6:22, pp. 16-18; with plans.

Rigotti, Giorgio, 'I Borghi dalle "Siedlungen" alle "Greenbelt towns." ' In *Urbanistica*, Jan.-Feb. 1937, vol. 6:1, pp. 3-18; with photos, maps, plans.

'Site Plans of "Greenbelt" Towns, Layouts of the Resettlement Administration's New Suburban Communities Now Under Construction near Washington, Cincinnati and Milwaukee.' In *American City*, Aug. 1936, vol. 51:8, pp. 56-59; with plans.

Stein, Clarence S., Special reports made for the Resettlement Administration, Nov.-Dec. 1935. Studies of operation-maintenance costs in suburban resettlement communities; studies of the relative improvement costs of various schemes of house grouping; studies of relative cost of construction and improvements of various schemes of house grouping. See Appendix and body of book.

Stephenson, Flora C., 'Greenbelt Towns in the United States.' In *Town and Country Planning*, Winter 1942-43, vol. 10:40, pp. 121-123; with photos, plan. Also in *Planning and Reconstruction Year Book*, 1943, pp. 216-218; with plan only.

U.S. Congress, 81st, 1st Session, House, Suburban resettlement projects. Hearings . . . on H.R. 2440, a bill to authorize the Public Housing Commissioners to sell the suburban resettlement projects . . . 1949. (See also S351.)

U.S. Congress, 81st, 1st Session, House, An act to authorize the Public Housing Commissioner to sell the suburban resettlement projects known as Greenbelt, Maryland; Greendale, Wisconsin; and Greenhills, Ohio . . . 1949. (Public law 65.)

U.S. Congress, 81st, 1st Session, House, Disposition of greentown projects. 1949. (Report no. 402.)

U.S. Congress, 81st, 1st Session, Sale of greentown suburban resettlement projects. Hearings . . . on S. 351 . . .; with tables. 1949.

GREENBELT, MARYLAND

Comey, Arthur C., and Max S. Wehrly, 'Demonstration Projects: Separate Communities: Greenbelt, Prince George's County, Md.' In their *Planned Communities*, Monograph 1, in U.S. National Resources Committee. Urbanism Committee. Supplementary report. 1939, pt. 1, vol. 2, pp. 75-76.

Fulmer, O. Kline, *Greenbelt*. Introduction by Lewis Mumford. Washington, American Council on Public Affairs. 1941. 46 pp.; photos on covers.

Greenbelt News Review (formerly *Greenbelt Cooperator*), an independent newspaper published every Thursday by Greenbelt Cooperative Publishing Assn., Inc., and delivered to every home in Greenbelt. Office, 9 Parkway, Greenbelt, Md.

GHVC News Letter, House Organ of the Greenbelt Veteran Housing Corporation, published monthly at Greenbelt, Maryland, and distributed to most residents.

Gutheim, Frederick, 'Greenbelt Revisited.' In *Magazine of Art*, Jan. 1947, vol. 40:1, pp. 16-20; with photos.

Larsen, Christian L., and Richard D. Andrews, *The Government of Greenbelt*. Bureau of Public Administration, University of Maryland. 1951. 78 pp. Tables.

Thorpe, Merle, 'Fever Chart of a Tugwell Town.' In *Nation's Business*, Nov. 1938, vol. 26:11, p. 13.

Walker, Hale J., 'Some Major Technical Problems Encountered in the Planning of Greenbelt, Maryland.' In *Planner's Journal*, Mar.-Apr. 1938, vol. 4:2, pp. 34-37; with photo.

Warner, George A., *Greenbelt: The Cooperative Community*. An Experience in Democratic Living. New York, Exposition Press, Inc. 1954. 232 pp.

GREENBROOK, N. J.

Mayer, Albert, 'A Technique for Planning Complete Communities.' In *Architectural Forum*, Jan., Feb. 1937, vol. 66:1, 2, pp. 19-36, 126-146; with maps, plans, sketch, diagrams, chart, photos.

GREENDALE, WISCONSIN

American Legion Community Development Corporation, *Greendale, the Answer to the Veterans' Housing Problem, a Plan Offered by the American Legion Community Development Corporation*. Greendale, Wis., the Corporation. 1948. 6 pp., Photo, map, sketches.

Crane, Jacob, 'Greendale: the General Plan.' In *Planners' Journal,* July-Aug. 1937, vol. 3:4, pp. 89-90. Discussion by Charles B. Bennett and Richard B. Fernbach, Nov.-Dec. 1937, vol. 3:6, pp. 160-161.

Greendale, Wis., *This is Greendale.* Greendale, Wis. 1948. 44 pp. Photos, map, plan, sketches.

Kroening, W. E., *The Story of Greendale.* A Government demonstration in community planning and public housing. Greendale, Wis., the author.

Lansill, John S., and Jacob Crane, 'Metropolitan Land Reserves as Illustrated by Greendale, Wisconsin.' In *American City,* July 1937, vol. 52:7, pp. 55-58; with maps.

Peets, Elbert, 'Studies in Planning Texture for Housing in a Greenbelt Town.' In *Architectural Record,* Sept. 1949, vol. 106:3, pp. 130-137; with plans, sketches.

Peets, Elbert, 'Greendale: the Town Plan.' A paper presented at the Milwaukee meeting of the American City Planning Institute, October 24, 1936. The Institute. 1936. 3 pp. mimeo.

Stein, Clarence S., 'Greendale and the Future.' In *American City,* June 1948, vol. 63:6, pp. 106-109; with photos, plan. Partially reprinted in this book and under title 'Greendale Revisited' in *Layout for Living,* Jan. 1949, no. 21, pp. 4-7; with photos, plan.

'Veterans Seek Purchase of Greendale and the City of Milwaukee Co-operates.' In *American City,* Jan. 1949, vol. 64:1, pp. 73-74.

Wisconsin. Historical Records Survey. Division of Community Service Programs. Inventory of the local government archives of Wisconsin. Village series, no. 141, Greendale, sponsored by the University of Wisconsin and State Historical Society of Wisconsin. Madison, *The Survey,* July 1941. 101 pp. mimeo; maps, chart.

GREENHILLS, OHIO

Greenhills, Cincinnati, Ohio, in article 'Farm Security Administration.' In *Architectural Forum,* May 1938, vol. 68:5, pp. 414, 424; with photos, maps, plans.

Hartzog, Justin R., 'Planning of Suburban Resettlement Towns: Greenhills.' In *Planners' Journal,* Mar.-Apr. 1938, vol. 4:2, pp. 29-33; with photo.

A planned community in Ohio provides housing, shopping, school and recreation facilities, in article 'Defense Housing.' In *Architectural Forum,* Nov. 1940, vol. 73:5, pp. 466-467; with photos, plan.

BALDWIN HILLS VILLAGE

Bauer, Catherine, 'Description and Appraisal, Baldwin Hills Village.' In *Pencil Points,* Sept. 1944, vol. 25:9, pp. 46-60; with photos, one colored; plans, cross-sections, tables.

Mumford, Lewis, 'Baldwin Hills Village.' In *Pencil Points,* Sept. 1944, vol. 25:9, pp. 44-45; with photo, colored.

SUPPLEMENTARY BIBLIOGRAPHY
FOR 1966 EDITION

The New Towns: The Answer to Megalopolis. Sir Frederic Osborn and Arnold Whittick, with an introduction by Lewis Mumford. Leonard Hall, London, 1965.

The definitive book on the background and growth of the New Town movement in Great Britain, and on the creation of each of the British New Towns, with plans and photographs. Sir Frederic Osborn has been a central participant in all phases of the movement and

its effective work, including the first prototypes of Letchworth and Welwyn Garden City, early in the century.

Community Planning in the 1920's: The Contribution of the Regional Planning Association of America. Roy Lubove. University of Pittsburgh Press, 1963.

This covers much more ground than just New Towns; it includes them as part of a total social-economic-physical community-regional conspectus. It gives an excellent background of the development and thinking in this country, intimately introducing the theories and achievements and influence of such men as Lewis Mumford, Henry Wright, Benton MacKaye, and others. A brilliant memoir.

Kitimat: A New City. Reprint of 3 illustrated articles in the *Architectural Forum,* July, August, October 1954.

The planners of Kitimat (Stein, Mayer, Whittlesey) explain the background and rationale, as well as the technical-economic-social-sociological process of actually building this new town in British Columbia, Canada.

"New Towns." *Architectural Record,* August 1964.

"The Role of Regional Policy." *Architectural Record,* September 1964.

Two articles by Albert Mayer and Clarence Stein.

These deal with both the fundamentals and the current issues in this country such as Land Ownership and Development. The September article contains the proposal of the Regional City as basic pattern for future cities as well as for Metropolitan development.

Town and Country Planning. Monthly publication of the Town and Country Planning Association, 28 King Street, London WC2, England.

A stimulating journal devoting much of its space to the British New Towns. Each January issue contains tables showing progress in growth of population, housing, industry, shops, schools, etc. Important source of current information and opinion. The January 1956 number contains articles and critiques of British New Towns by eminent critics from 11 countries, including the United States, as well as much other provocative material.

The Planning of a New Town. Based on a study for a New Town of 100,000 at Hook, Hampshire. Published in 1961 by London County Council. Hubert Bennett, Architect to the Council.

Excellent comprehensive and intimate study for a New Town, from site selection through all the planning phases, to economic and engineering detail; well illustrated. Useful for both professionals and laymen.

The Culture of Cities. Lewis Mumford. Harcourt Brace and Co., 1938.

This is one of three complementary books in which Lewis Mumford has brilliantly interpreted the relationship of man to his environment and to his cultural background throughout the ages. The others of the series are *Technics and Civilization,* 1934, and *The Condition of Man,* 1944.

REFERENCES

1 Bing, Wright and Stein: Preliminary Study. *For further details of this and other footnote references, see Bibliography, p. 249.*

2 Reports of Commission of Housing and Regional Planning, 1920-1926.

3 Tough: Production Costs.

4 Tough: Production Costs.

5 Bing, Wright and Stein: Preliminary Study.

6 Mumford: Green Memories.

7 Bing: Sunnyside Gardens: A Successful Experiment.

8 Tough: Production Costs.

9 Smith: A Town for the Motor Age.

10 Olmsted: Forty-Eight Years of Architecture.

11 Traffic Quarterly. *April 1948, p. 205.*

12 Wright: The Autobiography of Another Idea.

13 Report of the Special Evaluation Committee of the First Citizens' Association of Radburn.

14 Ascher: The Extra Municipal Administration of Radburn.

15 Hudson: Radburn, A Plan of Living.

16 Stein and Bauer: Store Buildings and Neighborhood Shopping Centers.

17 Wright: Rehousing Urban America.

18 Wright, Henry: The Architect and Small House Costs in Architectural Record, *December 1932, p. 391. See also* Architectural Record, *December 1931.*

19 Lewis: The Large-Scaled Planned Community as an Investment.

20 Lewis: The Large-Scaled Planned Community as an Investment.

21 Memorandum to Mr. John S. Lansill, October 1935. See Appendix, pp. 228 ff.

22 Memorandum to Mr. Lansill, November 1935. See Appendix, pp. 228 ff. for these memoranda.

23 Memorandum to Mr. Lansill, December 1935. Studies of Operation-Maintenance Costs in Suburban Resettlement Communities.

24 Memorandum to Mr. Lansill, December 1935. Notes on Cost of Local Government and Community Activity.

25 Report to Mr. Lansill, December 1935. Shopping Centers.

26 The New Exploration, *pp. 147 and 188.*

27 Agricultural Research Center of the United States Department of Agriculture. Agricultural Research Administration, U.S. Department of Agriculture.

28 H.R. 2440, Public Law 65, 81st Congress, Chapter 127, 1st Session.

29 81st Congress, 1st Session, Senate Calendar No. 292, Report No. 312, Disposition of Greentown Projects. (Report to accompany H.R. 2440).

30 Written in 1949.

31 Founded by the late Edward A. Filene to further the Consumers movement.

32 Shopping Centers: principles of planning and possible income to be derived from rental of stores. A Report by Clarence S. Stein for the Resettlement Administration, 1935.

33 Store Buildings and Neighborhood Shopping Centers, *by Clarence S. Stein and Catherine Bauer.* The Architectural Record, *February 1934.*

34 Studies of Operation-Maintenance Costs in Suburban Resettlement Communities. A Report by Clarence S. Stein for the Resettlement Administration, 1935. See Appendix.

35 See p. 57, District Heating in American Housing, National Building Studies, Special Report No. 7, London 1949.

36 From an article, Greendale and the Future, *written by Clarence S. Stein on the tenth anniversary of the town in 1948, and republished in the* American City, *June 1948.*

37 Store Buildings and Neighborhood Shopping Centers. *By Clarence S. Stein and Catherine Bauer.* The Architectural Record, *February 1934.*

38 Pencil Points *(now* Progressive Architecture*) September 1944.*

39 Pencil Points *(now* Progressive Architecture *September 1944. pp. 58-60.*

40 A Civic Survey and Plan for Edinburgh. *Prepared for the Town Council by Patrick Abercrombie and Derek Plumstead. Oliver and Boyd, Edinburgh, 1949.*

41 "America's Needs and Resources," by J. Frederic Dewhurst and Associates. The Twentieth Century Fund, *1947.*

PHOTOGRAPHIC CREDITS

INDEX AND LIST OF ILLUSTRATIONS

260

INDEX

The Economics of Financia
and Medical Identity Theft

L. Jean Camp • M. Eric Johnson

The Economics of Financial and Medical Identity Theft

 Springer

L. Jean Camp
Indiana University
Bloomington, IN, USA
ljeanc@gmail.com

M. Eric Johnson
Dartmouth College
Hanover, NH, USA
M.Eric.Johnson@tuck.dartmouth.edu

ISBN 978-1-4614-1917-4   e-ISBN 978-1-4614-1918-1
DOI 10.1007/978-1-4614-1918-1
Springer New York Dordrecht Heidelberg London

Library of Congress Control Number: 2012931930

Printed on acid-free paper

Springer is part of Springer Science+Business Media (www.springer.com)

List of Contributors
  Elaine Newton, RAND
  Bennet Yee, Google
  Barbara Fox, Microsoft
  Allan Friedman, Harvard University
  Ari Schwartz, Center for Democracy and Technology
  Paul Syverson, Naval Research Laboratory

Preface

Anyone who has ever bought a car, visited their doctor, rented an apartment, or had an on-line conversation that they would rather not see in their employee review may find this book of interest.

There is a collision occurring in identity management. Identity technologies are problematic. Some hope they see light at the end of the identity theft tunnel. Yet the innovation is driven by individual tendencies to seek convenience and business imperatives to minimize risk with maximized profit. The light may be an oncoming identity train wreck of individual exposure, social risk, and minimal privacy.

There are alternatives to erosions of privacy and increasing fraud. There is an ideal where individuals have multiple devices, including computers, tablets, and smart phones. Yet such a system requires coordination and is unlikely to arise in an adhoc environment where Facebook and Google compete to be unique identity providers.

There are strong near term incentives for low-privacy, immediately cheap and thus technically limited, expensive in the long term, identity systems. The expense is now, and the risk of fraud is in the future. The immediate loss of privacy becomes a systematic loss in security over time. Just as convenient credit cards have became convenient for criminals with the advent on e-commerce, the foreseeable diffusion of mobile commerce and pervasive computing will break many of the proposed Federated or centralized identity systems. There are better choices.

This book is organized with **five major components**, each more focused than the last.

The book begins with a discussion about how the digital networked environment is critically different from the world of paper, eyeballs and pens. Many of the actual effective identity protections are embedded behind the eyeballs, where the presumably passive observer is actually a fairly keen student of human behavior. Even a passive clerk notices when a two hundred and fifty pound man presents Emily Marie's credit card.

The second section takes the observations about the profound divide between ink and bits, and applies that to the immediate problem of identity theft. Identity theft best practices are included; but the core observation is that the average person can do nothing to avoid exposure to this risk.

The third section looks at defining the problem of security in the context of identity. The fourth examines medical identity theft and health information security in a section by Eric Johnson. With spending on healthcare nearing one fifth of the US economy in the next decade, criminals are fueled by poorly secured data and vast financial flows.

After the overview of the technology and proposals for identity management comes a series of possible futures. Examination of these futures indicates that there are two choices: surveillance, near term profits, and long term fraud versus near term expense, private secure credentials, and long term stability.

Acknowledgements

L. Jean Camp would like to acknowledge her excellent doctoral students, first and foremost: Allan Friedman, Warigia Bowman, Camilo Viecco, Debin Liu, and post doctoral fellow Alex Tsow.

She would like to acknowledge all the participants of an early identity workshop, where the idea for this book was born. The two-day workshop included public servants, technologists, policy analysts, and civil libertarians. The early publication from that workshop provided the clearest set of definitions, and thus clear thinking, that she has yet to see on this issue.

Also, Dave Farber whose *ip* list provided pointers to many of the anecdotes included in this book.

M. Eric Johnson acknowledges the wonderful collaboration with graduate and postdoc students Ajit Appari, Juhee Kwon, Nicholas Willey, and Xia Zhao. He also acknowledges the data collaboration of Tiversa Inc and the financial support of the National Science Foundation (Grant Award Number CNS-0910842, under the auspices of the Institute for Security, Technology, and Society (ISTS)).

Contents

Chapter 1
Identity in Economics, and in Context

Unique identification today is as much about money as was the wide adoption of last names centuries ago. Governments around the world adopted identity schemes to enable census and taxation. Today businesses are creating and using new identity systems in order to enable commerce. Identity allows for the creation and pricing of risky contracts. Victims of identity theft often wonder, "how can person I never knew in a state I have never visited create a debt with a bank with whom I have never done business, and which now I am expected to pay?" The creativity of such identity thieves knows no bounds. They can use identity to steal money, goods, or services. They can also use an identity to commit other forms of fraud against unrelated individuals, firms, or governments. Sometimes the schemes are simple—like using a stolen credit card to buy a laptop or an insurance number to steal healthcare. Other schemes are far more complex, involving an ecosystem of intermediaries. The factors that created this situation and the resulting challenges that must be addressed to extricate us are the focus of this book.

The economics of identity drive everything we discuss in the forthcoming chapters. The root causes and solutions start with simple questions, like how much is it worth to have an identity, to know someone else's identity, or to protect your own? Technology often disguises these core economic issues.

Current investments in identity management are targeted at increasing the speed at which human-readable identity information can move through data and financial processing systems. The result will likely be an even greater explosion in identity theft. However, there is another option: privacy-enhancing, hardware-based, fraud-preventing credentials. Yet this second option is expensive and threatens the traditional business models and practices of many firms from banking to data aggregators. Adopting the second option requires clarifying the profound confusion of identities, which work for humans, and credentials, which work for networked computers.

Identity is built and constructed within an economic context. Anyone who has ever left the office for the sidelines of a kid's soccer game knows what it means to changes shoes and economic roles on the way. In each sphere we might introduce ourselves differently (Vice President Jones to Jenny's Mom). Likewise, going from work to the bar indicates the switch from productive employee to indulging consumer.

At some times and in some places, the identity "Professor" or "employee" is relevant. In others, it may be "patient," "customer," or "parent". Each of these corresponds to economic and social roles. "Treasurer of the Parent Teacher Organization" may indicate a trusted volunteer who will likely not leave a job worth far more that the possible spoils of a stolen PTO treasury or a person poor in funds but rich in trust and time. Identities can be specific or general, and defined by role and context. For example, consider the incredibly specific and simultaneously generic, "darling". Identity is defined by context. A global identity, while intriguing to some, could be both remarkably dangerous and somewhat useless.

Even people with the most focused lives—those who publicly identify themselves either through their employment or parenthood—have private interests within which they use different identities. Employees rarely pay mortgages through the office accounting system, and peace in marriage can be grounded on separate checking accounts.

Changing jobs results in a new identity in the modern sense of the word. A change in position may result in a different credit limit and different privileges on different networks. A change in jobs frequently means a new place to live, with an entirely new set of identifiers sharing soft magnetic charges in an old wallet. Park Street Video and the Science Museum memberships are discarded for Horizon Video and the Discovery Museum along with the disposal of the old employee ID. Some things may not change with the new job, like retirement account or even frequent flyer membership. Linking the steady essentials to the transient creates economic risks. Some of us always pay our credit card bills on time. Linking the resulting right to get a new card with a telephone number allows someone to use the transient to access the constant—by getting a cell phone and pretending to be someone else.

In terms of identity and authentication, a change in professional affiliation results in a change in authorization in some contexts but not in others. When can that be a problem? It can be difficult to fully understand the risks associated with keeping information linked or discarding it. The risks of keeping all the information around, and the risks of deleting information are both very real. Sorting all credit card numbers and associated PINs in a single computer file enables a quick recovery in the case of a lost wallet. Many self-help books about managing your finances recommend it. For example, Microsoft Money will help manage accounts. Yet the existence of this handy file increases the risk of loss, and makes possible a larger loss in the case of a lost laptop. Keeping no records of credit card numbers and not writing down PINs decreases the risk of wholesale loss, and are recommended computer security practices. However, this also increases the difficulty of recovery if there is a loss. In fact, since many users do not keep such records, credit card companies sometimes authenticate individuals on the basis of a Social Security number thereby opening one path to fraud (using a false SSN) to address a good security practice (unique PINs and codes that are never recorded). The risks are cumulative and sometimes quite subtle until the worst case casts ugly highlights on the costs.

Today identity is more than anything economic. And the technology used to create, utilize, and protect identities is increasingly ill matched to the economics and uses of identities. To understand the problems with constructing economically viable and useful identity systems, it is important to begin with an examination of identity papers. Because of the familiarity of the tactile traditional identity paper, this model is often in mind when considering identity issues. Of course, the paper model is hopelessly flawed.

Where are Your Papers?

Identity papers are the technology that underlies many assumptions in digital systems. What makes paper and digital identifiers different? What do we want to keep about paper and what should we abandon? What are the paper-based assumptions that can be embedded in digital identity systems? Understanding the economically-challenged system of modern identifiers requires unpacking the various functions and characteristics of identity papers. With those functions in mind, we will be ready to examine the mismatches with digital technologies and the resulting threats of identity theft.

Before the invention of the press, authoring was simple compared to copying. Documents were created, but only the rare document was copied. An identifying document from a powerful ruler was a rarity. Each letter was valuable. Only the most pain-staking copying enabled the survival of information from ancient Hebrew texts through the Roman and Byzantine empires, through Arab universities and finally to Europe. Without laborious copying, any authored document would be lost. Each book copied consisted of a set of articles selected by the human copier. To copy was to edit, in that modern editing is the selection and ordering of material for inclusion.

Should somehow mass identity papers have been created; organizing records of them would have been similarly difficult. Even that most basic ordering—alphabetical order—was not standard before the printing press. As said by an innovator in the 16th century, "Amo comes before bibo because *a* is the first letter of the former and *b* is the first letter of the latter and *a* comes before *b* ....by the Grace of God working in me, I have devised this order.".

Outlining paper and identity theft provides a good introduction to the most pressing issues. The challenge of identity and its economics are a bit broader. To widen the lens, identity is considered as an analog to different kinds of problems. Is identity theft a plague upon a war or us? Each view presents a different kind of solution.

Identity theft is the misuse of private authenticating information to steal or commit fraud. Protecting identity requires protecting privacy. Proving identity requires exposing information. The next two sections first define privacy as multi-dimensional, and then pull forward the economics of privacy.

The economics of privacy are not the same as the economics of security. There are commonalities. For example, in both cases it is easy for merchants to make security and privacy claims, and hard for customers to verify the claims. And security suffers from the classic free rider problem.

This book is roughly broken into four major themes. The formal discussion of economics of security is the heart of the first theme leading us to look at identity in a new way. The second major theme examines how identity fails in the online environment. We then turn to a discussion of the technologies of identity. The final section sketches possible views of the future. It doesn't offer the "comprehensive solution" for an identity system, because, by this point it is likely clear that there is no such thing. But just as financial risk can be hedged through a collection of investment strategies, the risks of identity can be also be managed. Technologies offer solutions, but also bring new risks and subtle unintended consequences.

Digital identity failures underlie more problems than are immediately obvious. Failures may not only result in consumers who are unable to identify themselves, but likewise makes venders difficult to verify. Surely there a few legitimate Nigeria bankers, but most email appeals claiming to be so are fraudulent. The inability to distinguish a bank from a kiosk and a banker from a badly dressed fraudster indicate deeper flaws in identity than exposed by credit card theft. Identity ownership and flawed risk allocation underlie these problems. Spyware, bots, zombies and scams can make it difficult to identify a merchant; much worse, they may even make it difficult to identify your own actions. There are effectively three ways to prevent the kinds of fraudulent masquerades so popular on the Internet: third party assertions ("trust him"), first party assertions ("trust me") and social network judgments ("everybody trusts them"). The economics of these systems vary widely, and as a result these systems provide different kinds of economic signals.

There is a wide range of solutions to failed signals. These include anonymous credentials; which are the technical equivalent of presenting yourself well without an introduction in a conversation. Although anonymous credentials sound fancy, they are extremely common and simple. Everything from dollar bills to theatre tickets are anonymous credentials. Identity-based signatures are another technology for identity, one that proves group membership. Identity-based signatures can prove email from Bob@microsoft.com is really from Bob at microsoft.com. The following chapter discusses the often cited magic bullet of biometrics. Of course, placing biometric security in an economically broken system, results in a broken biometric system. We also describe reputations. Reputations allow groups to form identities through rating various providers, as in the social network descriptions above.

Technologies create identities that are embedded into economics. We will conclude the book with a discuss four vignettes that provide possible views of the future: single national identifier, business as usual; ubiquitous identity theft; and anonymous identifiers. Each of these snapshots of possible futures highlights the potential promise and pitfalls for identity systems.

Chapter 2
Modern Technological and Traditional Social Identities

Identity Within a Community

For much of human history, identity was linked to community. Within the community, identity was clearly understood and context defined all. Who you were and what others thought depended on where you sat: throne, bar stool, or the side of the field. Now, where you are sitting proves nothing.

Sitting at your computer you prepare to move some funds into bonds. Every year your retirement investing should become a little more conservative. So every year, the same week as your birthday, you reliably move 1% of your funds from the international equities market that has been so good to you, intro Treasury Bills. The return may be less, but it will also be less risky.

Opening the browser window you see the first sale. AOL/Time Warner is being sold. What? Who is selling it? This is not a managed account. You end up taking two minutes and going to Google to get your fund's 800 number, since all links to contact lead to email. While you listen to the hold music the accounts you have spent two decades building up are emptying.

FINALLY A HUMAN ON THE PHONE!

"Stop!! Thief!!" you cry. "lock my account"

"Sir, if you could just verify your identity. What is your mother's birthday?"

4/16

"I am sorry but that is incorrect."

"SOMEONE ELSE CHANGED IT!! FREEZE THE ACCOUNT!"

"Sir, can you tell me the name of your fist pet?"

Darn, was did a record the turtle or my cat. I can't remember.

"Bert"

"I am sorry but that is incorrect."

"WHO CARES, WHY ARE YOU WASTING TIME? SOMEONE IS STEALING MY RETIREMENT!!"

"I am sorry sir, let me place you on hold while I pass you to our fraud department..."

Not only is this imaginable, it is possible today. A victim cannot prove himself the owner fast enough, even were she to see the account being looted. Identity systems are broken, economically, and we all are paying the price. Both individuals and organizations experience the costs of a broken system and the failures are far more than simply technical.

During a vast swath of human history, lineage, location, and profession would have answered questions of rights and ownership. Choice of profession was a function of lineage and location. Potter, weaver, William's son, or the resident of the farm on the hill next to the manor could describe an individual with implicit and socially embedded information providing identity. But these names described the individual completely in one context because the context was small and the ability to track, confirm and share information was well within human abilities. Because the context was small, there were connections between everyone in the group. Such an environment today might be called a highly connected network or an information rich environment. Then it was simply reality that life was likely to be short, difficult, and extremely geographically constrained. Context mattered.

Indeed the adoption of these informal descriptions as last names was economic. The description weaver became the last name Weaver and William's son became Williamson because effective tax mechanisms required unique identification.

In that time, each name provided with it an evaluation of the person within the context of the community. Each description provided a reason to extend trust or not because each description provided a connection to this ubiquitous context, and to a reputation. Evidence of a 'good' family, wealth earned, a farm well tended, or a skill provided what would now be called information for a risk assessment and the potential to report any untrustworthy behavior to the community. Wealth was embodied in both tangible products and opportunity created from socially constructed identities. Today intangible production and wealth requires more carefully constructed identities.

Trust was based on identity, and identity was personal and family history. Such a history included an evaluation of behavior in past interactions and transactions. "An apple doesn't fall far from the tree," implies not that there were few distinct apples, but rather the larger tree defined each individual. It also meant no credit or quarter was given to the person identified as being part of a larger, distrusted family. As Snopes in the stories of Faulkner creatively illustrates, rising in the social and economic ranks was not made easier by association with a family that was not trusted as recently as the nineteenth century.

A person could improve his station in life to some small degree based on charisma, hard work, and luck to build a positive local reputation. Apparently good weather and surviving a plague helped too. Individuals could not necessarily access even greater opportunities by escaping a bad reputation. Both traditional community suspicion of wandering souls, and modern mathematical models illustrate that the only reputation worth escaping is a bad one.

Today, the Western world emphasizes the worth and reputation of individuals and not families. In the past, distinct identities were for strangers and emigrants, who entered without being integrated in the larger community. By contrast, today each of us is a package of identities in different contexts. Yet, these contexts are collapsed into a small set of identifying information, digital networked information, and because of this resulting complexity the financial and personal risks are increasing.

Yet the brutal reality of risk is that proof of self, much of which is inherently publicly available, requires knowing only public information: date of birth, mother's birth date, Social Security Numbers. Individuals have lost control of identifiers - all the data publicly available used for proof of self. We are living the midst of a terrible collision - traditional public community information is used to confirm identities in a world of networked digital commerce. How did this come to be?

Papers vs. Avatars

In the paper-based environment transactional histories were sparse and accessible to few. Community networks and common recollection, with little documentation, held personal histories.

In the paper world, the physical person is inherently linked to the action. A transaction requires the presence of a body. Thus the body and the identity are linked. This enables an enforcement system that depends in the extreme on bodily enforcement (such as imprisonment). Remote paper transactions required either self-verifying documents such as letter from a common friend, or a delay while paper documents were processed (e.g., a check being sent, cleared, and then credited).

Increasingly, important transactions are entering the digital realm. Accordingly, trust depends on transactional history—credit records, educational history, employment history, and criminal or medical history (depending on the rules of the state). The extension of trust is based on records or transactional histories associated with some common identifier. Across administrative domains that identifier is often the Social Security Number (SSN). Within administrative domains the number may be an employer identifier or membership number. These numbers, including the ubiquitous SSN, are difficult to remember. These numbers are often pass phrases or record identifiers, built to function for the computer. Neither pass phrases nor passwords are ideal for the individual who is being identified. The ability of humans to remember random information is quite limited unless the information is given some understandable framing. Thus digital identifiers often have some process for release to the person with whom the data are associated. Such a release of pass phrase or record identifier is most often based on information that can be easily remembered. Today a Social Security Number and a maternal family name prove worth for creditor, employer or, increasingly, authorization for the one-time purchase of discount goods from the web.

Computerization has made transactional histories detailed, and computer networks have made them available to many. The increased detail and availability of transactional history has made the value of the information on each specific transaction lower, while making the value of the entire compilation of data higher. Information about a specific transaction is easy to obtain, and thus less valuable. Information provides a detailed look into our daily lives, and thus the sum of information is more valuable.

The use of some small set of information to access a range of transactional records has two fundamental flaws. First, the correlation of information across different sources is the canonical privacy threat enabled by information and communications technologies. Second, the use of the same information in multiple arenas creates a security risk. That security risk is most clearly illustrated by *identity theft*. *Identity theft* is the misuse of information to masquerade as someone else to obtain resources.

The individual data that together forms a 'proof' of identity are hard to locate or extract in a paper-based system. Consider the difficulty of locating a mother's maiden name and a Social Security Number for a stranger before networked digital information. Access to that information would require access to paper records, records that could be managed and secured. In a computerized and networked environment, such individual datum is difficult to conceal. Once the individual datum is located, the access data can be created by a simple combination. Then the person with whom the data are associated has been subject to identity theft. Note that identity theft is not associated with physical impersonation. Rather identity theft is the compilation of information in order to access the rights and privileges associated with that information. The inclusion of a name is necessary but not central to identity theft. The problem is experienced by the victim as the loss of personal information, not the loss of an internal sense of self. Yet the use of personally identifiable information to construct interactions in the market is so ubiquitous as to cause the loss of key personal data to be an assault upon identity in daily transactional life.

Paper-based centuries-old concepts of identity are being imported into the digital age with unpredictable results. The same information - called identity - that links the achievement of a college degree, credit worth, health insurance risk, or a promotion sent via email and on-line purchase records at on-line merchants. The record of each web view can be traced to the login at a specific machine. Information entered into forms may remain on the machines in the users' profile or password manager. As the same identifiers are called to serve multiple functions with great variance in the value of the data, the diversity in resulting management practices increases. And as these identifiers are linked to one identity, the threat to privacy and risk to data integrity increases.

When a single set of data is used for multiple functions, this creates the problem of wildly varying management practices for the same data. Those who obtain low but nonzero value from identifying data obtain such data, and store it according to their own value calculations. In terms of identity and identifiers there is a tragedy of the commons.[1] Very high-value transactions and decisions—employment, professionals managing large transactions—use the same identity-specific data as very small transactions. Because the risk in low value transactions can be decreased using personally identifiable information at the most detailed level (e.g., social security numbers, universal identifiers, credit information) these managers keep data long term. Identifiers simplify price discrimination. Yet because the value of the transac-

---

[1] The tragedy of the commons occurs where there is some highly desirable shared resource that, if everyone uses it according to their own incentives, will be destroyed. The tragedy of the commons refers to the grazing commons, where it is in the interest of each farmer to add an additional sheep. However, if everyone adds sheep the commons will be over-grazed and destroyed. Similarly if everyone uses the same identifier, like a SSN, that identifier will be over-exposed, under-protected, and eventually made unreliable.

tional records is low the level of protection is low. Use of this data resembles use of the proverbial common—all parties have an incentive to use the data but only one has incentive to protect it according to the highest value. Any party seeking to subvert data will seek data or systems at the lowest level of protection and then use the data for authorization to subvert the security surrounding high value uses.

Many of the technical problems of anonymous transactions, linking identity to binary data, and access control have individually been solved. Yet adoption of the solutions has lagged. This is particularly problematic in e-government.[2] The services and purchases by government are significant, as the authority vested in enforcement and benefit agencies requires risk aversion in applications of policies.

Individuals, government and businesses suffer from the use of a single identifier for high value (e.g., Social Security benefits) and low value (recreational fishing license) transactions.

When the government uses an identifier the issues are more complex, because identity is far more problematic for governments. Governments both need to be able to identify their citizens, and need to be constrained from knowing their citizens too well.

Sometimes, the identity systems created for security results in a handy way to undermine security and thus exploit trust in the system. For example, in the Battle of Algiers, the story of the Algerian struggle against their French opponents is told, in all bloody tragedy. Terrorist opponents of France they were, or maybe freedom fighters. The French instituted a policy of identification papers to determine who was trustworthy to move around the city. After a particularly ugly bombing, the Captain was shouting at the private for letting in the terrorist. The private replies, "Sir, his papers were perfect." The Captain angrily replied, "Only the terrorists have perfect papers." The average guy forgets his papers, or loses them, spills coffee on the picture, or forgets which paper goes with which authority. Passwords may not be subject to coffee spills but they are far easier to lose.

A single bit of paper embeds many things at once, by the very nature of paper. Consider a passport. A passport includes an identifier, the passport number. It lists some attributes, including nationality, sometimes height and weight. It includes personal identifiers, including date of birth and name. It includes a biometric[3] method of identification—a photograph. Passports are used, therefore for both identification ("I am me") and identity authentication ("My government authenticates that I am me."). A passport links attribute authentication (citizenship) with identity authentication (name) to enable off-line identification (photograph and physical description data). All of these elements are combined in a single document, and that document must be shown in whole to provide authentication. This binding of attribute to identity for the purpose of authentication is made necessary by the power and limits of paper. A person cannot calculate the exponentials needed to make a public key

---

[2] Implementing the traditional paper-based functions of government using online interaction between governmental entities or between the government and citizens is e-government.

[3] A biometric is a physical, biological feature or attribute that can be measured. Examples of unique biometrics are fingerprints, iris patterns, and DNA sequences. Other biometrics are not unique and therefore not useful for authentication or identification, e.g., hair color, nose length, and height.

system work—this requires computers. An individual cannot check if an attribute identified only by a number is valid in a highly dynamic system—this requires a network and highly available data.

In fact, passport errors are not terribly rare. Jean's passport has been extended to July 6, 20011. However, it is not likely that she will be able to travel for the next eighty years on the same document much less the next eighteen thousand. Typos and errors in documents are accepted because the overall tactile form of the document. It is unlikely a terrorist would ever tolerate such an egregious typo.

The document holds up to scrutiny because, other than the typo, it holds together. It binds all the elements of what we think of as identity—identity, identifiers, and authentication. That collection of details inherently occurs with paper-based system but does not necessarily exist in digital systems. Assumptions about "document" which are really based on assumptions of "paper documents" can be misleading, and lead us into risk instead of security.

Clarity requires breaking the traditional paper system, the passport, the certification or the license, into its functional components and understanding the interaction of those components in a digital networked environment. Without that clarity, digital systems can be designed with vulnerabilities resulting from the fundamental concepts of identity and authentication embedded in technology. What are the parts of the passport or the national id? How can those parts be taken apart and put together so it works for the holder?

The Elements of Identity

An identity in an identity system is not about personality or style. An identity is a set of attributes corresponding to the appropriate identifier. An identifier distinguishes a distinct person, place or thing within a given context. A context of an identifier is often defined in the very name of the identifier-the student id number or the badge number defines where the identifier came from and where it is meaning. These contexts are called *namespaces* in digital systems and the difference between context and namespace is worth keeping. A context implies the larger world, the entire passport with the picture and the smell of the airport. A namespace is something smaller-just the number and the name and all the information inside the passport.

An automobile, an account, and a person each have identifiers. The automobile has a license plate and the account has a number. The person may be associated with either an auto or an account through additional information, e.g., serial number, or a certificate. One person, place or thing can have multiple identifiers. A car has a permanent VIN and temporary license plate. Each identifier is meaningful only in the namespace, and only when associated with the thing being identified. Therefore, each identifier can reasonably be thought of as having a <thing identified, identifier, namespace> set, e.g., <car, license plate, state motor vehicle database>.

In the human tradition, an identifier has been a name in a community. In this case the namespace is the community. Name space is literally the space in which the name is recognized. Identifiers can be strictly formal, with the case of an employee identification number. An identifier can be extremely causal, as with Jean's brother-in-law, who is "Uncle Mud" in his immediate family, "Uncle Mike" in our extended family, and "Butter Boy" to a certain niece.

In an identity management system, identity is that set of permanent or long-lived temporal attributes associated with an entity.

In a community, identity is a set of attributes associated with a person in community memory.

It is this very significant difference that underlies the use of identity today, which often threatens security and privacy. Identity in a computer is an identity in an identity management system. Identity to the human is a set of memorable authenticating facts or attributes. People and computers are so fundamentally different that there must be very different mechanisms for identity in a community and in a digitally networked system.

Attribute

An attribute is a characteristic associated with an entity, such as an individual. Examples of persistent attributes include eye color, and date of birth. Examples of temporary attributes include address, employer, and organizational role. A Social Security Number is an example of a long-lived attribute in the American government system. Passport numbers are long-lived attributes. Some biometrics data are persistent, some change over time or can be changed, (e.g., fingerprints versus hair color).

The attribute of the employee id number mentioned above is employment at the issuing company. The attribute of Uncle Mud is that he was once immemorially in the doghouse. The attribute of Butter Boy is that he once spilled drawn butter thrice during a family visit to a seafood buffet.

"Uncle Mud" is a personal identifier only in a very small namespace—that of one family. There are probably very many Uncle Muds in the many families given the many uncles in the world. The context defines *which* Uncle Mud and thus *who* is being identified.

Attributes are relationships or past actions. I am professor because of a specific University (Indiana or Dartmouth). I am an account holder because of my bank. In my house I am Mama or Dad, simultaneously the most unique and common attributes on the planet.

Personal identifier

Personal identifiers are linked to exactly one person. Persistent identifiers consist with that set of identifiers associated with an individual human that are based on attributes that are difficult or impossible to alter. For example, human date of birth and genetic pattern are all personal identifiers. Notice that anyone can lie about his or her date of birth, but no one can change it. Personal identifiers are not inherently subject to authentication.

The employer identification number is a personal identifier. There are common employer numbers, especially low numbers as it is common in start-ups to start with the founder as employee number "1".

Mama is an attribute. It is also a unique and deeply personal identifier in the context of one family.

Identification

Identification is the association of a personal identifier with an individual presenting attributes, e.g., "You are John Doe." Examples include accepting the association between a physical person and claimed name; determining an association between a company and a financial record; or connecting a patient with a record of physical attributes. Identification occurs in the network based on both individual humans and devices. Identification requires an identifier (e.g., VIN, passport number).

Identification is the claim of a personal identifier. It occurs in some namespace by implication. For example, the Kennedy School of Government employs a photographer. She is an excellent photographer. Her name is Martha Stewart. She is no relation to the (convicted felon) doyenne of décor and no one ever accidentally calls Martha Stewart Inc for a photograph. Martha Stewart identifies a photographer at the Kennedy School of Government.

Authentication

Authentication is proof of an attribute. Identity as it is constructed in modern systems is an attribute, e.g., "Here is my proof of payment so please load the television onto my truck". Identity is often used where an attribute is being authenticated, e.g., "Here is proof of payment for television 1245678, please load television 1245678 in this truck." A name is an attribute and an identifier, but it usually is not used to provide authentication.

The employer identification number authenticates a current state of employment. The possession of the identification card authenticates the association of the employee and the employee identifier. The employer's database authenticates the employee identification number.

A common argument is that authentication is who you are; authorization is what you can do. This means that identity is an explicit mechanism to connect authentication and authorization. Removing identity, or making identity authentication distinct from attribute authentication, means removing the threat of identity theft. Identity theft is enabled because of the confusion between authenticating identity (I am Jean) and authenticating attribute (I am a good credit risk in this transaction).

Identity Authentication

Identity authentication of identity is proving an association between an entity and an identifier: the association of a person with a credit or educational record; the association of an automobile with a license plate; or a person with a bank account. Essentially this is verification of the <thing identified, thing> claim in a namespace. "You are John Doe." is identification while "Your documents illustrate that you are John Doe." is identity authentication.

Uncle Mud cannot be authenticated to an outsider. If I was attempting to present a fabrication, and his family cooperated, there is no way to prove that Uncle Mud was ever used for my brother in law. However, I cannot prove to you either that I am telling the truth without an extended process of legal swearing. So Uncle Mud is a personal identifier in a namespace but it is an identifier that cannot be authenticated.

Attribute Authentication

Authentication of an attribute is proving an association between an entity and an attribute; e.g., the association of a painting with a certificate of authenticity. In an identity system this is usually a two-step process: identity authentication followed by authentication of the association of the attribute and identifier. The automobile is identified by the license plate; but it is authenticated as legitimate by the database of cars that are not being sought for enforcement purposes. Of course, the license plate check may find an un-flagged record in the database yet fail identity authentication if the license plate is visibly on the wrong car; e.g., a license plate issued to a VW bug on a Hummer. The person is identified by the drivers' license and the license simultaneously authenticates the right-to-drive attribute. Notice the difference between "your documents illustrate that you are John Doe" (identity authentication) and "your documents illustrate that you are a student registered at the University and have access rights in this building" (attribute authentication).

When Uncle Mud pulls out his credit card (which most assuredly does not bear that name) his physical possession of the card and the match between the signature on record and his signature confirm his right to use the card. That is an attribute authentication. The name is simply a claim. When the service provider also requires identification, ("May I please see your license?") then there is identity authentication that corroborates the attribute identification embodied in the physical credit card.

Authorization

Authorization is a decision to allow a particular action based on an identifier or attribute. Examples include the ability of a person to make claims on lines of credit; the right of an emergency vehicle to pass through a red light; or a certification of a radiation-hardened device to be attached to a satellite under construction.

After authentication, by credit card or a combination of credit card and personal id, then a charge is authenticated.

Anonym

(as in anonymous).

An anonym is an authenticated attribute that is not linked to an identifier. An identifier associated with no personal identifier, but only with a single-use attestation of an attribute is an anonym. An anonymous identifier identifies an attribute, once. An anonymous identifier used more than once becomes a pseudonym.

The most commonly used anonyms are the dollar and the euro. The most familiar anonyms are self-authenticating. The users authenticate the paper. The right to spend the paper is authenticated simply by the fact that it is presented. To hold a euro is to have an anonym that authenticates the right to spend that euro. These dollars, coins, Euros, and shillings are anonymous tokens. In contrast, credit cards and debit cards authenticate an identity; use that identity to authenticate the attribute. The attribute in this case is the right to make charges. Credit cards are identity-based payment systems. Cash is token-based anonymous payment.

Pseudonym

A pseudonym is an identifier associated with attributes or set(s) of transactions, but with no permanent identifier.

Uncle Mud (who I cannot but hope does not read this book) is a pseudonym. It is one where there may be many instantiations (or incidences, or examples of general nickname of Uncle Mud).

Telephone cards are pseudonyms. Telephone cards or pre-paid phones use an authenticator multiple times in one context.

Identity options exist in more than money or telephone minutes. Disney World offers season tickets, where a season ticket holder can authenticate by hand geometry. Alternatively, Disney World offers traditional tickets. These are tickets where the ticket itself authenticates the right to enter the park — anonyms that verify the right to enter the park. Disney stores offer insured tickets, where the ticket is linked to the identity via payment mechanism. These tickets look like anonymous tickets. However, if the ticket is lost, the purchaser can go to the Disney store or office, cancel the previously purchased ticket, and obtain a new valid ticket by presenting proof of identity. Then anyone who tries to use the canceled ticket is flagged. This is an identity-linked ticket, where the identity of the user is explicitly not checked during use except for dispute resolution. All the family tickets to Disney were linked to my identity and my credit card, yet clearly they were purchased for use by my entire family. I could have also sent them as gifts to any other person who could have used them, but who could not have reported them stolen. The insured ticket has an identifier that is linked, by Disney, to the payment process but identity is not authenticated for use.

In contrast, passports explicitly reject the possibility of providing anonymity. A pseudonymous passport that simply identifies you as a citizen is not available. In the digital world, in theory, a passport could present a citizenship claim, add a biometric to authenticate the citizenship/body claim and even enable a search of known criminals. In such a transaction the person remains anonymous assuming there is not a match between the unique biometric and the list of those sought by law enforcement. The binding between the citizenship authentication and the person physically present is much stronger than in the case with the paper passport, yet the roles of identity claims are minimized.

Identity systems must be trustworthy to be useful. The more critical the context or namespace in which identities are authenticated, the more robust the attribute authentication must be. Making certain that no one is holding explosives requires stronger attribution than making certain that everyone seated in the plane purchased a ticket. Adding identity into attribute authentication can weaken an identity system by creating a possible attack because it adds an extra step. When identity is added to authentication attribution then the authentication becomes as strong as the <identity, thing identified> link. If the authentication has two steps (identity authentication, then <identity, attribute authentication>) this creates another opportunity to subvert the authentication by subverting the first step.

Direct attribute authentication ("Do you have a euro?") is more reliable than identity-based attribute authentication ("Do you have a euro credit?") in any case where it is easier to create a fraudulent identity than it is to create a false attribute. If dollars were easier to counterfeit than identities to steal, identity theft would arguably not be the fastest growing crime in the United States. If the process of arrest and enrollment in the American criminal justice system relied on personal attribute (i.e., fingerprint) first, before identity authentication (i.e., name and ID), then criminal identity theft would not be useful. Identity theft is worthy of its own discussion.

Modern identities consist of informal, social identities as well as sets of credentials. The credentials may be short-lived (a ticket to go to a theater), long-lived (date of birth), independent (right to see a Disney movie) or interdependent (right to see an R-rated movie).

Current practices combine the dependence in a dangerous manner. Many proposed identity systems take advantage of network information to share information and compile identities without recognizing the risks that criminals have exactly the same advantages.

The next chapter in this book cover immediate information about identity theft, and possible practices to avoid them. Understanding identity theft will provide the groundwork for understanding the greater problems with an identity infrastructure.

Chapter 3
Identity Theft

The name of a thing is sometimes quite illustrative. The remote control offers the ability to implement preferences over a distance. A browser allows one to go lightly from one virtual space to another, browsing not committing to one thing as with the purchase of a paper. The transistor is characterized by changing, or transient, behavior in terms of electrical resistance. Fireplaces are places designed for fires, and compressors compress.

Yet identity theft is an odd moniker for a crime where, in the end, the victim is not required to pay for the items charged or stolen. Rarely are victims left bereft of their sense of self. Victims do not lose their memories, as in the science fiction version of the theme. They rarely lose jobs and even more rarely lose their lives.

The cases of fatal identity theft have been where stolen payment mechanisms have been used to purchase child pornography. Of the tens of people who committed suicide after a United Kingdom bust of 'child pornographers', based entirely on credit card purchases, only two killed themselves after being cleared. The guilt or innocence of the others is indeterminate. Most people; however, lose their credit scores, not their freedom or dignity.

In the case of medical identity theft, victims are sometimes subject to changes in their medical record that can lead to physical harm. For example, if someone receives treatment under a stolen identity, that treatment including data on test results, diagnosis, and prescriptions become part of the medical record. Later the victim may seek treatment and have that treatment influenced by these amendments to the medical record. A wrong blood type or incorrect allergy information can be harmful or even fatal. However, many variants of medical identity theft are closer to traditional financial identity theft. We will further explore the peculiarities of medical identity theft later in the book.

Financial "identity theft" in the U.S. typically refers to the misuse of Social Security Numbers by criminals to construct and utilize an alias that cascades through the financial systems. The trick is to obtain a correct name: Social Security Number match. The name: SSN match can be used to begin instant credit at any address.

After instantiation of a credit card it is possible to get utility service in the identity's new residence. Utility bills and a phone number can be used to provide proof of residence and obtain a state identity card, usually a driver's license.

Alternatively, the criminal could go to any of the thirty driver licenses authorities that have been found to have fraud. In particular, the entire New Jersey authority has been found to be rife with corruption. Corruption was so endemic that all the line employees were fired, and the name of the Bureau was changed. [35]

Begin with a Social Security Number move to cell phones, credit cards, and then all the other services that are based on "credit", funds extended on expectation of payment based on credit records, something very much like an old-fashioned good name. The phrase and the crime are an indicator of how deeply embedded the SSN is as authentication is today.

After obtaining a SSN and an associated address, the attacker obtains credit. Initially, the attacker pays only the minimum due. Such a practice provides the highest possible credit rating.

Identity theft is the major common individual risk because of identity-based systems. The efficacy of identity theft is based on the fragility of the SSN-based identity system. Social Security Numbers enable federated identity systems. Because of the federation of multiple identities, one authenticating element can be used to generate reams of credentials.

No one has one key for their entire lives — one that opens the car, the safety deposit box, the house, and the desk. Different keys are controlled by different entities. The bank issued the safety deposit box key; and an employer issues the key for the building, yet each of these places shares one key in the digital databases when ownership information is stored - the Social Security Number.

A SSN is required to obtain and sign a mortgage, or for a credit check to rent. A SSN is required to open a bank account and obtain a safety deposit box. A SSN is required as identification to get a job. A SSN is officially not required to obtain phone service; however, phone companies often simply refuse by not responding to requests with other identification. Having one key shared by all these organizations for all the locks in a person's life is unwise in terms of security and risk management, a disaster waiting to happen. It is this consistent relentless practice in the information realm that has caused identity theft.

Who would design a system where one key fits every lock in a person's life, and that person is required to give copies of the key to everyone with whom they have any chance of sharing a lock? It is tempting to explain this away with some false wisdom, like the jokes about committees where "None of us is as stupid as all of us." But in fact it is something more fundamental than the tendency of bureaucracy to use what works until it fails catastrophically. The one-lock-fits-all is based in part of the non-digital analog concept of identity that is deeply embedded in our humanity; that is, the idea that we have a single meaningful social and human identity.

Most importantly, the design is a result of *failure to design*. One system worked. Reliance on that system resulted in a collective failure to effectively move authentication and identifiers into the information age. The credit agencies and data brokers that profit dominate the resulting policy debate.

Paper-based identity systems link attribute, identity, and authentication into a single stand-alone document. SSNs worked fairly well in a paper-based system. The availability of networked data opens entire new vistas of possible systems. However, it simultaneously destroys the assumptions on which paper-based systems are built. Networked data is undermining the assumptions of "secret" information on which paper systems depend. "Secret" information is not information that is in every database, from Amnesty International donation records to the Zoo Family Membership.

The risks created by this shift are not equally distributed. Organizations can utilize the value of databases without protecting them. The value to the organization is in having the data; not in preventing others from having what is essentially public data.

Identity theft victims for a very long time were quite left in the cold. However, now that identity theft is the fastest growing crime, victims have some company and some legal support. There is Federal legislation making identity theft a crime. Before that legislation it was sometimes difficult to obtain a police report, as needed in recovery for identity fraud.

The Identity Theft Assumption and Deterrence Act, (918 USC 1028) in addition to prohibiting the construction of fake identification documents regardless of their use, requires the Federal Trade Commission record these complaints. However, the FTC does not investigate the complaints; rather the FTC keeps a database of cases, uses this database for research and tracking of cases, and provides a listing of law enforcement agencies that investigate complaints. The complaint numbers from identity theft victims obtained under the law must be provided to Federal officials in order to track the problem as it expands. For the tenth year in a row, in 2011 identity theft was the most frequent consumer complaint to the FTC. By January 2011, the FTC had over two and quarter million identity theft cases in its Sentinel Network database.

The Fair and Accurate Credit Transaction Act of 2003 defined identity theft as "fraud, attempted or committed using identifying information without authority". The FACT enabled ID theft victims to place 'fraud alerts' on credit files, and thus decrease the risk of loss in the future. FACT also created a National Fraud Alert system.

The 2004 Act greatly increased penalties for identity theft; however, the practices that lead to identity theft (in particular the use of Social Security Numbers by businesses) have not yet been eliminated. Interestingly enough, the 2004 bill included particularly stringent punishments for using identity theft in conjunction with a terrorist attack. This explicit recognition of the use of identity in terror attacks is almost as explicitly ignored in anti-terror programs, as some proposals depend on the assumption that identity theft is not possible.

State laws that cover identity theft also usually cover criminal identity theft. Yet some are too focused on identity theft as a financial act, rather than as a device to commit other crimes. For example, the Massachusetts law makes it criminal to obtain information in order to pose ("falsely represent oneself, directly or indirectly, as another person") as another person or to obtain financial gain or additional identity information.

Specific identity theft laws have been passed in the vast majority of the states. In the remaining states identity theft is covered under fraud statutes and prohibitions on providing false information in a police report. Yet no state has a comprehensive mechanism for recovering from criminal identity theft. Once a criminal assumes a trustworthy identity as an alias, that identity cannot be trusted.

Avoiding Identity Theft, Individually

The best investment in avoiding identity theft is not a shredder but a phone call. The best way to prevent identity theft is to limit dissemination of your credit information. Of course, credit reporting companies make money by selling information. It is therefore in the interest of credit reporting companies to sell as much individual information as possible. Providing false, outdated, or incomplete information has a disproportionate impact on individuals. Of course, the value of the credit bureaus' information is linked to its quality and thus the firm has some incentive to get it right. But the cost of bad information is far higher to the individual who is deprived of a mortgage, not selected for a job, or who experiences identity theft. Historically, this incentive problem has led to public outrage when it appeared that data accuracy was of too little concern to the industry Moreover, both the sellers' and users' preference is for more information, not less, even if that information is not relevant. In fact, at one time credit reporting companies reported prurient gossip until the Fair Credit Reporting Act prohibited the practice. Therefore it is a good practice to regularly confirm the data maintained by the agencies. Sadly, there is risk in trusting a company to be responsible or opting-out.

Avoid Unwanted Offers

Opt-out of offers of credit. A credit offer in the mailbox allows an identity thief to easily begin a range of thefts. To opt out of pre-approved credit offers call the three major credit bureaus or use their mailing address. Following is the contact information.

> FTC
> (888) 5OPTOUT
> Equifax, Inc.
> P.O. Box 740123
> Atlanta, GA 30374-0123
>
> Experian
> 901 West Bond
> Lincoln, NE 68521

Attn: Consumer Services Department

TransUnion
Name Removal Option
P.O. Box 505
Woodlyn, PA 19094

The sites that are at the top of the Google search, my-free-credit-report.com, will connect to sites that require signing up for an expensive credit-monitoring service. The only free credit reporting site is AnnualCreditReport.com.

Encouraging employees to make such a phone call is an excellent investment for managers. A person with a lost identity will have difficulty obtaining credit, traveling, and can even be prevented from traveling internationally. After identity theft it takes the average victim more than two thousand hours to recover. Thousands of hours or time will inevitably impinge on work as well as personal time.

To avoid other "offers" of questionable value, individuals can add their names to the Direct Marketing Association's Mail Preference Service. The Direct Marketing Association offers an on-line form at:

http://www.dmaconsumers.org/offmailinglist.html

The Federal government has provided a Do Not Call list, based on the failure of much-vaulted self-regulation in privacy. Information on the National Do Not Call list can be found at urlhttps://www.donotcall.gov/. Notice that charities are not prohibited from contacting numbers on the Do Not Call list; so all calls will not cease. Also, some companies with which you are doing business have a right to call individuals on the Do Not Call list.

Keep Your Information Close

In the case of banking transactions, lying about a Social Security Number is a crime. Refusing to provide the number will result in no service. However, in the case of video stores, grocery preference cards, the best approach is simply to refuse to provide social security information. In many cases, the business will back down on the request. If they argue, explain that the SSN could lead to identity theft. Such theft places them at risk — both from financial loss and with outraged customers. My children's school removed SSNs from an enrollment form when I made this case and pointed out the burden they faced in protecting the (unneeded) information. Explain that your counsel has recommended that it not be provided. Faced with determination, most companies will provide an alternative method for proving identity. Of course, these alternative methods will work far better to provide authentication of identity. These methods rarely provide the company with information that can be used to commit fraud. For example, a copy of a drivers' license on a fax will provide date of birth, address, certain disabilities (e.g., a need for glasses), and a drivers' license number. Since few organizations use such information without a SSN to authenticate, the information does not generate as much risk.

Unless you are paying for your medical services with Medicare or Medicaid, there is no law requiring that you provide your SSN to any medical provider.

No web site has any right to demand a Social Security Number. Request for a SSN should be a warning flag. As a general practice, never enter a Social Security Number in a web site, banks and other businesses have telephones.

Some companies essentially force requirement for SSNs. Some companies charge fees to customers withholding SSNs. A decade ago, providing a deposit was adequate to obtain phone service without a SSN.

Employers and providers of financial services need the Social Security Number of the individual to comply with money laundering laws, and to confirm taxation. No other organization, the phone company, the video rental store, the local charity — needs the information. Not sharing it is the best protection.

Protect Your Postal Mail

It is not possible to prevent banks from printing full account numbers on banking statements, and some argue that it is desirable. It is possible to make certain that the mailings, ripe for identity theft, are not readily accessible. An old fashioned mail slot into the house is far preferable to a standard open suburban mailbox. These mailboxes are easy to use, and require a key to extract the larger documents. The boxes are as easy to use for the recipient of the mail, but are not optimized for the carrier.

On the web, the Mailbox Guy offers mailboxes from traditional to deeply paranoid. $200 may seem a large investment for a mailbox, yet it is an order of magnitude cheaper than identity theft. The secure mailboxes also keep mail reliably dry.

One form of harassment or technique for implementing identity theft is to put in a short term change of address form. If this attack is used, then the documents will simply be lost. Change of address forms were traditionally protected only by the law, not by process. For example, at Cambridge Savings Bank a change of address requires that the bank send a letter to the old address. The account holder must receive the letter, and then return the enclosed form with account information added. The account information is asked for on the form but not provided by the bank. Sending a message and requiring a reply is called *challenge and response* in computer security.

The postal system handles many more magnitudes of change orders than Cambridge Savings Bank. So the approach adopted by the Postal Service is to send a notification to the address from which mail is being directed. The person at the address will receive a change of address at the time the change of address is implemented. So while some mail may be lost, a victim will be notified.

In the event of a malicious change of address, the avenue of response runs to the local Postal Inspector. Postal Inspectors are the police of the United States Postal Office. As filing a false change of address form is a crime, they will both investigate concerns and endeavor to find for the responsible party. There is a listing of postal inspection offices at http://www.usps.com/ncsc/locators/.

The final way to protect mail is to buy a shredder. Use the shredder to prevent mailings with valuable information from going out in the trash.

Check Your Records

First, obtain your Personal Earnings and Benefit Estimate. Currently the Social Security Administration is required to mail these documents. Since the SSA is required to *mail the documents*, the SSA must purchase mailing lists. The best mailing lists have error rates on the order of a tenth of a percent. The SSA must mail millions of reports, and with tens of millions of Americans, tens of thousands of reports are mailed to incorrect addresses. The policy places every person at risk, as the error may be a simple as a transposed house number. This policy was revised so that currently PEBES reports are mailed upon request. A request can be made at http://www.ssa.gov/statement/ (not available at the moment of writing due to budgetary cuts). The system requires that the requestor provide authenticating information including legal name, Social Security number, date of birth, place of birth, and mother's maiden name. Then the information is mailed to the requestor.

A second set of documents that would be of use is credit records. The previous numbers provided relief from pre-approved credit offers. The numbers below provide a way to order credit records and therefore check their validity. There are also credit-monitoring services that notify their subscribers every time credit is checked or an account is opened. Each agency has its own number.

Equifax provides a useful summary of the security freezes in their security freeze fees and requirements web page. This service provides a state-by-state listing of who is entitled to a freeze, at what cost, and under what conditions.

Beware Of Express Checks From Distant Purchasers

An increasingly common scam both directly obtains cash from a victim and provides banking information for the scammer, when completely successful. This scam applies to those selling high value items over the web. A foreign national contacts a victim and purchases the product by check, often from a UK or Irish bank. The victim deposits the check, waits seven days and then sends the shipping amount by Western Union and the goods by freight. The victim has become engaged in money laundering, in addition to being subject to plain vanilla theft of goods.

This result could be easily addressed. Funds could be made available as soon as checks clear, and not before. Customers could be provided with two numbers: current funds and funds pending. The customer could then know when the pending funds are in fact available. Even if the customer queries the bank, the teller will not provide them with the status of all funds. Given the vagaries of global banking, the teller may not know.

International checks often take two weeks to clear. Express clearing is one mechanism to address this type of fraud. Refusing to take payments over the amount of purchase is also reasonable. International checks can be created, fairly convincingly, on a high quality printer. Never send goods until the payment is cleared. Recently this fraud was expanded to sending checks to "winners" of "lotteries". Some part of the amount printed on the fake certified check is immediately available for withdrawal as a courtesy as soon as it is deposited, or shortly thereafter. However, the bank may not know the fact that the check is false for ten days or more.

PayPal presents a similar risk. PayPal offers assurance that a payment has been received before the sender has lost the ability to recall the payment. Purchase of high value goods on PayPal therefore requires either withdrawal of funds by the recipient, or patience by the person who is paying.

Protect Your E-Mail

The best immediate action most users and companies can take to decrease their risk of dangerous information exposure is to change browsers and email programs. This is a common suggestion, and many dismiss it as intra-IT politics.

Yet this is not a case of professional lack of courtesy. The American Department of Homeland Security's US Computer Emergency Readiness Team recommended using any browser but Explorer as early as 2002 for security reasons. The code in Explorer is so deeply embedded into the operating system, for marketing reasons, that there have been vulnerabilities that literally cannot be fixed without an entire operating system update. The Department of Defense has a report on its own use of open source systems including browsers, and the National Security Agency distributed a version of Linux optimized for security, at no cost to download. Explorer and Outlook are so intertwined with the underlying operating system that securing the operating system from either is problematic.

This is not American government politics. The German Federal Office for Information Security (BSI) told the Berliner Zeitung in September of 2004 that Internet users should switch to Mozilla or Opera. The Federation of German Consumer Organizations (Vzbv), the rough German equivalent of the American Consumers Union, recommends that users have extra care if they choose to stick with Explorer. Vulnerabilities make it such that Explorer and Outlook, particularly when combined, have cost customers or Dresdner bank their bankbooks.

You Are Helpless

The essence of the manner and the core problem of digital identity is that there is often little that you can do. The above are useful best practices. However, there is no way for an individual to completely protect himself or herself from identity theft. For example, birth announcements from newspapers are available on-line. This means that given a birth date and an ability to search the Internet, any person can find your mother's maiden name. Indeed, increasingly women do not change their names so that date of birth allows you to know mother's maiden name. When your parent dies, the survivors are listed. Every mother's obituary is a gold mine for identity thieves.

Social Security numbers must be given to rent a house or even a DVD. Employers, family members, and roommates have stolen identifying information and thus financial identities.

We can choose to live in a society without obituaries and without white pages. Or we can construct a new identity system that forces all of us to make changes. Passwords, user ID's and secret questions are designed to be easy for consumers and not be a deterrent to commerce. However, these simple systems put both parties at risk.

As individuals and organizations, we can muddle forward into identity confusion or we can design a system that works by not being shared.

Identity versus Risk Management

If a good name is valuable to an honest person, imagine how valuable it must be for a fugitive who could not only use it to obtain credit, but also remain free. A person engaged in some larger crime, or one more severely punished, can use a nice clean identity to save time and trouble during interactions with law enforcement. A clean identity can prevent a person wanted on one crime being held when stopped for another. A clean identity can result in a person committing a third violent felony from being held as a violent felon when stopped for a traffic ticket, or arrested for a misdemeanor. A nice clean identity in the hands of a criminal becomes an alias, and the original person identified by the authenticators claimed by the identity becomes a victim of criminal identity theft.

"Criminal identity theft" as it occurs in the United States is a multi-stage process that requires the systematic organizational failure in the use of a readily available database of biometrics (in other words, fingerprints). To begin, a criminal commits identity theft and obtains a drivers license. Then, when arrested, the criminal presents this false identification information. The data from the false authenticating documents are entered into the national fingerprint database under the claimed name. The fingerprints may not be compared with those already in the database because the system is keyed on claims of identity (name and date of birth) rather than the persistent identity-authenticating attribute (fingerprint). Of course, the criminal never shows up for the trial having escaped the net by using another's good name.

A warrant is issued in the name of the criminal identity victim. Eventually the unlucky victim is stopped in traffic, or an officer arrives at the victim's house. The criminal identity theft victim discovers the theft only after being arrested for another person's crime. At that time the victim's fingerprints are compared to the criminal's. Then the criminal's fingerprints are compared with all other fingerprints in the national fingerprint database, often but not always yielding a match.

Compare the entering of names (identities) with the direct entering of fingerprints (biometric attributes). The entering of a name asks the question "Is this claimed identity in the system?" The attribute authentication question, "Are the fingerprints of this body in the database of criminals?" offers a more reliable response.

Criminal identity theft illustrates that biometrics can deliver the wrong answer more quickly and with a greater degree of precision than paper-based identity systems. Biometrics is only as reliable as the process of enrollment.[1] If criminal's fingerprints are enrolled under a victim's name, then the police will seek the identity theft victim when the warrant is issued.

Fingerprints are not validated against an arrested person's assertion of identity during the arrest procedure. This failure to verify identity allows high-risk multiple-offense felons to be classified as the low-risk single-arrest identities they present. The failure to verify every fingerprint against possible identity theft not only puts law enforcement personnel inappropriately processing dangerous multiple offenders at risk; this failure also increases the value of stolen identities of the innocent.

Fingerprints are not validated because fingerprint validation and the corresponding process predate computers. Having humans search fingerprint records is expensive, and time consuming. Having computers search fingerprint databases is cheap, but requires a change in processes that have become culture.

One possible response to criminal identity theft is that every set of fingerprints is evaluated against a claimed identity then entered. Such a response would be far-sighted, rational, and embed an understanding of the value of biometrics as authenticating identifiers. It is not ubiquitous because of the cost.

Instead the various Criminal Identity Acts create a set of identification papers that victims of identity theft can show to officers in the covered jurisdictions. The victim of criminal identity theft obtains a document that verifies that a criminal uses the person's identity as an alias, and the bearer is not the criminal. The bearer of this certificate can then present the certificate to law enforcement to attest to his or her innocence.

The initial dependence on the constructed identity rather than the biometric attribute allows an attack on the law enforcement system and allows wanted criminals to escape from police custody by whitewashing their criminal records with others' good names. This creates an arms race, whereby the criminal can now create forged documentation claiming to be the innocent party, or more simply generate yet another false identity to use in the next legal interaction. The problems of international travel for victims of criminal identity theft have not been solved.

---

[1] Enrollment is the process of entering initial records with biometrics. A biometric is only useful if it is associated with attributes (e.g., criminal records). The creation of a biometrics: attribute record is enrollment.

Criminal identity theft and the legislative response to the problem illustrates more than the failure of a process for enrolling criminals in the national database of fingerprints. It illustrates the misunderstanding of authentication, identity, identification and attributes. Tragically this misunderstanding is being widely applied in the effort to secure America against terror. In seeking to provide security, multiple identification mechanisms are being implemented. Yet many confuse identification with authentication, thus creating risk rather than enhancing security.

At the Federal level in the US, there is a Transportation Security Administration "no fly list" and also a Computer Assisted Passenger Screening System (CAPSS) list. Without addressing the widely cited possibility that the no-fly list is used to limit efficacy of political opponents of the Bush Administration CAPSS can be addressed in terms of its efficacy in its stated goal. A similar list, the Computer-Assisted Passenger Pre-Screening System (CAPPS II), was developed by the TSA and Homeland Security. Notice that no system is perfect and in every system there will be failures, even in theory.

CAPPS II and CAPSS systems embody the perfect failures of static lists of identities. Static lists provide identifiers associated with people who have proven to be untrustworthy in the past, or who are expected to be untrustworthy in the future.

With a static list of identities, an individual is either on or off the list. It is not too hard to find out if you are on the list. Being on the list can be seen as a rating. A serious attack requires first avoiding security scrutiny. To implement the attack, the first round is to determine if the identity used for the attack is one that will result in scrutiny. Therefore, the obvious first effort is to determine a set of identities that will certainly not result in being subject to scrutiny. The less random the scrutiny, the easier it is to avoid.

Currently the no fly and security checklists are static. In addition, there are well-known factors that determine security scrutiny. Buying one-way tickets and having no frequent flyer number result in certain scrutiny. Having a frequent flyer number, buying a round trip ticket and flying coach will result in less scrutiny. These well-known flags create a brittle system that is deterministic and therefore easy to subvert.

The use of static lists of identities for security without randomization or comprehensive security tests requires both a flawless identity system and perfect knowledge of who will commit the next crime. Or, it creates a system with systematic flaws that are leveraged by criminals of all types, not just ideological criminal terrorists.

Consider the case of the no-fly list. If that were the sole protection, then by definition everyone who flies can be trusted. Of course, this is not the case. Every passenger is examined for metal and some for explosive residue. If the existence of an un-trusted (and thus by default a more trusted) list decreases the overall scrutiny of each passenger or person not on the list, overall security is decreased. The least trusted person could obtain a false identifying information offering verification as the most trusted.

An identity-based security management system must be able to predict the source of the next attack. Otherwise, a person who has not yet implemented an attack but intends to do so can pass through the security system unchecked. A failure to predict the identity of the next attacker causes a failure in an identity-based system.

Identity is being used to confer trust. That sounds nice in a culture where identification implies knowledge. Yet in a networked environment where identity implies only authentication of a credential, trust based on identity makes no sense.

Could the attackers, including a member of the large bin Laden family, be able to obtain an $80 card? If so, then the proposal increases rather than decreases risk by offering a security bypass to the most dangerous individuals.

Imagine that all people of Middle Eastern descent were denied this card. Then a tiny fraction of the millions of dollars could find someone who is highly trustworthy who never flies. That identity could then be used for travel, certain in the knowledge that the stolen identity purchases lower scrutiny. The criminal or attacker on the plane is the person who most values being trusted.

Consider the following examples of two parts of an institution protecting the same asset (people) against the same threat (car bombs).

The Kennedy School of Government occasionally hosts speakers from parts of the world characterized by protracted struggles with terrorists. The President of Turkey, the Prime Minister of the United Kingdom and Benazir Bhutto, have each spoken there in the past few years. As such, the Kennedy School is concerned with the threat of truck bombs.

One approach to this concern would be to check the identities of all drivers who approach the Kennedy School; another approach would refuse to allow any vehicle large enough to be a significant car bomb into the threat area. In fact, the Kennedy School of Government allows any vehicle to enter the parking area, but has installed large concrete "planters" that prevent any car from driving into the pedestrian or building areas.

Harvard University similarly considers itself a possible target for attack. Security at commencement was commensurate with this concern. Police officers were placed at every exit and entrance. During 2004 graduation cars were allowed into Harvard Yard lots based on the appearance of the driver. A female clad in rented academic robes was able to drive into parking areas in a Taurus wagon, with the back covered, with fully drivable access to the pavilion. The pavilion held all the graduates of KSG and Harvard, with their respective esteemed families. The credentials confirmed were race of the driver, gender of the driver, and possession of academic robes.

The KSG approach is to protect against car bombs; the Harvard approach is to identify untrustworthy drivers. Thus under the Harvard College approach the driver must get past identity scrutiny only, and can do so for the cost of a renting academic regalia.

KSG depends on specific *threat analysis* and *risk mitigation*. The Faculty of Arts and Science depend on *attribute authentication*, which imply some facts about identity.

The university example, CAPSS and CAPPS II illustrate the risks of using identity as a security management tool and the even more common use of trusting unauthenticated assertions of identity in risk management.

If only individuals who are known as current or future threats are subject to scrutiny, then any unknown future criminal will escape security examination. This is a general observation, and applies to traffic stops as well as airline travel. One would expect that most criminals do not speed when there is a body in the trunk.

In the United States, there is currently no legislation or case law requiring identification to travel by air, because the courts are not hearing cases that assert the right to travel without identification. However, the Supreme Court has confirmed the right of a police officer to demand identification of any individual he or she approaches, *Hiibel v. Sixth Judicial Court of Nevada*. In this case the state claims that the ability to demand an unauthenticated claim of identity increases officer safety. This particular case is an excellent illustration of the misuse of identity in risk management.

For identification of a subject at the beginning of an interaction with police to be valuable requires three conditions. First, the identification must be accurate. Second, the identification must immediately correspond to useful attributes. Third, the identification and information must address an identified threat; thereby providing guidance for the officer that will immediately enhance his or her safety.

Without an authenticated identity leading to the corresponding appropriate response to the threat model, identification does not decrease risk. False identities, if believed, lull officers into believing that there is a low level of risk in a high-risk situation. If assertions of low risk identities cannot be believed, then the officer must always assume he or she is in a high-risk situation. The information cannot be trusted, and cannot be used in risk management. False identities used by dangerous suspects, and the resulting false sense of security by officers, may lead to an increase in risk. It is exactly the same as the airport searches; those who most need to be trusted (criminals) will invest more into trust-creating identities.

Without identity management as a risk tool, the implication is that every officer should treat every traffic stop and every encounter as potentially dangerous.

Demanding a claim of identity is demanding an identifier. "Are you a criminal?" offline. "Are you my bank?" online. "Are you my customer?" online.

The claim of identity is simply a claim of a label or credential. What is often called identification is credential authentication. There is little or no direct way in which to confirm a simple claim of a name. In order to confirm the claim it will be necessary for the investigating officer to demand a list of associated claims that might authenticate the identity. For example, the officer would need to obtain date of birth and current address to confirm a claim of a name with driver's license records. In fact, the officer may need the drivers' license number itself depending upon the database access provided by the motor vehicle provider to confirm the claim. The criminal who is emptying a bank account will have the victim's Social Security Number and the victim's mother's birthday handy. The criminal will never forget your mother's birthday on the phone with customer service. However, you might.

Asking for a name is either asking for a completely unverified and therefore useless label from a potentially hostile party, or initiating a query for a data set that verifies any claim of identity. A completely unverified claim of identity is of no use in a criminal situation. Increasingly, the unverified claims of identity using public information online are useless. An innocent party will provide correct information while any suspicious party would mis-identify.

Criminal aliases were used before identity management systems in law enforcement, and their value to criminals in fraud and detection is well documented.

Even given the ideal technologies, the treatment of all interactions as potentially dangerous is the best possible practice for the police officer as well as the consumer, for the same reason that the treatment of all patients as bearing infectious disease is the best possible medical practice. In both cases, those identified as previously benign may suddenly change to hazardous. In both cases, professional practice of self-protection and wariness is the best defense for the professional on the front lines.

Identity systems that function best are those that identify an individual through an un-forgeable biometric (the capture of which is observed by law enforcement and processed appropriately) that is linked to a specific attribute. The use of other identity management tools has abetted criminals in committing fraud, escaping justice, and evading surveillance. Identity systems are best used only when the threat is one of misidentification, rather than for attribute forgery. When attribute or credential information is sought, then direct attribute identification is preferable.

Chapter 4
Defeating the Greatest Masquerade

Identity theft, medical identity theft, phishing, identity fraud, criminal identity theft and payment instrument frauds are all examples of malicious activity that requires a successful masquerade. Even confidence fraud is a masquerade, of a criminal who claims to be an honest person in a particularly difficult or powerful situation. While networks and databases have made it more difficult to maintain privacy, these technologies have also conversely made masquerade attacks easier. An examination of masquerade attacks can illuminate the importance of credentials, the threats that together create identity theft, and the relationship between privacy and security.

In the real-world context, an individual evaluates the amount of perceived risk in a specific context through familiarity of social and physical context. People infer knowledge about someone's "values and moral commitments on the basis of their clothing, behavior, general demeanor ... or a common background". [113] An individual will trust another individual or a merchant if the other person is significantly similar to them; the similarity and hence perceived familiarity "triggers trusting attitudes". [113, 108] Online, those social cues are absent.

Web Spoofing and Scams

Internet commerce is embedded in daily life. According to a study conducted by Pew Internet & American Life Project (PEW), online banking increased 127%, online auction participation has doubled, and e-purchasing expanded by 63% from 2000 to 2002, respectively [148]. As the popularity and prevalence of e-commerce transactions has increased so have malicious and fraudulent activities. As the criminal use of technologies has become more sophisticated, it has become substantially more difficult to evaluate web merchants.

Attacks are increasing social as well as physical. For example, common fraudulent activities come in the form of unscrupulous merchants and "phishing" sites. In the digital age, new types of fraudulent activities have emerged, such as "phishing" scams. A phishing site impersonates a trusted entity, for example a consumer's bank, in order to attain personally identifiable information. Such information includes passwords and account numbers, credit card numbers, and social security numbers.

Well before the instantiation of e-commerce, merchant fraud was a popular and profitable endeavor (e.g., [149]). Unscrupulous merchant practices include everything from the ill-mannered (misleading the consumer about the product quality), to the irresponsible (collecting and selling personally identifiable information) to the illegal (charging the consumer twice). Merchant misinformation is not unique to the Internet. However, the ease of masquerading attacks and ability to construct false business facades are so different in quantitative terms that there is also arguably a qualitative change. While there are a range of security protocols, Internet-based confidence scams are in fact increasing in popularity and sophistication as organized crime has become involved.

The Federal Trade Commission has reported that in 2004, 53% of all fraud complaints were Internet-related with identity theft at the top of the complaint list with 246,570 complaints, up 15 percent from last year. [71] PEW has noted that 68% of Internet users surveyed were concerned about criminals obtaining their credit card information, while 84% were worried that their personal information would be compromised. [149]

Banking institutions, Federal law, and criminal courts distinguish between these various sources and types of fraud. There are significant legal distinctions between instantiations of unauthorized use of authenticating information to assert identity in the financial namespace. Yet the risk for the subject of information is the same regardless of the mechanisms of disclosure. For example, when Choicepoint exposed 145,000 California users to an identity thief, it was because one criminal created 43 authorized accounts. Choicepoint did not experience a technical hack. The business model, not the security protocols, of Choicepoint was itself the threat to American consumers. When Bank of America lost unencrypted back-up tapes of personal account information that included 1.2M records, this was a security failure based on a flawed policy. When personnel information was stolen from a laptop at the University of California at Berkeley, it was theft of property and the existence of personal information on the laptop was a violation of university security policy. While policymakers should make these distinctions, there is no reason for any victim of theft from these incidents to make this distinction. The end result was the same. Similarly end users have been given a proliferation of tools that distinguish between privacy policies (Privacy Bird), key hierarchies (PKI), and some of which identify malicious sites of a certain category (e.g., PhishGuard). Will it be possible to defeat this masquerade?

Imagine a false PayPal Web page. It will look identical the authentic PayPal Web page. The domain name will be somewhat off, for example PayPal.com.cgi.bin.com. A false web site is a type of masquerade attack is called phishing. Phishing is possible because, despite the efforts in identifying consumers to merchants, there is less information for consumers to identify the merchants in return.

The lack of a proper Internet address may identify this as a scam, yet in the email the link to the address will say http://www.paypal.com. And of course a higher quality fraud would add the image of the lock and the image of the correct URL.

Note that a core part of the business plan of PayPal is to avoid the cost of fraud implemented over its payment system. For example, by using bank accounts rather than credit cards, PayPal makes disputing fraud more difficult and pays less overhead for fraud management. Thus risk is shifted to the consumer. PayPal is not without risks itself. But it does manage its subscriber's risks in order not to expose them to identity fraud.

Unlike PayPal, this website requests a Social Security Number. Of course, one should never ever provide a Social Security Number over email or web pages. This masquerade attack is taking advantage of the fact that PayPal has convinced its customers to enter their banking information. By obtaining access to a bank account through the PayPal password, the attacker can transfer funds to his or her own account. By obtaining a SSN, the attacker can implement another set of attacks.

First, the attacker masquerades as PayPal to the customers of PayPal. Second, the attackers use the information from the phishing attack to masquerade as the victim to credit-granting agencies. The individuals who fall for this attack are victimized at least twice. First, the victims lose access to established accounts. Second, the victims may be held responsible for accounts opened in their names by the attackers.

The ability to misuse individual information and the importance of never sharing a SSN underscore that fact that privacy is, in some cases security.

How can a person detect that this is false?

Notice that there is no browser lock, indicating that Secure Sockets Layer (SSL) is not in use. Therefore, in addition to the criminals implementing the masquerade attacks, all information entered on this web page is transmitted unprotected. This allows any group of criminals (they need not be affiliated with the phishing attack) to read the information from the Web form as it crosses the network.

In fact the Security Sockets Layer[1] (SSL) security system can be undermined. Criminals can obtain legitimate certificates. If the criminal is willing to pay for the certificate, the criminal can obtain one. Certainly these criminals are masters of identity theft, so they will have the information of a trustworthy person. This can be used to purchase a certificate with a domain that appears trustworthy. For example, an organization calling itself paypal.unfraud.com obtained thousands of valid credit cards through its trustworthy name and fine interface. Another way to obtain a certificate is to have a boring domain name, such as "cgi.com". The domain name will be sent to the victim as http://www.paypal.com.login.usr.bin.cgi.com/.

One variation of phishing spam targets people by sending mail as if "from" the victim to bogus accounts. So the user opens his mailbox and finds a list of replies from email he hasn't sent. Emails like this:

To :unlucky@isp.net

---

[1] The next section is this chapter provides more detailed information on the organizational issues associated with the use and distribution of SSL.

Subject : Undelivered Mail Returned to Sender
From :MAILER-DAEMON@cs.uni-potsdam.de (Mail Delivery System)

I'm sorry to have to inform you that the message returned below could not be delivered to one or more destinations.

For further assistance, please send mail to <postmaster>

If you do so, please include this problem report. You can delete your own text from the message returned below.

Unlucky is duly concerned. Why are those mails being sent to him? Has he a virus (maybe)?

And then the final mail from the ISP, the axe appears to fall. An email arrives that reads like this:

To :unlucky@isp.net

Subject : Account Termination Notice
From :admin@isp.net

You have violated your user agreement by sending out bulk email. Your account will be terminated in 24 hours.

If your account has been hijacked and you have not sent these emails, confirm your account at the following web page:

http://accountverify.isp.net

Enter your verifying information. Your account will not be terminated and a record of the hijacking of your account will be investigated.

For further assistance, please send mail to <administrator>.

The victim immediately goes to the account verification page, reports the hijacking and exhales with relief.

Unfortunately for the victim, the web page is a false pointer. Spammers who first sent out multiple emails targeted the victim, knowing he had received these "bounced" emails. If people complained to the victim's ISP, the ISP could see the underlying routing information and know the victim was not spamming.

The spammers knew they had targeted the victim (along with hundreds of others) and guessed that the victim did not know how to read the path of an email. The spam victim has given his personal information to the very people who spammed him.

Similarly a warning that your computer *"has been running slower than usual it may be infected with spyware. To scan your computer, click yes below."* Clicking simply delivers you to the page of the company that sent the heavily streamed ads that slowed your computer.

Beware of solutions that emerge immediately after the problem has been experienced, especially if the solution is to offer up your information. Again, security requires privacy.

Third-Party Assertions of Identity

The browser lock is an example of third party reassurance of the integrity of a website. Traditional providers of credentials for business include the Better Business Bureau and the Consumers Union[2]. Third party assertions of identity and attributes range from cryptographically secure to graphics that are trivial to forge.

There is no simple way for an end user to determine if the third party certification is secure; that is, if the authentication is weak or strong. Third party certification includes established organizations (e.g., Better Business Bureau) or Internet-only organizations (e.g., TRUSTe, Verisign). In either case, the third party organization is paid by the Internet entity that is trying to appeal to the customer. While there have been claims of security, even the highly vaunted Verisign security products have been subverted.

With the absence of familiar cues, users are likely to transfer trust by first extending trust to entities that have a real-world counterpart, those that have been recommended to them, or entities that have an established brand reputation. Third party certification, when it works, makes the market more competitive because it allows consumers to make an informed choice to trust previously unknown merchants.

The Secure Sockets Layer (SSL) is the ubiquitous security infrastructure of the Internet. SSL provides confidentiality during browsing by establishing a cryptographically secure connection between two parties (such as a customer and a merchant) that can then be used to conduct commerce transactions. The SSL layer ensures confidentiality, i.e. passwords, credit card numbers, and other sensitive information cannot be easily compromised by third parties through eavesdropping. SSL is excellent at meeting its design goal of preventing eavesdropping. It does *not* function as a reliable identification and credentialing service for web sites. The reason SSL fails in this function is, in part, the economics of the market for certificates.

SSL does not shelter the consumer's information from insecure merchant machines, nor does it prevent the merchant from exploiting the acquired information.

A claimed identity, called "owner's name or alias" in Internet Explorer (IE) documentation is linked to an SSL certificate. In January 2004, the number of trusted roots by default the IE version for Windows XP exceeded one hundred, it continues to grow. The listed entities are primarily financial institutions and commercial certificate authorities (CA) but also include a multitude of businesses that have associations with Microsoft, for whom it is convenient to be included as default. Noted cryptographer Matt Blaze has observed that the largest commercial CA, Verisign, protects consumers from anyone who will not give Verisign money.

Thus currently implemented CA's are problematic in multiple dimensions. First, the Internet Explorer default is a broad and fundamental inclusion of commercial entities as trustworthy, yet there has been no interaction by the customer. Indeed even competent and otherwise reliable merchants may have practices strongly disliked by a customer. Second, the CA bears no liability for the behavior of those parties they have certified. The certification only indicates that the CA authenticated the

---

[2] The Consumers Union publishes Consumer Reports.

claim of the requestor of a domain name. Most certificates do not have any implications for the business practices of organizations that are associated with the domain names. Therefore, there is a strong and consistent incentive for CA's to certify as many parties as broadly as possible.

Another common form of third party verification is third-party trust seals. Third party seals from organizations such as the Better Business Bureau, TRUSTe, and Verisign are used to indicate a compliance with specific business practices, fair information practices, as well as verify digital credentials. The seals are especially targeted to new Internet companies that do not have a reputation in the real world, but would still like to establish a relationship with clientele.

Unfortunately, several problems are inherent in the seal solution. First, the seals themselves are digital images that can be easily acquired and displayed by malicious websites, thereby effectively exploiting a customer's trust. Subsequently, once an online merchant has procured a seal, no one attempts to ensure that the merchant continues to comply with all the policies because the burden of such a task would be too great. Third, a certification by a third party will not make a site automatically trustworthy. The certification is only as trustworthy as the certifying party. Finally, the seals only confirm that the merchant complies with a privacy policy. Not only is there no confirmation of the quality of security of the merchants' site, but it is also the case that the site's privacy policy may be exploitive or consist of an assertion of complete rights over customer data.

For example, the TRUSTe seal indicates only that the site has a privacy policy and follows it. In many cases, this seal in fact implies an exploitive policy declaring users have no privacy. If the company complied with the Children's On-line Protection Act or with the European Privacy Directive then the company could obtain the EU privacy seal. Of course, any American business is required to comply with the law, so the EU seal is less than a gold standard. In effect, the most popular seal on the web is as much a warning sign on the state of privacy practice as a reassurance.

An empirical study examined the top web sites based on search rank for a series of common search terms. The author of the study, Ben Edelman, then checked two factors. First, he examined each web site's privacy policy. Second, he left his computer open so that any attempt from the web site to download spyware or malicious code would be detected. He found that those sites with TRUSTe web seals were significantly more likely to download malicious code and to have exploitive privacy policies than those without. So the most common mechanism for identification of web sites as trustworthy is sometimes a warning flag.

Identification must be mutual to be effective. I must be able to authenticate that I am communicating with a bank to confirm in any meaningful way that I am a customer of the bank. The combination of exploitive privacy policies and actual installation of malicious code from certified trusted sites are the perfect complement to the standard of identification that now exist: provide an unverified web site all your information, and you may be able to make a purchase. The current practices require us to prove identity through personal disclosure. It's not the only option, as described in later chapters. It is an option that minimizes security by minimizing privacy. It is prevalent because the alternatives require more investment in customers and technology.

Proving Identity Through Personal Disclosure

Information disclosure systems are those that allow a web-based entity to assert that its behavior is trustworthy, and the user of the site is left with the decision to believe those assertions or not. The assertions that are presented include privacy policies, and the automated evaluation of policies. Information disclosure is distinguished from third party certificates because the site asserts a claim with no centralized or secondary verification.

Privacy policies are assertions of trustworthy behavior by merchants. Privacy policies may be difficult to read, and may vary in subtle ways. The Platform for Privacy Preferences (P3P) was, according to the developers, designed to enable individuals to more easily evaluate and interpret a website's privacy policy.[3] P3P requires a vendor to generate an XML file which describes the information practices of the website; this file can then be automatically read by the web browser and compared with a user's preset preferences. Microsoft incorporated P3P into Internet Explorer 6.0. However, Microsoft's implementation is so limited that P3P primarily functions as a cookie manager.

AT&T created a plug-in for Internet Explorer called the "Privacy Bird" in hopes of encouraging utilization to the full potential of P3P. The Privacy Bird compares the privacy policy of a site with the expressed preferences of the end user. The bird provides simple feedback (e.g., by singing, changing color, issuing cartoon expletives) to end users to enable them to make more informed choices. The Privacy Bird is arguably the most effective user interaction mechanism for evaluating privacy policies to date. However, it responds to unsubstantiated claims and there is no mechanism to prevent post-transactional policy change.

The core problem with P3P is that the protocol relies on the vendor to provide an honest and thorough accounting of the information practices on the website, which again forces consumers to place trust in the vendor. The protocol does not have a mechanism for validation of the vendor's claims. So the Privacy Bird may mislead a consumer to trust an objectionable site. Also, in the case of IE 6.0 , poor implementation of the user interface counteracted the protocol's attempt to be simple yet informative. The IE 6.0's privacy thermostat used a privacy scale from "low" to "high" yet the differences between the settings are neither immediately apparent nor well-documented.

---

[3] Hochheiser, 2002 noted that the substantive result from P3P was the defeat of the proposed privacy rules for online businesses. To the extent that P3P was designed to enhance consumer privacy, it has not obviously succeeded. To the extent it was created by W3C to prevent privacy regulation under the self-regulation argument, it has been a remarkable success.

The automated evaluation of privacy policies may be effective in empowering consumers; however there is no mechanism for feedback or shared experiences in P3P.

Signaling Identities

Internet fraud, enabled by a lack of reliable, trusted sources of information, is a large and growing problem and is based primarily upon the inability of individuals to identify merchants. The prevalence of fraud makes consumers more suspicious of e-commerce.

As an example, consider the phishing attack discussed above. Phishing is difficult to prevent because it preys directly on the absence of contextual signals in trust decisions online. Absent any information other than an email from a self-proclaimed bank, the user must evaluate a website that is nearly identical to the site he or she has used without much consideration. Simultaneously, there is very little that an institution can do to show that it is not a masquerade site. If consumers continue to misplace their trust in the information vacuum, losses will accumulate. If they decide to avoid such risks, then the economy loses a valuable commercial channel.

Another form of attack is web sites that download malicious code, or exploit browser vulnerabilities to create zombies[4]. For example, a study by Microsoft using monkey spider browsers (browsers which spider the web but act like humans) found 752 sites that subverted machines via browser vulnerabilities. [204]

Individuals have been destroyed by information security failures. In Connecticut in the U.S., a substitute teacher named Julie Amero was under threat of forty years imprisonment for showing students pornography. Told "Do Not, Under Any Circumstances Turn off the Computer," she felt she had no recourse when malware began displaying obscene pictures to the classroom of seventh graders. [175]

In a more severe case, thirty-four people in the United Kingdom killed themselves after being charged with downloading child pornography based entirely on credit card purchases. Commodore David White killed himself within 24 hours after the charges, after which it was determined that there was no evidence on his own computer, cameras, or memory devices that he had ever downloaded such material. Another killed himself after being declared "innocent"[5] of downloading child pornography. In the two years of the investigation, he had been divorced, denied custody of his children, refused employment, and socially shamed for being a pedophile based upon the records of one computer transaction. [92] An emergency room doctor, in contrast, cleared his name when the judge declared that credit card records alone, with no pornography on the doctor's machines, was evidence only of credit card fraud. [14]

---

[4] Zombies are machines that are remotely controlled by malicious parties. These are usually home computers, which are utilized by criminals to phish, send spam, and commit other online crimes.

[5] The judge noted that the court could only declare him, "not guilty", but that he would rather that it be clear in this case the accused had been completely exonerated.

In the physical realm there are useful visual, geographical and tactile cues that indicate a merchant's professionalism, competence, and even trustworthiness. In e-commerce, parties to a transaction commonly are geographically, temporally, and socially separated.

Consider two places in the physical realm: Tiffany's and the Hong Kong Ladies' Market. These are both places where one might purchase pearls. Were these markets meters, as opposed to continents, apart there would still be no way to confuse the two.

In economic terms Tiffany's has the higher quality and is able to signal this quality through the construction of an impressive facade, location at a prestigious address, and a highly ordered self-presentation.

In contrast, the signaling in the Hong Kong Ladies' Market indicates high competition, low overhead, and strong downward pressure on prices. In the Hong Kong market, merchants may assure buyers that the pearls are real, perhaps even harvested in Japan. The buyer may be assured that the low prices are a result of once-in-a-lifetime opportunity, and that the buyer should not hesitate at this rare chance at owning such high quality pearls. The overall context of the transaction provides information useful in evaluating these claims.

Online these virtual sites would be distinguished only by the web site design, domain name, and corresponding SSL certificates. Imagine one of the merchants in the Hong Kong were named Tifanny. In February 2006, the domain name Tifanny.net was available for tens of dollars. In contrast, brick and mortar businesses can invest in physical infrastructure and trusted physical addresses to send signals about their level of prestige, customer service and reliability. For example, a business on the fiftieth block of Fifth Avenue (arguably the most expensive real estate in New York and thus America) has invested more in its location than a business in the local mall that has in turn invested more than a roadside stand. The increased investment provides an indicator of past success and potential loss in the case of criminal action. Information on such investment is far less available on the Internet. The domain "tifany.us" was available in 2007, but creating an equally believable offline version of Tiffany's requires far more investment.

Identity systems can be centralized or based upon social networks. (See Chapter 9 for more detail on social networks and reputations.) No identification can prevent confusion; and thus no system can prevent every fraud. However, targeted, user-centered systems could prevent the masquerade attacks discussed here by identifying the merchant or bank to the customer. Privacy-enhancing identification systems could prevent the phishing attacks described here from enabling identity theft. Privacy-enhancing identity thefts prevent attacks that can be leveraged into cascading failures of identification by limiting information use, and preventing re-use of information. Anonymous credentials that can empower consumers to protect privacy while improving authentication are described in Chapter 9.

Chapter 5
Secrecy, Privacy, Identity

Phishing attacks are so profitable because they enable cascading failures. Online identity systems that are built upon concepts of papers and identification enable these cascading failures in part because such systems do not protect privacy.

Privacy, confidence and trust are about the distribution of power. Privacy offers me the ability to act freely, as a citizen, in my own home without my government or employer watching me. Privacy offers me the power to protect myself. Privacy also allows me to use illegal drugs or commit acts of violence in my home, despite government prohibition and employer chagrin. Privacy can enable harming others.

Privacy is violated only when identifying information is associated with other data. There are no privacy issues with anonymous grocery cards, not because with work and determination the shopper cannot be identified. There are not privacy concerns because the work required is so much higher than the value of the identifying information. There are no privacy concerns in inventory or tracking purchase correlations (e.g., giving out cat litter coupons upon the purchase of cat food). Privacy is only an issue when there is identity in a record, or when identity can be easily extracted from the record.

Yet privacy is double-edged sword. One person's privacy can reduce another person's autonomy. A classic use of privacy to control is described in "The Unwanted Gaze" where Rosen discusses the dual problems of privacy in sexual harassment. Sexual harassment investigations allow for intrusive investigations, against both claimants and those charged. Yet the lack of sexual harassment laws created a sphere of privacy that was used for abuse of power. The pundit O'Reilly had his secret sexual fantasies exposed when his producer played the tapes of his obscene phone calls. Powerful men demanded women's bodies for the women to keep their jobs. Exploitation of this type, called quid pro quo, is now not only illegal but widely socially condemned. Bragging about sleeping with a secretary is as contemptible as driving drunk — another change in social mores based on the balance between individual autonomy and the good of others. Yet the practices of exploitive sex in the workplace was an element of the existence of privacy, just like domestic violence and child abuse. The relationship between my privacy and your security is complex.

Indeed it was the sanctity of the family that prevented child abuse laws to the point where the first successful child abuse prosecution was under laws against cruelty to animals. (In 1874 animals were legally protected but children were not. In the case of the horribly abused Mary Ellen McCormack, the first successful child abuse prosecution in the United States, the judge depended on cruelty to animal laws to sentence the mother to 1 year of prison. The next year the New York Society for the Prevention of Cruelty to Children was founded based on the model of the NY Society for the Prevention of Cruelty to Animals.) Child abuse laws were seen as invasions into the privacy of the family. Privacy can be the opposite of accountability. For example, Rosen defends a concept of privacy that is brutal. A perfectly private world risks being one where violence is never investigated, where identities can be snuffed out. Privacy that prevents a person from bearing witness to her own experiences does not create freedom. But privacy that makes every interaction recorded merchandise creates its own threats to freedom.

This balance in autonomy, the downside to privacy is widely heralded and embraced in discussions about security. No doubt children, though lacking full legal protection until age eighteen, are better off with child abuse laws than without them. No doubt the family that is wrongly accused might disagree, so the ability to accuse and investigate is tightly constrained.

Yet the balance between security and privacy is not so absolute. A lack of privacy can weaken security. Privacy cuts both ways in terms of security.

A lack of privacy can mean no autonomy. A life lived under surveillance is not a free life.

A lack of secrecy can mean a lack of security. Without privacy there is no secrecy. When all is exposed there are no secrets. Identity theft, phishing, and much computer crime, is enabled because there is no secrecy for the supposed private information. Indeed, an Illinois Appellate court has determined that sharing information, including names, addresses, and social security is not an invasion of privacy. The basis for the decision that cell phone companies can use subscriber information was that none of information shared (including — names, cell phone numbers, billing addresses, and social security numbers) were private facts. In this case, no privacy means no security. (Busse v. Motorola, Inc., 2004 Ill. App. LEXIS 738 (1st Dist. June 22, 2004))

Yet unlike secrecy (we all agree on the nature of a secret) there is great divide in people's perceptions of privacy. Age, gender, employment, and generally the person's place in the overall hierarchy affect their beliefs about the value and nature of privacy. Individual politics and belief systems alter our conceptions of privacy — a libertarian and a liberal have different views about government limits on business use of personal data. Yet both have the same understanding (albeit possibly different opinions) about classified or secret data.

The loss of privacy in the cases where security is decreased is deeply intertwined with identity and identity management.

On the surface, there is a seemingly inherent tradeoff between identity and privacy. Privacy-enhancing identity management is not an oxymoron. Privacy and ubiquitous ID systems can, together, serve to enhance individual autonomy. Of course, there is a conflict between the designer's desire to have information to make optimal use of the system and the subject's right to privacy, that is, their control of information about themselves. Yet carefully selecting information and deciding in the design stage who will have access to and control of information can enhance functionality while protecting privacy.

Making privacy function in identity design requires understanding the various dimensions of privacy. The technology implemented by a designer can vary based on the designers' conception of privacy (e.g., [30]). Thus in the following chapter I examine different conceptions of privacy, from Constitutional law to technical practice.

Laws of Identity

The debate on privacy in terms of identity was greatly enhanced by the creation and support by Microsoft of the "laws of identity". Obviously these are not laws, they are too vague and guarantee nothing. Yet they provide an excellent framework for considering identity systems. Are these the laws that should be adopted?

User-centric identity is a grand phrase. Yet can be a disaster. It depends on the details. Like use of SSNs user-centric identity, users can be effectively forced to consent. In the worst case user-centric identity simply extends the reach of personal data. Within a federated identity, there is a limit to the federation, so personal information flow is limited to the federation. User-centric identity can result in accelerated transmission of personal data as every party requires information from the user to interact.

User control and consent brings up the question of consent. In theory, we have all consented to the current state of data publicity. By interacting with companies that sell data to data resellers we consent to the use of our data. By providing information for a loan, we provide information for ChoicePoint to fax to identity thieves (upon valid payment). Consent has proven woefully inadequate thus far for the protection of authenticating and identifying information.

Minimal disclosure for a defined use is a foundation of privacy. In fact, few consent to resell of data. Yet when the choice is to sign the mortgage, close the loan and move or to pursue a fruitless search of banks for a reasonably privacy policy, we must consent. Minimal disclosure for defined purpose would imply that our identifying information would be provided only to obtain a mortgage, not to generate additional business in data resale for the lender.

Justifiable use is as difficult as consent. Marginal decreased use for the data collector justifies, for the collector, the request for data. After the data are all collected, profit inherently justifies resale.

Directional identity implies that identity can be proven to one party, so that the authenticating party cannot simply sell the information to others who may or may not be interested in various masquerade attacks.

The first four are privacy principles, the others are about good design practices.

Pluralism of operators and technologies is the final "identity law". This implies that no one party can own identity. In fact, forcing discrete agencies to create their own identities implies that each is responsible for that identifier. If the movie rental agency had to create its own records, the company might require a membership fee. However, the fee could be returned with consistent responsible behavior. Similarly, telephone companies require either a (refundable) deposit or a Social Security Number with the corresponding record.

Other identity requirements can be added. For example, user control as implied above, is meaningless without user empowerment. To the extent that these are "laws" then they should be instantiated in the technology and as difficult to violate as gravity. Anonymous credentials would fulfill the requirements of consent, exposure and disclosure in a technical mechanism. Yet this requires investment in a new infrastructure.

Privacy as Spatial

Doors exist to be as much to be shut as to be open. Doors, walls, structures, and neighborhoods create boundaries both in terms of appropriate behavior and trust. Boundaries both reinforce and support self defined choices and identities. Neighbors are trusted not only because of the self-sorting of modern neighborhoods but also because the cost of a dispute is so high.

Privacy in computing is often conceived of as an issue of boundaries. Many technology designers have adopted a concept of contested social spaces as articulated in the concept of privacy as process. Contested social spaces are spaces where you are not in secret but may or may not be identified. For example, in a train station or in the mall you may identify yourself for payment. There is a record created of the purchase that places you in one location. Or perhaps you may pay cash. There is no formal record of identification for being in that place. However, the place is not private in the sense that there are social behaviors that are inappropriate in these clearly public places.

Social spaces are now anonymous by choice of the designers or owners. Video systems are widely used. Video systems can be linked to face recognition. More likely, credit cards and identification will become wireless, so the mall or street or train station can continuously check to see who is present. The population of the mall could readily offer the specials, the pricing, and the sales especially to the extent that advertisements and pricing information is provided electronically. There is an incentive for identification of who is in the mall.

The boundary concept strongly parallels the early work on regulation of speech on the Internet, in which legal and policy scholars disputed the nature of cyberspaces.[1] In both digital speech and digital privacy, spatial metaphors were

---

[1] This debate was settled when Internet Service Providers obtained a Safe Harbor provision in the Digital Millennium Copyright Act that delineated appropriate ISP behavior with regards to copyright (a most troublesome modern speech/property conflict) and expression.

adopted because of the potential power of the heuristic. Spatial metaphors enabled the classification of contests with historical conflicts of speech. Spatial metaphors offer great subtlety. Like the speech debate, the spatial privacy discourse has integrated issues of social, natural and temporal spaces. Being at the mall at midnight when it is closed is quite distinct from being there at 8pm when it is open.

The difference between virtual and physical spaces is determined by the nature of the boundaries that divide them. Virtual boundaries are distinct in three dimensions: simultaneity, permeability and exclusivity. Simultaneity refers to the ability of a person to be two places at once: at work and at the mall. The mall might attempt to determine who is there. Should it be able to sell the information of who is at the mall to employers, in order to determine who is taking an extended lunch break December 22? What of the case when you are shopping at work?

Suzie,

Given that Joey has been having trouble in school I thought I might purchase the phonics package. What do you think of this resource?

http://www.dyslexia-parent.com/course.html

thanks,

Lucy

In this case the law argues that the business needs only to have a business need to read the email. However, sitting at the desk the individual is experiencing an interaction in multiple dimensions. Sitting at work, even on break, the person is an employee. Sending an email the person is both parent (to Suzie) and grandparent (to Joey). Examining the task and asking another person, the person is a consumer. Lucy identifies herself to the computer at work to access her web mail. She identifies herself to her web-based personal email provider via a password. She identifies herself to the recipient of the question by her originating email address. Lucy is in multiple spaces because the virtual spaces of the web-based email, the store, and the workplace are simultaneous. The employer may use application-level proxies. In this case the employer has every identifier. Of course, employers are not monolithic organizations but are entities made of human beings. Should the IT workers (somewhere on the globe) have access to all the identifiers and communications created by the complex interaction? In a physical space, the existence of boundaries allows for the separation of identifiers. The existence of multiple simultaneous virtual spaces can concentrate risk. A criminal IT support party can obtain all Lucky's identifiers — perhaps even her credit card depending on the operation of the firewall should Lucy choose to purchase the Multi-Modal learning package under consideration.

Permeability is the capacity of ICTs to make spatial, organizational or functional barriers more powerful, less powerful, or even invisible. The permeability of the work/home barrier is most clearly illustrated with telecommuting. Barriers can be so permeable as to be transversed without the knowledge of the person putatively moving across the boundary. For example, moving from a conference site to the payment processor or from a web site to an affiliate is intended to be seamless.

Similarly some blogs (a notably annoying feature dropped by e-commerce sites) keep a reader framed so that the reader cannot easily escape one blog into another. In one case the user crosses boundaries and experiences simultaneity, and in the other the user attempts to cross boundaries and is constrained by invisible ties. In case, identities and authentication information crosses boundaries and risk can be multiplied.

Exclusivity, in contrast, is the ability of ICTs to create spaces that are impermeable, or even imperceptible, to others. Intranets may offer exclusive access through a variety of access control mechanisms, and the creation of databases that are invisible to the subjects clearly illustrates the capacity for exclusivity.

In the physical sphere, the walled private developments offer an excellent example of exclusivity, yet it is not possible to make physical spaces so exclusive as to be invisible. In digital spaces discovery of places one is not allowed to view is itself problematic. Technologies redefine the nature of space, and digital networked technologies alter the nature of boundaries.

Exclusivity is possible for identities. Secure hardware, encrypted interactions, and protection of authentication information allows for exclusive identification. Exclusivity means that one lost identifier does not cause a cascading effect. For example, loss of a gym locker combination does not create a lack of security elsewhere. The locker is exclusive so that accessing the locker does not allow access into the home. In the virtual realm, loss of control of a computer desktop will allow access to other dimensions. Loss of information used for cross-domain authentication (e.g., Social Security Numbers) creates systematic failures. In the virtual world it is if whenever a locker is broke, one's keys and wallet are by definition in that locker at that movement. Physical exclusivity implicitly provides failure isolation. Virtual exclusivity can do the same.

Communities online are often imagined communities. For example, Facebook is considered an extension of the campus life. Students conceive of this as a safe place that is not going to be part of life after they graduate.

The share of users of high sensitivity to partner or sexual orientation who claim to be concerned about sexuality is nearly three-quarters. Yet fully half of these have posted that information on Facebook. Only one in five realize that anyone can search the data. 85% do not believe that Facebook will collect information from other sources. Three quarters do not believe Facebook will give away information. Yet the privacy policy is clear about resale and release of information.

Almost 70% suggest that *others* are putting themselves at risk when those others post behavioral information. Yet when asked why they put information up, the majority of users identify expressing themselves as having fun.

The students are imagining boundaries that do not exist. The students live in an imagined community. They believe the virtual information space is exclusive. The privacy policy is clear about compilation and resale of information. But the image of a virtual space is so strong, that they trust information they declare that they would not share.

Data Protection

Due to the complexity of the problem of privacy and ever increasing data flows, the European Union, Canada, and Australia have adopted data protection regimes. The Code of Fair Information Practice is the foundation of the dominant data protection regimes. The Code (and the related data protection requirements) has as its core *transparency, consent, and correction*. In terms of privacy, these are generally seen as a reasonable minimum. Transparency requires that no data compilation be secret.

Consent can be problematic even when the installation is clearly visible. Informed consent implies an understanding of the underlying sensor technology and the data that can be compiled. Consent includes not only awareness of the existence of data in sorted form, but also consent to the various uses of that data. Consent requires that data can be deleted or corrected when desired by the subject.

Data protection regimes have the advantage of mitigating the complex dimensions of privacy. In contrast, the multi-level jurisdictional approach has the advantage of illuminating the sometimes competing dimensions of privacy.

Data protection defines some data as inalienable (e.g., sexual orientation) and other data as subject to contract (e.g., name, address, date and amount of a purchase). The clean, carefully drawn lines about particular data elements in data protection are inadequate for the continuous data flow with probabilistic potential to detail all factors of our lives.

Data protection differs from identity principles. But data protection can limit the abuse and construction of identity. For example, Canadian identity principles require that identifiers justify the use of identity. Unfortunately, as long as all payment mechanisms are linked to identity, provision of easily stolen information is required for commerce. However, data protection also requires that there be a reason for identity information. Also, the resale of identifying information is not allowed under data protection requirements.

Autonomy

Autonomy has traditionally been a central concern of legal scholars in privacy. In the literature of democracy, privacy is autonomy. Privacy as a Human Right under the UN Universal Declaration of Human Rights is based on the freedom to act without the fear of surveillance. Surveillance can result in targeted retaliation. Similarly, the European Data protection regime recognizes informational autonomy by declaring that there are data that cannot be collected except under highly constrained circumstances, for example data on sexual preference. Legal monographs on privacy tend often focus exclusively on the autonomy concept of privacy.

Privacy is a form of autonomy because a person under surveillance is not free. In the United States, Constitutional definitions of privacy are based on autonomy, not seclusion. These decisions have instituted both sexual autonomy and, in the case of postal mail and library records, a tradition of information autonomy under the law.

This concept of information autonomy was altered under the USA PATRIOT Act but still remains central in American jurisprudence.

Autonomy is more than agency. Autonomy is the ability to act without threat of retaliation and thus refers to freedom of action and patterns of actions that are not mitigated by surveillance. In NAACP v. Alabama, the opinion sums up the requirement for autonomy for a legal regime, "a government purpose to control or prevent activities constitutionally subject to regulation may not be achieved by means which sweep unnecessarily broadly and thereby invade the area of protected freedoms." A technical modification may be "a technological purpose to control or prevent activities subject to surveillance may not be achieved by means which sweep unnecessarily broadly and thereby invade the area of preferred freedoms."

Autonomy as privacy became part of the popular discourse in the United States in 1965 because of two decisions by the Supreme Court that year. In the first, a unanimous Court struck down the Congressional statutory authorization of the Post Office to detain mail the USPS determined to be "communist political propaganda" and to release that mail only after the addressee notified the USPS in writing that he or she wanted that specific information. (Lamont v. Postmaster General) Later the Court reviewed an arrest of a Director of Planned Parenthood who was providing contraception and information about contraception to a married couple. The law prohibiting such communication was abolished in a split court with the decision Griswold v. Connecticut. These two decisions form the underpinning of the right to privacy. Both are decisions based on the availability of information. Of course the later decision Roe v. Wade, which secured the right to legal abortion, is the privacy law most prevalent in the American mind.

Privacy as autonomy, privacy as a human right, is inalienable. Only the concept of privacy as autonomy provides the theoretical underpinning for individuals' interest in data about themselves absent quantified harm. Recognizing that individuals have interests in data that extends beyond immediate harm is recognition of the right to privacy as autonomy.

In technical systems, privacy as autonomy is usually implemented as strong anonymity. Users who seek autonomy in a particular dimension will seek data deletion, anonymity or obfuscation.

In addition to the very real threats of crime and abuse of power, privacy is also trumped by speech in the United States. The First Amendment is absolute, "Congress shall make no law respecting an establishment of religion, or prohibiting the free exercise thereof; or abridging the freedom of speech, or of the press; or the right of the people peaceably to assemble, and to petition the Government for a redress of grievances." "No law" is taken by many to mean "no law". In contrast, privacy has no such absolute protection.

Property

Privacy in the United States is a subject of both civil (that is state law) as well as federal Constitutional law. Thus privacy is also a tort (or rather a set for four torts that need not be specified here) in the United States. Privacy as a tort defines privacy as essentially commercial, a wrong that can be set right by payment.

Privacy can yield economic advantage to select stakeholders. For example, data that provides demographic information and thus enables price discrimination can violate this dimension of privacy.

User behavior with respect to personal information, valuation of protection of information, and characterization of data types with respect to the subject identification are all topics of active economics research. [32]

The objection to privacy as property is that property rights are alienable. Under the property paradigm all subject interests in property are lost at the transaction. A data subject has no more right to limit secondary use of data than a seller of a home has a right to return and paint the kitchen after the closing.

In either case, the data are economically valuable and thus centralized authorities will have economic incentives to share those data. Users who see data as property will want payment for data. Alternatively, users may seek deniable pseudonyms in order to avoid future price discrimination or to prevent complete loss of control over personally identifiable data.

Sign on the Virtual Line

I reach out my hand and push the browser button down. In response, the task bar slowly fills from left to right. I have digitally signed a document.

I sign my name across the small black screen to authenticate my credit purchase. I have created a digitized record of my signature.

My fax is signed. I send it to authorize my purchase. I have sent a signature that was physical, digitized and then printed into an analog physical form.

Each of these actions has very different implications in terms of my own risk, and the ability of others to misuse the information sent to spend my money, or otherwise pretend to be me to obtain payment authorization.

The last is the easiest to understand and the only case where there is a true signature. But why would my handwriting be adequate to authorize a monetary transaction? I simply claim to be me and send a scrap of paper. Here is my handwriting, and it represents me. Why is sending a fax (possibly from a fax machine that can be accessed for a small cash payment) superior to making the same claim of identity over the phone? In part, this is because there are legal and organizational mechanisms that allow that signature to be verifiable later for dispute resolution.

Digital signatures or cryptographic signatures use the science of hiding information. The hiding of information using codes has long been the purview of government and high finance. Codes were not always mathematical. Caesar implemented one of the oldest recorded tricks for hiding information. He wanted to send a message through hostile territory via a messenger. But the messenger might be captured and killed or even subject to torture to obtain any secret message. Thus Caesar had to send a message that could not be read by the messenger or any person who intercepted the messenger. Having something unreadable by the messenger was simple; any illiterate slave would fill that condition. However, any slave would be unlikely to endure torment in order to protect an owner's secrets. In this case the solution was to write the message on the slave's head with strong ink and then, after having grown back his hair, the slave was sent with the message to the recipient. ("The Codebreakers" by Kahn is the canonical history of cryptography, and the source of this tale and other.)

Despite the fact that this approach is wildly inappropriate today, it achieves some of the same goals that mathematical cryptography does today. First, the bearer of the message cannot read the message. Neither the Roman slave nor the modern ISP is a reliable agent of the interest of the sender. In technical terms the message was *confidential*.

However, there is an effective attack against both systems. If the slave cooperates with any party intercepting the slave then the message may be read. That is, the slave may simply tell the messenger how to access the secret ("It's under my hair.") Then, the slave's head is shaved and voila! The attacker has the message. The slave is literally the man in the middle, and his cooperation can subvert security.

Similarly there are man-in-the-middle attacks online. In this case, the man-in-the-middle is the attacker and the transmitter of messages. Online, the man-in-the-middle masquerades as both parties, each to the other. The man-in-the-middle pretends to be the bank to the customer, and the customer to the bank. The man-in-the-middle sets up a web site that appears to be the bank site to the customer. The customer enters authenticating information: password, account number, or whatever else is needed. The man-in-the-middle sends this to the bank, and confirms to the customer that the information is correct. The man-in-the-middle then may even accurately perform actions on behalf of the user while the user is logged on. However, the man-in-the-middle will not log off and will certainly abuse the account information provided.

If the slave showed up with head shaved (unlikely if he were rewarded for cooperation, impossible if he were killed) then the recipient would know there was interference. In technical terms this means a loss of confidentiality is detectable. Thus writing on the head of person provides a secure communication system that is *tamper evident*. That means you can tell if the message had been altered or accessed without authorization. There is a nice feature of the shorn slave for the ancient royal correspondents. That is an advantage to writing on a slave as opposed to writing on the Internet — any loss of confidentiality is more easily detected in the head-writing case. However, the recipient may not know to expect a message. Caesar's representative, like the banking customer today, sits unaware while the cost of the lost message is amplified by use and time. In the case of digital information there is no readily available method to know if someone has seen the hidden information.

Both security mechanisms (hair and cryptography) share at least one weakness in that it is (relatively) time consuming. Adding a cryptographic signatures to a message causes some delays, because cryptographic operations are processing intensive. In this case the time is fractions of seconds added to other fractions of seconds, not weeks added to days.

Sadly there is a correspondence between modern security and the hygiene of ancient Rome that found hair-washing so unimportant. The slave may bring more than the message. The slave might arrive ill, bearing viruses and germs with the gift of information. Similarly secure systems in computers can be subverted and do more harm than good, particularly if subverted. Messages received may bear more than the content.

Chapter 6
Security and Privacy as Market Failures

Most software is sold as is, according to the end user licensing agreement. This means that the software is released with bugs, known and unknown. There is tremendous market pressure to push software out the door. Money flows in as soon as the software is written. Being first may mean market dominance.

The resulting software, with errors, may need to be repaired regularly. Indeed, one Tuesday a month for the life of Windows, Microsoft released patches to address failures in the software.

In part this is because the information economy is relatively new. Code is complex. Even line by line examination of code cannot detect every possible security failure. Some bugs, i.e. vulnerabilities, are a result of interaction between programs. The errors emerge in complex unforeseen ways. Some errors emerge not from interaction, but only from unique states in the program. There are bugs that occur only when tens of conditions are simultaneously met, so that they could not be detected even in the most rigorous testing.

The result is that the individual who does not keep his or her machine secure by patching every month is at risk. However, every machine that is not patched creates risks for everyone connected to the network. Like the industrial facilities and home toxins that poisoned communities in the first half of the twentieth century; software vulnerabilities and unpatched home machines poison the network and the information on which virtual life depends.

In formal terms, lack of security can be seen as a particular kind of market failure, an externality. [32] Computer security failures cause downtime and costs to the people other than the ones who either create or do not mitigate these failures. At the most obvious, stolen information enables identity theft. But at a more subtle level, the Internet is a network of trust.

Three common ways in which security from one system harm another are shared trust, increased resources, and the ability for the attacker to confuse the trail. Shared trust is a problem when a system is trusted by another, so the subversion of one machine allows the subversion of another. (For example, when passwords for one machine are kept on another). The use of cookies to save authentication information has made this practice extremely common.

The second issue, increased resources, refers to the fact that attackers can increase resources for attacks by subverting multiple machines. This is most obviously useful in brute force attacks, for example in decryption or in a denial of service attack. Using multiple machines makes a denial of service attack easier to implement, since such attacks depend on overwhelming the target machine.

Third, subverting multiple machines makes it difficult to trace an attack from its source. When taking a circuitous route an attacker can hide his or her tracks in the adulterated log files of multiple machines. Clearly this allows the attacker to remain hidden from law enforcement and continue to launch attacks. The last two points suggest that costs to hackers fall with the number of machines (and so the difference between the benefits of hacking and the costs increases), similar to the way in which benefits to phone users increase with the number of other phones on the network.

A fourth point is the indirect effect security breaches have on users' willingness to transact over the network. For instance, consumers may be less willing to use the Internet for e-commerce if they hear of incidents of credit card theft. This is a rational response if there is no way for consumers to distinguish security levels of different sites.

Because security is an externality, the pricing of software and hardware does not reflect the possibility of and the extent of the damages from security failures associated with the item.

Externalities and public goods are often discussed as if they are the same. They are two similar categories of market failures. A common example of a public good is national security, and it might be tempting to think of the analogies between national security and computer security. National security, and public goods, are generally single, indivisible goods. A pure public good is something which is both non-rival (my use of it doesn't affect yours) and non-excludable (once the good is produced, it is hard to exclude people from using it).

Computer security, by comparison, is the sum of a number of individual firms' or peoples' decisions. It is important to distinguish computer security from national security (i.e. externalities from public goods) because the solutions to public goods problems and to externalities differ. The government usually handles the production of public goods, whereas there are a number of examples where simple interventions by the government have created a more efficient private market such that trades between private economic parties better reflect the presence of externalities.

Identity management systems may be a public good. For identity management systems to work they either need to be dedicated to a specific use, or usable by all. If one person can subvert an identity management system, then everyone is at risk for subversion.

SoBig, a virus that made a splash, is an exemplar of security as an externality. SoBig was motivated by the ability to subvert the computers of naive end users in order to implement fraud through phishing and spam. The creator of SoBig has not been detected by law enforcement . In fact, the lack of consideration of agency in computer crime laws creates criminal liability for those with computers subverted by SoBig as they are, in fact, spamming, phishing or implementing DoS attacks from their own home machines.

Such an attack had been previously identified as a theoretical possibility the year before it occurred in the First Workshop on the Economics of Computer Security. But it became widely known after as SoBig.

The model of computer attacks as infection does not apply because the large financial motivation for subverting identity systems is not addressed. The model of computer crime as warfare fails in the SoBig example because the virus subverts but does not destroy.

In this case the assets are the availability of the network. There are providers who assist in preventing denial of service attacks and targeted assaults. For example, when Microsoft came under attack from the MyDoom worm, the company had an agreement with the Linux-based Akamai to provide content in the case of such an attack. However, few organizations will face a denial of service attack and those that do cannot call on content servers for assistance.

In this case the need is to protect assets and the threats are downtime and loss of confidentiality. Threat mitigation includes making internal billing for security prevention such that the externalities are addressed. For example, if every department is charged for spending time patching their computers, then departments will not want to address the constant stream of patches for Microsoft products.

Every first Tuesday of the month Microsoft issues a set of patches. These may be simply a wish list for Microsoft, containing repairs for functionality bugs that might have been fixed before shipping in the absence of market pressures. It may contain an update to the Digital Rights Management systems that will prevent the computers' owner from controlling music or videos on the machine. In fact, some Microsoft patches have code that defeats other code interoperability in order to increase the relative desirability of Microsoft's competing products. Microsoft patching is time-consuming and not always in the best interest of the user. Thus requiring departments and individuals to invest in this patching is irrational, in the most complimentary terms.

If departments are provided free patching support, and charged based on the vulnerabilities of the network, then the pricing reflects the externality. The new risk for changing this accounting system is that it creates incentives for managers to spend too much time looking for vulnerabilities and not enough time on other sources of internal risk.

For the individual, the result is push patching and automated zombie repair. Push patching means that the patch is "pushed" into a machine from Microsoft. This places much of the cost of patching onto Microsoft. Microsoft has to track the machines that are registered, check their status, and assure compliance. Starting with XP and continuing with Vista Microsoft also detects and removes known zombie code from home users' machines.

Economics of Security

Why, given the resources and programmers of Microsoft, would the company choose to release relentlessly flawed code resulting in the creation of a market of zombies? Microsoft is among the great winners of the computer and network revolution. If there were any company that wants to ensure ever-more adoption of broadband and high-speed machines at the home and the office it would be Microsoft. And why don't individuals secure their own machines? Why do we endless spam ourselves?

The reason most individuals do not secure their own machines is that security is invisible, complicated and the value is partially recovered by others. While we may spam ourselves as a nation of people with insecure machines, one person is unlikely to knowingly receive a spam from his or her own home machines. Microsoft accepts insecurity because we do.

Security is invisible. The value of a clean and secure machine may be as high as the value of a machine with a zombie network. In fact, once recruited into a zombie network there are benefits. Owners of networks of zombies (botnets) take care of their machines. Criminal owners may patch the machines to ensure that these resources are not stolen from the original thief. Zombies run processes in polite modes, so the physical owner does not notice the load on the machine. Since it is prohibitively expensive to obtain reliable patching at a reasonable cost from a legal service, being part of a high quality botnet may not be a bad deal for the individual home user. Of course, if the criminal controlling the machine installs a keylogger, then the transaction is a very bad one for the home owner.

Those attacks that undermine individual use result in more investment against the invisible threat of botnets. Anti spyware and virus technologies are found on far more machines than up-to-date patches.

Beyond downloading freely available firewalls and anti-spyware code, security is complex. Patching is time-consuming and complex. The result, staying out of a botnet, is of limited value. Indeed, sometime patches contain undesirable code, such as anti-competitive code that disables competing products under the guise of digital rights management.

Wireless routers can be plugged in, and work out of the box. These open routers have positive social value when they are used to share Internet access in a community. Of course, the open bandwidth also can have negative results. Individuals who use resources that others have provided such that the resources remain available to the owners are called free riders. As long as the free riders are polite, not downloading massive content and disconnecting when the connection becomes lower, open networks are valuable to everyone.

Yet when free riders are not polite, or even malicious, the owner of the system has significant risks. Those risks are not apparent. Frankly, the possible risks appear unbelievable until they occur. The teacher in Connecticut, who faces up to forty years in prison because malware caused pornography to pop up on the screen, since the firewall subscription was not renewed, can now define firewalls. Yet this twenty-something teacher never heard of firewalls until one particular failure effectively ended her career. The tens of people in the United Kingdom who killed themselves rather than face prosecution for purchasing child pornography on-line did not all live to see their names cleared. The solicitors of child pornography had utilized identity and credit card thefts to their detection and punishment for their crimes. Similarly, the home user who decides to share their wireless network, perhaps believing it safe out of the box, likely does not know MAC addressing[1] or encryption options. Free riders can download unlicensed copies copyrighted material, launch criminal attacks, connect long enough to command a botnet, or even download that most prohibited material, child pornography. Because the security is complex does not mean it is not necessary.

When default settings for the administrator account are not changed, wireless routers can distort the network view and an attacker can program a router to provide incorrect information; for example, giving those who use the router a fake page for the eBay login or for any known banking URL. Providing an incorrect network address for a correct URL is called pharming, a derivative of phishing. There is no current installed or available technology to prevent pharming.

Because of the problems of invisibility and complexity, security does not follow classical economics. Rational economics would argue that as risk goes up, so does investment in security. Also, as the education and capacity of the user increased the personal effort, i.e. the individual cost, to secure a router decreases. Reading complex instructions is easier, or lower cost, to a more educated individual. Similarly, increased wealth means increased risk exposure. Just as the wealthy are more likely to purchase risk-appropriate insurance, so rational economics would argue that the wealthy would be more likely to secure a wireless router. Loss of reputation and loss of income are greater monetary risks with more wealth.

Clearly exposure to criminals increases risk. Arguably, exposure to potential criminals increases risk. Assuming that every person is equally likely to be a criminal, those living in higher density locations face more risks. In high-density locations, there is also the opportunity to free ride outside of public view.

The economic argument suggests that wealth, education and housing density would increase likelihood of use of security. A study of more than three thousand home routers found none of these factors to make a discernable difference. [98] In fact, the only difference was the ease of use of the security of the routers. Ease of use includes both the usability (e.g., is there a security wizard?) and defaults (does encryption come on immediately?).

---

[1] MAC addresses are machine addresses. Wireless routers allow their owners to list the set of computers that can connect, based on the unique addresses of these machines. This is not foolproof. A machine can be programmed to misrepresent its MAC address, just like a person can lie about her own name.

Economics of Privacy

Monitoring and logging user actions are often seen as solutions to a generic security problem. However, security is best used when based on a clear threat model, and an understanding of the dynamics of security in society. Beyond the economic model, there are other conceptual models of security that can assist in understanding the complex technical, organizational, and legal interactions that have created identity theft.

Using a simple model from automobiles, is LoJack worth the investment? Yes, it prevents theft and solves a real problem. In addition it creates a positive externality, which is when Lojack is in use by some people car thefts go down for an entire neighborhood. What about car alarms? They do make noise. However, they are easily disabled and have not been shown to prevent auto theft. Car alarms also create a negative externality. They make neighborhoods less pleasant and decrease social capital. Privacy choices mechanisms are similarly complex.

Unlike the distinction between car alarms and silence, distinguishing between high privacy and low privacy domains can be very difficult. In economic terms, there are no reliable signals. In economics, signals, are difficult to falsify data that can be used to distinguish between types of otherwise indistinguishable goods. In this case the "goods" in questions may be Web sites, email (spam or legitimate warning?), or privacy policies. Ideally, identity systems can communicate structural information from social networks to create difficult-to-falsify signals. These signals could indicate that a web site has a history of reliable behavior, just as good grades indicate that a potential employee has a history of hard work.

First and foremost, the privacy market does not have adequate signals. At the most fundamental level, "protecting privacy" is a vague promise. For example, the privacy-enhancing technology market boom of the nineties included privacy protection that ranged from Zero Knowledge's provably secure and private email to Microsoft Passport's concentration of information in one (insecure) location. Even when privacy can be defined and specified, e.g., through machine-readable P3P policies, a signaling problem remains.

The privacy-signaling problem has been described in formal mathematical terms, and illustrates that the market for privacy cannot function without an external forcing function. A model of the market with fluctuating numbers of reliable privacy-respecting merchants illustrates that the market will not necessarily reach equilibrium where it is efficient for consumers to read privacy policies. As the cost of investigating the privacy policy increases, merchant respect of their own policies varies, and thus the reliability of what is read changes, there is no stable equilibrium under which consumers should read privacy policies.

Data compiled from privacy behaviors suggests that whatever the risks and why ever the reason, the risks of privacy are in fact discounted in consumer decision-making. In fact, individuals not only immediately discount privacy risk, but they increase their discount rate over time. That is, if there is an immediate small benefit and a great cost in the future, people choose the immediate benefit. This is particularly interesting considering the rapid rate of increase in identity theft that suggests the risks increase over time.

Privacy can be good or bad for individuals, if the information obtained by others' is used to lower prices or to extend privileges. In particular, the opposite of privacy in the market is not necessarily information; the opposite of privacy is price discrimination. In markets where there are zero marginal cost (e.g., information markets) firms must be able to extract consumer surplus by price discrimination. This means that the firms cannot charge what they pay, at the margin, but must charge what the consumer is willing to pay. What are privacy violations to the consumer may be necessary pricing data to the merchant. Accurate signaling information, while useful for the market may not be in the interest of firms and thus never receive support.

Imagine that a company produces some numbers of useful things, say software packages. After the code is written, the only cost is to write the software on a CD, or even host it on a web page. There are many people who will buy the software, and the trick to making the most money is to sell the software for the right amount. Knowing just how much a person or institution will pay for something means knowing about that person. So the opposite of privacy, for a company, is not surveillance. The opposite of privacy is extremely accurate pricing.

There are two things that enabled by exact price information: price discrimination and bundling.

Price discrimination is common to anyone who has purchased an airline ticket, or a sporting event ticket. Careful planners on tight budgets buy airline tickets early, and stay over Saturday. The company traveler or well-paid buying on a whim can pay a high price. In this way, the airplane is filled with the greatest possible revenue. Once the airline company has purchased the plane; built the infrastructure; and paid the people the cost of an additional seat is almost zero. So the airline can afford to fill a few seats with low-paying passengers. These low-paying passengers can sometimes pay less than the average fixed cost and still be profitable.

Yet someone has to pay above average fixed cost, or the system will not work. By having complex fare schedules, airlines can fill planes with the most people and the most profit. Simply charging everyone the higher fare would leave many of us at home, the seats empty; and the airline in a worse condition. Charging everyone the lower price would fill the seats, but not cover the cost of flying the plane. The reason selling those seats at a low price makes sense is that marginal cost of having one more person on the plane is extremely low.

Price discrimination is the ability to charge a person exactly what an item is worth to that person. One way to get price discrimination is to auction off everything. Each person could buy airline tickets, with the price fluctuating as individuals entered and exited the auction. Yet this requires coordination: everyone would have to buy at the same time. So instead, merchants have used timing, advertisement, packaging, and other mechanisms to attempt price discrimination.

Airlines are not the only industry to use timing for price discrimination. Those willing to pay higher prices and stay up until midmight could watch Harry Potter and the Deathly Hallows: Part II early. Similarly as each of the last four books arrived on the self these could be purchased full price by those staying up until midnight at the bookstore. Another way to obtain a cheaper copy was to wait until the book was resold as used. Those with more patience than cash could sign up to obtain a copy of the library. From full price to free, these options are available for an identical commodity item. Yet the line to pay full price was hours long for the final book in the summer of 2007. Indeed the book had become such a phenomenal that British Airways provided free copies to any child traveling internationally on the day that Deathly Hallows was finally released in book form.

Merchants can also sell distinct versions of an item. Those who waited months for the paperback paid less, at risk for learning of the death of great wizards on a blog before getting the book themselves.

Alternatively, all the *Potter* books can be packaged, for a larger total price of a lower price per book. Bundling allows producers to sell more goods to more people, by adding lower value goods in with higher value goods. Imagine that there are two books, call them *Philosopher* and *Sorcerer*, and each costs $10 to produce. One customer values *Philosopher* at $10, and *Sorcerer* at $30. The other customer values *Sorcerer* at $10 and *Philosopher* at $30. If each book is sold for $20, then the bookstore sells two books for $40. If they are sold in a package at $40, the store sells four books for $80. In this case, both the customers and the bookstore are better off with bundling.

Bundling becomes potentially more profitable for goods that have a high initial fixed cost for the very first item and low marginal cost for the additional items. For example, after a software package is written, it costs almost nothing to make copies. So obtaining an increase in marginal profit by selling more bundled goods is better for the producer, and often the consumer. Like the airline which is willing to accept less than the average fixed cost for a seat (because the flight is going regardless) the software producer would like to obtain more total income.

For the merchant, it would be ideal to be able to simply know the customer's type. Is this customer rich, with a tendency to take trips on a whim? Does this customer stand in line for each release of the Potter series and would pay double for a first night copy? One way to determine this is to be able to identify every customer, and have a copy of the customer's detailed personal data. A customer who has purchased six books on Anguilla; has a twenty-year wedding anniversary in March; and has a salary of six figures can be charged more for his vacation for two even if he stays over a Saturday night. Allowing that customer to book early, from the perspective of the airlines, is leaving money in the customer's wallet that could go to the airline profits.

The opposite of privacy is not exposure or risk; the opposite of privacy is price discrimination.

Chapter 7
Identity Theft in Healthcare[1]

To understand identity theft in healthcare you have to follow the money. And there is a lot of money in healthcare! Growing faster than the overall economy or the rate of inflation, U.S. health care costs are projected to nearly double in the next decade to $4.6 trillion, representing one-fifth of the entire economy by 2020.

Thus far we have examined how data breaches from hacking to phishing to inadvertent disclosure, lead to identity theft. In most cases, lost personal information translates directly into financial losses through fraud and identity theft. The healthcare sector also suffers many data hemorrhages, with a more frightening array of consequences. In some cases, the losses translate into privacy violations and embarrassment. In other cases, criminals exploit the information to commit traditional financial fraud and identity theft. In yet other cases, data losses result in unique crime including medical identity theft.

In this chapter, we consider the threats and vulnerabilities to medical data. We overview the consequences of data hemorrhages, including a look at how criminals exploit medical data—in particular through medical identity theft. We also describe the financial flows and the business models of healthcare criminals.

Data Hemorrhages and Patient Consequences

Data hemorrhages from the healthcare sector are diverse, from lost laptops to exposed servers. Losses include everything from business information and the personally identifiable information (PII) of employees to patient protected health information (PHI). Considering all data losses (Figure 7.1), some are related to business information, like marketing plans or financial documents, and do not involve patient identities. Any loss that identifies a patient results in privacy loss. We focus on these more disturbing releases of individually identifiable information that are pri-

---

[1] This chapter partially relies on: Johnson, M. Eric (2009) "Data Hemorrhages in the Health-Care Sector", *Proceedings of the Financial Cryptography and Data Security*, Barbados, February 22-25.

vacy violations (including violations of both state privacy laws and federal HIPAA regulation). These losses can also result in more negative patient experiences from fraud and theft to adverse health outcomes.

On one hand, healthcare data can lead to traditional identity theft. This occurs when leaked patient or employee information is used to commit financial fraud. For example, using social security numbers and other identity information to apply for fraudulent loans, take-over bank accounts, or charge purchases to credit cards. We have already covered this crime in detail earlier in the book. In this chapter, we focus on the unique fraud found in healthcare.

Fraud Models

Healthcare fraud is often conducted by bad actors within the context of legitimate healthcare organizations. Traditional healthcare fraud models typically involve billing payers (e.g., Medicaid/Medicare or private healthcare insurance) for something more than was provided. Such fraud is referred to as upcoding because it involves exaggerating the severity of the patient's illness and treatment resulting in larger payments (Figure 7.2). Upcoding is typically invisible to the patient. In a related model, criminals use stolen identities to bill for services never rendered. However, unlike upcoding, this approach requires a more complex ecosystem of identity providers (those who steal identities) and corrupt medical providers. While the corrupt healthcare providers may be purely virtual, providing no real medical services, many have some legitimate business to provide cover for the fraud. In one

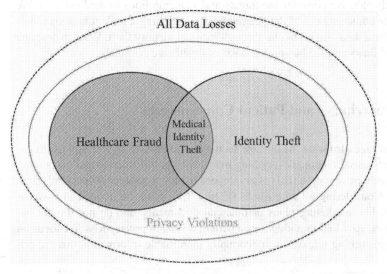

Fig. 7.1 Patient consequences of healthcare data loss.

of the most aggressive recent cases, criminals combined stolen doctor entities with stolen patient identities in an elaborate long-operating fraud. Using 118 fake health clinics in 25 states, prosecutors alleged that gangsters billed Medicare for over $100 million, collecting $35 million over a four-year period [212]. Notice that in this case, identity theft was committed against both the doctors and patients.

When stolen identities are involved, the crime is typically referred to as medical identity theft—shown in the figure as the intersection of medical fraud and identity theft. Like medical fraud, it involves fraudulent charges and like financial identity theft, it involves the theft of identity. It is unique in that it involves a medical identity (patient identification, insurance information, medical histories, prescriptions, test results...) that may be used to obtain medical services or prescription drugs [11]. Leaked insurance information can be used to fraudulently obtain service, but unlike a credit card the spending limits are much higher—charges can quickly reach tens of thousands or even millions of dollars. And unlike financial credit, there is less monitoring and reporting. Sadly, beyond the financial losses, medical identity theft carries other personal consequences for victims as it often results in erroneous changes to medical records that are difficult and time consuming to correct. Such erroneous information could impact care quality or impede later efforts to obtain medical, life, or disability insurance. The US General Accounting Office estimated that 10% of health expenditure reimbursed by Medicare is paid to fraudsters, including identity thieves and fraudulent health service providers [21, 115]. Overall estimates of US healthcare fraud have ranged from 3-10%. When you include overpayment and misuse, you end up with truly astounding estimates, with annual losses in the hundreds of billions of dollars.

Another recent form of medical identity (Figure 7.3) has involved the sale of health identities to uninsured patients [125]. In this case, stolen identities are sold to individuals who use that identity to obtain healthcare. These forms of theft are a problem impacting payers, patients, and healthcare providers. Payers and providers both see financial losses from fraudulent billing. Payers ranging from Medicare to private insurance pay the bills thinking the charges are legitimate. In other cases

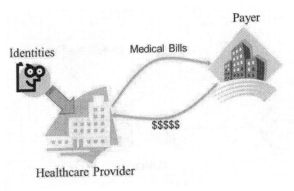

Fig. 7.2 Charging for exaggerated service or services never provided.

when the payer discovers the fraud, the provider is left with an unpaid bill. Patients are also harmed when they are billed (co-pays or uncollected bills) for services they did not receive, and when erroneous information appears on their medical record.

Illegal immigrants sadly represent a block of individuals with a clear motive to participate in such medical identity theft. In the case of a severe medical emergency, they will not be refused care in most instances. However, if an illegal immigrant requires expensive surgery, costly prescriptions, or other non-emergency care, they have few options. One of the most shocking and well documented cases comes from Southern California, where a Mexican resident fooled the state insurance program, Medi-Cal, into believing that he was a resident and therefore entitled to health care coverage [89]. Mr. Hermillo Meave, was transferred to California from a Tijuana, Mexico hospital with heart problems, but told the California hospital that he was from San Diego, and provided the hospital with a Medi-Cal ID card and number. Although the circumstances surrounding Mr. Meave's arrival were suspicious, the hospital went ahead and completed a heart transplant on Mr. Meave. The total cost of the operation was an astounding one million dollars. Only after the surgery did the hospital determine that Mr. Meave actually lived and worked in Tijuana and was therefore not entitled to Medi-Cal coverage.

Perhaps emboldened by the success of Hermillo Meave, a family from Mexico sought a heart transplant for a dying relative just three months later at the very same hospital. This time, fraud investigators were able to discover the plot before the surgery could be completed. While processing the paperwork for the patient who was checked in as Rene Garcia, Medi-Cal authorities found nine other individuals around the state, using the same name and ID number. The hospital had the family

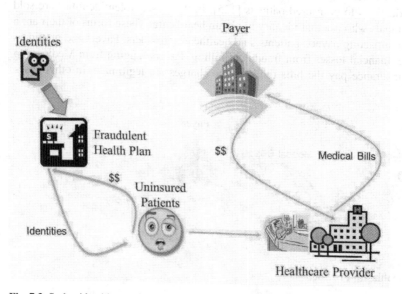

Fig. 7.3 Stolen identities used to gain access to medical care.

arrested and jailed for the attempted fraud, which had cost the hospital $200,000, despite the lack of surgery. The family told investigators that they had paid $75,000 in order to obtain the ID and set up the surgery. The trafficking of identities between Mexico and California is commonplace, but the sale of Medi-Cal identities adds a new dimension to the crime. The disparity in care between California hospitals and Mexican facilities makes the motivation to commit medical identity theft clear: falsified identification is a low-cost ticket to world-class care.

Between 1998 and 2006, the FTC recorded complaints of over nineteen thousand cases of medical identity theft with rapid growth in the past five years. Many believe these complaints represent the tip of the growing fraud problem, with some estimates showing upwards of a quarter-million cases a year [57]. Currently, there is no single agency tasked with tracking, investigating, or prosecuting these crimes [115] so reliable data on the extent of the problem does not exist.

The crime of financial identity theft is well understood with clear underlying motives. A recent FTC survey estimated that 3.7% of Americans were victims of some sort of identity theft [72]. Significant media coverage has alerted the public of the financial dangers that can arise when a thief assumes your identity. However, the dangers and associated costs of medical identity theft are less well understood and largely overlooked. Of course, PHI (including insurance policy information and government identity numbers) can be fraudulently used for financial gain at the expense of firms and individuals. However, when a medical identity is stolen and used to obtain care, it may also result in life-threatening amendments to a medical file. Any consequential inaccuracies in simple entries, such as allergy diagnoses and blood-typing results, can jeopardize patient lives. Furthermore, like financial identity theft, medical identity theft represents a growing financial burden on the private and public sectors.

Individuals from several different groups participate in the crime of medical identity theft: the uninsured, hospital employees, organized crime rings, illegal aliens, wanted criminals, and drug abusers. In many cases the theft is driven by greed, but in other cases the underlying motive is simply for the uninsured to receive medical care. Without medical insurance, these individuals are unable to obtain the expensive care that they require, such as complicated surgeries or organ transplants. However, if they assume the identity of a well-insured individual, hospitals will provide full-service care. For example, Carol Ann Hutchins of Pennsylvania assumed another woman's identity after finding a lost wallet [208]. With the insurance identification card inside the wallet, Hutchins was able to obtain care and medication on 40 separate occasions at medical facilities across Pennsylvania and Ohio, accumulating a total bill of $16,000. Had it not been for the victim's careful examination of her monthly billing statement, it is likely that Hutchins would have continued to fraudulently receive care undetected. Hutchins served a 3-month jail sentence for her crime, but because of privacy laws and practices, any resulting damage done to the victim's medical record was difficult and costly to erase.

Hospital employees historically comprise the largest known group of individuals involved in traditional medical fraud. They may alter patient records, use patient data to open credit card accounts, overcharge and falsify services rendered, create phony patients, and more. The crimes committed by hospital employees are often the largest, most intricate, and the most costly.

Take for example the case of Cleveland Clinic front desk clerk coordinator, Isis Machado who sold the medical information of more than 1,100 patients, to her cousin Fernando Ferrer, Jr., the owner of Advanced Medical Claims Inc. of Florida. Fernando then provided the information to others who used the stolen identities to file an estimated $7.1 million in fraudulent claims [191].

Another criminal business model involves using stolen identities to obtain prescription drugs or medical equipment that can be resold into black markets (Figure 7.4). Likewise, individuals abusing prescription drugs may use stolen identities to support their habit. Drugs obtained through this method may also be resold or traded. Roger Ly, a Nevada pharmacist allegedly filed and filled 55 false prescriptions for Oxycontin and Hydrocondone in the name of customers. Medicare and insurance paid for the drugs that Ly, allegedly, then resold or used recreationally [193]. The total value of drugs sold in the underground prescription market likely exceeds $1 billion [146]. Sometimes, the crimes involving prescription drugs are less serious; a Philadelphia man stole a co-worker's insurance identification card to acquire a Viagra prescription, which he filled on 38 separate occasions. The plan finally backfired when the co-worker he was posing as attempted to fill his own Viagra prescription and discovered that one had already been filled at another pharmacy. The cost to his company's insurance plan: over $3,000 [142].

Wanted criminals also have a strong motive to commit medical identity theft. If they check into a hospital under their own name, they might be quickly apprehended by law enforcement. Therefore, career criminals need to design schemes to obtain care. Joe Henslik, a wanted bank robber working as an ad salesman, found it easy to

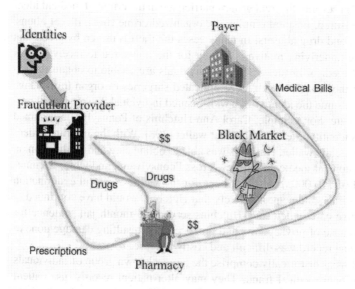

Fig. 7.4 Obtaining pharmaceuticals that are sold into black markets.

obtain Joe Ryan's Social Security number as part of a routine business transaction [26]. Henslik then went on to receive $41,888 worth of medical care and surgery under Ryan's name. It took Ryan two years to discover that he had been a victim of medical identity theft. Even after discovery, he found it difficult to gain access to his medical records, since his own signature didn't match that of Henslik's forgery.

Anndorie Sachs experienced a similar situation when her medical identity was used by a mother to give birth to a drug addicted baby [156]. Sachs had lost her purse prior to the incident and had accordingly cancelled her stolen credit cards, but was unaware of the risk of medical ID theft. The baby, which was abandoned at the hospital by the mother, tested positive for illegal drug use, prompting child services to contact Sachs, who had four children of her own. Fortunately, since Sachs did not match the description of the woman who gave birth at the hospital, the problem did not escalate further. If Sachs was not able to prove her identity, she could have lost custody of her children, and been charged with child abuse. Furthermore, before the hospital became aware of the crime, the baby was issued a Social Security number in Sachs name, which could cause complications for the child later in life. Like Sachs, few individuals consider their insurance cards to be as valuable as the other items they carry in their wallet. Moreover, medical transactions appearing on a bill may not be scrutinized as closely as financial transactions with a bank or credit card.

As these examples illustrate, medical fraud is often complex with criminals operating in rings, sometimes using elaborate ruses to gather the identities of hundreds of individuals. In a Houston case, criminals allegedly staged parties in needy areas offering medical deals as well as food and entertainment [192]. At the parties, Medicaid numbers of residents were obtained and then used to bill Medicaid for alcohol and substance abuse counseling. The scheme even included fraudulent reports, written by 'certified' counselors. The fraudulent company managed to bill Medicaid for $3.5M worth of services, of which they received $1.8M. In this case, no medical care was actually administered and the medical identity theft was committed purely for financial reasons.

In summary, there are many reasons why individuals engage in medical identity theft, including avoiding law enforcement, obtaining care that they have no way of affording, or simply making themselves rich. Many tactics are used including physical theft, insiders, hackers, and harvesting of leaked data. As we saw, PHI can be sold and resold before theft occurs—as in the case of the nine Garcias. The thief may be someone an individual knows well or it could be someone whom they've never met.

For healthcare providers, the first step in reducing such crime is better protection of PHI by: 1) controlling access within the enterprise to PHI; 2) securing networks and computers from direct intruders; 3) monitoring networks (internal and external) for PII and PHI transmissions and disclosures; 4) avoiding inadvertent disclosures of information. Often loose access and inadvertent disclosures are linked. When access policies allow many individuals to view, move, and store data in portable documents and spreadsheets, the risk of hemorrhage increases.

Chapter 8
Healthcare Data: Protections and Hemorrhages[1]

Hemorrhages of patient health data fuel identity theft and privacy violations. Given the fragmented nature of the US healthcare system, data hemorrhages come from many different sources—ambulatory healthcare providers, acute-care hospitals, physician groups, medical laboratories, insurance carriers, back-offices of health maintenance organizations, and outsourced service providers such as billing, collection, and transcription firms. While the US HIPAA legislation on privacy and security went into effect over five years ago, healthcare information security remains a significant concern as organizations migrate to electronic health records. The recent HITECH legislation aimed at accelerating this migration contained mandates for greater security, including the addition of new requirements on breach reporting. In this chapter, we overview both HIPAA and HITECH and examine their impact on data hemorrhages. We then take a look at the types of data that are lost and how these leaks occur in healthcare. To illustrate the issues, we include results from our ongoing research and a case study illustrating the disturbingly private patient information that is exposed.

HIPAA and HITECH

The 1996 Health Insurance Portability and Accountability Act (HIPAA) was enacted to reduce costs and improve quality through better use of information technology and to ensure portability and continuity of health insurance coverage. At its roots, HIPAA was designed to protect workers' health insurance coverage when they changed or lost employment. It also included standards for the transfer of healthcare information that are designed to protect the privacy of sensitive patient medical information. The Privacy and Security Rules of HIPAA require covered entities to ensure implementation of administrative safeguards in the form of policies, person-

---

[1] This chapter partially relies on: Johnson, M. Eric and Nicholas Willey (2011), "Will HITECH Heal Patient Data Hemorrhages?" Proceedings of HICSS-44, Hawaii, Jan 4-7 2011.

nel and physical safeguards to their information infrastructure, and technical safe-guards to monitor and control intra and inter-organizational information access [38]. Those rules were phased in over time with compliance maturing over five years ago (Privacy Rules in April 2003 and Security Rules in April 2005).

Unfortunately, compliance on these rules has been slow and uneven [2]. Variations in provider implementation may also make medical identity theft more difficult to track, identify, and correct. When a patient's medical record has been altered by someone else using their ID, the process used at different providers to correct the record can be confusing for the patient. The erroneous information in the medical file may remain for years. Also people who have been victims of medical identity theft may find it difficult to even know what has been changed or added to their record. Since the thief's medical information is contained within the victim's file, it is given the same privacy protections under the act. Without the ability to easily remove erroneous information, or figure out the changes contained in a medical record, repairing the damages of medical identity theft can be a very taxing process.

In theory, Health and Human Services (HHS) enforcement of HIPAA is a positive force in the fight against identity theft. It is true that institutions have been fined and required to implement detailed corrective action plans to address breaches of iden-tifiable electronic patient information [93]. However, until recently many observers note that very few cases have actually resulted in a fine. And while HIPAA could be used to prosecute offending medical professionals, which are historically the largest group of healthcare fraud perpetrators, few are ever prosecuted. So it is not clear that this protection of patient identities really discourages inappropriate use of medical information or reduces the chance of hemorrhages. Better compliance with both the security and privacy rules is certainly needed. Of course, HIPAA can do little to stop patients from disclosing their medical identities voluntarily to individuals posing as healthcare providers, or poorly managing their own computerized documents.

The recent Health Information Technology for Economic and Clinical Health (HITECH) legislation was enacted as part of the 2009 American Recovery and Rein-vestment Act (ARRA) to spur the adoption of Electronic Health Records (EHR). The act earmarked $20 Billion dollars to be used as incentives and investments in the creation of a digital health information infrastructure. It also created a new office—the National Coordinator for Health Information Technology, to oversee the transition to electronic health records, and enhance patient privacy. According to Congressional projections, the act should produce a rapid and expansive adoption of EHR technology, with 90% of doctors and 70% of hospitals employing the digital systems sometime in the next decade. The act also followed up on earlier HIPAA legislation to enhance privacy and security rules. It expanded the breach notification process by extending the parties covered under HIPAA, i.e. care providers and insur-ers, to include their business associates. It also defined new conditions and penalties for noncompliance.

Central to the legislation are a powerful set of incentives to encourage doctors and hospitals to switch to EHR technology as soon as possible. Beginning in 2011, independent physicians can receive a yearly payment of as much as $15,000. These incentive payments will decrease over time as the program is phased out over a maximum of 5 years of eligibility. According to the House Ways and Means committee, a Doctor qualifying for all incentives could be awarded as much as $65,000 for adequately demonstrating meaningful use of EHR technology over a 5 year period [194]. Similarly hospitals can receive large incentive payments for converting to EHR technology. Hospitals demonstrating meaningful use of EHR will receive a base amount of $2,000,000 for the initial year of EHR use. This amount will be adjusted upwards for hospitals discharging more than 1150 patients per year ($200 per patient), and scaled downwardly according to the fraction of total patients using the government run Medicare program. Like the payments to physicians, these incentives will be phased out over a 5-year period. Long-term care or rehabilitation facilities, such as nursing homes and psychiatric hospitals, are not eligible for incentives under the stimulus act.

The act also follows up on the federal government's HIPAA legislation and outlines plans for required privacy and security controls on EHR systems. While electronic health records can streamline admittance, billing, and the administration of care, the increased accessibility creates new risks. In a system where almost all PHI is digital, patient vulnerability to massive scams is a concern, thus driving stricter measures governing the transmission and storage of PHI. To address this issue, the initiative establishes protocols and certifications for health information technology products. Certification will be necessary for health providers to qualify for the aforementioned incentives, and the development of a certification program is being handled by the National Institute of Standards and Technology. Furthermore, Congress has established a protocol to be followed by health providers in the event of a PHI leak. This so-called breach notification process has varying response levels depending on the severity of the breach.

Following the passage of the HITECH act, the Department of Health and Human Services outlined their requirements for breach notification HHS [94]. The guidance lists the necessary steps to be followed in the event of a breach of *unsecured* public health information. The special definition given to "unsecured" by the HHS is information that is not secured with technology that renders PHI "unusable, unreadable, or indecipherable" to unauthorized individuals. In plain terms, EHR systems must use a form of encryption technology, and health practitioners must destroy unencrypted copies of health information after use. If health information is to be used for scientific purposes, only a "limited data set" of information relevant to the study is to be provided and such data must adequately obscure the identity of the patients. Furthermore, the Act extends the requirements on data security from parties covered under HIPAA, i.e. care providers and insurers, to also include their business associates. According to the guidance, affected individuals must be notified that a breach has occurred within 60 days after the discovery of the breach. If the HIPAA party does not have contact information for an individual then they must post the breach on their website or make media notifications (local newspaper, television station, etc.). If a breach is larger than 500 people, state media and government notifications are required. The Secretary of Health and Human Services maintains a web hosted list of entities involved in a breach affecting more than 500 people.

Groups covered under HITECH must also abide by several other new requirements [74]:

- Must honor an individual's request that information be withheld from health plan providers if care is paid for in cash.
- Must be capable of providing a 3-year audit trail of patient health information disclosures upon request.
- May not communicate with patients for marketing purposes resulting in monetary gain without the permission of the patient.

Additionally, HITECH increased the severity of HIPAA fines. The federal government imposed monetary penalties for both inadvertent and willful disclosure of unsecured patient information. The penalties under HITECH increased with the severity of the violation, ranging from $100 to $1.5 million [65].

Much of the debate around EHR and government incentives to adopt new systems have hinged around the words "meaningful use." Providers must be able to demonstrate meaningful use to receive incentive payments. On January 13, 2010 HHS issued a Notice of Proposed Rulemaking (NPRM) to implement provisions that provide incentive payments for the meaningful use of certified HER [66, 67]. The proposed rule included the definition of meaningful use following a three-stage definition phased in over time, along with other requirements for qualifying for incentive payments. That rule was finalized in July 2010 [68]. HHS maintains a website at healthit.hhs.gov, which provides funding announcements, tools, and information on health information technology. The Office has published an implementation plan which outlines the future goals of the office and its strategy for meeting its obligations under the Recovery Act [95].

The success of the HITECH Act will be highly dependent upon the attractiveness of the incentives to healthcare providers and their willingness to transition to digital technologies. The in-trenched and familiar paper systems supported by ad hoc digital systems like Excel spreadsheets will likely take time to disappear. For hospitals working with independent physicians, this likely means maintaining both legacy electronic and paper systems with new EHR during the transition phase, which could lessen the economic benefits that the recovery act hopes for. Furthermore, the government will need to work diligently to make sure that the sensitive data in transition into EHRs remain secured. Firms across all business sectors struggle with data security problems and it is unlikely that there is a prescribable out-of-box solution that will work for all parties handling EHR. Any platform that does become widely adopted will become a larger and larger target for parties seeking to exploit EHRs for personal and financial gains. In the end, the hope is that health professionals will respond to the offered incentives and that the HITECH Act will make healthcare faster, cheaper, and higher quality.

Data Hemorrhages

Despite the enactment of the Health Insurance Portability and Accountability Act (HIPAA) and the new disclosure requirements of HITECH, data losses in the healthcare sector continue at a dizzying pace. The public disclosures of breaches impacting over 500 individuals quietly clicked past 10 million patients in the spring of 2011. And few believe those disclosures represent anything more than the tip of the iceberg. While firms and organizations have invested to protect their systems against direct intrusions and hackers, many recent data hemorrhages have come from inadvertent sources. Organizations have mistakenly left many different types of sensitive information exposed on the web, from legal to medical to financial. For example, Southern California Medical-Legal Consultants mistakenly posted the medical records of 300,000 Californians on the internet. Simply using Google, anyone could see completed insurance forms with social security numbers and doctors' notes [160]. One case described a maintenance worker's broken ribs while another described a man's sexual dysfunction. A researcher stumbled upon the site in June of 2011 and notified the firm. But the damage was done. Likewise, Wuesthoff Medical Center in Florida inadvertently posted names, Social Security numbers and personal medical information of more than 500 patients [209]. Insurance and healthcare information of 71,000 Georgia residents was accidentally posted on Internet for several days by Tampa-based WellCare Health Plans [91].

The University of Pittsburgh Medical Center inadvertently posted patient information of nearly 80 individuals including names and medical images. In one case, a patient's radiology image was posted along with his Social Security number, insurance information, medications, and with information on previous medical screenings and procedures citeTwedt07. Harvard University and its pharmacy partner, PharmaCare (now part of CVS Caremark), experienced a similar embarrassment when students showed they could easily gain access to lists of prescription drugs bought by Harvard students [162]. Even technology firms like Google and AOL have suffered the embarrassment of inadvertent web posting of sensitive information [39, 141]—in their cases, customer information. Still other firms have seen their internal information and intellectual property appear on music file-sharing networks [52], blogs, YouTube, and MySpace [185].

Many of the largest data spills have come from lost and stolen equipment. For example, in 2011 nine computer hard drives disappeared from a Health Net data center. The drives contained patient information including health histories, financial information and Social Security numbers of 1.9 million Health Net insurance customers [160]. Laptops at diverse health organizations including Kaiser Permanente [23], Memorial Hospital (South Bend IN) [184], the U.S. Department of Veterans Administration [117], and National Institutes of Health [130] were lost or stolen—in each case inadvertently disclosing personal and business information.

In each case, the result was the same: sensitive information inadvertently leaked creating embarrassment, vulnerabilities, and financial losses for the firm, its investors, and customers. In a recent data loss, Pfizer faced a class action suit from angry employees who had their personal information inadvertently disclosed on a popular music network [200].

A Window into the Hemorrhages

In our past research, we showed that peer-to-peer (P2P) file-sharing networks represented a significant security risk to firms from banking [102, 103] to healthcare [107]. File sharing became popular during the late 1990s with the rise of Napster. In just two years before its court-ordered closure in 2001, Napster enabled tens of millions of users to share MP3-formatted song files. Through its demise, it opened the door for many new P2P file-sharing networks such as Gnutella, FastTrack, e-donkey, and Bittorrent, with related software clients such as Limewire, KaZaA, Morpheus, eMule, and BearShare. Today P2P traffic supports tens of million simultaneous users [124]. P2P clients allow users to place shared files in a particular folder that is open for other users to search. However, there are many ways that other confidential files become exposed to the network (see [104] for a detailed discussion). For example a user: 1) accidentally shares folders containing the information—in some cases confusing client interface designs can facilitate such accidents [88]; 2) stores music and other data in the same folder that is shared—this can happen by mistake or because of poor file organization; 3) downloads malware that, when executed, exposes files; or 4) installs sharing client software that has bugs, resulting in unintentional sharing of file directories.

While these networks are most popularly used to trade copyrighted material, such as music and video, any material can be exposed and searched for including databases, spreadsheets, Microsoft Word documents, and other common corporate file formats. The original exposure of this material over P2P networks is most likely done by accident rather than maliciously, but the impact of a single exposure can quickly balloon. After a sensitive file has been exposed, it can be copied many times by virtually anonymous P2P users, as they copy the file from one another and expose the file to more peers. Criminals are known to engage in the sale and trafficking of valuable information and data. In earlier studies using "honeypot" experiments (experiments that expose data for the purpose of observing how it is stolen), we showed how criminals steal and use both consumer data and corporate information [104]. When this leaked information happens to be private customer information, organizations are faced with costly and painful consequences resulting from fraud, customer notification, and consumer backlash.

Ironically, individuals who experience identity theft often never realize how their data was stolen. Worse than losing a laptop or a storage device with patient data [159], inadvertent disclosures on P2P networks allow many criminals access to the information, each with different levels of sophistication and ability to exploit the information. And unlike an inadvertent web posting, P2P disclosures are far less likely to be noticed and corrected (since few organizations monitor P2P and the networks are constantly changing making a file intermittently available to a subset of users).

In earlier work [107], we showed that disclosures of healthcare data made protected health information (PHI) readily available on P2P networks. Working with security firm Tiversa Inc, we found thousands of files leaking from the healthcare system containing tens of thousands of patients' PHI. The files ranged from internal marketing and personnel documents to patient medical histories, billing, and insurance information. We found files leaked throughout the healthcare supply chain including care providers, laboratories, back-office services, and financial partners. Clearly, such data hemorrhages violate the privacy and security rules of HIPAA, which call for healthcare organizations to ensure implementation of administrative safeguards (in the form of technical safeguards and policies, personnel and physical safeguards) to monitor and control intra and inter-organizational information access. We also demonstrated that malicious users are searching P2P networks for sensitive files. However, these P2P leaks are not the focus of this chapter. These examples simply provide a window into the overall problem and allow us to examine the types of data that seep out of the healthcare sector. The same types of patient data that are leaked in file-sharing networks are exposed by stolen storage devices or laptops.

Case Study of a Data Hemorrhage

In our analysis of leaked files, we found many that were the result of health IT usability issues and the complex nature of the healthcare supply chain. For example, in one particular case, we found that a large hospital system had outsourced collection of overdue payments. Figure 8.1 shows part of a spreadsheet containing data that was shared with the collection agency. Rather than provide the agency with secure access into the organization's patient record system, the data was dumped into a large spreadsheet and sent (without even Excel password protection) to the agency. The spreadsheet was later leaked by the collection agency onto a P2P network. Evidently a collection agency employee was using a P2P client on a work machine that also held the spreadsheet. The spreadsheet contained vast PHI on over 20,000 patients. Up to 82 fields of information were recorded for each patient— representing the contents of the popular HCFA form. One field included the diagnosis code (IDC code) for each patient. For example, code 34 is streptococcal sore throat; 42 is AIDS; 151.9 is malignant neoplasm of stomach (cancer); 29 is alcohol-induced mental disorders; and 340 is multiple sclerosis. In total the file contained records on 201 patients with different forms of mental illness, 326 with cancers, 4 with AIDS, and thousands with other serious and less serious diagnoses.

In this case, the hemorrhage came from an outsourced collection agency working for the hospital. However, besides the patients and hospital system, many other organizations were comprised. The data disclosed in this file well-illustrates the complexity of US health care with many different constituencies represented, including

4 major hospitals, 335 different insurance carriers acting on behalf of 4,029 patient employers, and 266 different treating doctors (see Figure 8.2). Each of these constituents was exposed in this disclosure. Of course, the exposure of sensitive patient health information may be the most alarming to citizens.

Data hemorrhages from the healthcare sector are clearly a significant threat to providers, payers, and patients. The inadvertent disclosers we describe point to the larger problem facing the industry. Clearly, such hemorrhages may fuel many types of crime. While medical fraud has long been a significant problem, the crime of medical identity theft is still in its infancy. Sadly, many of the well-documented crimes appear to be committed out of medical need. However, with the growing opportunity to commit more significant crimes involving large financial rewards, more advanced schemes have developed. Stopping the supply of digital identities is one key to halting this type of illegal activity. Likewise, better financial controls by payers such as Medicare and Medicaid are instrumental in reducing the motivation for identity theft.

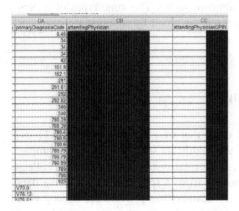

Fig. 8.1 A section of a spreadsheet for a few (of over 20,000) patients showing IDC diagnosis codes. Personally Identifiable Information has not been included in the illustration to protect the identities of the patients and physicians.

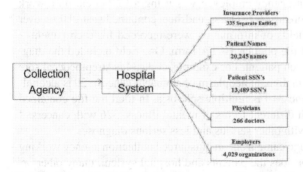

Fig. 8.2 A single data spill exposes a large array of healthcare constituents.

Tighter controls on patient information are a good start, but consumers still need to be educated of the dangers of lost healthcare information and how to secure their information on personal computers. Hospitals and others concerned with medical identity theft have begun to undertake measures in order to curb medical identity theft. One of the simplest and most effective measures put in place by hospitals is to request photo identification for admittance to the hospital. In many cases, when a request for photo identification is made, the individual will give up on obtaining care and simply leave the hospital, never to return again. Of course, this measure will likely lose its efficacy in time as criminals become aware of the change in policy. Once a few personal identifiers have been acquired, such as date of birth and Social Security number, a criminal can obtain seemingly valid photo-ID. In the future, insurance companies may need to begin issuing their own tamper-proof photo identification to help stop medical identity theft. Many of the solutions examined in this book apply to healthcare.

Finally, healthcare providers and insurers must enact better monitoring and information controls to detect and stop leaks [7]. Information access within many healthcare systems is lax. Coupled with the portability of data, inadvertent disclosures are inevitable. Better control over information access governance [216] is an important step in reducing the hemorrhages documented in this report.

Chapter 9
Technologies of Identity

Trusting Code and Trusting Hardware

by Bennet Yee

Should we trust hardware any more than we trust code or software? Why? What are the differences?

In order to trust a device or system to perform actions on our behalf, whether it is some form of local data processing (e.g., word processing) or an electronic commerce activity (e.g., ordering goods via the Internet), we have to have trust in the devices that perform these actions on our behalf. Certainly, we are confident that our Selectric typewriters will remain uninfected by viruses. By contrast, we cannot have the same level of trust in our word processors regarding viruses. On the other hand, a Selectric has far fewer features than a word processor.

Observing that all software has to run on some hardware and that hardware is often useless without software to run on it, we might think that the distinction between software and hardware is easy to make. With the possible exception of quantum computing, there is no difference between what, in principle, can be computed by systems that perform more (or less) of their work in hardware versus software. The *speed* at which the results are arrived at will, of course, vary, but what is computable is identical.

There are, however, important qualitative distinctions between software and hardware—and "firmware"—that should be taken into account. Hardware tends to have a more limited set of behaviors. This is because what hardware can and cannot do is basically fixed by the design. Software, on the other hand, is changeable and thus has a potentially infinite range of behavior; a software-driven device's behavior cannot be determined once and for all: not only does its behavior depend on what software was originally installed on the device, it also depends on how that software has been modified afterward. That software may be dynamically updated, perhaps by authorized software updates and patches, or perhaps maliciously through computer viruses.

Embedded software (firmware, such as you might find in an automobile) lies somewhere in the middle. Devices controlled by embedded software can sometimes be updated, if the embedded software is stored on chips that allow such updates, e.g., using flash memory or EEPROM chips as opposed to ROM chips, then that embedded software is also vulnerable to being maliciously updated. Yet despite the complexity, there are malicious programs which target firmware. For example, the pharming attack on the wireless router described above is an attack on the embedded software.

The flexibility of software or the ease with which software can be updated is both is its blessing and curse. The positive side is that when a security problem is identified, it is also relatively easy to install more software to fix the problem.

The ease with which software can be changed also makes security more difficult. First, the malleability of software creates an economic incentive for producers to release software before it is fully debugged. Purveyors to ship flawed products, knowing these can be easily fixed in the field. Software malleability also makes it difficult to evaluate any given computer. In order to decide whether to trust a particular device requires a security review or evaluation to determine the vulnerabilities that the device may have, and the current state of the code. Changing the device invalidates the security review or evaluation performed earlier, since new vulnerabilities may have been introduced.

Hardware devices, by their immutable nature, rarely require a re-evaluation. Of course, the ability to trust hardware is also a function of progress in process control. For example, the vaunted steel hull of the Titanic was made with flawed steel. Modern detailed examinations of the wreckage suggest that impurities and weaknesses of the steel made the Titanic far more fragile than any of its designers could have predicted. The steel bucked and cracked because the process controls were inadequate and materials science is as much alchemy as established academic domain. Today even the most complex micro-electronic cans and are examined at every stage of production. Thus hardware is re-evaluated based on if the operating environment changes beyond what the original evaluation covered, or when the requirements change.

Complex devices can—and do— surprise us even when they cannot be maliciously changed. It is also far easier to build complex applications using software than using hardware, and complex applications will be harder to specify, harder to implement, harder to debug, and harder to analyze for security vulnerabilities. Complex systems embed flaws, just as the massive production of steel for the Titanic embedded impurities. Software enables the construction of very complex systems.

In engineering, the "KISS principle" adjures designers to Keep It Simple, that is, to look for simple and elegant solutions and avoid complex and baroque ones. Despite the wisdom in this engineering acronym, software designers have developed an industry-wide tendency to add complex features. This complexity often leads to decreased reliability and consequently decreased trustworthiness.

Identity systems suffer from this same systematic problem. *An* identity system designed to resolve a specific problem explodes until it is more dangerous than useful. For example, public key systems designed to share a specific credential, later became the Public Key Infrastructure which was intended to identify all humans in all contexts.

While software-oriented designs are not inherently less trustworthy than hardware-oriented designs *if they solve the same problem*, software is used to solve larger and more complex problems. Expansion of the code is easier, both initially and after introduction. The inherent complexity of the corresponding solutions makes such systems less trustworthy.

The design, implementation, and deployment of trusted systems can ideally include some hardware components in the Trusted Computing Base (TCB). Currently, most computers include trusted hardware that, when properly protected, can be completely trustworthy throughout the hardware's life cycle. The core reason that the TCB can be trustworthy is that it has tamper-proof hardware. Because of the cryptographic strength of this hardware, home users can be more lax. While companies can continue to invest in more carefully controlled-access facilities, limited network access, and proper procedural security; home users with a TCB can ensure that the hardware's integrity is not violated.

Recall that the hardware and software cannot be perfectly separated. Implementing protections for the software components of the TCB is complex. Not only does the underlying hardware have to be properly protected, but its access to that hardware must be carefully controlled. Properly detecting and controlling physical access to hardware is a far easier task than detecting and controlling accesses to software. No homeowner is without some perimeter defense, even if she never thinks of it in those terms. The relative simplicity of the defense mechanism for hardware makes the maintenance of trustworthiness easier.

However, the Trusted Computer Base is also called the Treacherous Computing Base. Storing identity information in a TCB allows correct identification over the network. However, stored identity information may also require correct identification. Anonymous access to information can be prohibited. In fact, the first documented goal of TCB was not protecting the identity of the computing homeowner, but rather ensuring that any machine on the network was linked with an identifiable entity. A TCB may strip the homeowner of any anonymity, to ensure that the price is always right. Or a TCB may secure cryptographic secrets to limit identity leakage and protect the individual. The technology can be used either way.

Technologies of Identity

Identity management at the most common is the connection between a personal name, address or location, and account.

The most common identity management mechanisms today are focused on the certification of a person known in an organization to interact with enterprise systems. With enterprise identity systems, this has expanded into an integrated system of business processes, policies and technologies that enable organizations to facilitate and control their customers' access to critical online applications and resources while protecting confidential personal and business information from unauthorized users. Many companies and some governments already have this level of identity management. Companies are interested in charging for individual services, interacting across organizational lines, targeting of advertisement, and leveraging corporate partnerships.

At the second level identity management is the ability to authenticate a set of permanent, long-lived or temporal attributes unique to each individual. The confirmation and use of attributes enables the identified to take actions and interact with others in a safe secure manner. For the purpose of the converged network (text, voice, video, mobile, and fixed) the critical functionality of identity management at this level is to securely deliver customers their content anywhere, anytime, and on any device. For the purpose of digital government, identity management is to securely deliver services to their citizens anywhere, anytime and on any device. The technical requirements are not unalike.

Identity management, at the most profound, is the systematic identification of a person, role, or payment on the network. Effective identity management at this level implies leveraging confirmation of identity to serve the end points of the network. For the purpose of the government, this means leveraging the unique features of government in the identity realm to manage the nation.

Identity management has three possible depths. Identity management can be *per interaction*, the depth where institutions without enterprise identity management are currently operating. Identity management is internal, and may depend on a single point of identification for each application. Identity management is used for specific elements of the organization where each point of information is targeted to a particular task. Identity management can be *ubiquitous*, where there is a core set of attributes for each account or identified entity within an account.

Identity management can have different technical strengths. Identity management depends on authentication. The underlying authentication determines the strength of an identity management system.

Authentication is based on three factors. First, it can be something you know. A person may know anything from a weak four digit PIN, to a complex password, or even a cryptographic secret stored in a human readable form.

Second, authentication can be based on something you are. In security literature this corresponds to biometric identification such as a fingerprint or an iris. It may also correspond to something more temporary; for example, landline telephone and pay television authentication is based on location. Are you at the location determined to be subscribing is a question of something you are, i.e., where.

Third authentication can be based on something you have; for example a car key or a smart card.

These elements can be combined. For example, a person holding a remote for a cable TV box in a living room, and entering a PIN to authorize a purchase has all three. The remote is what the customer *has*, the location is where the customer *is*, and the PIN is what the customer *knows*. Each of these elements can be strengthened independently. However, that which the customer has (the remote) is available to anyone who is present at the location, so the combination is weaker than if the two were independent. For example, a visiting minor may pick up a remote and purchase a video on demand. Efficacy of identity management depends upon the reliability of the authorization of the critical attribute: age, willingness to pay, location, etc.

A strongly authenticated attribute or identity can be more effectively leveraged at a lower risk than weakly identified identities. Even a strongly authenticated identity can have weakly or strongly authenticated attributes. For example, an address may be strongly authenticated by physically visiting a location, such as by placement of customer equipment on the premises. However, the ability of the person holding the equipment to authorize release of information may not be as well authenticated. An example of this is telephony. Wireline telephones are placed into a home, and the line in the home can be identified. Yet a friend can make an expensive call while visiting, or a child can accept a collect call from a relative.[1] Thus while the billing address is strongly authenticated the right to authorize payment is weakly authenticated.

Identity management may be strong or weak, centralized or decentralized, ubiquitous or dedicated to a specific purpose. These dimensions are independent and orthogonal. The long-term optimal identity management system is strong, decentral-

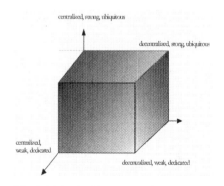

Fig. 9.1 Identity Management Dimensions

---

[1] For example, the high cost of phoning from prison is a serious problem in the US. Families may lose their breadwinner, and then the phone shortly thereafter based on the high cost for collect calls from parties that hold the contracts to provide phone services from prisons. The result is economic and communications isolation.

ized, and narrowly targeted in order to avoid relying on other systems. The economic incentives are for weak, centralized or federated and thus highly interdependent systems.

The third dimension of identity management is its concentration. Identity management systems can be highly distributed or highly centralized.

A highly centralized view of the world concentrates on a single database. This point of leverage is used to distribute owned or contractually controlled services to a previously identified and associated population.

A decentralized approach leverages customer identification with a set of identified partners to use the customer data to better offer a series of services. This is a service-based rather than a box-centric approach. The ability to bill for services offered by others and delivered by the network is the promise of this approach.

The most decentralized, also called an open approach, leverages information to produce a set of open services that can be utilized (and paid for) by any individual using the open service. For example, a database of authenticating information can be used to evaluate claims of attribute association by any member of an alliance would be an open identity architecture.

Anonymous Identifiers

I know where you live.

This statement implies a threat that any failure in interaction can be met with an expansion beyond the scope of the transactions. That is a mouthful for your average bully. But the simple threat above is based on spheres of activity.

"Anonymous" is the opposite of "uniquely identified." A face in the crowd is anonymous depending on the size of the crowd and the feasibility of the technology to examine the crowd given its size. Today, a face in the crowd will be identifiable to the extent that there is video technology, and the individual facial geometry is recorded and unique.

Anonymity is the opposite of identity. Yet anonymity does not mean that there is no accountability. This is most richly explained in the scenarios. Anonymity means that credential authentication does not depend on the intermittent step of identity authentication.

Cookies can be anonymous or identifiers. Cookies save state. Cookies can be totally anonymous, linking only one request for information to the next.

A cookie linked to your New York Times registers on-line reading habits, as does one from Washington Post. That cookie may be linked to personal data entered during registration. That would make the cookie closely associated with person-ally identifiable information. However, entering one of the well-known and widely shared identifiers based on a favorite blog, a local soccer club or just a common well-known login also yields an identified. In this case the identified is an *anonym*, instead of an I.D. It links your reading habits to others with the same ID, but you each have a unique cookie. Using these group identifiers is an expression of a desire for privacy.

A cookie that is linked to a widely used ID identifies you are part of a statistical group. A blog, it identifies the number of readers who come from the blog and stay. In the soccer club, it identifies everyone associated with that soccer club. If this is a neighborhood club then people in that club are likely to have similar incomes, and increasingly similar political alignment. The cookie on your machine identifies you as part of a group and an individual in that group. But it does not provide an identifier that can link you to other transactions, domains, or credentials. You are provided a low quality anonymous identifier.

The value of identifying a person as a group member is that it enables targeted ads. By associating yourself with a group, you provide statistical information. The statistical information from the group enables more perfectly targeted advertise-ment.

The inherent value of the cookie itself is its functional. The cookie distinguishes each browser from the other. Without cookies, it would be impossible to fill a virtual shopping cart and then pay for the goods, as the thread of browsing connections over time would be lost.

When your cookie is linked to purchases and records from one site to another site, then that cookie subverts your anonymity by making connections across domains.

Identity stands in for difficulty of physical credential reproduction in the digital realm. Digital anonymous credentials prove that this need not be the case. Identity also provides several secondary effects — a lack of privacy, more efficient marketing, a risk of identity theft, and the ability to reclaim your charge cards in a remote city using only the knowledge in your head.

Cryptography is the art of hiding information using mathematics. Therefore, while the slave's hair may have effectively hidden information, the use of mane instead of math places that particular technique outside the range of encryption. Cryptography can solve the problems of privacy and security simultaneously, while ensuring accountability.

Modern cryptography, using machines and codes too complex to break by even the most brilliant sleight of mind, was born in the turmoil before World War II. First the Italians stole the American substitution code, providing it to the Germans. This provided critical information even before the US entered the war, enabling the brilliance of at least one German general. Before Pearl Harbor, Colonel Bonner Frank Fellers, West Point Graduate and former personal assistant to MacArthur, provided detailed timely information to Washington about British plans. He was diligent from his post in Cairo to investigate every plan of the British Empire. By doing so he provided the information to Field Marshall Erwin Rommel as well. No doubt Rommel would have agreed with the post-war citation given to Fellers that noted, "His reports given to the War Department were models of clarity and accuracy." The historical record argues that the accurate information encrypted in weak American ciphers enabled at least one massacre of British forces. The War Department valued Fellers' sufficiently that they cleared his security practices in a review in June 1942 despite British complaints. Fellers was recalled in July of 1942, after the British provided decryptions of his reports to the surprised Americans. Thus on October 23 the 8th Army attack on the German positions led by the Dessert Fox came as a complete surprise. The fox has lost his seventh sense.

Later the tables turned with the well-known breaking of the Enigma machine and the Purple code. Alan Turing is rightly famed for designing the first computer, which vastly sped the cracking of specific keys for the German Enigma machine. William and Elizabeth Friedman were the less known husband and wife team who decoded the Enigma-based machines used by the Japanese for their communications before and during World War II.

The ability to read Axis codes allowed the Allies to target and shoot down the plane of Admiral Isoroku Yamamoto 18 April 1943. Yamamoto was educated at Harvard and served as Naval Attaché to the United States in 1925-28. He commanded the Japanese Combined Fleet, and planned the Attack Pearl Harbor as well as being in command at the Battle of Midway. The Battle of Midway was to be a surprise attack, following a feint at Alaska. Because of the breaking of the Japanese code, the feint was doomed to failure and the US Navy attacked and broke the Japanese naval superiority at Midway. Taking advantage of the opportunity required the perseverance, bravery, sacrifice and skill of the forces at Midway should not be understated. The cryptographers made it possible for there to be a the possibility of an advantage.

Yamamoto's intelligence and his understanding of American warfare were of such value to the United States that the US risked identifying that the Purple codes were broken through this ambush. How could the Japanese possibly believe sheer luck lead the Americans to Yamamoto's lightly escorted flight? A change in codes could have been disastrous. However, the Japanese were so confident that the Purple codes could never be broken that the codes were never updated.

Similar arrogance is embedded in many schemes today, where the risks are lower but the technology more complex. Individuals are assured of perfection in digital signatures and identity schemes. Obviously less is on the line today than global domination in terms of numbers of lives. But the destruction of individual lives in terms of false life-shattering arrests for child pornography based on a stolen credit card, or false convictions of theft based on the perfection of ATM machines is nonetheless terrible for the individuals involved. Yet the level of oblivion to past major risks suggest that systems designers cannot be relied upon to carefully plan for the risk of failure. Systems are oft designed to fail completely or succeed completely, with the risk sometimes going to the party least capable of defending himself — the Unlucky User.

In the physical world there are local failures that feel catastrophic — losing a wallet being the classic. A lost wallet requires contacting any entity that is represented in your wallet. Most importantly, for financial reasons, most people first contact the bank and the credit card company. Yet many of the material in a wallet or purse are anonymous, which is two-sided.

Physical keys are anonymous. Some have stamped numerical identifiers on them. The occasional hotel key still allows the holder to identify the room. Most of us carry keys that cannot be associated with the locks they open.

Anonymous credentials take a different tack on the problem of authentication. By credentials being anonymous, the possible influence of subversion is lost. For the imperial Japanese losing Purple was a critical element of losing World War II because the codes encrypted all confidential traffic. For the Unlucky User losing a Social Security Number is the core of losing an identity, because that number is the key to all the financial controls associated with a person. Because of the link to the person and financial records, originally social security numbers were prohibited as identification numbers. For verification, this limitation was printed on every card.

Note the bottom line: NOT FOR IDENTIFICATION.

Fig. 9.2 Social Security Card

It is not the number itself that makes identification the problem. Not the top line, it is the second line. The top line provides a number, and that number links taxes paid to benefits due. The second line links all of these to the person associated with the number.

Anonymous credentials in the physical world are very common. Basically any bit of valuable paper without identifying information is an anonymous credential. A dollar is an anonymous credential that proves the right to spend that amount. It is truly a meaningless bit of paper with green ink and some embedded counterfeit protection. Yet it is valuable because the producer, the person holding it, and the merchant, agrees upon its value. US currency is accepted many places where the US government has no power: in developing countries, in enemy countries, even in the Soviet Union before its collapse. Other examples of anonymous credentials include tickets to Broadway performances, movie tickets, most bus passes, coupons and those authenticating tags that are not supposed to be removed until the mattress makes it home.

Anonymous credentials are difficult in the digital world because copying is cost-less, easy and ubiquitous in the digital world. To open a file is to make temporary copies in the cache, after calling the longer-lived copy from the hard drive. Physical anonymous credentials depend on being difficult to copy to maintain their value. If it were trivial to Xerox dollars, inflation would be have to be measured daily.

Some credentials that could clearly be anonymous are linked to identity. Grocery store coupons could be anonymous. Most coupons are anonymous — 50 cents discount for the purchase of chocolate chips if you buy butter. Yet coupons printed for the customer when the customer uses a grocery store discount card are not always anonymous. The value for the customer is printed on the coupon, in large obvious print. The value for the merchant is knowing their customer. Their customer may provide statistical information for other customers: what else did that customer buy? What promotions should be linked? Knowledge can guide advertisements: are there customers more likely to own cats or dogs? The knowledge of the customer can be linked to other databases: what movies appeal to people who fit the profiles of their customers, and thus where should they place ads?

Airline tickets were once effectively anonymous. Airline travel now requires the provision of a government-issued i.d. Of course, the criminals have most reliable identification. The major result of requiring identity in airline travel has been to prevent the resale of tickets. Before 2001, tickets could be easily transferred if one person could not use a ticket and wanted to resell it. There was a small industry of people buying cheap "travel in advance" tickets and selling them. Online auctions changed the potential of that industry from small retail services to wholesale arbitrage. If you have a ticket, then the online auctions can match you with a buyer.

Linking identity to airline travel does not in any way crease safety. If the more trusted passengers were indeed given less scrutiny any attacker would begin planning by obtaining a more trusted identity. By creating a list of "more trusted" passengers based on untrustworthy documents the security of air travel is decreased. All of the 9-11 hijackers flew under assumed identities, identities of valuable Saudi customers. The failure on 9-11 was a systematic failure to take precaution, and the ability of attackers to take advantage of business as usual. The check-in agents flagged the hijackers in Maine, and made them check in again in Massachusetts. Yet the there was no heightened alert. There was no basis for the agents to refuse boarding. Changing business as usual to create a group of trusted passengers presents another vulnerability in business as usual.

Why then does airline travel require identification? Adding identifiers to airline tickets makes them non-transferable. It does not prevent crime. It prevents commerce.

As long as an airline ticket was an anonymous credential (that is, there was a name but the passenger did not have to prove association with that name) there was a secondary market in airline tickets. Brokers could buy tickets two or three weeks in advance and then resell them. If the broker bet correctly and was able to resell all the tickets purchased, then the broker made money. If the broker could only sell a few, the broker lost money. The advent of widespread consumer-to-consumer commerce, first on Usenet and now on dedicated web sites, made the chances of that broker selling all the tickets very high. Effectively broker's opportunities for arbitrage were vastly increased by the reduced search and transactions cost of the Internet. Adding identity confirmation for airline travel reduced the opportunity for arbitrage, made the market less fluid, and did nothing what so ever for security in airline travel.

Similarly, proposals to demand identification for bus passes prevent people from sharing bus passes. Currently two or three people could purchase a bus pass and trade it off. With an identification requirement, this becomes impossible.

There is nothing wrong with the airlines or the buses setting prices and insisting that customers stick to the contract. A deal is a deal, after all. Airlines could pursue resellers of named tickets. Bus companies could give drivers the authority to demand identification with the use of a bus pass.

Yet the treatment of identity in these economic situations as if identity were being used to increase security, instead of profit margins, is a very serious problem. By claiming security as the reason, private companies recruit the government to do the identity checking. When government is watching people travel, and purchase, and trade that is a significant threat to privacy. It is one thing for the bookstore to ask that I not resell a book at risk of being charged a resell premium. It is another for the government to obtain a database of my reading, travel, and leisure time.

The pretense of security places the customer at a bargaining disadvantage. Wanting a grocery store card that is anonymous because Unlucky User doesn't want to risk identity theft is a reasonable option. Wanting a grocery store card that is anonymous when such anonymity is a risk to national security is clearly less reasonable. After all, with an anonymous card the terrorist could buy a large number of over the counter chemicals to produce a toxic chlorine to gas a crowd. Of course, the fact that such a purchase would not be flagged and indeed every such purchase thus far in American history has been intended to clean filth from the bathroom makes such theoretical arguments obviously flawed. And the ease of mis-representation of identity gives the security claim for the lie that it is.

Identity is used today to increase profit by placing risk on consumers of identity theft, fraud, and even wrongful criminal prosecution. Systematic exposure of citizenry to these risks does not enhance national or personal security.

Identity misuse is the pollution of the information age. Everyone breathes and lives in a little more risk so that very few people can obtain marginally increased profit margins. Using identity in a way that exposes Unlucky to harm is as wrong as dumping chemicals in his drinking water.

Anonymous digital credentials illustrate that living without privacy is no more necessary in the information age than living without clean air was necessary in the industrial age.

As with tickets to the theatre and passes to the rides at the fair, there are anonymous generic tickets available on the Internet. No person has to show identification to get into the movie (assuming they are old enough to watch what they have chosen). When we purchase a roll of tickets at the fair, there is no protocol for transferring the right to ride to the children.

The equivalent of paper passes exist on the Internet: unlinked to identity tokens. These are either called digital tokens or proof of work, depending upon how they are made. A distinct reliable party mints tokens. Proof of work tickets are generated by the person who wants to present them.

Anonymous tokens are digitally linked to some value, like one dollar. (These links are constructed using public key cryptography, which is described in the next section.) Anonymous tokens are strings of bits rather than rectangles of paper. A token is digitally signed, just as money is traditionally "signed" by the Treasurer of the United States and by the Secretary of the Treasury. Each US dollar also has a series number, and those numbers are unique and sequential. The issuer, usually a bank, signs an anonymous digital token. The bank then keeps a copy of the digital token. When it is spent it goes to the merchant and then goes back to the bank. Because of the way the token was signed, the bank will recognize it as being signed but cannot connect it to a merchant. The essential observation is that a third party, usually a centralized trusted party, verifies anonymous tokens. Digital tokens can be very strongly authenticated. However, even with the centralized elements, digital tokens can be decentralized. Merchants choose to take tokens or not. Consumers hold their own tokens before they are spent. And of course this is very private.

Tickets are different than tokens. Tickets are generated by evidence of effort. While anonymous tokens are money, tickets are more analogous to manners. As payment is a universal phenomenon, so is appropriate address upon introduction. Liberty Alliance offers the option of being the universal introducer. Tickets allow us to do the digital equivalent of dressing well and being on time. Using computational power, memory accesses, or human interaction to show that a request for services is made in good faith generates tickets.

Tokens, like dollar bills, are relatively expensive to create. A token is associated with the party that signs it. While the spender of a dollar or user of a coupon or distributor of a digital token is not identified, the producer of the dollar, coupon or token is well known.

While a token might be used for an arbitrary payment, tickets scan be used to defeat misuse of identifiers by adding a cost to digital introductions. For example, consider spam. Spam is on its own a significant problem in that it consumes vast network and human resources. If the Internet is an attention span economy, then spam is wholesale theft. CipherTrust estimates in 2005 the volume of global email as exceeding 50 billion messages per day. Spam is so profitable that estimates of spam as a percentage of all email has increased even as the total volume of email increases. Estimates of the percent of email sent (not delivered) range from 56% in 2003 to 80% in 2006. Spam is a malicious network activity enabled by the otherwise virtuous cycle of network expansion. As the network expands, spam becomes more profitable, and thus increases. Spam is also a vector for other activities: distribution of malicious code, phishing attacks, and old-fashioned fraud.

The core challenge in defeating spam is that the sender bears almost no cost to send email. The cost is borne by the network service providers and the recipients. In order to solve this problem, proof of work was designed to alter the economics of spam by requiring that the sender commit to a per-email cost.

The core enabling factor of spam is that spam is cheap to send. The negligible cost of sending spam makes solicitations with response rates in the tens of a percent profitable. Proof of work was deigned to remove the profit from spam.

Proof of work comprises a set of proposals. Different proposals require email senders to require fungible payment, perform a resource-intensive computation, [60], perform a series of memory operations [59], or post a bond, for each message sent. This section describes the initial proof of work proposal, and details different analysis.

In 1992, the first computational technique for combating junk mail was presented by Cynthia Dwork and Moni Naor. Their fundamental contribution was to link the economics of email with the security and privacy threat of spam. They did this by proposing that to send an email require the computation of some moderately hard, but not intractable, function of the message and some additional information in order to initiate a transmission. Sending an email means initiating a network transmission. Initiating a transmission means gaining access to the resources: the network for transmission, the recipient's storage in an inbox, and the recipient's attention span if the transmission is accepted.

The essence of POW is that "if you want to send me a message, then you must prove your email is worth receiving by spending some resource of your own". Currently, email is a market that has been almost completely broken. Therefore the key property of the POW functions is that they are very expensive for email sender to solve, but it is comparatively cheap for email recipient to verify the solution.

Of course, the time investment in any processing-intensive POW system depends upon the specific platform. Work that might take 20 seconds on a Pentium IV could take several minutes or more on a Pentium II, and be completely infeasible on a mobile phone. To address this problem, a POW pricing functions based on accessing large amounts of random access memory as opposed to raw processing power was originally proposed by Cynthia Dwork, Andrew Goldberg, and Moni Naor, with later work creating additional memory-bound mechanisms. Since memory speeds vary much less across machines than CPU speeds, memory-bound functions should be more equitable than CPU-bound functions. While processing speeds can vary by orders of magnitude, Dwork claims a factor of four between fastest and slowest memory operations. The current Microsoft implementation, Penny Black, is designed to be agnostic about the form of work and requires only some form of work.

POW offers one way to prevent spam that allows each of us to select with whom we will openly share our inboxes. Imagine each of us had our own histories and lists of people we have communicated with in the past. Each person who wanted to connect would have to do some work as an introduction. If we didn't like the email, labeling it as spam or even rather rude, no more email from that address would reach us. This would entirely alter the economics of spam. And it would alter those economics using our own social networks. For example, some people love getting Chicken Soup for the Soul. Others embrace the latest update on wiretapping legislation and practice. No one wants to be fraudulently separated from his or her money.

The alternative anti-spam network technologies are all based on hierarchies. There is no hierarchy that determines who we invite to dinner, and into our cars. Each of us has a right to be absolutely arbitrary and wrong about sharing our individual resources. This autonomy should continue on the network.

Right now, anyone can use a network identifier with very little investment. Your email, your web address, and the commonly shared bandwidth over the Internet are all resources that can be abused by identity stealing network criminals. Either each all contribute a bit to proof of work; or we can built a universal identifier to enable exact numerical assertions of trust for every person on the Internet. Of course, this new identifier is likely to end up being as much as new vector of attack, while anonymous tickets evaluated by each user will be much more difficult to profitably subvert.

Digital Signatures

Digital signatures, and the digital keys that create these signatures, are an important tool in creating an infrastructure that could prevent identity theft. A digital signature is based on two digital keys: a secret key and a public key. The individual holds the secret key, and only the individual can know that secret key. Each key is a special kind of number that is very large, consisting of hundreds of digits.[2] The keys must be created in pairs, so that for every secret key there is one corresponding public key.

The public key can decrypt or unlock anything encrypted with the secret key. The secret key can decrypt anything encrypted with the public key. Encrypting twice with either key only makes it necessary to decrypt twice with the other key.

Imagine a drop box. A drop box that is open to the public, where anyone can use the public key to open it and place material in. By its nature as a drop box, putting something in is simple. Everyone has the capacity to drop; everyone has access with the key to the drop box. The drop box, the key and the information dropped in it, are of course, all bits. In the digital dimension, dropping in the box is encrypting with the public key. Only the person with the matching secret key can unlock the encrypted material.

Imagine that each drop box has a number associated with it. You have a check to deliver to a particular person. How do you know in which place to drop it? The association between individual and key created by the public key infrastructure — is a way for everyone to know which drop box uniquely belongs to which individual. Thus the infrastructure that associates the key pair to the individual is critical for digital signatures to work.

Retrieving the material requires the individual's single-person secret key that is the other half of the unique pair. In digital terms, this means decrypting that material that was dropped in through encrypting with the associated public key.

The ability to retrieve is created by the knowledge of the secret key. The association of the secret key, the public key and the person who knows the secret key is created by the public key infrastructure — the PKI.

PKI can be implemented in practice to mean a single identity for all uses in the digital realm: to send and receive email, to authorize payments, to log in at work, or at a government website. In the original vision, PKI would have been ubiquitous in that there would be a single great identity hierarchy, like one giant phone book for everyone and every institution on the Internet. Anyone who has tried to look up an old friend using Internet white pages realizes how difficult it is to associate exactly one name with one unique number and have no confusion or overlap.

In the original PKI vision, each person would have one pair of keys (a secret and the corresponding public key) that corresponds to his or her "true name." Obviously that has not and cannot happen; however there are many smaller implementations

---

[2] The secret key can be held on any type of computing device: a smart card, a computer, or a mobile phone. The key can be unlocked by any type of authentication; for example, biometrics on a smart card or a pass phrase on a computer.

of smaller PKIs in companies and commerce. For example, the lock on the browser window is a result of a set of competing PKIs created by companies that sell the authentication of the websites with these locks.[3] The proposals for a single national ID all depend on this fundamental idea.

A PKI has two core things: a cryptographic record of the public key of the key pair, and a way to link that record to a larger database of attributes, credentials or identifiers. Recall that the possession of the secret key authenticates the link between the public and the secret key. However, computers are not as seamless as human beings. So linking a person to a computer record to a larger database is not so easy if you are linking in human terms.

Developing a system that identifies humans in computer terms is not trivial. We identify each other by context, by integrating information. Humans build on context. Computers determine by categorization and parsing. People integrate, computers parse.

The Public Key Infrastructure

A PKI can prevent identity theft by having secure key storage and specified uses. Or a PKI can make identity theft worse though weak security for key storage and strong liability for digital signatures. PKI can enable weak, centralized identity systems or decentralized strong dedicated identity systems. Taking public keys and stapling them onto off-line identities should not be the goal of a Public Key Infrastructure. Obviously, no one suggested an Infrastructure in this manner. Instead, PKI was described as a "digital signature". "Digital signatures" is a powerful metaphor; in fact, too powerful. The signature metaphor implies that everyone has exactly one for every occasion, like a hand written signature. Cryptographic keys can be thought of as physical keys, for all the possible different locks and doors in life. Cryptographic keys can also be thought of credentials, for movie tickets to lifetime memberships.

Public keys are widely used today, for example, to generate the confidentiality as indicated with the lock icon on the browser. Public key infrastructures are a way to connect those numbers (e and d above) to a meaningful person or entity. The problem is that the meaning was not considered before the infrastructure was built.

The original suggestion was for a single digital PKI. The original proposal for PKI was X509. The original linking of public keys, which can provide authentication for authorization, was the link to identity from a public key. Of course, in the physical would few people have exactly one key? The history of certificates in PKI provides, in condensed form, what the future history of identity might be.

X509 was the original PKI proposal. X509 proposed that each person has a "distinguished name" and an associated public key. Each person would have a set of attributes associated with an identity. The key would be linked first to identity then

---

[3] The browser lock indicates that the transmissions are being encrypted and thus cannot be simply read off the wire. The most common use of this encryption technology (Called Secure Sockets Layer) is to protect credit card numbers as they are transmitted over the Internet.

to the associated attributes. The attributes would then determine the rights of the identified person: employee, Girl Scout, professor.

X.509 was the original all-digital secure identity infrastructure proposal. It failed in the marketplace. No one party was trusted by every other party to set up the system. Even if the system was constructed, companies did not want employee access to depend upon the same key that is used by the Girl Scouts. There are different risks, requirements for confidentiality, and organizational structures associated with different credentials.

X509 assumed a centralized enrolling party. Consider your own enrollments. Mine include an employer, video rental by mail, various online publications, blogs, domains that I administer, and a grocer. No single party can verify each and every attribute for all possible uses. My employer needs to authenticate me very well for me to alter my benefits. However, the worst case for the movie rental company is that someone absconds with three DVDs. My employer also has no basis for investigating my DVD rentals. Yet, with one identifier, the history of DVD rentals might be as much a part of the employment process as are credit checks today.

Physical credentials allow delegation (unfortunately, at times accidental delegation). A movie rental card that is dropped is as useful as a movie rental card that is handed to the teenager in the home. Delegation is common in the online world as well, as every assistant with a supervisor's password knows so well. X509 necessarily limited delegation. Because there was one key per person, delegating your one secret key of the key pair would give anyone all your rights. Any delegation key under X509 was a delegation for your entire identity. So to give a colleague the right to sign internal memos in your name meant giving that colleague all your rights (credit cards, health record access, etc) for all time or until you re-establish your identity. Parental rights would be delegated with movie rental rights, there being only one key pair.

The concentration of all identity information with a single public key would have created significant recovery problems. If all data are digital, and the digital identifier is lost or no longer valid, how is recovery possible? The ideal of the single PKI was fundamentally flawed.

While the single universal PKI in the form of X509 did not succeed, there are many distinct PKI instantiations. Different companies built and control their own authentication mechanisms, and these include both devices and humans. Devices clearly do not have "distinguished names" in the form of machine addresses, serial numbers, and retailer-provided identifiers. The ubiquitous UPC code has been expanded so that not only every computing device but also every pair of socks and disposable razor can have unique identifiers. Since socks and razors do not have autonomy they don't interact in different social spheres, but these unique identifiers can be quite useful in a supply chain.

Recall that, like the common UPC on socks, credentials do not have to be associated with identity. One proposal includes privacy-enhanced credentials. In various instantiations (most famously by Stephen Brands) a public key can be linked to a set of credentials. In this case, the individual only shares information on the relevant credential. There is still one key, but the key is used to authenticate attributes, not identify a person in order to imply attributes.

Brands' system allows individual's choice in what attributes are shared with whom, even if another party stores the attributes. This resolves, in a limited way, the problem of recovery. Losing a purse is a terrible thing. However, you are unlikely to lose your purse, cell phone, wallet and change your address at the same time. If this happens, then recovery should be expensive. Recovery should be difficult and require physical presence because this event is extremely rare. Using these blinded credentials has an advantage. It is possible to use a phone or PDA to sign specific credentials. Sometimes, it is only one credential that matters.

> On vacation, I went to Cozumel one week with my children, then one and five. We stayed in an all-inclusive resort with wonderful children's' programs, and diving off the pier. Relaxation was the operative word. On the flight back we were sitting up front. All around me were a group of contractors who were consuming alcohol and flirting with the flight attendant. The children were good, but this required active parenting as the adults became louder and somewhat inappropriate. One of the things these other passengers were bragging about was their acumen in avoiding taxes, including writing off the cost of this particular trip as a business expense. After some time one turned to me and asked, in a gregarious if drunken manner, what I did. Having a dry sense of humor, I told him I was an auditor for the IRS. After a bit of silence, he replied, "Really?" I laughed and explained that actually no, I was a professor at Harvard with expertise in Internet commerce. I was just joking. They insisted on selecting a drink, carried my luggage from the plane to the baggage carousel, and praised my kids on the flight. Finally, I told them what happens in Mexico stays in Mexico and that I could honestly say that I would never, ever audit them. (Given that I did not know their names, even had I wanted to change careers, I would not have been able to audit them.)

The point of this tale is that the other passengers had a set of credentials. The other passengers on the flight with me knew my identifier: Jean. The passengers knew that I had two children, and where I spent my vacation. Having spent something like an hour next to me, they had a pretty good idea of my parenting style. Yet they could not use this rich set of credentials to ascertain another (my job). This kind of isolation of credentials can make identity theft more difficult.

Affiliation is powerful. Credential cryptography [4] is a type of public key cryptography that is particularly useful at proving affiliation. A cryptographic key in the world of identity is itself only a number or a series of letters. All by themselves, these numbers prove nothing. Credential-based cryptography can prove, for example, that I am an IU professor and not an IRS auditor.

As with other public keys, there is a need for some connection between the key and the associated attribute. With credential cryptography, that means that there is some third party which authenticates the claimed affiliation or credential. In the case above, that third party would be the university. The university could generate private keys associated with each credential: professor, student, etc. The ability to use the private key generated by the third party would prove the affiliation.

---

[4] Credential cryptography is usually called "identity cryptography", since any random string including a name can be used as the public key. However, the use of the phrase "identity cryptography" would be quite confusing, so I utilize the less widely used phrase credential cryptography.

Any third party can use credential cryptography to confirm any particular credential or attribute using a simple string. For example, the ISP can confirm that you come from a stable Internet address. A credit card company can confirm that you have the right to charge without the requirement that you provide your charge account number, or any information that could be reused in a manner that creates risk.

Using credential cryptography instead of filling in forms, all that would be needed to guarantee payment would be a signed email. That email may be signed with a simple cryptographic credentials, e.g. Fandango, can provide a ticket to the movies without having anything from the purchaser but a digitally signed email. The cost of the movie ticket would be authorized using credential cryptography but Fandango need not develop a profile that enables anyone who can obtain access to steal your credit card. Using this system, a person can change emails as often as desired, but then authenticate that email to the credit providing authority. Ideally, if the credit authority errs in accessing a charge, the credit card company could then be liable.

Emails have an advantage over passive provision of reusable information in that they are interactive. Instead of pushing a button on one screen, there can be a requirement for an exchange. You receive and respond to an email in order to enable a credit charge. This is a transaction where there is increased privacy, increased interaction and increased security. The cryptographic credential would require interaction in this case. So identity theft would not be invisible — it is easy to fake an email address from an account. It is impossible to fake a digitally signed email without the secret key. And it is very close to impossible for anyone to prevent an

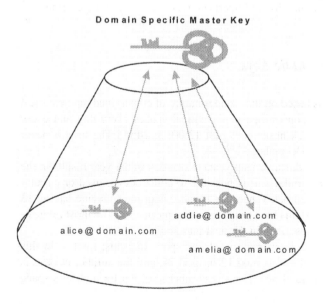

Fig. 9.3 Identity Credentials Cryptographically Confirmed with Email

individual from receiving an email. (A trusted insider working for the recipient's email provider could delete the email after it was received.) So, the individual with the email would get a message with every attempt to charge.

Anyone can create multiple emails so that the failure of one credential would not harm the others. Recall each credential can be linked to an email, or one email linked to many credentials. With purely digital transactions Jean the professor would not be linked to Jean the parent; and indeed no first purchase need be linked with a second.

The reliability of this system depends upon the ability of the credit charging entity to enroll the correct email with the correct account. And enrollment fraud is the essence of identity theft. Enrollment is critical to any successful identity system.

Identity based cryptography can link many emails to one attribute (can charge things to the VISA international clearinghouse) or many attributes to one email. Because the signatures can be compound, any email can prove as many or as few things as the sender wants. For example, the AARP and MasterCard might sign an email. Alternatively, you might carry a phone filled with credentials just as your phone is filled with telephone numbers. Some of these will be anonymous, as with digital cash. Some of these will reflect a debit account, such as a check. Others will indicate your right to draw on a line of credit. Large or unusual purchases may require additional authentication, through interaction over email or proving to your phone that it is indeed you.

The biometrics primer of Chapter 9 describes how biometrics are particularly useful when they are distributed as opposed to centralized. If you have to authenticate yourself to your phone with a fingerprint, using your stolen phone would be more difficult. If that digitized fingerprint record were then stored centrally then anyone could steal the data that digital fingerprint record and forge fingerprints.

End Note: What Are Public Keys

Public key cryptography is based on the circular nature of constrained mathematical spaces. Of course, we use constrained mathematical spaces every day and every minute. The time on the clock never goes past 12:00, or 24:00. The time is never 24:01, and the date is never December 32nd.

Adding 365 days (or 366 during a leap year) to one day in the year results in the same date, one year later. Similarly, it is possible to construct a closed or circular counting system with any number. When that number is prime (imagine having 13 hours) then the counting systems have some amazing properties. The most interesting, in credential terms, is described in the next paragraph.

First, for ease of reading, represent any closed space like this: mod n. In this case, the clock can be thought of as mod 12 or mod 24, and the number of days is a non-leap calendar year is mod 365. For any number (call it a for any) in a space defined a by prime number (p for prime, so mod p).

$$a^{p-1} = a(mod\,p) \qquad\qquad (9.1)$$

It is possible to combine two prime numbers, and creating a larger but still constrained space. This is like combining months to create a larger, but still constrained, year. To use some small number examples, 13 is prime, so: $4^{12} = 13 \times 16777215 + 1$. Similarly $3^6 = 7 \times 104 + 1$.

Ron Rivest made a magnificent recognition that it is possible to combine two of these[5]. The result was that for any message M there can be two numbers e and d, so that $M^{e \times d}(mod(p-1)(q-1)) = M(mod(p-1)(q-1))$. These two numbers, e and d, are the heart of public key cryptography. In this case, e is the secret key and d is the public key.

Basically, Ron Rivest found a way to wind the clock forward and backwards in a consistent way. Every person has a different set of clocks, two complementary clocks. And winding up one required unwinding the other. One clock is public; one is secret.

Because of their complementary nature these clocks or keys solve the problem of key distribution. Two people can communicate without needing to set up a unique key. Public keys do *not* solve the problem of identification. That I can have a public key does not prove any of my attributes except that I do, in fact, have a public key.

Recall that for public key cryptography, keep one number secret and publicize the other. Thus anyone can communicate in a secure manner with anyone else because the initiator of the communication can simply use the public key of the recipient. Just as anyone can send mail to anyone else, the initiator simply has to know the recipient's email. However, as phishing and spam so painfully illustrate, understanding the connection between the key to communication and the person with whom you think you are communicating is not trivial.

---

[5] This is a vast and gross, but potentially useful, simplification.

Strengths and Weaknesses of Biometrics

Elaine M. Newton[6]

Introduction

In general, there are three approaches to authenticating an individual's identity. In order of most secure and convenient to least secure and convenient, they are as follows:

Something you are: a biometric such as a fingerprint.

Something you know: a PIN, such as an ATM bank account password.

Something you have: key, token, card, such as an ID card.

Any combination of these approaches can potentially further heighten security.

Facial recognition software, fingerprint readers, hand geometry readers, and other forms of biometrics appear increasingly in systems with mission-critical security. Given the widespread consensus in the security community that passwords and magnetic-stripe cards accompanied by PINs have weaknesses, biometrics could well be ensconced in future security systems.

This document begins with a definition of biometrics and related terms. It then describes the steps in the biometric authentication process, and reviews issues of template management and storage. The appendix concludes with a brief review of mainstream biometric applications.

Overview

A biometric is any *measurable, robust, distinctive* physical characteristic or personal trait that can be used to identify, or verify the claimed identity of, an individual. Biometric authentication, in the context of this report, refers to automated methods of identifying, or verifying the identity of, a living person.

The italicized terms above require explanation.

Measurable means that the characteristic or trait can be easily presented to a sensor and converted into a quantifiable, digital format. This allows for the automated matching process to occur in a matter of seconds.

The robustness of a biometric is a measure of the extent to which the characteristic or trait is subject to significant changes over time. These changes can occur as a result of age, injury, illness, occupational use, or chemical exposure. A highly robust biometric does not change significantly over time. A less robust biometric does

---

[6] as adapted from John D. Woodward, Katherine W. Webb, Elaine M. Newton et al., Appendix A, "Biometrics: A Technical Primer," "Army Biometric Applications: Identifying and Addressing Sociocultural Concerns," RAND/MR-1237-A, Santa Monica, CA: RAND 2001. Copyright RAND 2001.

change over time. For example, the iris, which changes very little over a person's lifetime, is more robust than a voice.

Distinctiveness is a measure of the variations or differences in the biometric pattern among the general population. The higher the degree of distinctiveness is, the more unique the identifier. The highest degree of distinctiveness implies a unique identifier. A low degree of distinctiveness indicates a biometric pattern found frequently in the general population. The iris and the retina have higher degrees of distinctiveness than hand or finger geometry.

The application helps determine the degree of robustness and distinctiveness required. The system's ability to match a sample to a template is sometimes referred to as the biometric's reliability.

Systems can be used either to identify people in a consensual or non-consensual manner — as when faces are scanned in public places — or to verify the claimed identity of a person who presents a biometrics sample in order to gain access or authorization for an activity. The following section expands on this issue.

"Living person" distinguishes biometric authentication from forensics, which does not involve real-time identification of a living individual.

Identification and Verification

Identification and verification differ significantly. With identification, the biometric system asks and attempts to answer the question, "Who is X?" In an identification application, the biometric device reads a sample and compares that sample against every template in the database. This is called a "one-to-many" search (1:N). The device will both make a match and subsequently identify the person or it will not make a match and not be able to identify the person.

Verification is when the biometric system asks and attempts to answer the question, "Is this X?" after the user claims to be X. In a verification application, the biometric device requires input from the user, at which time the user claims his identity via a password, token, or user name (or any combination of the three). This user input points the device to a template in the database. The device also requires a biometric sample from the user. It then compares the sample to or against the user-defined template. This is called a "one-to-one" search (1:1). The device will either find or fail to find a match between the two.

Identification applications require a highly robust and distinctive biometric; otherwise, the error rates falsely matching and falsely non-matching user's samples against templates cause security problems and inhibit convenience. Identification applications are common where the end-user wants to identify criminals (immigration, law enforcement, etc.) or other "wolves in sheep's clothing." Other types of applications may use a verification process. In many ways, deciding whether to use identification or verification requires a trade-off: the end-user's needs for security versus convenience.

In sum, biometric authentication is used in two ways: to prove who you are or who you claim you are and to prove who you are not (e.g., to resolve a case of mistaken identity).

Three Basic Elements of All Biometric Systems

All biometric systems consist of three basic elements:

1. Enrolling an individual—the process of collecting biometric samples from an individual, (the "enrollee")— and subsequently generating her template.
2. Creating templates–the data representing the enrollee's biometric.
3. Matching — the process of comparing a live biometric sample against one or many templates in the system's database.

Performance refers to the ability of a biometric system to correctly match, or identify individuals.

Enrollment

Enrollment is the crucial first stage for biometric authentication because it generates a template that will be used for all subsequent matching. Typically, the device takes three samples of the same biometric and averages them to produce an enrollment template. Enrollment is complicated by the fact that a users' familiarity with a biometric device usually improves performance because they know how to place themselves in front of or onto a sensor, but enrollment is usually the first time the user is exposed to the device.

Environmental conditions also affect enrollment. Enrollment should take place under conditions similar to those expected during the routine matching process. For example, if voice verification is used in an environment where there is background noise, the enrolling system should capture voice templates in the same environment.

In addition to user and environmental issues, biometrics themselves change over time. Many biometric systems account for these changes by continuously averaging. Templates are averaged and updated each time the user attempts authentication.

Templates

The biometric device stores the data captured when enrolling a person as a template. The device uses a proprietary algorithm to extract features appropriate to that biometric from the enrollee's samples. Templates are only a record of distinguishing features, sometimes called minutiae points, of a person's biometric characteristic or trait. For example, templates are not an image or record of the actual fingerprint or voice. In basic terms, templates are numerical representations of key points taken from a person's body. They can be thought of as very long passwords that can identify a body part or behavior.

The template usually occupies a small amount of computer memory (and is smaller than the original image) and thus allows for quick processing, a key feature of making biometric authentication practical.

The template must be stored somewhere so that subsequent templates, created when a user tries to access the system using a sensor, can be compared. Some biometric experts claim it is impossible to reverse-engineer, or recreate, a person's print or image from the biometric template.

Matching

Matching is the comparison of two templates: the one produced at the time of enrollment (or at previous sessions, if there is continuous updating) and the one produced "on the spot" as a user tries to gain access by providing a biometric sample via a sensor.

There are three ways a match can fail:

Failure to enroll / Failure to acquire.

False match.

False nonmatch.

Both failure to enroll (during enrollment) and failure to acquire (prior to matching) are failures to extract distinguishing features appropriate to that technology. For example, a small percentage of the population fails to enroll in fingerprint-based biometric authentication systems. There are two primary reasons for this failure: the individual's fingerprints are not distinctive enough to be picked up by the system, or the distinguishing characteristics of the individual's fingerprints have been altered because of the individual's age or occupation, e.g., as might happen with an elderly bricklayer.

False match (FM) and false nonmatch (FNM) are frequently referred to by the misnomers "false acceptance" and "false rejection," respectively, but the latter pair of terms are application-dependent in meaning. FM and FNM are application-neutral terms that describe the matching process between a live sample and a biometric template.

A false match occurs when a sample is incorrectly matched to a template in the database (i.e., an imposter is accepted). A false nonmatch occurs when a sample is incorrectly not matched to a truly matching template in the database (i.e., a legitimate match is denied). People deploying biometric systems calculate rates for FM and FNM and use them to make tradeoffs between security and convenience when choosing a system or tuning its parameters. For example, a heavy security emphasis errs on the side of denying legitimate matches and does not tolerate acceptance of imposters. A heavy emphasis on user convenience results in little tolerance for denying legitimate matches but tolerates some acceptance of imposters.

Template Management, Storage and Security

Template management is critically linked to privacy, security, and convenience. All biometric authentication systems face a common issue: biometric templates must be stored somewhere. Templates must be protected to prevent identity fraud and to protect the privacy of users. Privacy is affected when additional information is stored about each user along with the biometric template.

Possible locations template storage include

- the biometric device itself,
- a central computer that is remotely accessed,
- a plastic card or token via a bar code or magnetic stripe,
- RFID (Radio Frequency Identification Device) cards and tags,
- optical memory cards,
- PCMCIA (Personal Computer Memory Card International Association) cards, or
- smart cards.

In general, transmitting biometric data over communications lines reduces system security. Such transmission renders the data vulnerable to the same interception or tampering possible when any data is sent "over the wire." On the other hand, a network or central repository may be needed for some applications where there are multiple access points or when there is a need to confirm information with another node or higher authority. Biometrics are more secure when stored under the control of the authorized user, such as on a smart card, and used in verification applications. Cards have varying degrees of utility and storage memory.

Smart cards are the size of credit cards and have an embedded microchip or microprocessor chip. The chip stores electronic data that can be protected using biometrics. In terms of ease of use, there are two types of smart cards: contact and contactless smart cards. The term "smart card" implies a standard card that must be inserted into a reader. American Express Blue is an example of a smart card that requires reader insertion. A contactless or wireless smart card only has to be placed near an antenna to carry out a transaction.[155] This is particularly useful for passing through an area where the person carrying the card may pass multiple times a day, or where their may have secondary tasks that require the use of the person's hands. Yet the convenience also can create risks, as the signal is broadcast. This risk is physically small albeit in an extremely small range. The risk can also be completely mitigated by encrypting the interaction between the card and the reader. The option of smart-card based encryption for authentication has become eminently feasible with the decrease in the cost of computing power.

The number of uses of the database also affects security for template database storage: will it have a unique use or will it be used for multiple security purposes?

For example, a facilities manager might use a fingerprint reader for physical access control to the building. The manager might also want to use the same fingerprint template database for his employees to access their computer network. Should the manager use separate databases for these different uses, or is he willing to risk accessing employee fingerprints from a remote location for multiple purposes?

Additional security features can be incorporated into biometric systems to detect an unauthorized user. Because unauthorized users malicious entities appearing to be harmless, they are sometimes called "wolves", as in *a wolf in sheep's clothing*. For example, a "liveliness test" tries to determine whether the biometric sample is being read from a live person versus a faux body part or body part of a dead person. Liveliness tests are done in many ways. The device can check for such things as heat, heartbeat, or electrical capacitance.[7]

Other security features include encryption of biometric data and the use of sequence numbers in template transmission. A template with such a number out of sequence suggests unauthorized use.

In general, verification applications provide more security than identification applications because a biometric and at least one other piece of input (e.g., PIN, password, token, user name) are required to match a template and the corresponding record. In essence, it is a second layer of security.

Verification provides a user with more control over his data and over the process when the template is stored only on a card. Such a system would not allow for a clandestine, or involuntary, capture of biometric data because the individual would know each time, where, and to what system s/he were submitting their biometric. Verification applications with storage (and possibly matching, too) of a biometric template on a card are potentially more palatable to the public (for privacy, convenience, and security concerns) and more secure than identification applications or applications with a repository for many reasons:[8]

There is no large centralized storage location of templates, which could be abused or hacked. An administrator should regard even distributed databases as "honey pots" for hackers and leave open the possibility of abuse.[9] They require the user's consent to capture data.[10] Being in possession of a card adds a layer of security Further, requiring a password can also enhance security. For example, image files of fingerprints may be of interest to an organization (such as the FBI or a bank) because of their law enforcement or security applications. In the case of fingerprints, the military may want to keep both electronic image files of the fingerprint as well as the biometric templates. The image files are too large to be used for biometric applications but would be useful for forensic purposes. Moreover, an organization

---

[7] Electrical capacitance has proved to be the best and least reproducible method for effectively identifying a live person.

[8] Security also depends on other factors, such as the care taken to safeguard tokens and passwords and to ensure that transmissions of biometric data are adequately protected.

[9] This primer does not cover standards for interoperability or so-called "plug and play" applications because this subject is tangential to the project. This appendix relies heavily on the following sources: [90] and [205]. See also [100].

[10] See, e.g., Appendix B, Program Reports, Fort Sill Biometrically Protected Smart Card.

might want to store image files to give it greater technical flexibility. For example, if the FBI did not keep image files of enrollees, it might have to physically reenroll each individual if the FBI decided to change to a different proprietary biometric system. .[11]

Because the search seeks only a match against one template in the database, verification applications require less processing time and memory than identification.

Biometric Applications

Most biometric applications fall into one of nine general categories. First there are financial services (e.g., ATMs and kiosks) to limit risks by using biometrics to provide authentication to data. The second large class is to evaluate the right of individuals to make certain movements and cross borders. These are most widely proposed for immigration and border control (e.g., points of entry, pre-cleared frequent travelers, passport and visa issuance, asylum cases).

The use of biometrics where the physical entity is authenticated is broad. In social services, biometrics provide fraud prevention in entitlement programs. In health care, biometrics offer security measure for privacy of medical records. Biometrics are used for physical access control for a variety of institutions, (e.g., institutional, government, and residential).

Biometrics are also used for narrow replacements for traditional problems of verification. Applications here include time and attendance where biometrics are used as, a replacement of time punch card. Biometrics are widely proposed as solutions to problems in computer security including personal computer access, network access, Internet use, e-commerce, and e-mail authentication.

In addition, biometrics have been proposed as an enabling underlying service in telecommunications to limit mobile phone fraud, authenticate callers into call centers, strengthen the security of phone cards, and enable televised shopping.

Finally biometrics have been embraced by law enforcement for us in criminal investigation, national ID, driver's license, correctional institutions/prisons, home confinement, and are integrated into smart gun designs.

Biometrics are any measurable physical feature that can be used to identify or classify a single person or set of people. Some biometrics are considered attributes, for example, age is a biological attribute that is not generally used for authentication. In the physical realm, age is often authenticated by observation, as anyone who has reached the age of being to purchase alcohol without proof of maturity can affirm.

Biometrics have increasingly come to refer to the basic authentication that is possible when an individually is properly enrolled. Biometrics have different relative strengths, but the entropy provided by a biometric in all cases is less than that of a weak password. What is unique about biometrics is that these are fundamentally tied to the body.

---

[11] Image files are also known as raw data or the corpus.

The tie to the body does not confirm the accuracy of a corresponding digital record. Enrollment is to no small degree more difficult in biometric systems. Enrollment requires physical presence and a readable biometric. While the most obvious failure to enroll would be loss of limb or eye, there are more chronic difficulties. Particularly the elderly have difficulties in enrollment. The aged frequently do not have readable fingerprints. They are more likely to have cataracts or other medical problems that prohibit the use of retinal scans. While biometrics are the most effective at preventing duplicate enrollment; biometrics also have the most problematic enrollment.

Protection is not possible with biometric data. In any place the body is, the biometric can be read. Fingerprints are left on glasses, and can be reproduced with a heating element and a gummy bear. Retina scans are more intrusive, and are unlikely to be made surreptitiously. Corporations may choose to use the same biometrics for different risks. For example, fingerprints and hand geometry are collected at Walt Disney World. The same data should not then be used to protect a person's life savings. Raw biometrics cannot be recovered. Biometrics are "the password you can never change."

Unlike the case with asymmetric authentication, raw biometrics with centralized storage require that authenticating data be provided for authentication to occur. Therefore, each time authentication occurs with the biometric, the recipient obtains the information required for identity appropriation. An alterative to centralized biometric authentication is smart-card based authentication. In this case, the smart card is imprinted with the biometric, so that only the individual who has imprinted the card may use it. The use of a distributed smart-card based infrastructure has a very different recovery and protection profile than a centralized system.

In technical terms, biometrics are weak. The entropy in a biometric identifier is low. Protection is difficult. Biometric data are highly distributed; we inherently share biometric data everywhere. Yet biometric systems can be built centralized; thus increasing the threat of catastrophic failure.

However, biometrics are the only mechanism which link a body to a claim of identity. For that reason, organizations that deal with bodies reasonably advocate for and use of biometrics. Fingerprints have proven extremely valuable in law enforcement; and the US Department of Defense maintains DNA records in order to identify remains.

Mainstream Biometrics

While there are many possible biometrics, at least eight mainstream biometric authentication technologies have been deployed or pilot-tested in applications in the public and private sectors:[12] (The leaders are listed as the top four.)

---

[12] For a detailed discussion of these mainstream biometrics, see [100].

Fingerprint

The fingerprint biometric is an automated, digital version of the old ink-and-paper method used for more than a century for identification, primarily by law enforcement agencies. Users place their finger on a platen for the print to be read. The minutiae are then extracted by the vendor's algorithm, which also makes a fingerprint pattern analysis. Fingerprint template sizes are typically 50 to 1,000 bytes.

Fingerprint biometrics currently have three main application arenas: large-scale Automated Finger Imaging Systems (AFIS) (generally used for law enforcement), fraud prevention in entitlement programs, and physical and computer access.

Iris Scan

Iris scanning measures the iris pattern in the colored part of the eye, although the iris color has nothing to do with the biometric. Iris patterns are formed randomly. As a result, the iris patterns in your left and right eyes are different, and so are the iris patterns of identical twins. Iris scan templates are typically around 256 bytes.

Iris scanning can provide quick authentication for both identification and verification applications because of its large number of degrees of freedom. Current pilot programs and applications include ATMs ("Eye-TMs"), grocery stores (for checking out), and the Charlotte/Douglas International Airport (physical access). During the Winter Olympics in Nagano, Japan, an iris scanning identification system controlled access to the rifles used in the biathlon.

Facial Recognition

Facial recognition records the spatial geometry of distinguishing features of the face. Different vendors use different methods of facial recognition, however, all focus on measures of key features. Facial recognition templates are typically 83 to 1,000 bytes. Facial recognition technologies can encounter performance problems stemming from a number of factors, including uncooperative user behavior and environmental variables such as lighting.

Facial recognition has been used to identify card counters in casinos, shoplifters in stores, criminals in targeted urban areas, and terrorists.

Hand/Finger Geometry

Hand or finger geometry is an automated measurement of many dimensions of the hand and fingers. Neither of these methods takes actual prints of the palm or fingers. Only the spatial geometry is examined as the user puts his hand on the sensor's surface and uses guiding poles between the fingers to properly place the hand and initiate the reading. Hand geometry templates are typically 9 bytes, and finger geometry templates are 20 to 25 bytes. Finger geometry usually measures two or three fingers. During the 1996 Summer Olympics, hand geometry secured the athlete's dormitories at Georgia Tech. Hand geometry is a well-developed technology that has been thoroughly field-tested and is easily accepted by users.

Voice Recognition

Voice or speaker recognition uses vocal characteristics to identify individuals. It involves their speaking a pass-phrase so that the sample they used when enrolling can match the sample the use at the time of attempted access. A telephone or microphone can serve as a sensor, which makes it a relatively cheap and easily deployable technology.

Voice recognition can be affected by environmental factors, particularly background noise. Additionally, it is unclear whether the technologies actually recognize the voice or just the pronunciation of the pass-phrase (password) used. This technology has been the focus of considerable efforts on the part of the telecommunications industry and NSA, which continue to work on improving reliability.

Retinal Scan

Retinal scans measure the blood vessel patterns in the back of the eye. Retinal scan templates are typically 40 to 96 bytes. Because the retina can change with certain medical conditions, such as pregnancy, high blood pressure, and AIDS, this biometric might have the potential to reveal more information than just an individual's identity.

Because end-users perceive the technology to be somewhat intrusive, retinal scanning has not gained popularity with them. The device shines a light into the eye of a user, who must be standing very still within inches of the device.

Dynamic Signature Verification

Dynamic signature verification is an automated method of examining an individual's signature. This technology examines such dynamics as speed, direction, and pressure of writing; the time that the stylus is in and out of contact with the "paper"; the total time taken to make the signature; and where the stylus is raised from and lowered onto the "paper." Dynamic signature verification templates are typically 50 to 300 bytes.

Keystroke Dynamics

Keystroke dynamics is an automated method of examining an individual's keystrokes on a keyboard. This technology examines such dynamics as speed and pressure, the total time taken to type a particular password, and the time a user takes between hitting certain keys. This technology's algorithms are still being developed to improve robustness and distinctiveness. One potentially useful application that may emerge is computer access, where this biometric could be used to verify the computer user's identity continuously.

Classifying Biometric Applications

Biometric applications may be classified in many different ways. James Wayman of the National Biometric Test Center suggests the following seven categories for classifying biometric applications, explained below.

1. overt or clandestine
2. cooperative or uncooperative
3. habituated or not habituated
4. supervised or unsupervised
5. standard or nonstandard environment
6. closed or open system
7. public or private.

Overt versus clandestine capture of a biometric sample refers to the user's awareness that he is participating in biometric authentication. [13] Facial recognition is an example of a biometric that can be used for clandestine identification of individuals. Most uses of biometrics are overt, because users' active participation improves performance and lowers error rates. Verification applications are nearly always overt.

Cooperative versus uncooperative applications refers to the behavior that is in the best interest of the malicious entity, sometimes called a "wolf" in the biometric literature. Is it in the interest of malicious entities to match or to not match a template in the database? Which is to the benefit of the malicious agent, to re-enroll of additional benefits or to be mis-identified as a legitimate employee? This is important in planning a security system with biometrics because no perfect biometric system exists. Every system can be tricked into falsely not matching one's sample and template-some more easily than others. It is also possible to trick a biometric device into falsely matching a malicious sample against a template, but it could be argued that this requires more work and a sophisticated hacker to make a model of the biometric sample.

In systems that store user information in a database, a malicious entity may try to trick the system into divulging biometric samples or other information. One way

---

[13] James Wayman uses the term "covert" instead of "clandestine", making the distinction between "covert" and "overt".

to strengthen security in a cooperative application is to require a password or token along with a biometric, so that the attacker must match one specific template and is not allowed to exploit the entire database for his gain.

To gain access to a computer, an attacker would want to be cooperative. To attempt to foil an INS database consisting of illegal border crossing recidivists, an attacker (recidivist) would be uncooperative.

Habituated versus not habituated use of a biometric system refers to how often the users interface with the biometric device. This is significant because the user's familiarity with the device affects its performance. Depending on which type of application is chosen, the end-user may need to utilize a biometric that is highly robust. As examples, the use of fingerprints for computer or network access is a habituated use, while the use of fingerprints on a driver's license, which is updated once every several years, is a not habituated use. Even "habituated" applications are "not habituated" during their first week or so of operation or until the users adjust to using the system.

Supervised versus unsupervised applications refer to whether supervision (e.g., a security officer) is a resource available to the end-user's security system. Do users need to be instructed on how to use the device (because the application has many new users or not habituated users) or be supervised to ensure they are being properly sampled (such as border crossing situations that deal with the problem of recidivists or other uncooperative applications)? Or is the application made for increased convenience, such as at an ATM? Routine use of an access system may or may not require supervision. The process of enrollment nearly always requires supervision.

Standard versus nonstandard environments are generally a dichotomy between indoors versus outdoors. A standard environment is optimal for a biometric system and matching performance. A nonstandard environment may present variables that would create false nonmatches. For example, a facial recognition template depends, in part, on the lighting conditions when the "picture" (image) was taken. The variable lighting outdoors can cause false nonmatches. Some indoor situations may also be considered nonstandard environments.

Closed versus open systems refer to the number of uses of the template database, now and in the future. Will the database have a unique use (closed), or will it be used for multiple security measures (open)? Recall the fingerprint example from "Template Management-Storage and Security" for employees to enter a building and log on to their computer network. Should they use separate databases for these different uses, or do they want to risk remotely accessing employee fingerprints for multiple purposes?

Other examples are state driver's licenses and entitlement programs. A state may want to communicate with other states or other programs within the same state to eliminate fraud. This would be an open system, in which standard formats of data and compression would be required to exchange and compare information.

Public or private applications refer to the users and their relationship to system management. Examples of users of public applications include customers and entitlement recipients. Users of private applications include employees of business or government. Both user attitudes toward biometric devices and management's approach vary depending on whether the application is public or private. Once again, user attitudes toward the device will affect the performance of the biometric system.

It should be noted here that performance figures and error rates from vendor testing are unreliable for many reasons. Part of the problem is that determining the distinctiveness of a biometric accurately requires thousands or even millions of people. To acquire samples over any amount of time in any number of contexts from this number of people would be impossible. To test for the many variables in each type of application would be impossible in most cases, and too costly in the few where it is possible. Operational and pilot testing is the only reasonable method to test a system. Additionally, vendor and scientific laboratory testing generally present only the easiest deployment scenario of a biometric application: overt, cooperative, habituated, supervised, standard, closed, and private.

Salient Characteristics of Biometrics

The table below compares the eight mainstream biometrics in terms of a number of characteristics.[14]

The first of the four characteristics are if the technology is suitable for verification as well as identification.

The second characteristic is the measure of change in the biometric, e.g. robustness.

The third characteristic is if the biometrics themselves are distinction; and the fourth is how intrusive a direct interaction is required.

As the industry is still working to establish comprehensive standards and the technology is changing rapidly, however, it is difficult to make assessments with which everyone would agree. The table represents an assessment based on discussions with technologists, vendors, and program managers.

Half of the systems in the table below can be used for either identification or verification, while the rest can be used only for verification. In particular, hand geometry has been used only for verification applications, such as physical access control and time and attendance verification. In addition, voice recognition, because of the need for enrollment and matching using a pass-phrase, is typically used for verification only.

Robustness and distinctiveness vary considerably. Fingerprinting is moderately robust, and, although it is distinctive, a small percentage of the population has unusable prints, usually because of age, genetics, injury, occupation, exposure to chemicals, or other occupational hazards. Hand/finger geometry is moderate on the distinctiveness scale, but it is not very robust, while facial recognition is neither highly robust nor distinctive. As for voice recognition, assuming the voice and not the pronunciation is what is being measured, this biometric is moderately robust and distinctive. Iris scans are both highly robust (because they are not highly susceptible to

---

[14] The authors compiled this table from various sources at the SJB Biometrics 99 Workshop, November 9-11, 1999, including [90]. See also [100].

Table 9.1 Comparison of Mainstream Biometrics

Biometric	Identify or Verify	Robust	Distinctive	Intrusive
Fingerprint	Either	High to Moderate[a]	High	Touching
Hand/Finger Geometry	Verify	Moderate	Low	Touching
Facial Recognition	Either	Moderate	Moderate	12+ inches
Voice Recognition	Verify	Low	Moderate	Remote
Iris Scan	Either	High	High	12+ inches
Retinal Scan	Either	High	High	1-2 inches
Dynamic Signature Verification	Verify	Low	Low	Touching
Keystroke Dynamics	Verify	Low	Low	Touching

[a] This is a function of the population using the system.

day-to-day changes or damage) and distinctive (because they are randomly formed). Retinal scans are fairly robust and very distinctive. Finally, neither dynamic signature verification nor keystroke dynamics are particularly robust or distinctive.

As the table shows, the biometrics vary in terms of how intrusive they are, ranging from those biometrics that require touching to others that can recognize an individual from a distance.

Biometric Conclusions

Where previous evaluations identified temporal and pose variations as two key areas for future research in face recognition, the FRVT 2000 showed that progress had been made with respect to the former, but developing algorithms that can handle a year or more variation between image capture is still a very imperative research area. In addition, developing algorithms that can compensate for pose, illumination, and distance changes were noted as other areas of needed research. Differences in expression and media storage do not appear to be issues for commercial algorithms.

The FRVT 2000 experiments on compression confirm previous findings that moderate levels of compression do not adversely affect performance. Resolution experiments find that moderately decreasing the resolution can slightly improve performance, which is good news since many video surveillance cameras do not acquire high quality images - especially aged cameras. In most cases, compression and reducing resolution are low pass filters, and suggest that such filtering can increase performance.[15]

---

[15] Although not covered here, vendors, city governments, and airports have conducted scenario evaluations of face recognition systems to determine their efficacy in specific locations when used by the general population or the airport employees. Overall, these pilots have shown very poor performance.

Reputation

All the identity technologies discussed previously assume you exist in some hier-archy. In fact, there are many hierarchies. Yet there are more social networks than hierarchies. Even within a hierarchy there can be putative authorities that are sub-servient to social networks. The classic example of this is the new minister in the established church. The minister leads the flock, but every party is aware that the established families determine if the flock follows.

Social identities online may exist simultaneously and exclusively. My role as a good neighbor is something of which I am proud, yet it can only be authenticated by my neighbors. The State of Indiana can authenticate my ownership of my home; but cannot comment on my quality as a neighbor. Yet my classification as a decent neighbor, who brings by cookies and invites everyone over for an annual party, is not something that can be centrally authenticated. My relative success in the en-deavor of building a social network is a function of the community of neighbors. This community is disinterested in my reputation among my academic peers.

Similarly my standing in the academy is a function of the respect of my peers. Every workplace has some combination of hierarchy of official power and social awareness of competence.

Proving Identity Through Social Networks

Social networks are a powerful tool and can be used to enrich the online experi-ence. Social networks can be used to create reputations. Reputations can be used to authenticate specific attributes or credentials.

Referrals made through an existing social network, such as friends or family, "are the primary means of disseminating market information when the services are particularly complex and difficult to evaluate ... this implies that if one gets positive word-of-mouth referrals on e-commerce from a person with strong personal ties, the consumer may establish higher levels of initial trust in e-commerce". In 2001, PEW found that 56% of people surveyed said they email a family member or friend for advice [149].

Several commercial websites, such as Overstock.com and Netflix.com, utilize social networking and reputations. These sites have created mechanisms to en-able users to share opinions, merchandise lists, and rating information. Using these mechanisms, Overstock.com attracted more than 25,000 listings in six months after the implementation of a friends list.

Public forums (perhaps on the vendor's site) and rating systems provide a natural incentive for merchants to act in an honorable manner or otherwise face economic and social consequences. The cost is greater if the sources of the reputation infor-mation are trusted. The opportunity for retaliation (through ratings or direct pun-ishment) is an important predictor of behavior in repeated trust games, so venues where merchants cannot "punish" customers have advantages.

As has been demonstrated by game theoretic experiments, data provided from the FTC [71] and PEW [149] social constraints do not by any means guarantee trustworthy behavior. Yet reputations can be used to authenticate (sometimes weakly) specific practices or characteristics. Today reputation systems are used to support evaluation of vendors, users, products and web sites.

Reputation systems attempt to enforce cooperative behavior through explicit ratings. However the design of the reputation system is not trivial. If the reputation system itself is flawed it might inadvertently promote opportunistic behavior. Consider the case of cumulative ratings, as on eBay. On eBay, a vendor who has more than 13 transactions but cheats 25% of the time will have a higher rating than a vendor who has had only ten honest transactions. Vendors game the system by refusing to rate customers until the vendors themselves are rated, thus having the implicit threat of retaliation.

Reputation systems may be centralized, with a single authority ensuring the validity of the reputation, as with eBay. Reputation systems may be distributed, with multiple parties sharing their own reputation information. Like other identity systems, reputations provide weak or strong authentication. Reputation systems may be dedicated (e.g., eBay) or widely utilized (e.g., credit scores).

Reputation systems are community centered or peer produced identity systems. These systems are the result of the merger of two distinct computing traditions: the scientific and the corporate. The most common form of description of these systems is peer production or P2P. The more recent, and more broadly applicable description is peer production. Peer production includes blogs, file sharing, massively parallel community processing, and gaming.

People can come together and do amazing things with no centralized identifying authority. Reputation systems allow individuals to build verifiable records of reliable and trustworthy behavior over time. The American credit rating is an example of a hieratical reputation system. The reputation of who is reliable in a pinch exists in every community. If you recall the opening chapter, identities were all once community-based. In general, community-based reputation failed to scale in the industrial revolution. The connectivity and communications of the information revolution enables utilizing the wisdom of neighbors.

Many technologies are presented as if centralized attribute authentication were the only option. However, social networks can be used to verify claims of attributes ranging from identity to reliability.

In the history of the network, computation has cycled, from distributed on the desktop to concentrated in one centralized location. Peer production systems are at the decentralized end of the continuum. P2P systems utilize the processing power or data storage capacities at the end points of the Internet.

The fundamental basis of P2P is cooperation. Therefore P2P systems require trust, and are an excellent example of reputation. P2P systems also require some level of social trust, because the Recording Industry Association of America has a policy of policing unlicensed music downloading through lawsuits.

P2P systems are fundamentally about sharing resources. Cooperation is required to share any resource, whether it is two children splitting chocolate cake or two million people sharing files. Peer production through P2P therefore requires some degree of trust and security.

P2P systems are powerful because they are able to leverage computers that are not consistently identified by domain name or IP address; and are not always connected to the network. Peer production can leverage machines that have highly variable processing power, and are not designed to have particular server capabilities other than that provided by the peering network. The systems are built to withstand high uncertainty and therefore can accept contributions from anyone with even a modem.

After considering the generic issues of P2P systems, specific systems are described: Napster, SETI @home, Gnutella, Freenet, Publius, Kazaa and Free Haven. Limewire and Morpheus are implementations of Gnutella. These specific systems are used to illustrate problems of coordination and trust. Coordination includes naming and searching. Trust includes security, privacy, and accountability. [28]

These systems provide different examples of accountability through identity or credential management. The range of systems includes both the centralized and the decentralized. Some carefully authenticate results (e.g., SETI @home) and others weakly authenticate. All have dedicated reputation systems; which are not portable between systems.

Functions and Authentication in P2P Systems

The essence of P2P systems is the coordination of those with fewer, uncertain resources. Enabling any party to contribute means removing requirements for bandwidth and domain name consistency. The relaxation of these requirements for contributors increases the pool of possible contributors by orders of magnitude. In previous systems sharing was enabled by the certainty provided by technical expertise of the user (in science) or administrative support and control (in the corporation). P2P software makes end-user cooperation feasible for all by simplification of the user interface.

PCs have gained power dramatically, yet most of that power remains unused. While any state of the art PC purchased in the last five years has the power to be a web server, few have the software installed. Despite the affordable migration to the desktop, there has remained a critical need to provide coordinated repositories of services and information.

Peer production is a decentralized model of processing and resource sharing. Peer production mechanisms provide different functions, and each function requires its own type of authentication. The series of examples that follow connect the function of the peer production system with the associated enabling authentication and identification. The systems vary from centralized and strong to weak and decentralized. All the systems use unique dedicated reputation mechanisms, tailored to the specific function of the system.

There are three fundamental resources on the network: processing power, storage capacity, and communications capacity. All of these are shared without centralized authentication and policing. In fact, resources are shared despite centralized resources focusing on the prevention of resource (e.g., music and video) sharing. All of these require some sort of trust, and thus some authentication. However, the authentication may be of results, reputation of a particular computer, or reliability of a node. P2P systems rarely depend upon identity. Yet these systems manage to perform all the functions expected of the networked system.

Peer production systems function to share processing power and storage capacity. Different systems address communications capacity in different ways, but each attempts to connect a request and a resource in the most efficient manner possible.

There are systems to allow end users to share files and to share processing power. Yet none of these systems has spread as effectively as have peer production systems. All of these systems solve the same problems as P2P systems: naming, coordination, and trust.

P2P systems created reputation-based widely distributed mechanisms for peer production. Reputation, in this domain, is broadly construed.

Mass Storage

As the sheer amount of digitized information increases, the need for distributed storage and search increases as well. Some P2P systems enable sharing of material on distributed machines. These systems include Kazaa, Publius, Free Haven, and Gnutella. (Limewire and Morpheus are Gnutella clients.)

The Web enables publication and sharing of disk space. The design goal of the web was to enable sharing of documents across platforms and machines within the high-energy physics community. When accessing a web page a user requests material on the server. The Web enables sharing, but does not implement searching and depends on DNS for naming. As originally designed the Web was a P2P technology. The creation of the browser at the University of Illinois Urbana-Champaign opened the Web to millions by providing an easy to use graphical interface. Yet the dependence of the Web on the DNS prevents the majority of users from publishing on the web. Note the distinction between the name space, the structure, and the server as constraints.

The design of the hypertext transport protocol does not prevent publication by an average user. The server software is not particularly complex. If in fact, the server software is built into Macintosh OS X. The constraints from the DNS prevent widespread publication on the Web. Despite the limits on the namespace, the Web is the most powerful mechanism used today for sharing content. The Web allows users to share files of arbitrary types using arbitrary protocols. Napster enabled the sharing of music. Morpheus enables the sharing of files without constraining the size. Yet neither of these allows the introduction of a new protocol in the manner of http.

The Web was built in response to the failures of distributed file systems. Distributed file systems include the network file system, the Andrew file system, and are related to groupware. Lotus Notes is an example of popular groupware. Each of these systems shares the same critical difficulty — administrative coordination is required.

Massively Parallel Computing

In addition to sharing storage P2P systems can also share processing power. Examples of systems that share processing power are Kazaa and SETI @home. Despite the difference in platform, organization, and security, the naming and organization questions are similar in clustered and peering systems.

There are mechanisms to share processing power other than P2P systems. Such systems run only on Unix variants, depend on domain names, or are designed for use only within a single administrative domain. Meta-computing and clustering are two approaches to sharing processing power. Clustering and meta-computing systems, in general, rely on centralized mechanisms for authentication.

Examples of Community-Centric Systems

In this section the general principles described above are discussed with respect to each system. For each system the discussion of design goals, and organization (including centralization) are discussed. Mechanisms for trust and accountability in each system are described.

Given the existence of a central server there are some categorizations that place SETI @home and Napster outside of the set of P2P systems. They are included here for two reasons. First for theoretical reasons, both of theses systems are P2P in that they have their own name spaces and utilize heterogeneous systems across administrative domains in cooperative resource sharing. Second, any definition that is so constrained as to reject the two systems that essentially began the peer production revolution may be theoretically interesting but is clearly flawed.

P2P systems are characterized by utilization of desktop machines characterized by a lack of domain names, intermittent connectivity, variable connection speeds, and possibly even variable connection points (for laptops, or users with back-up ISPs).

Napster

Napster began as a protocol, evolved to a web site, became a business with an advertising-driven value of millions, and is now a wholly owned subsidy of Bertelsmann Entertainment. Yet the initial design goal was neither to challenge copyright law nor create a business. The original goal was to enable fans to swap music in an organized manner. Before Napster there were many web sites, ftp sites and chat areas devoted to locating and exchanging music files in the MPEG3 format, yet Napster simplified the location and sharing processes. The goal of Napster was to allow anyone to offer files to others. Thus the clients were servers, and therefore Napster became the first widely known P2P system.

Before Napster sharing music required a server. This required a domain name, and specialized file transfer software or streaming software. The Napster client also allowed users to become servers, and thus peers. The central Napster site coordinated the peers by providing a basic string matching search and the file location. As peers connected Napster to search, the peers also identified the set of songs available for download.

After Napster the client software was installed on the peer machine and contacted napster.com, Napster the protocol then assigned a name to the machine. As the peer began to collect files it might connect from different domains and different IP addresses. Yet whether the machine was connected at home or at work Napster could recognize the machine by its Napster moniker.

Thus Napster solved the search problem by centralization, and the problem of naming by assignment of names distinct from domain names. Napster provided a list of the set of music available at each peer, and a mechanism for introduction in order to initiate file sharing.

When a peer sought to find a file, the peer first searched the list of machines likely to have the file at the central Napster archive. Then the requesting peer selects the most desirable providing peer, based on location, reputation, or some other dimension. The connection for obtaining the file was made from the requesting peer to the providing peer, with no further interaction with the central server. After the initial connection the peer downloads the connection from the chosen source. The chosen source by default also provides a listing of other songs selected by that source.

Accountability issues in Napster are fairly simple. Napster provided a trusted source for the client; therefore downloading the client is not an issue of trust. Of course, the Napster web site itself must be secure. Napster has been subject to attacks by people uploading garbage files but not by people upload malicious files.

In terms of trust, each user downloads from another peer who is part of the same fan community. Grateful Dead fans share music, as do followers of the Dave Matthews Band. Each group of fans shared music within their communities. It is reasonable to assert that Napster was a set of musical communities, as opposed to a single community of users.

Not only did Napster make sharing of ripped files common; it also created a mechanism for implicitly rating music. Obscure bands that were next to popular materials may be downloaded, heard, and thus advertised when these tunes would not rate radio play. Niches and subcultures could more effectively identify and share preferences, with members self-identifying by the music they choose to share.

Reputation in Napster was based on the number, perceived desirability, and availability of music. Like being a good neighbor, reputation was implicit but observable. Yet this weak reputation system initiated a fundamental change in the nature of the music business.

The success of Napster illustrates that even a weak reputation-based credential system can be powerful. Napster's reputation system is an example of weakly authenticated, centralized, and dedicated credentialing information.

Facebook

Facebook is a social networking site, initiated at Harvard and then available to other campuses. Facebook indicates to those who sign up that they are on a campus-like space. Facebook presents, for example, people at Indiana with an Indiana-themed space.

Facebook makes money by harvesting peer-produced information. The flaw of Facebook is that the authentication mechanisms are weak. Specifically, the authentication of the core Facebook credential (association with a university) is weak.

Facebook has a series of privacy-sensitive default questions for its configuration.

The first four questions are relationship status, standards for dating if you are single, gender and sexual orientation. The next information you are invited to fill out includes your religion. Religion may include a large selection of Christian denominations or simply Jewish according to the definitions provided by the Facebook pop-up. After this you are requested to identify the political candidates you sup-

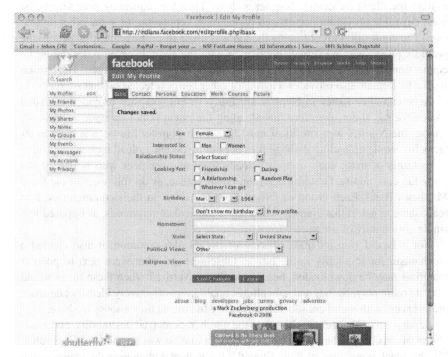

Fig. 9.4 Facebook Basic Information

port. Increasingly political candidates themselves have Facebook sites in order to identify and connect with a base of supporters on campuses. These are centralized, unauthenticated, self-asserted credentials.

Notice that this information is distinguished from other, personal information. Facebook identifies this as basic information, as if these attributes were the ones most often shared. Facebook creates a space where the attributes most often discussed are those not socially acceptable to ask. For religion, politics, and martial status, the basic identity attributes are also exactly those that cannot be determined in a job interview. However, this information is readily available to other Facebook subscribers.

Facebook information is widely available. Anyone with an email address in an .edu domain can obtain a Facebook account. This means that alumni of a university can view Facebook. Also, anyone who is attending any university in any capacity, including retirees at extension schools and hobbyists taking specialized coursework, can obtain a Facebook account. In fact, there are many university email addresses that are public — for example announcement addresses. It is possible to register with Facebook using one of those addresses, and thus registers anonymously. These weakly authenticated credentials in this imaginary world can have real world impacts.

Facebook uses a social networking mechanism to allow individuals to assert connectivity in a community and also relative placement in the social hierarchy. Social networking forms the Facebook reputation system. Those with more "friends" are seen as having more social capital than those with fewer friends. Those active in online groups and with many tagged pictures are perceived as having a higher status. Thus the individuals who join and utilize Facebook perceive that there is a functioning reputation system. However, that reputation system does not provide an additional authority or abilities. The reputation system in Facebook is not used to authenticate identifiers or credentials.

MySpace

MySpace is a centralized corporate system that nonetheless utilizes peer production. The genius of MySpace is that is made peer production easy. The critical flaw is that this peer production uses indirect and weak reputation mechanisms. While MySpace is similar to Facebook, MySpace is more targeted towards high school and middle school students. Facebook targets college students. MySpace indicates when logging on that it is a space for you and your friends.

Unlike Napster, which authenticated only musical taste via tunes offered for download, MySpace and Facebook do appear to be authenticating identity. However, both are based on self-asserted credentials and identification.

In 2006, a reporter for Wired searched MySpace using the databases of registered sexual offenders. He located nearly five hundred identified sexual offenders with MySpace pages. In one case, the offender had multiple links to fourteen-year-old MySpace participants and a space filled with sexual chat. Before Wired ran the article, this particular offender was arrested based on a sting operation. The response by MySpace was to request that the Federal Government require that every sexual offender have a registered email address.

MySpace would then bear no cost, and no liability. By calling for a government identity system, MySpace is seeking to externalize the cost of risk mitigation. MySpace seeks to transfer the costs to limiting the risk to government, and thus to us all. Notice that MySpace could have implemented exactly the same search as the Wired reporter, but choose not to. MySpace could use its own reputation system and examine behavior to develop a stronger mechanism for preventing the use of its systems by sexual predators. Instead, MySpace would create a system where first sexual offenders, and perhaps eventually everyone, would have to register an email address. This is a classic example of the economics of identity. A centralized identity system paid for by an entity other than MySpace, creating privacy risks for all, would be optimal in terms of MySpace profit.

The current information in MySpace's reputation system can be used to approach the particular threat of sexual predation. However, that reputation system would cost money. It would be isolated to MySpace, so it would not be a very useful reputation system to subvert. Therefore individuals would have little incentive to subvert the system; and the credentials would be of little use for committing identity fraud. MySpace's political call to create special registered addresses for sex offenders creates risks for others and is not as potent as a targeted system. However, the MySpace proposal would reduce risk and responsibility from MySpace.

It would be expensive for MySpace to police its users. Any policing system would have false positives and false negatives. To the extent that all successful detection of predators were published, MySpace would be safer but it may be perceived as more dangerous.

eBay

eBay is a reputation system that is worth real money. As such eBay has been subject to repeated attacks. Some of those things that consumers might consider attacks are not malicious by the standards of eBay and its sellers. [33]

eBay has a reputation system that provides unreliably glowing recommendations to eBay merchants. In fact, many customers of eBay are unhappy with some element of the purchase. Telephone surveys of eBay customers have found discontent and disappointment to be as high as thirty percent. Yet the eBay reputation system indicates only a few disappointed customers. This is because the eBay reputation mechanism is designed to reflect well upon eBay and the merchants. It is organized to enforce positive recommendations and acceptance of unreasonable shipping terms on customers. Claims of quality are often misleading. [101]

eBay is an auction house. After a merchant offers a good for sale, a buyer bids. The winning bidder agrees to purchase the item for a specific amount. The merchant then adds an unconstrained amount for shipping and handling. If the shipping and handling is excessive the buyer has a limited right to withdraw the bid. Mutually agreed upon withdrawal does not constrain the buyer. However, few merchants will agree that their shipping and handling is excessive. For low-value transactions the shipping and handling is often a multiple of the amount of purchase. Buyers are limited in the number of bids that they are allowed to withdraw, and excessive shipping and handling is not one of the accepted reasons for withdrawal.

Search for Intelligent Life in the Universe

SETI @home distributes radio signals from the deep space telescope to home users so that they might assist in the search for intelligent life. The Arecibo telescope sweeps the sky collecting 35Gbyte of data per day. SETI @home is a supercomputer built from potentially untrustworthy peers. SETI @home created a reputation system with each machine rather than each individual having an identifier. [16]

While other examples of peer production in this chapter are analogous to customers rating a merchant; SETI @home is analogous to a merchant evaluating customers. In terms of its use as a reputation system, SETI @home is more similar to eBay than Napster. The reputation system is of course dedicated; but it indicates cumulative ratings of past behavior.

To take part in this search, each user first downloads the software for home machine use. After the download the user contacts the SETI @home central server to register as a user and obtain data for analysis. Constantly connected PCs and rarely connected machines can both participate.

There are other projects that search for intelligent life via electromagnetic signals. Other programs are limited by the available computing power. SETI @home allows users to change the nature of the search, enabling examination of data for the weakest signals.

SETI @home is indeed centralized. There are two core elements of the project — the space telescope at Arecibo and the network of machines. Each user is allocated data and implements analysis using the SETI software. After the analysis the user also receives credit for having contributed to the project.

SETI tackles the problem of dynamic naming by giving each machine a time to connect, and a place to connect. The current IP address of the peer participant is recorded in the coordinating database.

SETI @home is P2P because it utilizes the processing power of many desktops, and uses its own naming scheme in order to do so. The amount of data examined by SETI @home is stunning, and far exceeds the processing capacity of any system when the analysis is done on dedicated machines. SETI is running 25% faster in terms of floating point operations per second at 0.4% of the cost than the supercom-

---

[16] In July 2002 there were updates to the SETI software in Bulgarian, Farsi and Hebrew. For four years the Iranians and Israelis have been cooperating in the Search for Intelligent Life in the universe. There has been no conflict between the peoples of those nations, at least in this domain. It helps that this is a highly specialized endeavor which requires no trust. It requires no shared trust because of the distribution of the processes.

puter at Sandia National Laboratories. (The cost ratio is .0004). SETI @home has been downloaded to more than 100 countries.

The software performs Fourier transforms — a transformation of frequency data into time data. The reason time data are interesting is that a long constant signal is not expected to be part of the background noise created by the various forces of the universe. So finding a signal that is interesting in the time domain is indicative of intelligent life.

The client software can be downloaded only from SETI @home in order to make certain that the scientific integrity of code is maintained. If different assumptions or granularity are used in different Fourier analyses, the results cannot be reliably compared with other result using original assumptions. Thus even apparently helpful changes to the code may not, in fact, be an improvement.

SETI @home provides trustworthy processing by sending out data to different machines. This addresses both machine failures and malicious attacks. SETI @home has already seen individuals altering data to create false positives. SETI @home sends data to at least two distinct machines, randomly chosen, and compares the results. Given the number of machines this is difficult. Note that this cuts the effective processing rate in half, yielding a cost/processing ratio of 0.002 as opposed to a 0.004. However, the cost per processing operation remains three orders of magnitude lower for SETI @home than for a supercomputer.

SETI @home strongly authenticates the results of processing. SETI @home weakly authenticates the machines, enough to enable strong authentication of results.

SETI @home has also had to digitally sign results to ensure that participants do not send in results multiple times for credit within the SETI @home accounting system. (Since there is no material reward for having a high rating the existence of cheating of this type came as a surprise to the organizers.) SETI @home can provide a monotonically increasing reputation because the reputation is the reward for participation. In addition to having contributions listed from an individual or a group, SETI @home lists those who find any promising anomalies by name.

Cooperative, weakly authenticated resource sharing is being used to create the largest, cheapest super computer on the planet. SETI does not depend upon identity verification, but rather results verification. SETI @home moves beyond attribute authentication to validate the results, without requiring any other cooperative information. By having a centralized reputation and results authentication mechanism, SETI @home has created a trustworthy supercomputer out of many untrustworthy machines.

Ubiquitous Anonymity: Your Credentials Please

Under this scenario the tools of crypto-anarchy serve the ends of business and e-government. The most effective tools for ensuring anonymity are linked with particular assertions, for example, the assertion of veteran status. Yet financial transactions and information requests can be made entirely anonymously.

Universal National identifier

The idea of a national identifier gained popularity in the United States in the wake of 9/11. The adoption of Real ID makes the construction of national ID as shown in this scenario quite likely, as national identifier program is moving forward through the coordination of the fifty state drivers licenses' authorities. A similar implementation can be seen in some identity management systems, which concentrate all data in a single account. Currently the Social Security Number is widely used as an identifier. This scenario is the equivalent of a single universally recognized "credential."

Sets of Attributes

In this scenario, instead of having only one credential, each person has a set of identifiers stored in secure hardware or in a series of devices. If the single credential is analogous to a signature, then the set of attributes is analogous to the key ring. In this case, the multiple PKIs and devices will have some limited interoperability and potentially complex risk cascading issues. This scenario draws heavily on reputation technologies.

Ubiquitous Identity Theft

This is a world where the information used to prove identity over distance — Social Security Numbers, address, zip code, credit card numbers — are all readily available to identity theft. Driven by the extreme criminalization of sharing copyrighted information, this scenario envisions a future in which identity swapping over the Internet becomes as common as file swapping is today.

Chapter 10
Identity Scenarios

Scenario I: Your Credentials Please

Paul Syverson

Introduction

Under this scenario the tools of anonymity serve the ends of business and e-government. Service providers can only link transactions to identifiers of individuals when needed for a specific service. These identifiers generally are not linkable to each other: They are service-specific. Most transactions are authorized without the need for even these identifiers by means of anonymous credentials. For example, a person can show that she is authorized for a service as a county resident, or as a veteran, or as disabled, or as having some combination of these without needing to identify herself.

Remote access to services is made over anonymity preserving infrastructures, such as onion routing [56]. Face-to-face transactions are comparable to cash transactions, except that they may be accompanied by some authenticator, for example, presenting a token, knowing a secret, having a personal physical property (biometric), or combinations of these.

The State of Identity

There are many kinds of transactions that can be made more private and anonymous. Most obvious of these are credit transactions. Consider the largest credit transaction that most of us will make in our lives, the purchase of a home.

John buys a house.

John is 30 years old, single, and wants to buy a house. In applying for a mortgage, he presents certificates showing that the same employer has employed him for the last five years. His income has been at least $50,000.00 per year during his employment. He has been renting for the past three years and paying (on time) $1,000.00 per month in rent. No third party can link these facts to each other. However, he can prove that these certificates are all held by the same person and can prove that he is that person. The verifier to whom he has demonstrated that proof can show that he has received such a proof, but cannot reproduce the proof by himself without John's cooperation. Thus, the verifier can show to a third party (such as an auditor) that he has adequately checked John's credentials. Nonetheless, he is not able to take those credentials he has been shown and reproduce the proof itself (so cannot try to pass as John or get credit for John's properties). [36, 24, 27]

Unfortunately, John has a twin brother who is not as productive a citizen as John. His name is Jim. Jim is no stranger to the court system and in fact has outstanding criminal default warrants against him for not appearing in court. The last time that Jim was arrested he used John's name and social security number because he knew that he was in default and that John had no criminal record. If the local court processed Jim under John's name, he could skip out and John would be left holding the bag.

John has faithfully filed his tax returns for the past five years. This year, as in the past, he is entitled to a state and federal refund. John's state has a law that authorizes the state's department of revenue to hold state tax refunds for scofflaws, those with child support arrearages, and those with outstanding criminal default warrants.

In an earlier decade, Jim's act of unspeakable brotherly love would have succeeded: the court would have issued a default warrant in John's name. When John's bank did a routine credit check on him, the State's lien against his tax refund would pop up. When John went to the local court to clear the matter up, he would be arrested as Jim. The local court would have an imaged picture of Jim on file. Since Jim and John are twins, the imaged photograph of Jim looks like John. John would then be held without bail on the default warrants.

Fortunately John is living in a more enlightened age. As the technology to allow anonymous transactions became more pervasive, society came to realize that authentication is important. Neither the courts nor credit agencies will now respect the sloppy identifiers of an earlier age that could let someone else pass responsibility on to an innocent victim. If John had been living in the first years of the twenty first century, there is a chance that he would have both a credit problem and a criminal record that would lead to his arrest on many occasions, despite carrying documents at all times from his district attorney explaining his circumstances [170, 180].

Instead, Jim's attempt to claim that he is John is caught by his failure to properly authenticate that he is John. More significantly, the laws and incentive structures have been formed so that any future risk stemming from incorrectly associating John with this arrest would not be his, but be born by those elements responsible for the misidentification, such as the credit reporting agencies. Indeed, in this future scenario the restructuring of law and regulation to more properly assign costs will have been as much responsible for the increased attempt to authenticate correctly and assign culpability accordingly as will be the technology that made it possible. [173, 181]

Notice that much of the public value of the information is maintained with this scenario. It is still possible to look at the prices of local houses before you buy your own. All the information on property value is readily available here, as it is today. However, the property listings are not longer indexed by ownership.

Fred gets arrested for speeding.

Fred speeds towards Cape Cod and gets stopped by a police officer. The officer checks the history of the car license on the Automobile Police Registry (APR). The register shows the car has not been reported stolen, taken part in any violent crime, or committed unlawful pass on highway tolls. The APR shows information on all types of events linked to the car's current license and that the license is currently attached to the VIN of the car that was stopped, but no information about the car's (current or former) owner. In this scenario, information about EzPass-type mechanisms are linked to the car, and not its owner. (See [30] for anonymous payment methods.) Any time a person buys a new car, he or she must jointly include the EzPass serial number in the registration of the new car, which gets later updated at the company's database. Additionally, information on the APR cannot be shared with any third party (public or private).

Once the car has been cleared, the officer asks for Fred's driving license and registration. An online check by the arresting officer reveals he has a valid driving license. The driving license is issued by a State agency and provides links to defined biometric characteristics of the license holder, but it does not link to his identifiers in form of name or social security number1. Similarly, Fred is able to show that he is the current registration holder for the car without linking explicitly to other identifiers. There is uniformity of license issuing mechanisms across states. The combination of biometric indicators used in issuing driving licenses cannot be recorded, asked, employed by, or shared to any other public or private entity other than similar driver's database of another state.

Once the validity of the driving license has been assured, the officer checks on the criminal record database for any information associated with that license (speeding, crashes, driving under the influence, etc.). While there is no mention of the identity of the license holder, there is a recorded history about previous incidents by each class. In the case of speeding, Fred's record shows an entry for the same highway two years ago, of speeding at 80 miles/hour. Today's arrest is included on his record, setting up a warning on it so the license gets yanked if he is caught in one additional speeding infraction. If the police vehicle is offline at the time of the new entry, the record gets queued and gets submitted automatically when online again.

If a person wants to renew a license in the same state, the only changes made are regarding the expiration period and update of biometric indicators. If the person moves to another state, the totality or part of his or her old registry gets downloaded to the new state's database. The difference between the totality or part of the driver's history is made by the differences between legal frameworks of both the old and new state regarding (a) confidentiality of information, and (b) validity and prescription of acts done in places outside the state.

In this scenario, issuing of a driver's license involves a biometric check that no other state has a currently issued driving license to someone with that biometric. However, states' records indicate only whether a license exists and if so what number. This may be checked for redundant assurance at the time of an arrest if the system is online. Otherwise, the relevant data can be briefly stored for check at a later time. Inconsistencies trigger further response. Issuance of new licenses may include transferring a previous driving record to the new license, canceling a previous license after additional checks that there are no errors about the bearer of the license, etc.

The provision of responsibility and allocation of risk are the critical factors that make this possible. The technologies necessary to make this scenario a reality already exist.

The Path to Today

One available mechanism for anonymity is simply lying about identity, or using shared credentials. For example, bugmenot.com is a web site that provides to those who would rather not be tracked by what they read in the paper shared login identifiers for major news entities and other popular sites. As Bob Blakley has so eloquently put it, "Privacy is the ability to lie about yourself and get away with it." This does not imply a right to lie, but if you can lie about some aspect of yourself and get away with it, then that aspect is effectively private.

Anonymity in the past was also provided to a limited degree because of the lack of ability to link databases with a single identifier. Information was effectively in silos in most cases. Because databases were not linked to each other, there was generally not a way to view all information in a single format. Up until recently, laws concerning privacy and information ownership have been less of an issue because there are bureaucratic and technological hurdles that have limited privacy violations or even enable anonymity.

Payment represents an example of how technology affects anonymity. Thirty years ago, if I wanted to buy a book I would generally walk into a store and pay in cash for that book. The bookstore would know that someone had bought the book, but they would not have the identity of that person, or be able to sell the person's name and preferences. Even if they did keep track of regular customers who willingly gave shipping addresses or gave a phone number to be notified when a book came in, this would be kept locally and in a paper index file. Twenty years ago, I would walk into the store and buy that book with a credit card. The bookstore would know that the book had been purchased, but by keeping track of the credit card numbers, they could also track all the books that I bought and do profiling. Similarly, the credit card company would also know that I had bought a book (or likely had, as the charge had come from a bookstore). Beginning about ten years ago, if I wanted to purchase a book from Amazon, I would create an account to do so. Amazon would know both the books I bought and the information about me: credit card, mailing address, email address, etc. In addition, they kept track of other addresses to which I shipped so they would know who my friends and relations were too, unless I took the precaution and inconvenience of shipping everything to myself first.

Amazon knows who I am, because I give up that anonymity for convenience, so they know both the books (and now toys and electronics and clothes...) that I buy and identifiers and other information about me. They have created a single view of two kinds of information about me that had been separate. Previously my anonymity was protected by the division of two pieces of information: my identity and the kinds of things I buy (and for whom, and when, and...). Now, by contrast, a single business has all that information in a single database. One person can easily access a list of all of the books that I have bought, and know quite a lot about my interests, my relations, not just an anonymous number. If in ten or twenty years all of the physical bookstores go away, or cash is no longer accepted at all, then it will become impossible to conveniently and simply make an anonymous purchase of a book.

There are online book merchants that do not require an account to make a purchase. And one can easily make purchases online using single-use credit card numbers—even at Amazon, as I can attest from the many expired numbers it tracks and shows me whenever I make a purchase. While this somewhat reduces my financial risk from exposure of my credit card to the merchant, all other information about me is known, and arranging payment and shipping without revealing significant information about me would be difficult at best. iPrivacy was a company begun at the turn of the millennium that attempted to provide privacy of purchase through the entire process from order, through payment, and even to delivery. iPrivacy was designed to proxy selection, purchase and payment through their system and to use PO boxes for delivery. The consumer still had to largely trust iPrivacy with his personal information and centralized otherwise-separate purchase information at iPrivacy, but it gave the consumer a relatively simple and straightforward means to be anonymous to online merchants in a practical sense. Today, iPrivacy is gone without ever having significant deployment. We can only speculate as to why. They may have failed for any number of reasons not specific to the service they offered. Or it may be that consumers do not pay for privacy unless they can recognize its impact personally and immediately [173].

The Technology and Policies

Laws creating barriers of anonymity are becoming necessary because advances in technology are removing the old barriers of anonymity. Information was too hard to cross-reference in order to violate anonymity. With technology making violations of anonymity ubiquitous, policies are necessary to prevent what the lack of interoperability used to prevent.

Fifty years ago, you went to one doctor and that doctor knew all of your medical issues. Now, people change jobs, insurance companies, etc. with frequency, and their information has to be available for payment as well as treatment. HIPA was instituted in large part because of the vast amounts of information that health care companies hold, but more because of the ease of access and the large number of people with that access. Fifty years ago your family doctor knew all of the same health information that Blue Cross knows now. Additionally, your family doctor knew your identity, as much as Blue Cross does. The new policies become necessary because the information is no longer trusted to a single doctor and receptionist. Given the vast health consortia, information about individuals and their health history is technologically available to far more people than one person could trust (or even know).

Policies need not dictate the handling of personal data per se to have an effect. Laws that first appeared in California and are now being imitated throughout the US require the disclosure of security breaches at a company if personally identifiable information may have been exposed. One impact has been to make privacy risk increasingly visible, widely recognized, and personal as thousands of people are notified after each exposure, and as the media plaster the names of offending companies across the headlines. It may be that iPrivacy was simply ahead of its time. Companies are given a public relations incentive to be more careful with sharing data, more aware of what data they have where and how it is protected, and possibly even what data they bother to collect and store. We cannot yet know whether this will have a significant lasting affect on companies or whether the frequency and size of these breaches will lead to fatalistic complacency.

Closing

This chapter has looked briefly at where anonymity and privacy are today and how they got there. Primarily we have sketched some scenarios of what is possible in a future world where identifiers are generally not needed to make purchases or interact with government service providers and authorities. Communication and transactional infrastructures are anonymous. This reduces the risk both of privacy and of liability for managing information. If an identifier is required for a transaction it typically need only be pseudonymous, and more importantly, should only come into play someplace removed from the point of transaction. The trend toward trusting every store clerk or online customer-service representative with complete information about you is curtailed. There can still be picture IDs and biometrics that show a person is the owner of a token, and the token can be used in authorizations and the tracking of reputation in various ways. What does not have to happen in this future world is that the "ID" tell the provider of a service who the recipient is.

Scenario II: Universal National Identifier

Allan Friedman

Introduction

Fears of terror, the promise of efficiency, and the potential for commercial gain make the prospect of using a single identifier look very attractive. Some believe that every individual in the United States should have a single, unique identifier that is bound to their person by the strength of law, a carefully constructed infrastructure and a robust biometric. The adoption of the Real ID Act and the requirements for RFID in passports indicate a perception of policymakers that identities are too fluid and uncertain.

While expensive and difficult to implement, a universal identifier makes control of personal information much easier, both for governments wishing to provide services and protect citizens, and potentially the individuals themselves trying to control their personal information. But, others note (source) the implementation of a single, unique identifier can also generate dangers for a democratic society including blows to privacy, the erosion of civil liberties, and the strengthening of a central government.

The State of Identity

In the Age of Information, it makes sense to have identifiers that come closer to meeting the needs and potentials of information technology. Thus, each individual is assigned a unique, universal identification number. This aspect, while not trivial, represents only one small part of the identifier challenge; a large infrastructure is necessary to bind the individual to that identifier. This is done in three levels, with increasing security and trust in that binding at each level. This UID serves as a key to access both public and private databases, as well as, being the base for security and privacy policies in those databases.

A UID number should not be a secret, any more than a name is a secret. This was one of the great failures of the Social Security number as an identifier: it was widely employed as both an identifier and a verification mechanism. It is unlikely that a stranger will know another's name, and less likely that the stranger will know her UID number. Yet having knowledge of that number should not give the stranger any more power than having a name (and in some cases, less power). The number space should be large enough to avoid redundancy, and ideally leave space for an error bit or other administrative information, yet be small enough to allow an individual to remember the number, if he or she has been prompted for it repeatedly. Alternatively, alphabetic characters could be used to increase the space with fewer digits. This number could be used as a stand-alone for transactions that do not require any large amount of trust. A call to a technical support center, for example, just needs a key to a database so that the technician can pull up the right software specifications that an individual purchased.

Most transactions, however, require confidence in the participants. Rather than simply knowing what can essentially be treated as public knowledge, a basic level of trust could be conferred on having something. In this case, a smart card is the most likely choice, since it can hold protected information and can be signed by trusted institutions or government agencies for an added degree of security. A swipe of the card could produce an ID number, providing a basic level of verification. More importantly, a swipe could securely reveal to a concerned merchant or government official whether or not an ID holder is a member of a group. Is a consumer in the over-21 group or a traveler in the wanted-for-questioning group? A card reader can send an encrypted query to a trusted database and gain the necessary knowledge, and only the necessary knowledge. This builds a series of protections. A merchant must have appropriate permission to query the database, and each query can be tracked. The cardholder can be more confident that only the necessary information about her is drawn from remote databases, and little personal information actually has to be kept on the card itself.

To fully protect the link between identifier and individual, however, a biometric is necessary. Situations arise where a transaction party may wish to be certain that the person in possession of an ID card is actually the person identified by the card in previous transactions. Essentially, this question is seeking to determine whether the user of the card is the same person who has used the card all of the previous times. This can be asserted recursively with a biometric enrollment on issuance of the card; occasional matching of the cardholder with the biometric on file will help verify that the original individual-identifier link is still valid. This assumes that a biometric will be stable throughout the course of a lifetime; the UID drafters ultimately chose iris recognition. Biometrics are secured only occasionally, and in accordance with the risks of a mismatched identity and the necessary expenses. Obviously, the harm caused by a minor obtaining cigarettes are not on the same order of magnitude as the harm caused by a house purchased in some one else's name. It may be far too inefficient to check the biometric of every flier all the time. Since immigration and customs already performs a biometric check on entering the country (human assessment of a photo ID), a biometric scan dramatically simplified and improved the process.

The Path to Today

The path to a universal identifier was not terribly surprising. In an information age, the United States was a society with terrible information management systems. By relying on inefficient analog-world identifiers such as name or social security numbers, systematic abuse was inevitable. Police might arrest an innocent man based on a shared name with a terror suspect and knowledge of a social security number was seen as proof of identity. Integrated into massive but decentralized databases, this information was often inaccurate, and extremely hard to correct, or even verify with any degree of confidence. Even before the major crises of the beginning of the 21st century, government administrators were working to standardize and secure forms of identification.

Two major social problems focused political attention onto the problem of identification, and began to mobilize popular support for what had been the rather unpopular idea of a universal identifier: terrorism and identity theft.

Motivation: Terror and Fraud

After the tragic attacks of September 11, the United States looked around and saw itself as a society poorly equipped to defend itself against an embedded enemy willing to use suicide bombers and independent terror cells. The knee-jerk response of the Patriot Act raised alarms in countless civil libertarians' minds, but despite a period of calm, failed to prevent a second wave of smaller bombings and sabotage projects. Patriot II was hastily introduced, but its shortcomings were actively debated as a series of trade-offs that simply didn't offer adequate protection. Attacks continued on a smaller scale, striking deep into American life, in malls, sporting events and other public venues. Security experts predicted that the nation would be forced to begin approaching domestic security much like other terror-besieged countries such as Israel, and that we lacked the necessary public infrastructures to protect ourselves. Absent a comprehensive, nation-wide system of identification, the United States government would be forced to track everyone actively. With a robust ID system, it was argued, the average American would be freer of invasive surveillance and it would be harder for the bad guys to hide among the good. Politicians were interested in taking *some* major steps to show that the US government could fight domestic terrorism, and began exploring the idea of UIDs in depth.

At the same time, the criminal impersonation and fraud known as identity theft continued to grow. Lax standards in ID documents and no incentive to coordinate or improve ID verification made it easy to obtain papers "proving" that an individual was really someone else. The increasing number of digital transactions even began to make that step irrelevant, as just a few pieces of information were all one needed to remotely obtain credit, make purchases or even commit crimes in some one else's name. Insecure commercial databases were raided for this express purpose. Too soon, however, what was a crime that one individual committed using the personal information of a handful of helpless victims grew into massive fraud schemes run by organized criminals with vast resources. ID fraud grew by 100% in 2002 and cost an estimated $2.5 billion. Over the next few years, increased criminal activity and more sophisticated exploits caused the problem to grow by an order of magnitude. The financial industry and merchants simply could not continue to absorb these losses. The final blow to the system was a series of lawsuits that finally recognized that the fraud hurt not only financial institutions but also the individuals whose lives were significantly and adversely affected as they found themselves unable to erase the mistake from the myriad of information stockpiles. These decisions identified financial and information institutions who could be targeted for civil suits seeking damages and compensation as vehicles of fraud through negligence, even if they had lost money themselves.

Early Efforts

The initial response to many of these issues was to shore up the current system. The Patriot Act mandated minimum standards of identity verification, but these in turn rested on government-issued ID and flawed data collections. A few pieces of information or illegally obtained papers could be used to obtain legitimate proofs of ID. The process of authentication simply didn't have a source of trust. The same problem existed for a harder-to forge driver's license or a "trusted traveler" program: it was fairly easy to break, and once broken, it was very hard to identify the security breach.

Private sector attempts to normalize their databases also met little success. Credit agencies fought with banks, while the myriad of stakeholders, including insurance firms, hospitals and merchants, all attempted to influence the system to their own advantage whilst shifting liability onto other actors. Even steps as simple as altering the consumer credit system produced attempts to change the business model in the status quo or lock-in proprietary standards and produced long court battles. Privacy advocates saw little good that would come out of an ID system designed to meet the needs of private business and opposed almost all proposals. It looked like the only solution would be a massive nation-wide ID system.

A National ID System

The first consensus was that biometrics had to be involved. A short search yielded the iris scan as the most desirable option. It had the best error rates of anything so far tested and further examination bore this out. It was simple to use, and incredibly difficult to directly deceive. Moreover, it had properties appealing to privacy advocates, who started to recognize that a UID was going to move forward, and wanted a seat at the design table. Iris images are difficult to obtain clandestinely or against the will of the subject: it would be much harder to use this for mass public surveillance. The public however, was not very comfortable—especially at first—with using the eyes as identification. Despite the relatively unobtrusive measurement abilities (one meter, minimal light requirements) there is a general sensitivity to having one's eyes "scanned." This, activists hoped, would limit the number of biometric measurements taken.

Bringing privacy advocates into the design process early was a very sage move from the directors of the program. The Attorney General placed the project under the direction of the Department of Justice, but knew that a larger, more neutral ground was needed for administration, so she tapped the Office of Management and Budget and the General Accounting Office to oversee the development coalition. In addition to bringing in a wide array of e-government experts and technologists, the development team sought insight from a range of private industry experts. The understanding from Day 1 was that this UID would serve both public and private roles, and the public and private sector would need to supervise each other within the constraints of data protection legislation. Privacy activists were brought on board to help increase legitimacy and improve public support for the project.

A major concession the privacy community won was the adoption of a data protection regime. Despite continued resistance to the implementation of data protection legislation for some time, citing the Privacy Act 1976 as sufficient protection, it was finally conceded that much had changed in the ability of organizations to access and disseminate private information since then. In 1976, personal computers were not widespread, the Internet was not invented and the processing power of computers was nothing like as great as it is now. All these issues pointed towards the Privacy Act no longer being sufficient to protect citizens. The PATRIOT Act and the Military Commissions Act have supplanted the Privacy Act. The Privacy Act remains the single most coherent statement of privacy goals, even if these have been temporarily put aside in the name of terror.

Modeled after the EU Directive and the UK's Data Protection Act 1998, this system ensured that whilst a single identifier would be used to create complete information profiles, individuals would be able to ensure that this information was only used for reasons made explicit by the holders of that information. In this way, all parties were protected, the individual is protected from abuse of their information, and organizations were protected from lawsuits by gaining prior permission from the data subject.

In addition, the holders of personal information were also protected against the devastating lawsuits that continued to emerge from victims of identity theft. In some cases, ongoing class action suits were even settled out of federal coffers, to ensure the support of a few peak associations. A federal guarantee system was set up to cover losses directly attributed to failures in the ID system. In addition to helping secure industry support, it was believed that this provision would require stringent enforcement mechanisms. Commercial interests already operating ethically discovered that there was little that needed to change in their business practices to comply with the legislation and yet discovered that international trade particularly with the EU was considerably enhanced by the introduction of data protection legislation.

Politically, the coalition building was a great success. This success in turn furthered the project, since the sunk costs of actual and political capital investment propelled politicians and private sector firms alike into continuing to pursue the goal of a robust UID.

Phase-in

One of the most difficult aspects of the program was the society-wide adoption. Several test programs were successful, if a bit hasty. The first nationwide attempt to enroll all federal employees highlighted a few key problems, such as hardware incompatibility and coping with disabilities. However, the detection of several major cases of fraud among Medicare administrators and the capture of a highly-placed intelligence mole were hailed successes attributable to the system, so general population enrollment went forward.

A conveniently timed wave of tragic attacks increased America's patience with the inconvenience of enrolling. The few stories of Midwestern grandmothers being unable to prove who they were made national press, but were countered with examples of how several terror attacks might have been prevented. A 5 year time line was established, with a sixth "grace year" to accommodate latecomers. Meanwhile, biometric readings were integrated into both the child-immunization and immigration processes and a new generation of Americans came into this country already identifiable. Local officials received federal grants to aid with enrollment record verification; over 20 people were jailed or deported for attempting to obtain fraudulent breeder documents under the new system, with an undetermined number successfully enrolling in the new system using illegal documents or assumed identity. At the late stage of ID rollout, administrators began to pepper their speeches with phrases like "no system is perfect" and "mistakes will be made". This created a call for the administration to admit its mistakes gracefully but without having to concede to liability or compensation. Opinion polls showed that most Americans understood that the system would not eliminate terrorism, but the majority felt it would go far in fighting terror and crime. Based on these polls and recent attacks, few politicians were willing to take a stand against the UID as it began to be implemented.

From the services side, government offices were the first to be equipped with card readers and biometric scanners, since they were also the first enrolled in the system. Again, bugs were ironed out in this initial national introduction phase: banks soon followed as secure sites for biometric readers while security issues were ironed out. The private sector's desire for a successful program helped head off a few disasters, and delayed over-eager administrators from prematurely implementing key aspects of the system. Finally, more general institutions like hospitals and liquor stores began installing card readers and the occasional iris scanner. The American people remained on the whole a little skittish about use of biometric identification, and cash purchases increased somewhat.

As noted below, digital cash plans, unpopular in the age of ubiquitous credit cards, gained more popularity. A few key court battles determined that for certain purchases like plane tickets or guns, the federal government could require some ID trail. A small industry grew specializing in digital cash that linked to an individual's UID in an encrypted database, and claimed that only a subpoena could force them to divulge the link.

The final challenge was how to allow identity authentication from the home, or any other remote site. Given the sheer number of participants in e-commerce and e-government, this problem demanded a solution. The computing industry was already in the middle of a revolution of its own, as the security and content industries pushed towards trusted computing. A version of Intel's Trusted Computing Platform Architecture (TCPA) was adopted and operating systems were tailored to accommodate secure code and hardware devices on these architectures. (See the appendix.) While commercially available biometric devices remained fairly expensive, the card-readers rapidly became affordable, and were soon adopted as access control devices as well.

The universal ID has been adopted with much less trouble than initially predicted. Mission creep was evident from the early days, an expected result of "Deadbeat Dad Syndrome." Once in place, it was very difficult to argue against applying the power of a UID to some important social problems, such as tracking dead-beat dads. It did make fraud easier to detect across federal databases and private information stores as well. Among other side benefits, a more standardized information system has made government information management not only less prone to error, but far more efficient.

The Technology and the Policy: Privacy Protection

The Supreme Court defined modern privacy rights in *Katz v United States* (1967), where concurring Justice Harlan established the test of "reasonable expectations." Essentially, this case held that actions that are conducted publicly couldn't later be termed "private." There are, however, certain *sanctum sanctorums* where we can act freely without fear of unwarranted government surveillance. While much has been written on the full implications of a reasonable expectation of privacy in a technologically dynamic world, there is no question that popular and legal definitions of what is public and private would dramatically shift under a universal identifying regime. The government has the potential ability to glean information about every transaction using the ID infrastructure. We instead have come to rely on statutory protections of personal data and dignity.

The introduction of data protection legislation as indicated previously was modeled largely on those introduced in the EU during the 1990's and consists of six key tenets.

Personal data shall be processed fairly and lawfully.

Personal data shall be obtained for only one or more specified and lawful purposes and shall not be further processed or used beyond that purpose.

Personal data shall be adequate, relevant and not excessive in relation to purpose for which it was collected.

Personal data shall be accurate and up-to-date.

Personal data may only be kept for as long as needed for the purpose collected.

Appropriate technical and organizational measures shall be taken against unauthorized or unlawful processing of personal data and against accidental loss, destruction or damage to personal data.

Further, it was recognized that a key technical protection against a complete erosion of privacy is the division between disparate government databases. Although much has been done to improve the compatibility between databases, they remain in separate jurisdictions with separate rules and no one system contains all the total amount of information. Indeed, the preferred way of accessing information across databases is sending the same signed, Boolean queries to an agency. This drastically reduces the harm a rogue operator can commit by compromising on a data access point. Cross-referencing is still possible, and may even be desirable, but it would simply be very expensive to pick up and reorganize government databases again. Internal politics and jurisdictional issues would also make such a task extremely difficult from a policy perspective.

Nonetheless, we are now more dependent on statutory data protections. Our data and personal information is safeguarded in the private sector by the force of law: and within the public sector by the same standards with caveats where issues of security are predominant. Without such protection commercial actors would otherwise be very tempted to exploit the information that is now in their possession. The introduction of data protection legislation however produced unexpected results in that it removed completely the need for the provision of 'Safe Harbor' in order to conduct trade in personal information between the EU and the US. This reduction in the amount of 'red tape' considerably outweighed the administrative costs of implementation of the data protection legislation, and has increased trade by an order of magnitude that surpasses initial costs of compliance.

As social concerns come to the forefront of the American political scene, the temptation will be strong to rely on personal information in seeking a solution to other social ills, in this way the problems mission creep has become an issue requiring further consideration. On the other hand, in the face of such ubiquitous government information control, the right of citizens to check the reliability and accuracy of the personal information held is of paramount importance. Clearly, any system that contains large amounts of personal information with the intention that it provides government agencies with a source of intelligence, by its nature must ensure its accuracy or risk failure in its application.

There remains however, a general concern about the ease with which one may be monitored. Not surprisingly, much of the discomfort centers on potentially embarrassing behavior that many wish to avoid publicizing. This may involve those who frequent gay bars or the birth control choices of individuals.

After a decade of losing ground to the credit card, cash has seen a mild resurgence. Since use of a credit card almost always is accompanied by an ID card swipe, and the occasional iris scan, this can leave an electronic trail. Despite some legal data protections for UID purchases, the comfort of being as anonymous possible when purchasing a controversial book has led many to pay with cash. Digital cash vending machines add the convenience of plastic to the anonymity of cash, much like a debit card but without traceability. After languishing in the prototype phase for years, several competing companies now offer digital cards that can be loaded with money anonymously, and are accepted wherever credit cards are taken.

The Department of Justice feared that cash purchases might put a stop to exactly the sort of information gathering they hoped to perpetrate under a UID system, and urged Congress to act. A number of suspicion-arousing transactions, from weapons to pornography, were declared to require UID registration. Some of these, such as nitrate fertilizer that can be used to make explosives, were accepted without a fight. Others, particularly those that tread on the toes of proponents of the First and Second Amendments, were challenged in the courts. Data policies were fine-tuned based on specific applications and interest group pressure. The UID could be used for firearms background checks, for instance, but no record of the purchase could be kept in government databases.

Trust and Administration

A key weakness in any secure data system, especially one controlled by the state, is the centralized power of administrators. A system in which administrators have little power is a system that cannot be administered with any degree of efficiency or flexibility. Records will always need to be updated or corrected, added or deleted. Yet if every administrator could interact with the UID system with impunity, fraud would be easy and incredibly hard to detect. The solution, then, is to bring account-ability to the administrators by keeping a careful record of each action. If a record is changed, deleted or added, the administrator signs the transaction with his or her information, including jurisdiction or perhaps even his or her own UID. It should be almost impossible to change something without any trace. This protects the system against bad information by error or malice by allowing audits and error checking.

In the event that there is a dispute between what an individual piece of informa-tion in a UID database and the claim of an individual identified by that information, an audit trail should be clearly evident. While all disputes may not be able to be settled in this fashion, a large number of them can be, such as explaining discrepan-cies between two databases. At the very least, it offers a starting point for conflict resolution, even enabling some of the process to be automated.

We can imagine a rather narrow set of constraints under which true identity must be protected for reasons of public interest, such as witness protection, undercover policing or (state) espionage. Not every person with access to auditable records needs to know, or even should know that records have been altered. Still, we can imagine a series of protected files, with some amount of security protection that can be used to record all but the most sensitive of these actions. The ability to make untraceable changes should be guarded as fiercely as possible; allowing only a very few people to have that authorization.

The Future of UID

As the system grows more and more trusted, those with a bolder social agenda have encouraged exploiting a reliable identity system for programs that would otherwise be much less feasible. Some drug reformers, for example, have urged rehabilitation of addicts with some sort of prescription of addictive drugs to avoid the disincentive of cold-turkey withdrawal, a very painful process. While there are many criticisms of such a plan, a major obstacle to implementation is making sure that the drugs go to the addict in treatment and that addict alone. A greater amount of trust in an identification system would make such a system more likely.

The problem with increasing the trust in ID authentication systems is that it increases the incentive to subvert the system. The incentive for fraud is much higher when a valid ID can permit access to more desired goods and services. However, it should be easier to detect those seeking to engage in active fraud, like obtaining government benefits, or claim large sums of money from a bank because of the nature of the biometric on file. The very fact that they are placing themselves into a smaller, select group should make detection less difficult. A UID makes validating a claim of identity easier to the extent that the security of the UID is acceptable to the party asking the identity question. Yet to the extent that it can be abused against the interest of the actual person whose identity is being identified a UID is a threat not a promise.

Scenario III: Sets of Attributes

Barbara Fox

Introduction

We live in a world where it's impossible to maintain a single identity. Our family, our schools, our friends, our bank, and even our government assign us different roles and titles, which come with different identifying names and numbers. We contribute to the confusion by choosing our own pseudonyms for online transactions. We manage the complexity that comes with this plethora of personal identifiers because we wish to remain in control of our identity.

The perception of being in control drives us to reject a national identity card due to its potential for abuse by privacy-invasive applications from both industry and government, as well as its potential to increase the risk of identity theft. This scenario projects how we will continue to manage our multiple identities as priorities of privacy and security in national consciousness evolve. While we anticipate the potential for law and policy to make great strides, the unrelenting advance of technology is certain to ensure that we will continue to face tough policy questions around our identities in 2014.

The Evolution of Identity

Surprisingly, the average American citizen has only a handful of transactions with the government for which s/he needs an identifier. Identification cards and numbers are used much more frequently outside our interactions with government. These transactions are described in the following two subsections that describe how identifiers are used in 2040 and how they were used in 2004. Changes center in how government issued IDs may be used by industry and how the firms that collect it may share identifying information. The few changes in the identification infrastructure are highlighted in the following text.

How IDs are used in 2040

In 2002 there were 162,000 reported cases of identity theft, almost double the 86,000 reported the year before. A quarter million cases of fraud resulting from identity theft would be reported in 2003. These doubled again in 2004. [71] In 2006, identity theft insurance, identity theft management, and even advertisements on television addressed this now ubiquitous problem.

However, concerns from fraud would be overshadowed that summer when an investigation into a serial rapist led to a Boston pool hall at which each victim's driver's license had been scanned to reveal not only their age, but their name and home address. A search of the perpetrator's apartment revealed lists of purchases made by victims at merchants with which the pool hall shared information. This explained how the perpetrator had found the victim's homes and sent gifts to the victims before each crime, facts that had led investigators to believe that the victims had known their attacker. Extensive press coverage ensured that the consumer backlash not only hit those who collected information, but those who shared it.

In October of 2015, Congress made two unprecedented moves to guarantee individual privacy. It effectively repealed the USA Patriot Act (HR3162) passed in the wake of the September 11, 2001 terrorist attack and extended federal pre-emption of state privacy laws under the Fair Credit Reporting Act, by passing the Consumer Privacy and Safety Act (HR1984). The Act:

1. Mandated that states either update driver's licenses, or provide additional proof of age identification cards that did not reveal the holder's address.

2. Made illegal the collecting, selling, purchasing, or other exchange of consumer information without a separate opt-in contract, in a standard format issued by the federal government. Conglomerates faced regulations that limited the consumer information that could be shared across business units.

3. Mandated that social security numbers could no longer be requested, stored, or exchanged for non-governmental use other than tax accounting.

4. Mandated that payment and other transaction information could only be shared if the consumer granted permission for each transaction at the time of the transaction. This not only enabled the continuation of frequent flyer and other affinity programs from large firms, but also ensured that small firms could work together to bundle products and verify that products were indeed sold together. This allowed them to continue competing with larger firms that produced the full complement of products.

Critics of the bill argued that consumers in many states lost important privacy protections with its passage. But public response to a single federal agency accountable for every aspect of identity theft management was overwhelmingly positive.

Because of minimal changes with existing governmental IDS, little changed in the way citizens interacted with their government. The most noticeable change was that more technology was introduced into police cars to retrieve driver information that was no longer on licenses from remote sources.

Despite a major outcry from businesses, the majority of changes came in the level of disclosure provided from businesses to customers about information practices. In order to be able to continue to maintain merged records, firms rushed to get consumers to opt-in to existing sharing arrangements. These individual credit availability numbers (or I-CANs) were introduced before the legislation went into effect in late 2005, as a non-governmental identifier to replace the social security number for use in non-government transactions.

I-CANs were the product of an open international competition sponsored by the National Institute of Standards. Some proposals contained only a means for uniquely assigning numbers to individuals, leaving the authentication problem to be solved later. Others proposed detailed specifics of smart-cards designs containing digital signature and encryption technologies that not only enabled identity authentication, but also offered delegation and the ability to audit. The I-CAN authentication problem drove demand for low-cost, easy-to-use secure "identity storage appliances." These now-ubiquitous devices are easy to connect to personal and public computers. The devices hold a virtually unlimited number of unique identity enablers (private digital signature keys and associated certificates.)

While the final I-CAN standard and the I-CAN program became an unqualified success, it remained completely voluntary and covers only twenty percent of the US population. A full ten years later, the question remained of whether it should be extended, this time at government expense, to I-CAN2.

For practical purposes, the technology issues associated with a national identifier are off the table. I-CAN proved that we have the technology. What we are left with is the more difficult legal and policy questions that plagued us in 2004. Does the promise of digital government demand that we step up to answering them?

Chapter 11
Scenario IV: Ubiquitous Identity Theft

Ari Schwartz

This scenario offers a view of the world that most observers today would consider a worst case. Identity theft, characterized by law enforcement as the fastest growing crime in the United States, [86] has grown exponentially. Identity theft grew beyond epidemic proportions as confirmed by the Federal Trade Commission. [71] Due to continued weaknesses in identity frameworks, increased demands for information upon using and purchasing content and increased weaknesses in security, it is quite common for individuals to feel comfortable assuming the identity of others simply to protect themselves. For example, the medical database begun under Bush has no meaningful privacy protection. [144] Obtaining care at a pharmacy or minor emergency center that might result in future refusal to insure or personal embarrassment requires a credit card and id in a false name.

Assertions of identity are still utilized for social protocol and historical necessity. Yet the assumptions about individual identity to information links on which so many systems have been built have been broken down. Continuing ad-hoc methods of authentication are attempted, but subverted as soon as they are widely implemented.

The State of Identity

Interacting with the government in a world of ubiquitous identity theft is a confusing and frustrating endeavor. Some agencies still have complex authentication, verification and authorization schemes in place that just do not work and burden the process. Other agencies have given up completely, preferring instead to rely on face-to-face transactions. Most service agencies have learned to live with high rates of fraud and exposure of citizen information to snooping.

New laws have been put in place to harshly punish the worst fraud offenders. While the deterrent does not seem to work for small time theft, it has been somewhat effective for large-scale long-term repeat offenders where prosecutors can build up a case. This has relieved enough pressure on the judicial system to make most believe that this is all that can be expected from law alone at this point. Most of the culprits of widespread fraud are beyond the reach of American law, in Nigeria or Eastern Europe. The credit card processing companies have no interest in investing to reduce such fraud, because the investments may cost as much as the fraud. In addition, the cost of much fraud can still be pushed to the consumer through the use of PIN systems as with the United Kingdom.

One example of the repeated failures in authentication systems is the online Personal Earnings Benefit Estimate Statement online at the US Social Security Administration (SSA). Originally, beneficiaries could get an online statement describing working history and long term benefits by filling out a detailed form providing explicit personal information such as mothers maiden name, date of birth and address as listed on their last paycheck. Soon after going online, it was recognized that this information was far too easy for anyone to get. The SSA tightened security by sending a confirmation email message with a password. Soon after this measure went into effect, it became an increasingly easy and common practice for identity thieves to hijack email accounts. Then SSA switched to telephone "call backs" where they would ask "out-of-wallet questions" such as employment history, salary information and more. This process had the down side of being expensive (to pay for call centers) and cumbersome (true beneficiaries often could not answer the out of wallet questions correctly), but it did work for a few years. Eventually, however, even this measure has failed. Insiders in call centers of this kind began to regularly misuse and share the transaction information and it is quite simple and common to set up a phone in another person's name for a short period of time.

RealID was an expensive debacle that increased the flow of citizen information and ease of information theft. Driver's license authorities continue to be valuable sources of false identities, only those now work uniformly across state lines. The rate of identity fraud, and the economic necessity of credentialing illegal immigrants doomed the project from the start.

Other government offices have simply stopped providing services that require authentication. For example, individuals can no longer reserve a campground space in a national park in advance. Secondary markets and the ease of identity fraud caused the cost of popular campsites to skyrocket, and organized crime had become involved. Campsites had to return to first come, first serve.

Obviously many government agencies do not have the ability to reduce services in this way. For example, while most benefit offices have abandoned hope of providing benefits electronically over distances, they still need to provide basic services that require authentication. Beneficiaries are now expected to come into the office where large amounts of biometric data (via photographs and DNA samples) are taken about each visitor. The biometric information does not help in authenticating individuals. Identity thieves were able to duplicate and falsely populate biometric databases long ago. Instead the biometric information is used to help in fraud cases in the new, specially created, district fraud courts used to prosecute egregious offenders.

The Path to Today

How did we get ourselves into such a situation? As we look back at the choices made at the beginning of the 21st Century it seems that the problems we currently encounter were almost unavoidable. Trust in the system at first crumbled on the edges and then a critical mass of failures brought the system down upon itself.

As early as 2001, the US Federal Trade Commission (FTC) was reporting that identity theft was growing at alarming rates, almost doubling every year. [70] Yet, awareness of the problem was not commensurate with its scope and impact. [86] Several factors played critical roles in the slow decay that began in the 20th Century and played it self out in the next. These factors included:

Weaknesses in "Breeder Documents" - Historically, authentication systems relied on a small number of documents used to verify an individual's identity. These documents are often called "breeder documents" because a few of them are used to create all other individual identity credentials and then make it possible for an individual to open banking accounts, establish credit and generally live under a real or assumed identity. Yet, as a greater reliance was placed on the small number of breeders not suited for the purpose, problems (previously know and unknown) started to arise. In particular, many problems can be seen with the following breeder documents:

Birth Certificates

The first individual identity document given to people born in the United States is the birth certificate. Many other documents rely upon it. However, since municipalities control the issuance of the certificate, there are literally thousands of issuers with no set security or information standards for the certificate. Identity information often used in later identity authentications is not as helpful at birth as it is with adults since eye and hair color are not set and fingerprint ridges are too close together to read. Also, many individuals are not born in hospitals, making verification of individuals at birth very difficult for the localities. Finally, early implementations of biometrics stored raw biometric data, so the affluent early adopters have completely lost control of their own information. The documents have been easy to forge and localities have had no incentives to continue maintaining a relationship with the holder of the birth certificate making databases of current information practically useless.

Social Security Numbers (SSN)

The SSN was created in 1936 as a means to track workers' earnings and eligibility for Social Security benefits. Although the number was not originally intended to be a National ID number, it has been used for almost every imaginable purpose. The Privacy Act of 1974 was written, in part, to cut down on the federal government's reliance on the SSN, yet it has not stopped most uses. Meanwhile, use of the SSN by state governments and the private sector has continued to grow. Aside from the fact that the number was not properly designed to be used as an authenticator for such varied purposes. The overuse and public use of SSNs have made the numbers widely susceptible to fraud. Since the Social Security Administration is not generally in the business of verifying SSNs for the private sector criminals have made up plausible nine digit numbers or, more frequently, begun using a real person's SSN.

Driver's Licenses

While driver's licenses were created for the purpose of insuring safety on state roads, the license has become a de facto photo government issued identification card. Yet, the system is clearly not designed to issue universal photo identification for multiple reasons:

Since the driver's license is not given to someone at birth and non-US born individuals must also be allowed to obtain a license, the state issuer must rely on a series of other documents to authenticate the individual.

The authorities providing driver's licenses serve drivers and non-drivers, citizens, legal residents, and temporary visa holders so there are many issuers within a state, putting strain on communications and weakening security. The desire for service prevents a high degree of verification.

Employees are underpaid, disrespected, and overworked creating an atmosphere ripe for high levels of bribery and corruption.

States have various physical security concerns including a number of break-ins where computers and blank cards were stolen to make fake cards.

If the value of a driver's license is as high as the value of American citizenship, the cost of fraud prevention is not as high as the market value for a fraudulent license.

These problems and others led to a system where fake cards and falsely issued driver's licenses are common. As early as 1999, it was estimated that California alone wrongly issued 100,000 per year. [118, 167] By 2003, corruption was so rampant in New Jersey that the DMV fired the entire staff of the Newark branch office. [35]

Generally speaking, the agencies distributing breeder documents have little investment in their secondary use. By the time the agencies themselves were implicated, they were unable to stem the tide of use of the documents for authorization, marketing and other purposes.

The Growth of Identity Card Information "Swiping" - Continued use of information storage on the magnetic stripe of cards and the low cost of portable magnetic stripe readers led to a rampant increase in the theft of personal information directly from identification cards. In early 2003, only identity thieves and a few rogue businesses (bars and clubs) were using readers, but their popularity grew quickly and fair information practices were ignored. Calls for legislation to prohibit the practice went unheeded and collecting information off of cards for legal and illegal uses became routine.

Another driver to the world of ubiquitous identity theft was the lack of a coherent public records policy. The advent of networked technology brought the knowledge that an individual's life, activities, and personal characteristics can be found scattered throughout the files of government agencies. Companies quickly constructed a detailed profile of an individual using only publicly available, individually identifiable information from government records. As more of this information became available in electronic form, individuals began skipping the information aggregators and building their own profile database of friends, neighbors and others.

While the types of records available from jurisdictions may vary, the information available on a given individual (and a likely source of the information) can include:

1. Name and address (drivers license)
2. Social Security Number (driver's license number in some states)
3. Home ownership (land title)
4. Home loan (land title)
5. Assessed value of home (property tax)
6. Size of home, price, physical description (land)
7. Parents (vital statistics)
8. Sex (drivers license; vital statistics)
9. Date of birth (drivers license; vital statistics)
10. Selected occupations (occupational licenses)
11. Voting frequency (voter registration)
12. Political Party
13. Political contributions (Federal Election Commission)
14. Selected hobbies (hunting/fishing licenses; town web site access)
15. Boat/Airplane ownership (license)

Court records detail much more information. In particular, companies routinely collect the information of individuals who have interacted with the courts as a criminal defendant, as a plaintiff or defendant in civil litigation, as a juror, through divorce proceedings, in bankruptcy proceedings, as a beneficiary of a will, or in other ways through court records. Additional information is also available about individuals who are required to file information on stock ownership with the Securities and Exchange Commission; political candidates and government employees required to file ethics disclosure forms with state or federal offices; recipients of student loans, housing loans, small business loans, and other forms of government assistance; and employees who have filed workers compensation claims.

Information on the driver's license was forbidden to be shared by the Driver's Privacy Protection Act in the late '90s, yet some states continued to push the limits of the distribution of information, selling information to private data marketers. (AP, 2003) This information includes:

1. Make and model of automobile owned (motor vehicle)
2. Automobile loans (motor vehicle)

3. Driving record (drivers license)
4. Selected medical conditions (drivers license)
5. Social Security Number (drivers license)
6. Height and weight (drivers license)

As public information was made more available in electronic form, concurrent with the advent of intelligent search tools made all of this information easier to sort through, data aggregators were no longer needed and individuals began to build their own databases on friends, colleagues, neighbors and others.

A Lack of Incentives to Fix the Problem in the Marketplace

As the costs to society of greater identity theft began to increase, so did the cost to business, yet not enough for companies to take actions to stem the problem.

By 2002, cases involving thousands of victims were becoming routine with insider fraud and poor security at financial and medical companies the main culprit. [1] On a smaller scale, many major financial institutions were routinely giving out confidential customer account information to callers, using security procedures that authorities said, even at the time, were vulnerable to abuse by fraud artists. [138]

A report issued by the Tower Group in 2002 estimated that identity theft cost companies at least $1 billion in fraud. The report claimed that banks had no means to positively identify individuals. Yet banks and other companies were simply unwilling to spend money on possible preventive resources for such a complex problem.

Privacy Protections Did Not Keep up with Technology

The legal framework in the United States did not envision the pervasive role information technology would play in our daily lives. Nor did it envision a world where the private sector would collect and use information at the level it does today. The legal framework for protecting individual privacy reflects "the technical and social givens of specific moments in history." [170, 180] A relevant example — the Privacy Act, passed in 1974, covers only groups of records "under the control of any agency from which information is retrieved by the name of the individual or by some identifying number, symbol, or other identifying particular assigned to the individual." Yet the law does not take into account the fact that an agency may be collecting information in a distributed database that is not currently retrieving information by an

---

[1] In November 2002, a Massive identity theft ring broken up misusing Ford Motor Credit credentials, with 30,000 victims. In December, theft of medical information on 500,000 military-related from TriWest Healthcare Alliance on 14 Dec 2002 See Peter Neuman's Risk Report for these and other examples.http://www.csl.sri.com/users/neumann/illustrative.html#33

identifier. It also does not address protections for government subscription services to information brokers that are maintained by the private sector. [128, 168]

Vestiges of a pre-Internet, pre-networked world, stressed the privacy framework. Foremost among these was a belief that the government's collection and use of information about individuals' activities and communications was the only threat to individual privacy. This was the antiquated notion that a solid wall separated the data held by the private and public sector; and that the Internet would be used primarily for a narrow slice of activities. Finally there was a presumption that private and public digital networked "spaces" were easily demarcated.

Creating privacy protections in the electronic realm has always been a complex endeavor. It requires an awareness of not only changes in technology, but also changes in how citizens use the technology, and how those changes are pushing at the edges of existing laws and policies. While there were several pushes for a comprehensive privacy law, such a law never took hold.

Requirements of identity for copyright purposes became routine as liability law continued to shield providers of flawed technology creating a vacuum of responsibility Bolstered by court rulings such as RIAA v. Verizon,[2] intellectual property holders pressured companies to identify users of content. Rather than fight, ISPs and software companies began allowing anyone with an intellectual property claim to request identity information from users. Meanwhile, the constraints on security research embodied in the DMCA allowed providers of identity systems (Netiquette, Sun, and multiple start-ups) to hide the security flaws. Finally Microsoft required compliance with its own single sign-on standards to access any Web Server using NT. Combining a situation where individuals had to turn over personal information for every transaction online with the systemic security flaws in the single sign on, identity became liquid and readily available to almost anyone online.

A policy focus on identity theft came, but far too late in the spread of the problem. The focus was also not on restructuring the root causes of the theft, but on criminal penalties and awareness. Since it takes individuals 14 months on average to determine that their identity has been stolen, outrage always lagged behind action. [86]

Eventually, identity theft grew from a problem where everyone knew a victim to one where everyone was a victim, multiple times over. The way to fight back was not to report the crime, but to steal someone else's identity instead. Corporate practices of requiring identification to purchase a CD; requiring information for every use of payment instruments; and increasing interruption-based marketing left consumers with little capacity to protect their privacy. The systems meant to prevent consumers from providing misinformation to marketers instead drove otherwise law-abiding people into identity thieves. The distinction between the criminal and common was the purpose and extent of use.

---

[2] The most relevant opinion, RIAA v. Verizon opinion can be found at http://www.dcd.uscourts.gov/03-ms-0040.pdf. Please also see CDT's statement on the case http://www.cdt.org/copyright/030130cdt.shtml.

Chapter 12
Closing

The four scenarios show that there are really only two choices: decentralized, often anonymous credentials or ubiquitous identity theft. Within the range of reasonable anonymity there are different choices for breeder, foundational documents. The question is "who are you" in a social paper world becomes "what are your credentials" in a digital networked world. Confusing those questions will create another generation of identity theft with the same convenience of easy credit at the same costs in broken records and hindered lives.

The question of who you are is profoundly distinct from the question of the identifiers you may require. The confusion between these two basic ideas, identity versus credentials, creates very real risks. The question of who you are is not distinct from the risks you already face from a chronically inadequate identity system.

What problem are corporate and national identifiers supposed to solve? What new problems will the new identity systems create? Considering identity management more broadly, it is possible to conceive of an environment where there is one central key? What myriad of keys will be needed for the different identity puzzles? Each of the systems above has strengths, and none is appropriate for all environments.

Today we are headed more to the last scenario than any other. Surveillance for terror, crime, money and copyright policing is exploding. A study of home wireless use of students at IU found that a year of intensive education reduced rather than increased use of security mechanisms for student home wireless systems. Security seemed to be authority, offering the students only non-repudiation.

Even a theoretically technically perfect identity system will create new problems, particularly to the extent that it fails by design to solve a specified unique problem. Each system, even in the few above, has very different failures and strengths. Biometrics are incomparable at preventing duplicate enrollment. Biometrics are fundamentally flawed at verification of unique identity over a network. Card Space is decentralized, but may not be fully documented. Liberty Alliance is fundamentally an enabler of corporate data sharing. Reputation systems can be strong in cryptographic terms, but the distribution of enrollment responsibility means that they are inherently weak in organizational terms.

Identity management is not magic. With millions of people on the Internet, no one can know who each one is. Criminals already have anonymity through identity theft, botnets, and fraud. In pursuing these malicious few, identity systems are both removing autonomy from the innocent and ironically creating ever more opportunities for the malicious.

Generic identity architectures are being built with so many purposes as to have no functional purpose in terms of security; but are highly effective at violating privacy. Privacy plus security is not a zero sum equation. Just as no structure would be an ideal home, a perfect school, and an optimal office, no single identity structure will address identification of duplicate enrollment for fraud, distinguishing age, verification of financial status, graceful degradation, seamless recovery, and optimal availability. A set of distributed systems, that are purpose-driven rather than ubiquitous, with the strongest appropriate authentication offers the best potential for being supple enough to allow society and designers to recover from our inevitable mistakes.

These are risks for the future. Today, identity is simply used to shift risks. New modes of interaction are clearly needed. We are replacing implicit human identification with explicit inhuman identity management. This has proven inadequate.

Current identity systems are designed to increase the concentration of data and minimize the liability of the purveyors of those systems. From Yahoo! providing the name of a Chinese blogger to Amazon experiments with variable pricing, liability is being paced on those with the least control. Identity systems violate privacy in order to increase the profits of the corporate or national entities paying for the ID systems. Without privacy controls, we all lose.

At the level of implementing the software, each person entrusts critical information to software providers. Yet, why trust e software providers when they have proven untrustworthy? Today, providers of software have escaped even the minimal common law requirements for selling a functional good as promised. Yet these goods are sold with exploitive end user license agreements.

Education has been presented as the solution to everything from computer crime to identity theft. Yet the asymmetry in power means the customer can do little about identify theft. Educating the consumer can do little when the consumer is structurally helpless.

Until the discussion of identity management is expanded to include anonymity management, forward movement is limited. Spam is a good example of a difficult identity problem. Spam is not one problem; it ranges from the level of theft equivalent to stealing a donut from the office lounge to Enron levels of international criminal fraud.

Identification without anonymity is neither reliable, nor desirable. Online identity is inherently an oxymoron. Our identities, which we are, are part of the physical world. Credentials are digital; people are not. Until there is considerably less money to be made off the illusion that we can be represented with perfection online, that fiction will continue to endanger our finances, our reputations, and even our freedom.

References

1. Abric JC, Kahan JP (1972) The effects of representations and behavior in experimental games. European Journal of Social Psychology 2:129–144
2. AHIMA – The American Health Information Management Association (2006) The State of HIPAA Privacy and Security Compliance. Available at http://www.ahima.org/emerging_issues/2006StateofHIPAACompliance.pdf, last accessed on Nov. 2008
3. Akerlof GA (1970) The Market for Lemons: Quality Uncertainty and the Market Mechanism. Quarterly Journal of Economics 84:488–500
4. American Association of Motor Vehicle Administrators (2002) Fighting Fraud: One Document at a Time. Move Magazine. Winter 2002
5. Anderson R (1994) Why cryptosystems fail. Comm. of the ACM Nov 37(11):32–40
6. Anderson R (2002) Unsettling Parallels Between Security and the Environment. Workshop on Economics and Information Security, Berkeley, CA
7. Appari A, Johnson ME (2009) Information Security and Privacy in Healthcare: Current State of Research. International Journal of Internet and Enterprise Management 6(4):279–314
8. Associated Press (2003) ACLU Says Florida Illegally Sells Driver Records to Companies. Sun Sentinel. April 9, 2003
9. Avery C, Resnick P, Zeckhauser R (1999) The Market for Evaluations. American Economic Review 89(3):564–584
10. Axelrod R (1984) The Evolution of Cooperation. Basic Books, New York
11. Ball E, Chadwick DW, Mundy D (2003) Patient Privacy in Electronic Prescription Transfer. IEEE Security & Privacy. March/April, pp. 77–80.
12. Barney J, Hansen M, Klein B (1994) Trustworthiness as a source of competitive advantage. Strategic Management Journal 15:175-190
13. Basel Committee on Banking Supervision (2005) Basel II: Revised international capital framework
14. BBC (2004) Doctor Acquitted of Porn Charges. available at: http://news.bbc.co.uk/2/hi/uk_news/england/humber/3647207.stm. 21 April 2004
15. Beth T, Borcherding M, Klein B (1994) Valuation of trust in open networks. In: Gollman D (ed) Computer Security — ESORICS '94 (Lecture Notes in Computer Science), pp. 3–18, Springer-Verlag Inc., New York, NY
16. Becker LC (1996) Trust in Non-cognitive Security about Motives. Ethics, October, 107:43–61
17. Bikchandani S, Hirshleifer D, Welch I (1992) A Theory of Fads, Fashion, Custom and Cultural Change as Informational Cascades. J. Pol. Econ. 100(5):992-1026
18. Blaze M, Feigenbaum J, Lacy J (1996) Decentralized Trust Management. Proceedings of the IEEE Conference on Security and Privacy, Oakland, CA
19. Blaze M, Feigenbaum J, Ioannidis J, Keromytis A (1999) The role of trust management in distributed systems security. LNCS Secure Internet Programming 1603:185-210. Springer-Verlag Inc., New York, NY, USA

20. Bloom DE (1998) Technology Experimentation, and the Quality of Survey Data. Science 280(5365):847–848
21. Bolin JN, Clark LS (2004) Avoiding Charges of Fraud and Abuse: Developing and Implementing an Effective Compliance Program, JONA (34:12), 546-550.
22. Boston Consulting Group (1997) Summary of Market Survey Results prepared for eTRUST. The Boston Consulting Group, San Francisco, CA
23. Bosworth MH (2006) Kaiser Permanente Laptop Stolen: Personal Data on 38,000 Members Missing. Consumer Affairs. Nov 29. Available at http://www.consumeraffairs.com/news04/2006/11/kaiser_laptop.html
24. Brands S (2000) Rethinking Public Key Infrastructures and Digital Certificates. MIT Press, Cambridge, Massachusetts
25. Burrows M, Abadi M, Needham RM (1990) A Logic of Authentication. ACM Transactions on Computer Systems 8(1):18-36
26. BW (2007) Diagnosis: Identity Theft. Business Week. January 8, 2007
27. Camenisch J, Lysyanskaya A (2001) An Efficient System for Non-transferable Anonymous Credentials with Optional Anonymity Revocation In Advances in Cryptology – EUROCRYPT 2001. In: Pfitzmann B (ed), 2001, Springer-Verlag LNCS 2045, pp. 93-118
28. Camp LJ (2001) An atomicity-generating layer for anonymous currencies. IEEE Transactions on Software Engineering. March, 27(3):272–278
29. Camp LJ, McGrath C, Nissenbaum H (2001) Trust: A Collision of Paradigms. LNCS Proceedings of Financial Cryptography. Springer-Verlag Inc., New York, NY, USA
30. Camp LJ, Osorio C (2003) Privacy Enhancing Technologies for Internet Commerce. In: Petrovic O, Posch R, Marhold F (eds) Trust in the Network Economy. Springer-Verlag (Berlin). pp.317-329
31. Camp LJ, Tsang R (2001) Universal service in a ubiquitous digital network. Journal of Ethics and Information Technology. 2(1). (Previously presented at INET 1999)
32. Camp LJ, Wolfram C (2004) Pricing Security. In: Camp LJ, Lewis S (eds) The Economics of Information Security. Chapter 2, Vol. 12, Springer-Kluwer
33. Caulkins (2001) My reputation always had more fun than me. Richamond Journal of Law and Technology 7(4)
34. Cassell J, Bickmore T (2000) External Manifestations of Trustworthiness in the Interface. Communications of the ACM, December, 43(12):50–56
35. Center for Democracy and Technology (2003) Tracking Security at State Motor Vehicle Offices. http://www.cdt.org/privacy/030131motorvehicle.shtml. project initiated April 14, 2003
36. Chaum D (1985) Security without Identification: Transaction Systems to Make Big Brother Obsolete. Communications of the ACM. October, 28(10)
37. Chaum D, Fiat A, Naor M (1988) Untraceable Electronic Cash. In: Goldwasser S (ed) LNCS Advances in Cryptology CRYPTO '88. Springer-Verlag, Berlin, Germany
38. Choi YB, Capitan KE, Krause JS, Streeper MM (2006) Challenges associated with privacy in healthcare industry: Implementation of HIPAA and security rules. Journal of Medical Systems 30(1):57–64
39. Claburn T (2007) Minor Google Security Lapse Obscures Ongoing Online Data Risk. Information Week. January 22
40. Clark D, Blumenthal M (2000) Rethinking the design of the Internet: The end to end arguments vs. the brave new world. Telecommunications Policy Research Conference, Washington DC
41. Coleman J (1990) Foundations of Social Theory. Belknap Press, Cambridge, MA
42. Compaine BJ (1988) Issues in New Information Technology. Ablex Publishing, Norwood, NJ
43. Computer Science and Telecommunications Board (1994) Rights and Responsibilities of Participants in Networked Communities. National Academy Press, Washington, DC
44. Computer Science and Telecommunications Board & National Research Council (2003) Who Goes There?: Authentication Through the Lens of Privacy. National Academy Press, Washington, DC
45. Computer Science and Telecommunications Board & National Research Council (2001) IDs - Not That Easy. National Academy Press, Washington, DC

46. Council for International Business (1993) Statement of the United States Council for International Business on the Key Escrow Chip. United States Council for International Business, NY, NY
47. Cox TH, Lobel SA, McLeod PL (1991) Effects of Ethnic Group Cultural Differences on Cooperative and Competitive Behavior on a Group Task. Academy of Management 34(4):827–847
48. Cranorm LF, Reagle J (1998) Designing a Social Protocol: Lessons Learned from the Platform for Privacy Preferences Project. In: MacKie-Mason JK and Waterman D (eds) Telephony, the Internet, and the Media. Lawrence Erlbaum Associates
49. Daugman J (2003) The importance of being random: Statistical principles of iris recognition. Pattern Recognition 36(2):279–291
50. Davida GI, Frankel Y, Matt BJ (1998) On Enabling Secure Applications Through Off-Line Biometric Identification. IEEE Symposium on Security and Privacy, Oakland, CA
51. Dawes RM, McTavish J, Shaklee H (1977) Behavior, communication, and assumptions about other people's behavior in a commons dilemma situation. Journal of Personality and Social Psychology. 35:1–11
52. De Avila J (2007) The Hidden Risk of File-Sharing. Wall Street Journal. Nov. 7, D1
53. Dellarocas C (2001) Analyzing the Economic Efficiency of eBay-like Online Reputation Reporting Mechanisms. Proc. 3rd ACM Conf. on Electronic Commerce
54. Dellarocas C (2002) Efficiency and Robustness of Mediated Online Feedback Mechanisms: The Case of eBay. SITE'02
55. Dingledine R, Molnar D (2001) Accountability. Peer-to-peer: Harnessing the power technologies. ch. 16. O'Reilly & Associates, Cambridge, MA
56. Dingledine R, Mathewson N, Syverson P (2004) Tor: The Second-Generation Onion Router. In Proceedings of the 13th USENIX Security Symposium. August 2004, pp. 303–319
57. Dixon P (2006) Medical Identity Theft: The Information Crime that Can Kill You. The World Privacy Forum
58. Donath J, Boyd D (2004) Public displays of connection. BT Technology Journal 22(4)
59. Dwork C, Goldberg A, Naor M (2003) On Memory-Bound Functions for Fighting Spam. In: Boneh D (ed) Advances in Cryptology-CRYPTO 2003, LNCS 2729, Springer Verlag, pp. 426–444.
60. Dwork C, Naor M (1992) Pricing via Processing or Combating Junk Mail. In: Brick EF (ed) Advances in Cryptology-CRYPTO 1992, LNCS 740, Springer Verlag, pp. 139–147
61. Ellison C (2003) Implications with Identity in PKI. In: Camp LJ (ed) Identity: The Digital Government Civic Scenario Workshop, Boston, MA. http://www.ksg.harvard.edu/digitalcenter/conference/papers/pki.htm
62. Ericsson KA, Simon HA (1984) Protocol analysis: Verbal reports as data. MIT Press, Cambridge, MA
63. Evensky D, Gentile A, Camp LJ, Armstrong R (1997) Lilith: Scalable Execution of User Code for Distributed Computing. Proc. of The 6th IEEE International Symposium on High Performance Distributed Computing, HPDC-6, Portland, OR, pp. 123–145
64. FBI (2007) 2006 Financial Crime Report. Federal Bureau of Investigation. [Online] 02 28, 2007. Available at: http://www.fbi.gov/publications/financial/fcs_report2006/financial_crime_2006.htm. Cited: 02 04, 2008.
65. Federal Register (2009) / Vol. 74, No. 209 / Friday, October 30, 2009 / Rules and Regulations, 56123–56131. Available at: http://www.hhs.gov/ocr/privacy/hipaa/administrative/enforcementrule/enfifr.pdf. Retrieved: February 1, 2010.
66. Federal Register (2010) Medicare and Medicaid Programs; Electronic Health Record Incentive Program; Proposed Rule/ Vol. 75, No. 8 / Wednesday, January 13, 2010 / Proposed Rules, 1844-2011. Available at: http://edocket.access.gpo.gov/2010/pdf/E9-31217.pdf. Retrieved: February 27, 2010.

67. Federal Register (2010) Health Information Technology: Initial Set of Standards, Implementation Specifications, and Certification Criteria for Electronic Health Record Technology; Interim Final Rule/ Vol. 75, No. 8 / Wednesday, January 13, 2010 / Rules and Regulations, 2014–2047. Available at: http://edocket.access.gpo.gov/2010/pdf/E9-31216.pdf. Retrieved: February 27, 2010.

68. Federal Register (2010) Medicare and Medicaid Programs; Electronic Health Record Incentive Program; Final Rule / Vol. 75, No. 144 / Wednesday, July 28, 2010 / Rules and Regulations 44314–44588. Available at: http://edocket.access.gpo.gov/2010/pdf/2010-17207.pdf.

69. Federal Trade Commission (2002) ID Theft: When Bad Things Happen to Your Good Name

70. Federal Trade Commission (2002) Information on Identity Theft for Consumers and Victims from January 2002 Through December 2002. Available at http://www.consumer.gov/idtheft/reports/CY2002ReportFinal.pdf. Cited 11 April 2003

71. Federal Trade Commission (2005) FTC Releases Top 10 consumer Complaints for 2004. http://www.ftc.gov/opa/2005/02/top102005.htm. Cited 10 February 2005

72. FTC (2007) 2006 Identity Theft Report. Federal Trade Commission. November, 2007. Available at http://www.ftc.gov/os/2007/11/SynovateFinalReportIDTheft2006.pdf. last accessed on June 18, 2008

73. Feldman M, Lai K, Stoica I, Chuang J (2004) Robust incentive techniques for peer-to-peer networks. Proc. of EC '04

74. Freedman, LF (2009) The Health Information Technology for Economic and Clinical Health Act (HITECH Act): implications for the adoption of health information technology, HIPAA, and privacy and security issues, Nixon Peabody. February 23, 2009. Source: http://www.nixonpeabody.com/publications_detail3.asp?ID=2621 Retrieved: July 1, 2009.

75. Friedman B (ed) (2001) Human Values and the Design of Computer Technology. C S L I Publications

76. Friedman B, Millett L (2001) Reasoning About Computers as Moral Agents. In: Friedman B (ed) Human Values and the Design of Computer Technology. C S L I Publications

77. Friedman B, Kahn PH Jr., Howe DC (2000) Trust Online. Com. of the ACM. December, 43(12):34–40

78. Friedman E, Resnick P (2001) The Social Cost of Cheap Pseudonyms. J. Economics and Management Strategy 10(2):173–199

79. Fernandes AD (2001) Risking trust in a public key infrastructure: old techniques of managing risk applied to new technology. Decision Support Systems 31:303–322

80. Foley MJ (2000) Can Microsoft Squash 63,000 Bugs in Win2k?. ZDnet Eweek. on-line edition, 11 February 2000

81. Foner LN (1997) Yenta: A Multi-Agent, Referral Based Matchmaking System. First Int'l Conference on Autonomous Agents (Agents '97), Marina del Rey, California

82. Fukuyama F (1996) Trust: The Social Virtues and the Creation of Prosperity. Free Press, NY, NY

83. Garfinkle S (1994) PGP: Pretty Good Privacy. O'Reilly & Associates, Inc., Sebastopol, CA, pp. 235–236

84. Garfinkle S (2000) Database Nation. O'Reilly & Associates, Inc., Sebastopol, CA

85. Gefen D (2000) E-commerce: the role of familiarity and trust. Int'l Journal of Management Science 28:725–737

86. General Accounting Office (2002) Identity Theft: Greater Awareness and Use of Existing Data Are Needed. GAO-02-776, Washington, DC

87. Goldschlag D, Reed M, Syverson P (1999) Onion Routing for Anonymous and Private Internet Connections. Communications of the ACM 42(2)

88. Good NS, Krekelberg A (2003) Usability and privacy: a study of Kazaa P2P file-sharing. Proceedings of the SIGCHI Conference on Human Factors in Computing Systems. Ft. Lauderdale, Florida, April 05-10.

89. Hanson G (1994) Illegal Aliens Bilk Sick U.S. system. Insight on the News. April 18, 1994.

90. Hawkes P, Hefferman S (1999) Biometrics: Understanding the Business Issurs in Just One Day. Presentation, SJB Biometrics '99 Workshop, Nov. 9 1999

91. Hendrick   B   (2008)   Insurance   records   of   71,000   Ga.   families made   public.   Atlanta   Journal-Constitution,   April   08.   Available   at: http://www.ajc.com/metro/content/metro/stories/2008/04/08/breach_0409.html

92. Herbert I (2005) No evidence against man in child porn inquiry who 'killed himself'. Available via The Independent. http://news.independent.co.uk/uk/legal/article316391.ece. 1 Oct 2005

93. HHS (2008), HHS, Providence Health & Services Agree on Corrective Action Plan to Protect Health Information. U.S. Department of Health & Human Services, News Release. July 17. Available at: http://www.hhs.gov/news/press/2008pres/07/20080717a.html.

94. HHS (2009) Guidance Specifying the Technologies and Methodologies That Render Protected Health Information Unusable, Unreadable, or Indecipherable to Unauthorized Individuals for Purposes of the Breach Notification Requirements under Section 13402 of Title XIII (Health Information Technology for Economic and Clinical Health Act) of the American Recovery and Reinvestment Act of 2009; Request for Information. Office of the Secretary, Department of Health and Human Services. April 17, 2009 Source: http://www.hhs.gov/ocr/privacy/hipaa/understanding/coveredentities/hitechrfi.pdf. Retrieved: February 1, 2010.

95. HHS (2009b) Health Information Technology American Recovery and Reinvestment Act (Recovery Act) Implementation Plan. Office of the National Coordinator for Health Information Technology. Source: http://www.hhs.gov/recovery/reports/plans/onc_hit.pdf. Retrieved: July 5, 2009.

96. Hochheiser H (2002) The platform for privacy preference as a social protocol: An examination within the U.S. policy context. ACM Trans. Inter. Tech, Nov. 2002, 2(4):276–306

97. Hoffman L, Clark P (1991) Imminent policy considerations in the design and management of national and international computer networks. IEEE Communications Magazine. February, pp. 68–74

98. Hottell M, Carter D, Deniszczuk M (2006) Predictors of Home-Based Wireless Security. Fifth Workshop on the Economics of Information Security. University of Cambridge, England, June 26-28

99. Hsu S, Fears D (2007) As Bush's ID Plan Was Delayed, Coalition Formed Against It. Washington Post. February 25, 2007, Page A08

100. Jain AK, Bolle RM, Pankanti S (eds), Biometrics: Personal Identification in Networked Society. Kluwer Academic, December 1998

101. Jin GZ, Kato A (2005) Price, Quality and Reputation: Evidence from an Online Field Experiment. RAND Journal of Economics, Accepted. Available at SSRN: http://ssrn.com/abstract=917315

102. Johnson ME, Dynes S (2007) Inadvertent Disclosure: Information Leaks in the Extended Enterprise. Proceedings of the Sixth Workshop on the Economics of Information Security, Carnegie Mellon University, June 7-8

103. Johnson ME (2008) Information Risk of Inadvertent Disclosure: An Analysis of File-Sharing Risk in the Financial Supply Chain. Journal of Management Information Systems 25(2):97–123

104. Johnson ME, McGuire D, Willey ND (2008) The Evolution of the Peer-to-Peer File Sharing Industry and the Security Risks for Users. Proceedings of HICSS-41, Jan 7-10, Hawaii

105. Johnson ME, McGuire D, Willey ND (2009) Why File Sharing Networks Are Dangerous. Communications of the ACM 52(2):134–138

106. Johnson ME (2009) Data Hemorrhages in the Health-Care Sector. Proceedings of the Financial Cryptography and Data Security, Barbados, February 22-25

107. Johnson ME, Willey N (2011) Will HITECH Heal Patient Data Hemorrhages?. Proceedings of HICSS-44, Hawaii, Jan 4-7 2011

108. Kalakota R, Whinston AB (1997) Electronic Commerce. Addison Wesley, Boston, MA, pp. 251-282

109. Keisler S, Sproull L, Waters K (1996) A Prisoners Dilemma Experiments on Cooperation with People and Human-Like Computers. J. of Personality and Social Psych 70:47–65

110. Keize G (2004) Do-it-yourself phishing kits lead to more scams. Information Week. August 2004

111. Kephart JO, Chess D, White SR (1993) Computer Networks as Biological Systems. IEEE SPECTRUM. May 1993

112. Kerr NL, Kaufman-Gilliland CM (1994) Communication, Commitment and cooperation in social dilemmas. Journal of Personality and Social Psychology 66:513–529

113. Kim K, Prabhakar B (2000) Initial trust, perceived risk, and the adoption of internet banking. Proceedings of the Twenty First International Conference on Information Systems

114. Krackhardt D, Blythe J, McGrath C (1995) KrackPlot 3.0: User's Manual. Analytic Technologies. Columbia, SC

115. Lafferty L (2007) Medical Identity Theft: The Future Threat of Health Care Fraud Is Now. Journal of Health Care Compliance; Jan/Feb, 9(1):11–20

116. Lessig L, Resnick P (1999) Zoning Speech on the Internet: A Legal and Technical Model. Michigan Law Review 98(2):395–431

117. Levitz J. Hechinger J (2006) Laptops Prove Weakest Link in Data Security. Wall Street Journal, March 26

118. LoPucki LM (2001) Human Identification Theory. 80 Tex. L. Rev. 114

119. Luhmann N (1979) Trust: A Mechanism For the Reduction of Social Complexity. Trust and Power: Two works by Niklas Luhmann. New York: John Wiley & Sons, pp. 1–103

120. Lyon D (2001) Surveillance Society - Monitoring Everyday Life. Buckinghamshire: Open University Press, 2001

121. Mansfield T, Wayman JL (2000) Best Practices in Testing and Reporting Performance of Biometric Devices. Version 1.0. Available at http://www.afb.org.uk/bwg/bestprac10.pdf

122. McAdams RH (1995) Cooperation and conflict: The economics of group status production and race discrimination. Harvard Law Review, March, 108(5):1003-1084

123. Meadows CA (1995) Formal Verification of Cryptographic Protocols: A Survey. Proc. of ASIACRYPT: Advances in Cryptology – ASIACRYPT: Int'l Conference on the Theory and Application of Cryptology. IEEE Computer Society Press, Washington DC

124. Mennecke T (2006) Slyck News — P2P Population Continues Climb. June 14, Available at: http://www.slyck.com/news.php?story=1220

125. Messmer E (2008) Health Care Organizations See Cyberattacks as Growing Threat. Network World, February 28

126. Microsoft Research (2006) Biometric ID: Technical Overview. Available at http://download.microsoft.com/download/d/6/b/d6bde980-5568-4926-8c71-dea63befed64/biometric_id.doc. Cited 12/06

127. Microsoft Research (2006) Microsoft Tamper resistant Biometric ID Cards. Available at http://research.microsoft.com/msbit/Factsheet.doc. Cited 12/06

128. Mulligan D, Berman J (1999) Privacy in the Digital Age: Work in Progress. Nova Law Review, Winter 1999, 23(2)

129. Musco TD, Fyffe KH (1999) Health Insurers' Anti-fraud Programs. Washington D.C. Health Insurance Association of America

130. Nakashima E, Weiss R (2008) Patients' Data on Stolen Laptop. Washington Post, March 24, A1.

131. National Research Council (1996) Cryptography's Role in Securing the Information Society. Nat'l Academy Press, Wash, DC

132. Newell A, Simon HA (1972) Human problem solving. Englewood Cliffs, NJ: Prentice-Hall

133. Newton EM, Woodward JD (2001) Biometrics: A Technical Primer. In: Woodward JD, Webb KW, Newton EM et al. Appendix A, Biometrics: A Technical Primer. Army Biometric Applications: Identifying and Addressing Sociocultural Concerns. RAND/MR-1237-A, Santa Monica, CA

134. Nikander P, Karvonen K (2001) Users and Trust in Cyberspace. Security Protocols - 9th International Workshop. Springer LNCS, Verlag, Berlin, Germany

135. Nissenbaum H (2001) Securing Trust Online: Wisdom or Oxymoron. Boston University Law Review, June, 81(3):635–664

136. Nissenbaum H, Felton E, Friedman B (2002) Computer Security: Competing Concepts. 30th Research Conference on Communication, Information and Internet Polic. Washington, DC
137. Miller N, Resnick P, Zeckhauser R (2002) Eliciting Honest Feedback in Electronic Markets. SITE '02
138. O'Harrow R Jr (2001) Concerns for ID Theft Often Are Unheeded. Washington Post, July 23, 2001, Page A01
139. Office of Technology Assessment (1985) Electronic Surveillance and Civil Liberties OTA-CIT-293. United States Government Printing Office, Gaithersburg, MA
140. Office of Technology Assessment (1986) Management, Security and Congressional Oversight OTA-CIT-297. United States Government Printing Office, Gaithersburg, MA
141. Olson P (2006) AOL Shoots Itself in the Foot. Forbes, August 8
142. PA (2006) Pennsylvania Attorney General. Attorney General's Insurance Fraud Section charges former SEPTA employee with using co-worker's ID to obtain Viagra. Harrisburg: s.n., July 6, 2006
143. Paoulson K (2006) MySpace Predator Caught By Code. Wired News, 6 Oct 2006. Available at http://www.wired.com/news/technology/1,71948-0.html
144. Pear Robert (2007) Warnings over Privacy of US Health Network. New York Times, 16A, columns 3-5, February 18
145. Perlman R (1999) An overview of PKI trust models. IEEE Network, Nov/Dec, 13:38–43
146. Peterson M (2000) When Good Drugs Go Gray; Booming Underground Market Raises Safety Concerns. The New York Times, 12 14, 2000, pp. 1.
147. Pew Internet and American Life Project (2005) Trust and privacy online: Why Americans want to rewrite the rules. PEW Internet & American Life Project, NY, NY
148. Pew Internet and American Life Project (2002) On-line rating Systems. PEW Internet & American Life Project, NY, NY, February 2002
149. Pew Internet and American Life Project (2002) What consumers have to say about information privacy. PEW Internet & American Life Project, NY, NY, February 2002
150. Phillips PJ, Martin A, Wilson CL, Przybocki M (2000) An Introduction to Evaluating Biometric Systems. IEEE Computer, February 2000, pp. 56-63
151. Phillips PJ, Moon H, Rizvi S, Rauss P (2000) The FERET Evaluation methodology for face-recognition algorithms. IEEE trans. PAMI 22(10)
152. Pierce D (2003) Opinion: Swiping driver's licenses-instant marketing lists?. Seattle Press, March 31, 2003
153. Rangan PV (1988) An Axiomatic Basis for Trust in Distributed Systems. Proc. of the 1988 IEEE Sym. on Security and Privacy. pp. 204–211. IEEE Computer Society Press, Washington, DC
154. Raul AC (2002) Privacy and the Digital State: Balancing Public Information and Personal Privacy. Kluwer, Norwell, MA
155. Ratha NK, Bolle RM (1999) Smartcard based authentication. In: Jain AK, Bolle R, Pankanti S (eds) Biometrics: Personal Identification in Networked Society. pp. 369—384, Kluwer Academic Publishers, 1999
156. Reavy P (2006) What Baby? ID victim gets a jolt. Deseret News (Salt Lake City). May 2, 2006
157. Regan P (1995) Legislating Privacy: Technology, Social Values and Public Policy. Business Ethics Quarterly 8(4):723–724
158. Resnick P, Zeckhauser R, Friedman E, Kuwabara K (2000) Reputation Systems. CACM, Dec., 43(12):45–48
159. Robenstein S (2008) Are Your Medical Records at Risk?. Wall Street Journal, April 29
160. Robertson J (2011) New data spill shows risk of online health records. Associated Press, August 21
161. Rubin L, Cooter R (1994) The Payment System: Cases Materials and Issues. West Publishing Co., St. Paul, MN
162. Russell J (2005) Harvard fixing data security breaches: Loophole allowed viewing student prescription orders. Boston Globe, January 22

163. Schneider F (ed) (1999) Trust in Cyberspace. National Academies Press, Washington, DC
164. Schneier B (2002) Computer Security: It's the Economics, Stupid. Workshop Econ, and Information Security, Berkeley, CA
165. Schneier B (1995) Applied Cryptography. Second Edition, John Wiley & Sons, Inc., New York, NY
166. Schneiderman B (2000) Designing Trust into Online Experiences. CACM, Dec., 43(12):57–59
167. Schwartz A (2002) Driver's License Security. Testimony Before the House Committee on Transportation and Infrastructure Subcommittee on Highways and Transit. September 5 2002
168. Schwartz A (2000) HR 4049 Privacy Commission Act. Testimony Before The House Committee on Government Reform Subcommittee On Government Management, Information and Technology. April 12, 2000
169. Shostack A (2002) Privacy Invasion Infrastructure Subsidies. CACR. Toronto (CN), March 13, 2002
170. Sullivan B (2003) ID Theft Costs Banks $1 Billion A Year. Available via MSNBC.com http://www.msnbc.com/news/891186.asp. Cited: April 15, 2003
171. Seamons KE, Winslett M, Yu T, Yu L, Jarvis R (2002) Protecting Privacy During On-line Trust Negotiation. In: Dingledine R, Syverson P (eds) Privacy Enhancing Technologies 2002. Springer-Verlag, LNCS 2482, Berlin, Germany
172. Seligman A (1997) The Problem of Trust. Princeton University Press, Princeton, NJ
173. Shostack A (2003) Paying for Privacy: Consumers and Infrastructures. Wrksp on Econ and Info, Sec., College Park, MD
174. Slovic P (1993) Perceived Risk, Trust, and Democracy. Risk Analysis 13(6):675–681
175. Smith G (2007) Teacher Guilty in Norwood Porn Case. Norwich Bulletin. Saturday January 6. Available at http://www.norwichbulletin.com/apps/pbcs.dll/article?AID=/20070106/NEWS01/701060312/1002/NEWS17
176. Sophos (2002) Melissa was 'a colossal mistake' says author. Sophos Prsss Release. Available at http://www.sophos.com/virusinfo/articles/melissa2.html
177. Sproull L, Kiesler S (1991) Connections. The MIT Press, Cambridge, MA
178. Stubblebine SG, Syverson PF (2000) Authentic Attributes with Fine-Grained Anonymity Protection. In: Frankel Y (ed) Financial Cryptography (FC 2000). Springer-Verlag, LNCS 1962, Berlin, Germany
179. Su J, Tygar JD (1996) Building blocks for atomicity in electronic commerce. Proc. of USENIX Security Symposium. USENIX Association, Berkeley, CA
180. Sullivan B (2003) The darkest side of ID theft. Available at http://www.msnbc.com/news/877978.asp?0si=-&cp1=1
181. Syverson PF (2003) The Paradoxical Value of Privacy. Workshop on Economics and Info Security. College Park, MD
182. Tang L (1996) Verifiable Transaction Atomicity for Electronic Payment Systems. Proc. of the 16th Int'l Conf. on Distributed Computing Systems. IEEE Computer Society Press
183. Taylor N (2002) State Surveillance and the Right to Privacy. Surveillance & Society (1):66–85
184. Tokars L (2008) Memorial Hospital loses laptop containing sensitive employee data. WSBT, Feb 7, Available at http://www.wsbt.com/news/local/15408791.html.
185. Totty M (2007) Security: How to Protect Your Private Information. Wall Street Journal, January 29. R1
186. Twedt S (2007) UPMC patients' personal data left on Web. Pittsburgh Post-Gazette, April 12
187. Tygar JD, Whitten A (1996) WWW Electronic Commerce and Java Trojan Horses. Proc. of the Second USENIX Workshop on Electronic Commerce. Oakland, CA, pp. 243–249
188. Tyler TR (1990) Justice, Self-Interest, and the legitimacy of Legal and Political Authority. In: Mansbridge JJ (ed) Beyond Self-Interest. The University of Chicago Press, Chicago and London
189. Tyler T (1990) Why People Obey the Law. Yale University Press, New Haven, CT
190. USA PATRIOT Act (2001) [Section 326, among others]

191. USDC (2006) United States of America vs. Fernando Ferrer, Jr. and Isis Machado, 06-60261, s.l., United States District Court Southern District of Florida, September 7, 2006

192. USDJ (2007) US Department of Justice. Six Indicted for Health Care Fraud Scheme in Southeast Texas. Houston, TX: s.n., 2007. Press Release.

193. USA (2007) United States Attorney, District of Nevada. Las Vegas Pharmacist Charged with Health Care Fraud and Unlawful Distribution of Controlled Substances. Las Vegas, United States Department of Justice, 2 23, 2007

194. US House (2009) Title IV Health Information Technology for Economic and Clinical Health. Majority Staff of the Committees on Energy and Commerce, Ways and Means, and Science and Technology. January 16, 2009, Source: http://waysandmeans.house.gov/media/pdf/110/hit2.pdf. Retrieved: July 1, 2009.

195. United States Senate Committee on Governmental Affairs Subcommittee on Oversight of Government Management (2002) Restructuring, and the District of Columbia, Hearing: A License to Break the Law? Protecting the Integrity of Driver's Licenses, April 16, 2002. (Witness List: http://www.senate.gov/ gov_affairs/041602witness.htm)

196. Useem J (2007) Fortune 500: The Big Get Bigger. Fortune Magazine, 155, 8, April 30, 81. Wall Street Journal, March 26

197. Van den Hoven J (1997) Privacy and the Varieties of Informational Wrongdoing. In: Spinello, Tavani (eds) Readings in Cyberethics, Jones & Bartlett: Sudbury, pp. 430–442

198. Varian H (2002) System Reliability and Free Riding. Economics and Information Security Workshop, Berkeley, CA

199. Viega J, Kohno Y, Potter B (2001) Trust (and mistrust) in secure applications. CACM, February, 44(2):36

200. Vijayan J (2007) Personal data on 17,000 Pfizer employees exposed; P2P app blamed. Computer World. Available at: http://www.computerworld.com/action/article.do? command=viewArticleBasic&articleId=9024491.

201. Yahalom R, Klein B, Beth T (1993) Trust relationships in secure systems—A distributed authentication perspective. Proc. of the IEEE Symposium on Research in Security and Privacy. pp. 150–164

202. Wacker J (1995) Drafting agreements for secure electronic commerce. Proc. of the World Wide Electronic Commerce: Law, Policy, Security & Controls Conference, Washington, DC, pp. 6

203. Walden I (1995) Are privacy requirements inhibiting electronic commerce. Proc. of the World Wide Electronic Commerce: Law, Policy, Security & Controls Conference, Washington, DC, pp. 10

204. Wang Y, Berck D, Jiang Z, et al. (2006) Automated Web Partol with Strider Honey Mondekeys. Proc. of Network and Distributed System Security. ISOC Publishing, Washington DC

205. Wayman JL (1995) Confidence Interval and Test Size Estimation for Biometric Data. National Biometric Test Center, San Jose State University, CA, Oct. 1995

206. Weick KE (1990) Technology as equivoque: Sense-making in new technologies. In: Goodman PS, Sproull LS (eds) Technology and Organizations (pp. 1–44). Jossey-Bass, San Francisco, CA

207. Weisband S, Kiesler S (1996) Self Disclosure on computer forms: Meta-analysis and implications. Proc. of the CHI '96 Conference on Human-Computer Interaction, Vancouver, BC, Canada

208. Wereschagin M (2006) Medical ID Theft Leads to Lengthy Recovery. Pittsburgh Tribune-Review, 10 24, 2006

209. WFTV (2008) Medical Center Patient Records Posted On Internet. August 14, Available athttp://www.wftv.com/news/17188045/detail.html?taf=orlc.

210. Whitten A, Tygar JD (1999) Why Johnny Can't Encrypt: A Usability Evaluation of PGP 5.0. Proceedings of the 8th USENIX Security Symposium. USENIX Association, Berkeley, CA

211. Williams M (2001) In whom we trust: Group membership as an affective context for trust development. Academy of Management Review 26(3):377–396

212. Wilson M, Rashbaum WR (2010) Real Patients, Real Doctors, Fake Everything Else. New York Times, Oct 14, A3

213. Winslett M, Yu T, Seamons KE, Hess A, Jacobson J, Jarvis R, Smith B, Yu L (2002) Negotiating Trust on the Web. IEEE Internet Computing, November/December 2002

214. Wit AP, Wilke HAM (1992) The Effect of Social Categorization on Cooperation in Three Types of Social Dilemmas. Journal of Economic Psychology 13(1):135–151, March, 17

215. Yee B, Blackley R (2003) Trusting Code and Trusting Hardware. In: Camp LJ (ed) Identity: The Digital Government Civic Scenario Workshop, Boston, MA. Available at http://www.ksg.harvard.edu/digitalcenter/conference/papers/codeanHW.htm

216. Zhao X, Johnson ME (2008), Information Governance: Flexibility and Control through Escalation and Incentives. Proceedings of the Seventh Workshop on the Economics of Information Security, Dartmouth College, June 26-27

217. Zwicky ED, Cooper S, Chapman DB (2000) Building Internet Firewalls, Second Edition. O'Reilly and Associates, Sebastopol, California